MILLENARIAN MOVEMENTS IN HISTORICAL CONTEXT

Michael J. St. Clair

GARLAND PUBLISHING, INC. • NEW YORK & LONDON
1992

© 1992 Michael J. St. Clair
All rights reserved

Library of Congress Cataloging-in-Publication Data

St. Clair, Michael, 1940–
  Millenarian movements in historical context / Michael J. St. Clair.
    p. cm. — (Garland reference library of social science ; v. 763)
  Includes bibliographical references and index.
  ISBN 0–8153–0218–5 (acid-free)
  1. Millennialism—History. I. Title. II. Series.
BT891.S8 1992
236'.9'09—dc20   91–36655
                                                                CIP

Printed on acid-free, 250-year-life paper
Manufactured in the United States of America

*for Roslin, Forrest, and Travis
with much love and affection*

Contents

Preface ix

Introduction:
The End of the World, the Millennium, and Religious Groups .. 3

Chapter One:
The Jewish Origins of Millenarian Ideas and Groups 23

Chapter Two:
Early Christianity as a Millenarian Movement 49

Chapter Three:
Continuing Millennial Hopes, Montanism, and Monasticism ... 75

Chapter Four:
Reformers and the Revival of Prophetic Prophecy 95

Chapter Five:
The Taborites and Adamites of Czechoslovakia 119

Chapter Six:
Thomas Müntzer and the Millenarian Anabaptists 153

Chapter Seven:
England's Fifth Monarchy Men 191

Chapter Eight:
France from the Seventeenth to the Nineteenth Century 223

Chapter Nine:
England from the Seventeenth to the Nineteenth Century ... 239

Chapter Ten:
America, The Land of God's Chosen: The Early Period 267

Chapter Eleven:
America, Part Two: From Millerism to Flying Saucers 305

Conclusion 345

Selected Bibliography 357

Index 369

Preface

My interest in millenarian movements was initially caught by the enthusiasm and apparent extremism of those who were waiting for the End Time. Desperate people in difficult times were prepared, with non-rational fervor, to go to extraordinary lengths for their beliefs, to do whatever was necessary to prepare for the millennium, to remove whatever obstacles stood in the way of the Second Coming. What I began to learn, however, is that millenarianism may, at times, be the religion of despair and desperation or the religion of hope. Because of its emotional intensity and sometimes alien appearance and violence, millenarianism needs to be studied in context.

The finished book is not the book that I started out to write. What was to be a book on religious fanaticism and prophetic madness expanded to consider the history of millenarian movements, a tradition that was to prove more complex than I had expected. The more I learned, the more I came to appreciate the diversity and complexity that existed among millenarian groups and the relative normalcy of millenarian ideas during some periods. Some groups were fanatical and indeed went to excesses. Other groups in a quietist way computed the expected time before the end and patiently waited. Some groups were mass movements; others comprised a handful of devotees. No neat categories and patterns fit all cases. Increasingly it becomes clear that each group arises amid a specific context, at a specific time and under specific conditions.

Along with the millenarian movements is a scholarly tradition. Over the past thirty years numerous scholars have studied and argued over the causes and experiences of millenarian groups. To read the work of these scholars is enormously rewarding and interesting. Because it would take more than one lifetime to gather and master the overwhelming amount of original material containing the story of millenarian movements, this current work frequently has depended on the work of these scholars.

My work is intended as an overview, the beginning of a synthesis, a step in the direction of more comparative and comprehensive approach to millenarian groups. Perhaps the image of a map best describes this work, a guide for a journey through many of the groups and some of the scholarship that has illuminated them.

Firstly then, I am in debt to those marvelous scholars who got me interested in this area and from whose patient labors I benefited.

I wish to acknowledge gratefully the following for permission to quote material in copyright: to Review and Herald Publishing Associates, for material from Francis D. Nichol, *The Midnight Cry* (Washington, D.C.: Review and Herald Publishing Associates, 1945); to Dover Publications, for material from Edward Deming Andrews, *The People Called Shakers: A Search for the Perfect Society* (New York: Dover Publications, 1953, 1963); to Johns Hopkins University Press for material from Clarke Garrett, *Respectable Folly: Millenarians and the French Revolution in France and England* (Baltimore and London: Johns Hopkins University Press, 1975). Specific references are given in the text.

I wish to thank several colleagues and friends who read portions of this manuscript and gave me comments, specifically John Corcoran, Anthony Saldarini, Donald Logan, Margaret Hutaff, Barbara Radtke, and Robert Faulkner. Errors and difficulties are mine. I owe special thanks to Thomas McClure for assistance in production.

If this book brings anything that is original to the study of enthusiastic religion, it is the attempt to provide a vantage point with which to recognize the diversity and continuity of millenarian movements. A few themes emerged which deserve special treatment but which this

Preface xi

book can just touch upon, such as the special role of women in some of these movements, the rise of millenarian movements with secular ideologies, the role of prophetic ecstasy in some movements. . . .

Millenarian Movements
in
Historical Context

Introduction
The End of the World, the Millennium and Religious Groups

The Present

Early in 1990 a religious sect of over two thousand people gathered in Paradise Valley in Livingston, Montana, where they were preparing to spend years in underground shelters safe from a nuclear Armageddon that they believed was imminent. The members of this group, called the Church Universal and Triumphant, had sold their homes, closed out bank accounts and said goodbye to relatives. They expected the imminent destruction of most of the rest of the world but believed that they would survive in the special concrete and steel shelters that the church had built in Livingston.

The leader of this religious group, Mrs. Elizabeth Clare Prophet, told her followers that the world was in a "dangerous period," and that most of the world would be destroyed by nuclear explosions. In response to Mrs. Prophet's words, her followers from North and South America swarmed into an area of 33,000 acres along the Yellowstone River in Montana. Arriving in packed cars and loaded rental trucks, they transported personal possessions and survival gear. They stockpiled subterranean shelters with dried food, medical equipment, blood supplies, generators and cookware.

Mrs. Prophet had predicted the end of the world several times. She encourages her followers to pray intensely to lessen the chance of Armageddon. Indeed, members of the group claim that the lessening of world tensions is due to their prayers. The group began about 1981 when Mrs. Prophet began making her doomsday prophecies on the basis of a mix of New Age ideas and biblical fragments. One young man, Steve Hoemberg, who had been a member of this survivalist sect since 1983 was convinced that "the world's coming to an end."[1]

This North American group is but one more of those religious movements that make dramatic predictions about the approaching end of the world. Indeed, it is highly likely that as the decade of the '90s ends and the twentieth century fades into the third millennium, there will be more such groups and more such predictions. These kinds of movements frequently take their form from the sense that the world has gotten so bad that there can be no hope. Using parts of the Bible to interpret the signs of their own times, members of these groups believe calamitous destruction is near. Some groups believe that the survivors of such doom will attain new life and that they indeed are the chosen elect.

The central religious insight of these groups is a valuing of the future and seeing the present evils of the world from the vantage point of a coming time when the shape of society will be transformed into an ideal world. The future becomes the genuine level of reality by which the present is interpreted, evaluated—and generally devalued. This underlying anxiety about time's end being near has its roots in the ancient Hebrew sense that history is going somewhere and has an ultimate purpose, and thus these groups offer their followers a kind of theology of history.

Religion and the End of the World

Over the centuries, religious people developed many conflicting interpretations about the end of history. The Christian tradition is replete with attempts, some lasting but many of short duration, to gather devout believers into communities totally committed to God's way and to preparing for the coming of the end of the world and the expected return of Jesus Christ. Usually these efforts were a minority effort, and such groups have often been regarded as strange or heretical, for they held up to the world a vision of what the Christian life ought to be which contrasted with what the Christian life had become in ordinary society.

The focus of this book is on those Christian groups which, guided by their reading of the Bible, saw in their contemporary times the signs of the end. They acted on their beliefs by dramatic changes in their lifestyle; an important part of their expectation was about the kind of world that was to follow the end of the world as they knew it.

These Christian groups have taken different forms. Some are called apocalyptic groups, because they base their predictions on the apocalyptic literature of the Bible. Some groups are called adventist groups because they emphasize the second advent or coming of Christ which is associated with the end time. Others are known as millenarian groups because they expect a period of earthly paradise known as the millennium after the destruction of the present world order, a central concern being the transformation of the earth. This book uses the term millenarian group or movement to cover these basic kinds of groups. Most of these movements seek to correlate current historical events with a presumed timetable for the end of history. The end of history, depending on how the believer reads certain passages of the Bible, may variably bring the return of Christ and a thousand-year period associated with the defeat of Satan, the last judgment of humanity, and the earthly glory of the elect.

Millenarian groups and movements have varied in their extremism. Some were radical and violent, such as the medieval Münsterites of Germany; others simply wished to be left in peace, such as the ninteenth-century Shakers. Some counted thousands as followers, such as the Millerites of the eastern United States, and some numbered just a handful, such as the medieval Adamites of Czechoslovakia. A few groups, such as the Jim Jones' People's Temple which committed mass self-destruction in Guyana in November 1978, manifested clear signs of psychological disturbance.

But there remains an obvious fact: the world has not yet ended. All of these groups have had to face this contrast between their expectations and the ineluctable reality of the world's continued existence. How did they deal with this? Some dealt with it and have continued on their path of faith. Others have quietly faded from history. The major conclusion to be drawn, however, is that the millenarian impulse will continue; that is, believers will continue to use the apocalyptic passages of Scripture to find in their times signs of the end of time, the Coming of Jesus, or perhaps signs of an apocalyptic struggle with Satan.

In Europe, millenarianism has been a steady but not central impulse, although the most destructive of twentieth-century secular distortions of millennial schemes was Adolf Hitler's promise of a thousand-year Reich. By contrast, in America and England to a lesser extent, rather than being merely a marginal impulse toward eccentricity and pathology, millenarian concerns have been a constant part of the cultural experience. Indeed, the millennial myth in American life has proven so resilient and malleable that some scholars have moved it from the periphery to the center of the nation's self-understanding. America seems to offer unusually favorable conditions for a wide variety of both native groups and immigrant groups that are concerned about the end of the world and the coming of the ideal age of the millennium. More than a century ago, for instance, William Miller led a movement that numbered upwards of 50,000 Americans who expected the coming of the last days. By a recent estimate as many as 40 million present-day Americans share a belief that the end times are near. But it is not the mainstream apocalypticism or academic millenarianism that is the focus here but more the dramatic groups that gathered togeth in shared belief about the end time.

America has been receptive to a variety of immigrant communitarian and utopian sects such as the Hutterites and Amish who have maintained their religious and cultural distinctiveness in a rural environments where it has been easier to preserve the boundaries of the community apart from the perceived chaos of the larger society. But even mainstream America has developed a kind of secular millenarianism. The Presidential addresses of Woodrow Wilson, Franklin Roosevelt, John Kennedy and Lyndon Johnson reveal an explicit although secularized millennial pattern in which they offer the hope of a New Freedom, New Deal, New Frontier, or a Great Society.

Introduction 7

The Theme

This book is about the persistent return of the millenarian impulse: the periodic emergence of fervent groups and movements that expect the end of the world and the coming of a millennial period and an earthly paradise. This book looks at some of these diverse groups and deals with the source of their inspiration, their interpretation of the apocalyptic portions of the Bible.

But numerous other questions arise. Not all Christians have interpreted the Scriptures so narrowly or with this emphasis. Sometimes these groups have become radicalized and violent. What prompted this escalation, while other groups, also expecting the end of the world, have kept quietly to themselves? Most interesting is the question of what happened to these groups when the deadline for the end of the world passed and they were confronted with the continued existence of everyday life.

Over the centuries these groups have emerged in different forms, sometimes violent and revolutionary, sometimes quiet and separatist. The millenarianism impulse, however, has emerged in too many varied forms to be lightly dismissed. For example, to contrast two threads, one can consider the scholarly stream of millenarianism which reached its peak in the seventeenth century. This included the respectable study and interpretation of biblical prophecy by such luminaries as Isaac Newton, Joseph Priestly and Jonathan Edwards. Contrasting with this was a more popular and adventist stream unafraid of enthusiastic displays. But even the followers of Richard Brothers in England included a number of scholarly individuals.

Sometimes the excessive behavior of groups is in response to the aggressiveness of their critics and enemies. The medieval Taborites and Münsterites were destructive, but the threats they faced were real. Oftentimes the only information available about a group is from their critics, such as information about the Montanists or the extreme Adamites. With groups that exist at the fringes of society, observers easily can label them as strange and alien. Some stories are either distortions or simply not true, such as the story that the Millerites climbed up trees and on barn roofs dressed in their white ascension robes so as to be closer to Jesus when he came again. But Thomas Müntzer did preach to his followers that they would be able to catch the cannon balls of their enemies in their sleeves and not be hurt by human weapons.

Perhaps whatever pathology is present in millenarian groups and other cults is the handing over by individuals of their personal autonomy to some prophetic authority who leads the group. Once individuals abrogate personal responsibility they can get caught up in carrying out to its extreme an otherwise worthy principle. And pathology was present in the arbitrary killing of John of Leyden at Münster and the self-destructiveness of Jim Jones' followers in Guyana.

One finds, however, such a recurrence of the millenarian impulse that one can only conclude to the potency, if not the normalcy, of the millenarian impulse. The only certain conclusion that one can draw is that, despite the utter failure of all past millennial programs in their predictions of the end of the world, more groups and predictions will appear.

The book, then, scrutinizes and describes in their historical contexts some of the principal Christian millenarian groups that emerged in Europe and North America. These groups tend to be short-lived, loosely organized cult-like movements with a world view primarily drawn from the apocalyptic literature, principally the Book of Daniel and the Book of Revelation. But nothing, however, is neat or simple in studying groups that expect the end of the world and a millennium of peace. Categories and terms seem to overlap or not apply precisely. Accordingly it may assist the reader to have a preliminary overview of millenarian movements and the apocalyptic literature which inspires them.

The Millennium

The word millennium is from two Latin words *mille* and *annum, mille* meaning a thousand and *annum* referring to years. The millennium, a period of a thousand years, specifically refers to an idea in the Judaic-Christian tradition that suggests that perfect period of peace

Introduction

and righteousness that is described in the 20th Chapter of the Book of Revelation. Millenarian or millennial movements are religious groups or cults that expect millennial salvation to be imminent.[2]

Millennialism has spawned its own technical vocabulary. Some speak of millenarianism rather than millennialism. Though in a narrow sense the terms are synonymous, millenarianism sometimes refers to belief in a future salvation from present turmoil, a salvation involving the cataclysmic destruction of the powers of evil, but such a belief is not necessarily identified with the Christian expectation of the Second Advent of Christ. Some variants of millennialism are clustered under the rubric of adventism because here the focus is on the expected literal return of Christ rather than the details of Christ's anticipated thousand-year reign. Another term is chiliasm, derived from the Greek word for one thousand, which simply refers to the second coming of Christ and the expected thousand year reign.

In the narrow sense, millenarian groups refer to various Jewish and Christian groups of the Greco-Roman period in Palestine, approximately from 169 B.C. to 135 A.D. In the wider meaning of the term, millenarianism refers to hundreds of groups that sprang up in the wake of Christianity. In its broadest and most amorphous meaning the term is sometimes used to refer to such movements as Melanesian cargo cults, for example, or various fundamentalist revival groups. Also the blurred use of words like cult and sect causes some confusion, especially since the organization of a group is distinct from its millenarian ideology. To bypass some of the difficulties of church-sect-cult terminology, which often does not adequately cover millenarian experiences, the term millenarian group or movement will be used.[3] The discussion in these pages focuses only on the main millenarian groups of Europe and North America and excludes many smaller movements as well as the various cargo and nativistic cults of the Third World.

History offers up a rich diversity of millenarian movements, each with its own uniqueness and distinctness, and yet these movements do possess some common features in greater or lesser prominence. Groups with millenarian features have sprung up prior to the origin of Christianity and continue to spring up in the present day.

Anthropologists suggest some characteristics of millenarian groups that can be used in a preliminary way for description. These preliminary characteristics of millenarian groups come primarily from anthropological studies. There is only a partial overlap of millenarian and apocalyptic notions, and so it is also important to distinguish between the anthropological descriptions of millenarian movements and the scholarly study of Jewish-Christian apocalyptic literature. At this stage, the bare bones of seven features of millenarian groups—or points of comparison—can be briefly described and they will be fleshed out in later chapters. The concern here is not to strive for a rigid schema but rather to offer in a preliminary way open categories for the sake of comparing and discussing different groups.

Points of Comparison

Millenarian groups typically draw their inspiration from the *apocalyptic literature* of the Bible. Apocalyptic literature may inspire millenarian groups but does not necessarily "cause" them.

Apocalyptic has come to mean different things. The word apocalyptic has sometimes been used to suggest a world view or religious attitude which is only vaguely defined but which has an identity independent of specific texts or books.[4] It is more accurate, however, to speak of Jewish-Christian apocalyptic literature and to see how millenarian groups have drawn upon this literature for inspiration and for assistance in reading the "signs of the times." One or more of the apocalyptic books of the Bible have typically inspired in varying degrees Western millenarian groups.

A word about apocalyptic ideas and themes. Apocalyptic literature is a genre of religious literature that became an increasingly popular and widespread during the Greco-Roman period in Palestine. Apocalypses usually presented a comprehensive but pessimistic view of the world as a basis to exhort or console. The Book of Daniel, for example, seems to have provided support for believers in the face of persecution, and the Book of Watchers provided reassurance in the face of a shock to the culture. Most, if not all, millenarian groups base their

Introduction

expectations on the varying apocalypses, especially the Book of Daniel and the Book of Revelation. These books interpreted contemporary history and envisioned the destruction of pagan Babylon and Rome while offering a vision of the future where tribulations and sorrows would give place to triumph and peace. This kind of literature will be examined in more detail in the next chapter.

Because of their reliance on apocalyptic literature, the *dominant belief* of millenarian groups involves the expectation of heaven on earth soon, with the consequent destruction of the present social order.

Inspired by apocalyptic literature millenarian groups expect the arrival of a salvation that is imminent and of this world, a new heaven on earth. This imminent, total salvation will involve the overthrow, sometimes violently, of the present social order and the lifting up of the believers or members of these cults to a special status in the new kingdom. Initially early Christians, on the basis of the Book of Revelation (especially 20:4-6) and other writings of the New Testament period, believed Christ would return in their lifetime and set up an earthly kingdom. Believers of this period understood the millennium as a limited, transitional period that preceded the final judgment at the end of time, but later enthusiasts sometimes believed in an indefinite millennium period, not always limited to a thousand years.[5] For members of millenarian groups, the end of present time is near and the believing Elect tensely expect and prepare for a new, completely changed order in which they will be liberated from sin and evil.[6] Believers view the present order as evil and needing to be radically overturned to make way for the new order.

Another aspect of the belief of a few millenarian groups involves expectation of a messiah.[7] A few millenarian groups are messianic and are sometimes called messianic movements. A messiah is soon to bring salvation and establish his messianic kingdom. As will be discussed below, the Christians and later believers transformed messianic ideas found in the Old Testament and literature from the Inter-testamental period. Originally the messiah would be a warrior, but early Christians transformed the notion of messiah and believed that Jesus would return and inaugurate the new order. He is the redeemer and the representative of the divine. In fact, the very word

Christian comes from the Greek form of the Hebrew word for messiah.

Commonly millenarian groups are oppositional movements that stand against the majority culture. The ideology of any movement helps an observer to distinguish political, terrorist, fanatical or nationalistic movements from those that are essentially religious.[8] In these pages the millenarian cults investigated have an ideology that is concerned with the coming of the millennium. How each locates the millennium with reference to Christ's coming is another matter. *Pre*millennialists believe Christ is to return *before* the perfect age, while *Post*millenialists expect Christ to return *after* the elect has established the millennium either by preaching the Gospel or perhaps by fire and the sword.[9] Some groups, such as the Church Universal and Triumphant, have no clearly worked-out view of the millennium period but are an amalgam of Eastern religions, Christianity, and New Age faiths.

Perhaps the most fascinating feature of many groups is the terrific *release of emotional energy*. This emotional intensity gives some of these movements a dramatic confidence and compelling sense of certainty about their own mission.

People of the ancient world used various terms to express religious passion and the occasional ecstatic and sometimes uncontrolled behavior of devotees. When the ancient Greeks described the possession of a believer by a god they called it enthusiasm. Plato, for example, speaks of the poet inspired and possessed by the divinity, how the god speaks through the poet and robs him of his senses so that he is out of his mind. Ecstasy suggest an intense experience during which people leave their normal ways and good sense. The words *entheos* and *enthousiasei* from which the English enthusiasm is derived, suggest the idea of "being filled with the god" who causes the resulting excitement. Perhaps the most common non-Biblical term to describe intense religious feelings is *mania*, prophetic madness or frenzy. Frenzy can refer either to the outbursts of the individual or the ritual collective frenzy, especially of the women of a city during a festival. Euripides' *Bacchae* depicts the enthusiasts of Dionysus in such a frenzy. The enthusiasts, possessed by the divine, were filled with wild and intense feelings that transformed them and carried them along, sometimes even to a violent frenzy during which they might tear a victim from limb to limb. Euripides' depiction seems not to have been merely imaginative. The festival of Bacchus, often celebrated with new wine, caused the transformation of normal people, whether from hysteria or the effects of the wine. The excesses of some women devotees seem to have caused ancient authorities to attempt to prohibit some Bacchic revels. The various terms for religious feelings as found in classical literature as well as the New Testament were used, of course, in a general, not technical way.

The ancient Jews understood God to communicate through his people through prophets who were possessed. One dramatic example occurred when Moses led the Jews from captivity in Egypt, many of the Jews grumbled. Moses gathered seventy men of the elders. "Then the Lord came down in the cloud and spoke to him, and took some of the spirit that was upon him and put it upon the seventy elders; and when the spirit rested upon them, they prophesied," (Num. 11:25). God sent the prophet Samuel to a place where "you will meet a band of prophets coming down from the high place with harp, tambourine, flute, and lyre before them, prophesying. Then the spirit of the Lord will come mightily upon you, and you shall prophesy with them and be turned into another man" (1 Sam. 10:5-6). Although the Jews had the experience of ecstatic possession, they did not emphasize this kind of religious experience as the Greeks did. The New Testament, although using somewhat different words than the classic Greek writers did for intense religious experience, nevertheless suggests the intensity of the religious feelings of the early Christians. Early Christian writings, in general, however, are more quiet about intense religious feelings and reproach the frenzied madness of some of the pagan cults. Certainly Paul looked askance (1 Cor. 12:1-14:40) at the extraordinary manifestations among the Corinthian community, especially the gifts of prophecy and speaking in tongues.

Some millenarian groups tend to become prophetically ecstatic and antinomian, that is, counter to traditional rules and customs. Membership in the movement and the hope of redemption permits an elation, a terrific release of emotions and intense feelings. The extreme fervor may involve ecstatic religious practices, just as the total dedication may prompt excessive actions. The elation and fervor sometimes prompt a loss of self-control and consequently religious practices of believers become enthusiastic to the point of frenzy and group hysteria. Intense feeling may be expressed by speaking in tongues or in violent, shaking dancing. Obviously, such practices as religious dancing can of themselves generate religious feelings. In a smaller number of cases, religious fervor gets expressed in an opposite extreme, an excess of self-control and extremes of asceticism. In their attempts to bring about the new order of things, group members manifest supreme confidence that they act according to divine plan and will therefore ultimately triumph.[10] Intensity in some movements manifests itself in self-discipline, strict conformity to rules, and ascetic behavior.

Movements vary greatly in the extent to which members believe they have a part in bringing about the millennium. The passive ones believe that supernatural forces alone will bring the promised time. The more active believe that members can contribute to the advent of the millennium, although the kinds of activites will vary greatly from actions of a purely symbolic nature to active rebellion.

Related to frenzied emotional displays and extreme religious practices is a strong antinomian tendency, the feeling that membership gives the freedom to be beyond all previous taboos and traditional norms and rules. This sometimes means questioning the legitimacy of such social institutions as marriage and private property. The Adamites, for example, shocked their contemporaries by their nakedness and uninhibited sexual behavior which they linked to the freedom of the Garden of Eden. Needless to say, such intense feelings and attitudes can only threaten contemporaries and authorities who might label them as dangerous, heretical or simply mad.

Occasionally a group's leader demands a rejection of and rebellion against established authorities. On the basis of their intense and supremely confident commitment, members divide the world easily into good (us) and evil (them) realms. Of course, they feel God is on their side, and that means that their enemies are against God. Their elated sense of freedom sometimes expresses itself in uninhibited aggression or sexual abberations, either in the form of extremes of asceticism or sexual excesses. When religious hopes and political aspirations become linked, savage violence and aggression are not uncommon. As we shall see, often the violence tends to rise as frightened authorities grow more strenuous in their efforts to repress opposition which they see as non-rational or out of control. The excesses at Münster, in part, probably were triggered by the anxiety of authorities attempting to regain control. Similarly the savage fighting of the Taborites was out of fear and self-preservation as well as firmness of conviction. Modern extremists or terrorists may have a political motivation, but the passions that drive them to their terrorists acts are religious in their intensity and single-mindedness.

Although millenarian groups display dramatic and extreme emotions, to the point that their enemies often see them as pathological and signs of group madness, it is most important to understand the inner world and religious ideas behind the seemingly mad and frenzied behavior.

The leader of a millenarian group is usually—but not always—a charismatic and energetic figure.[11] *Leadership* of groups can vary, sometimes involving more than one leader, for example, when an inspired prophet is assisted by a practical organizer. The groups usually disintegrate unless there is strong leadership often based on private inspiration. Usually the leader or leaders is distinct from the figure of the Messiah, with the leader serving the Messiah, preparing his way, prophesy in his name. In many cases the leader is so much the focus of group identity that if he dies the movement disintegrates.

Because millenarian groups are often at the fringe of their society, social norms are broken and fringe members can begin to take on roles that society does not allow ordinarily. This is especially true of women who at first appear in the role of prophetesses but by the seventeenth century began to take on leadership roles in various religious movements.

A millenarian group may be a stable, exclusive sect-like group. But more typically, because of the nature of the millenarian message, many millenarian movements are amorphous in *organization*, with a core of leaders and ardent believers and an ill-defined body of followers. The hope of an imminent redemption arouses great hopes which pull a large number of followers into the group. The spiritual expectation of salvation and radical transformation very powerfully unite disparate groups into one chosen people.

The group faces a crisis if a definite date, fixed for a spectacular happening or cataclysmic ending, passes and nothing happens. Often the life span of the movement is very brief, sometimes because the expected new order or imminent salvation does not arrive when it was predicted. We shall return to the crisis of the nonappearance of the End Time (or *eschaton*) and how groups must establish institutions to preserve their vision.

Cults differ from other religious groups by making a radical break with the religious traditions of society. For example, sects tend to split off from mainstream churches and are schismatic movements concerned with preserving a purer form of the traditional faith. Because they remain within the major religious tradition of society, sects differ from cults. Many major religions begin as cults. Once a cult is born, organizational changes can then sweep the movement along. Cultic groups which are successful soon turn their attention to the problem of maintaining themselves as an organization. The difficulty with millenarian groups is that some look more like sects, others are more cult-like, although they may share much of the millenarian ideology. Hence, the use of the term group or movement in this book.

The difficult question about the organization of a group or movement is that many of the questions posed about a group reflect modern interests. The danger is to place an arbitrary or theoretical structure on what few facts may have survived. In seeking to explain the past there is the effort to provide a link with the present.[12]

Why do such groups arise? There is considerable scholarly musing on just what *social conditions* foster the emergence of millenarian groups. Periods of social transition or crisis, such as the stormy period preceding the destruction of the Temple at Jerusalem or the break up of the cultural homogeneity of the Middle Ages, gave birth to a variety of millenarian, messianic and renewal movements. More specifically, millenarian groups can often have their origin amidst social conditions of relative deprivation or social disorganization of some sort.

People join a movement for various reasons, depending on the conditions which give rise to the movement and how the movement answers the needs of potential members. Two issues intertwine in response to the questions of Who joins and Why? Social dissatisfaction and deprivation have often bred millenarian groups. Usually some form of deprivation, whether religious or social or political or a combination of all three, is present when millenarian groups blaze up. Such groups can flare up when there is a cumulative deterioration in the quality of life with likelihood of further declines. Sudden crises, disasters like plagues and famines, often supply the right fuel for flare-ups. When a more advanced culture comes in contact with another culture or one society encounters another radically different system of values and culture, the rapid social changes with attendant cultural disintegration produce the conditions for the emergence of messianic or millenarian movements.

A common interpretation of millenarian movements views the movement as providing compensation for or seeking a remedy for oppressive conditions or suffering. Scholars with a Marxist approach interpret millenarian movements as protest of the economically and politically oppressed who seek the overthrow of the existing order.[13] Other scholars have interpreted millenarian movements as responses to the disruption of social and cultural patterns, although some cases, such as colonial societies, include both oppressive and disruptive elements.[14] An epidemic, famine or war might provide such an acute disruption. Following such a disaster people feel vulnerable, confused and full of anxiety, and they may turn to millennial beliefs in order to account for the otherwise meaningless events. They interpret the disaster as the prelude to the millennium, and thereby their despair gives way to hope. What is important is that millenarian groups arise out of a complex of social, religious and political beliefs and actions.

Who makes up the *membership*? Membership more often than not is from the needy of society, from among those who have nothing to lose and everything to gain. But that is not always true, as illustrated, for example, by the Church Universal and Triumphant, which seems to be composed of the relatively affluent or at least the middle class who can afford the various trucks and equipment they were bringing to Montana. Sociologists who investigate modern groups may find that membership likely includes a broader range than just the poor and oppressed, that is, those who experienced themselves as isolated or powerless in their society. The difficulty is with historical groups, where sociological data is largely absent and where groups were mercilessly eliminated for their heretical or revolutionary elements.[15]

But social stress alone does not bring forth a millenarian movement; it requires a complex psychic and religious style of response.[16] There must exist the possibility of some remedial change. When societies have people who experience stress and emptiness, the promise of being filled by means of total this-worldly salvation presents a powerful appeal. Often it is the oppressed peasants, the poor, the marginal people in a society, those without hope, those with nothing who have everything to gain, who make up the membership of millenarian movements. Millenarian movements draw their membership from the deprived people in a society, even if that deprivation is only a matter of a perceived discrepancy between what they might legitimately expect and what they actually have.[17] The movement is a means to overcome the deprivation, the felt discrepancy between the way things are and the way they should be.

But it is not always clear just how millenarian groups serve this social function. Norman Cohn,[18] for example, feels millenarian movements serve society as a safety valve during times of disorientation and intense anxiety and despair. Most likely the key element is the intense concern with change. Religious movements often produce social changes, changes that are not always foreseen. Because millenarian ideas evoke such an intense commitment and emotional fervor, millenarian groups generate revolutionary power that can sweep aside barriers and produce far-reaching social changes. The energy demands social transformation. When the context of a millenarian group is some social or natural disaster, the break in accustomed patterns of human existence triggers the formation of a movement to make up in some way for the sense of loss and deprivation.

Members' commitment to the expected coming salvation and millennium is often so intense and total that the shock of disappointment does not shatter their hope, but rather the non-materialization prompts vigorous proselytizing or missionary activity. Sometimes movements develop theories to account for the delay, and they keep the hope alive. Despite repeated failures of the expected salvation to appear, millenarian hopes persistently re-appear.

Introduction

Similar conditions seem to breed similar but independent reactions, and certain historical periods seem to provide the right conditions for the emergence of millenarian groups. Such times of social crisis and transition as the stormy period preceding the destruction of the Temple at Jerusalem or the ending of the Middle Ages gave birth to a variety of millenarian, messianic and renewal movements. Christianity took root, with characteristics of a millenarian sect, amidst the rich variety of first-century Judaism, which generated revival, messianic and millenarian movements such as the Essenes, the Zealots and Christianity. Of all the millenarian activities of this period, only Christianity coalesced into a structured movement and became an established religion, while other movements remained ephemeral and passing outbursts.

Summary

Apocalyptic ideas played an important role in various Jewish resistance groups, in the early stages of Christianity and also in many of the millenarian groups that arose in later centuries. Apocalyptic literature is a complex literary genre that lends itself easily to partial interpretations and misreading. It is understandable that in difficult times many pious people turned to the Scriptures for comfort and used the texts to understand the "signs of the times." Sometimes the interpretation of texts was narrow and led to behavior that was marginal and extreme—but always interesting.

NOTES

1. *New York Times*, March 15, 1990, pp. 1, B6, and *Boston Globe*, March 14, 1990, p.3.

2. Sylvia L. Thrupp, "Millennial Dreams in Action: A Report on the Conference Discussion," in *Millennial Dreams in Action*, ed. by Sylvia Thrupp (The Hague: Mouton, 1962), p. 12.

3. J. Gordon Melton, "What Is a Cult?" in *Encyclopedic Handbook of Cults in America* (New York & London: Garland Publishing Inc., 1986), pp. 3-6; Geoffrey K. Nelson, "The Spiritualist Movement and the Need for a Redefinition of Cult," *Journal for the Social Sciences of Religion*, 8 (1969): 152-160; G. K. Nelson, "Cults and New Religions: Towards a Sociology of Religious Creativity," *Sociology and Social Research* 68 (1983/84): 301-302; Anthony F. C. Wallace, "Revitalization Movements," *American Anthropologist* 58 (1956): 275-276; Roy Wallace, "Ideology, Authority, and the Development of Cultic Movements," *Social Research* 41 (1974): 299-327. For church-sect categories see Max Weber, *The Protestant Ethic and the Spirit of Capitalism* (New York: Scribners, 1930) and Ernest Troeltsch, *The Social Teaching of the Christian Churches* (London: Allen and Unwin, 1931).

4. John J. Collins, *The Apocalyptic Imagination: An Introduction to the Jewish Matrix of Christianity* (New York: Crossroad, 1984), pp. 205-206.

5. Yonina Talmon, "Millenarian Movements," *Archives Européennes de Sociologie*, 7 (1966): 166. I follow Talmon's lead in discussing these areas of commonality.

6. Yonina Talmon, "Pursuit of the Millennium: The Relation between Religion and Social Change," *Archives Européennes de Sociologie*, 3 (1962): 125-148.

7. Yonina Talmon, "Millenarian Movements," p. 168; Stephen Fuchs, *Rebellious Prophets: A Study of Messianic Movements in Indian Religions* (New York: Asia Publishing House, 1965), p. 1.

8. James T. Richardson, "An Oppositional and General Conceptualization of Cult," *Annual Review of the Social Sciences of Religion* 2 (1978): 33.

9. *Pre*millennialists expect Christ's thousand-year reign will end in a final battle of good and evil at Armageddon. Premillennialism has little interest in the social order and avoids social reform since the world itself is thought to be an arena of Satan and would be subject to destruction when Christ returns. The task of pious premillenialists is to proclaim the gospel of the coming of Christ and rescue a righteous remnant from the clutches of a sinful world. *Post*millenialism, expecting Christ to return *after* the elect has established the millennium, is more optimistic than premillennialism, because of this expectation of mankind's gradual progress toward goodness and victory over the forces of evil before Christ's return. Cf. Charles H. Lippy, "Millennialism and Adventism," in *Encyclopedia of the American Religious Experience: Studies of Traditions and Movements* ed. by Charles H. Lippy and Peter W. Williams (New York: Charles Scribner's Sons, 1988), Vol. 2, pp. 831-844.

Introduction

10. Yonina Talmon, "Millenarism," *International Encyclopedia of the Social Sciences*, p. 350. Cf. Michael Barkun, *Disaster and the Millennium* (New Haven: Yale University Press, 1974), p.117, and Yonina Talmon, "Pursuit of the Millennium," p. 529.

11. Yonina Talmon, "Millenarian Movements," p. 169.

12. E.J. Hobsbawn, "History from Below—Some Reflections," in *History from Below: Studies in Popular Protest and Popular Ideology*, ed. by Frederick Krantz (Oxford and New York: Basil Blackwell, 1988), pp. 25-26.

13. See, for example, Peter Worsley, *The Trumpet Shall Sound* (London: Maggibon and Kee, 1957) and Eric Hobsbawn, *Primitive Rebels: Studies in Archaic Forms of Social Movements in the 19th and 20th Centuries* (New York: W.W. Norton & Co., 1965).

14. See, for example, Michael Barkun, *Disaster and the Millennium* (New Haven: Yale University Press, 1974); Michael Adas, *Prophets of Rebellion: Millenarian Protest Movements against the European Colonial Order* (Chapel Hill: University of North Carolina Press, 1979).

15. Cf. Natalie Zemon Davis, "The Rites of Violence: Religious Riots in Sixteenth-Century France," *Past and Present* 59 (1973): 83; Yonina Talmon, "Pursuit of the Millennium," p. 129.

16. Weston LaBarre, "Materials for a History of Sketches of Crisis Cults: A Bibliographic Essay," *Current Anthropology* 12 (1971): 23; Joseph A. Dowling, "Millennialism and Psychology," *Journal of Psychohistory* 5 (1977): 126.

17. David F. Aberle, "A Note on Relative Deprivation Theory as Applied to Millenarian and Other Cult Movements," in *Millennial Dreams in Action*, ed. by Sylvia Thrupp, p. 209.

18. Norman Cohn, *The Pursuit of the Millennium* (New York: Oxford University Press, 1957, 1970).

Chapter One
Apocalyptic Literature and Jewish Millenarians

Introduction

The spiritual ancestors of millenarian groups are those Jewish and Jewish-Christian groups that began in Palestine during the tumultuous period from roughly the Defilement of the Temple in 167 B.C.E. to the Destruction of the Temple in 70 C.E. It was roughly during this period that Jews responded in diverse ways to military, social and spiritual oppression. As part of their response there appeared various books of apocalyptic spiritual literature for comfort and encouragement in time of oppression and violence.

The apocalyptic way of thinking implies that the world is dominated by destructive evil, but the hour will come when the saints of God, a holy and chosen people, will rise up and—often by force and violence—gain dominion over evil and the world. This time will be the culmination of history, and God's saints will enter into a kingdom of glory and will inherit the earth.[1] Apocalypticism was an aspect of Judaism in the tumultuous centuries when Jews struggled to retain their religious identity against the religious syncretism of Hellenism and the military oppression of the Romans. Apocalyptic ideas played an important role in various Jewish movements, in the early stages of Christianity and also in most of the millenarian groups that arose in later centuries.

Threats to Jewish Religion and Identity

For centuries foreign powers dominated the Jewish people. First the Assyrians, then the Medes and Babylonians gained control of the Kingdom of Israel. Nebuchadnezzar of Babylon deported the Jews to Babylon between 598-582 B.C.E., taking the very heart of the nation into exile. Often the burdens of being dominated or persecuted brought about religious reform and revivals among the Jews and that was true during their exile in Babylon. What enabled these thousands of exiled Jews (cf. Jer. 52:28-30) to retain their identity as a people was their religious practices, such as circumcision and the observance of the Sabbath.

Nebuchadnezzar, in his turn, succumbed to Cyrus the Great of Persia who mastered the Medes and captured Babylon in 539. In the first year of his reign Cyrus permitted the Jews to return to Palestine (Ezra 1:1-2). Intense religious activity continued among the Jews on their return, and they began to rebuild the Temple. During this period the Torah became more central and authoritative within Judaism. The Torah, containing the oral and written religious traditions of the Jews, increasingly took on supreme authority for the Jews as more emphasis was placed on the preservation and study of the Law. To be sure, the cultic worship in the Temple continued to be important, but temple ritual had to be carried out in conformity with the Law. The Law regulated and ordered worship and, in addition, gave sense to the temple worship as a whole. Increasingly Jewish faith focused on the Torah which became the symbol of Judaism, and the Jews became the people of the Book. Religious leaders like Ezra (Ezra 7:7) put an emphasis on the Torah which provided for the proper ordering of temple worship as well as rules for ritual purity. By emphasizing the complete separation of God's holy people Israel from the "unclean" Gentile nations around them and by emphasizing ritual purity, the priestly leaders like Ezra fostered obedience to the Law and faithful-

Jewish Origins

ness to the covenant which God had made with Moses at Sinai.[2] To give emphasis to the Jews as a people separate from other nations and chosen by God, Ezra (Ezra 10:2-44), for example, compelled returned exiles who had married foreign women to separate from them. Jewish identity was linked to their fidelity to their religious traditions and observances.

As the Assyrians and the Babylonians had toppled and declined, so in their turn did the Persians when Alexander the Great of Greece and Macedonia brought the Near East under his rule in 331. In the wake of his conquests, Alexander unleashed a heritage of Greek ideas and culture, a pervasive influence covered under the term Hellenism, which spread throughout the eastern Mediterranean and Near East. From a very early stage the Jews must have felt the impact of this culture on their manner of life and particularly on their religion because Hellenism tended to reduce the divinities of local peoples to alternative expressions of classical Greek gods and goddesses. In short Hellenism, as a form of cultural imperialism, exerted a universalizing and homogenizing pressure which threatened both the Jewish people's traditional practices and their sense of themselves as special people.

Greek fashions and ways penetrated even Jerusalem. To give but one example of the pervasiveness of Hellenism and its threat to Jewish religious practice, Greek fashion dictated that athletes exercise nude in the sport places and the gymnasium. Because the Greek spirit craved beauty of form and took delight in the natural body, Greek culture regarded the Jewish practice of circumcision not merely as unaesthetic but as a barbaric mutilation. For this reason some Jews neglected those Jewish religious rites which appeared unaesthetic to the Greek eye. In abandoning Jewish practices these Jewish athletes succumbed to "gentile custom, and removed the marks of circumcision, and abandoned the holy covenant" (1 Macc. 1:11-15; also 2 Macc. 4:10-15).

Not all Jews, of course, reacted to Hellenism with enthusiasm. The pious passionately rejected any threat to their faith. The Hasideans (1 Macc. 2:42-48), for example, reacted to the threat to their religious culture and became fanatically devoted to the Law. At the start of the Maccabean uprising, the Hasideans observed the Sabbath with such rigor that they allowed themselves to be killed rather than desecrate it by taking up weapons. In general, conservative Jews held on to their dietary laws and the religious prohibitions against graven images—so at odds with the Greco-Roman artistic traditions—even forbidding the use of images on coins.

After Alexander's death, his successors divided up his empire. Palestine, a comparatively small part of that empire, in the third century came under the government of the Greek dynasty of the Ptolemies whose capital was Alexandria in Egypt. In 198 B.C.E. the Seleucid King Antiochus III defeated troops of Ptolemy V at Panion near the sources of the river Jordan, and once again the master of the Jewish people changed. Palestine passed from control of the Ptolemies to domination by the Greek dynasty of the Seleucids whose capital was at Antioch in Syria. For a number of reasons the relations between the Seleucid kings and their Jewish subjects deteriorated. Motivated by a desire to foster the Hellenization of Judea, the Seleucid king Antiochus IV Epiphanes enacted a series of decrees in 168 B.C.E. that forbad certain central Jewish religious practices. Even more offensive to the Jews, Antiochus IV Epiphanes in 167 B.C.E. attacked Jerusalem for the second time and set up the "abomination that makes desolate," the altar to Zeus Olympius, (Dan. 11:21-45).

These abominations of Antiochus IV led to the outbreak of a violent revolt in Judea, ably led by brothers belonging to the priestly Maccabean family. The Maccabees, skillfully exploiting the chaotic state of the Seleucid kingdom after the death of Antiochus IV Epiphanes, achieved political independence for Judea, and the last surviving brother Simon was crowned king in 141 B.C.E. By this time Rome began to make encroachments into the Near East, and the Maccabees diplomatically allied themselves with the ascendant Roman colossus.[3] The Maccabean or Hasmonean dynasty held power in Judea down to 63 B.C.E. In that year the Roman general Pompey, exploiting the civil war in the country, took Jerusalem for Rome. Pompey deposed the last Hasmonean king and established a pro-Roman dynasty, the Herodians. The Herodians (Antipater, Herod and Herod's sons, the last of whom was Archelaus) ruled Judea and the surrounding area as vassal kings of Rome for three generations, down to 6 C.E. Because the Herodians aroused such intense hatred and because there were growing messianic expectations among the Jews, the Romans had to act lest Palestine become even more unstable and

Jewish Origins

inflammable. Judea came under direct Roman rule, governed by a prefect, later a procurator, who was subject to the authority of the Roman governor of Syria. The corrupt rule of the procurators combined with an increased intensity of messianic expectation among the Jews to produce chronic instability in Roman Palestine. The ancient Jewish writer Josephus chronicles this situation in his *Jewish Antiquities* and *Jewish War*.[4] The revolt that flared up in 66 C.E. culminated in the Roman destruction of Jerusalem and the Temple in 70 C.E.

This period, from the profanation of the Temple in 167 B.C.E. by Antiochus IV to the destruction of the Temple in 70 C.E. by the Romans, was a time of religious and political turbulence that severely tried Jewish religious traditions and the Jews' special sense of themselves as a people. Judaism could not help but be linked with various nationalistic and prophetic movements seeking to resist foreign cultural, political and religious domination. The complex and changing Judaism of this period reflects the Jewish response at different levels to the stresses and threats to their very existence and identity as a people. On a political level there were various movements, ranging from armed insurrections and messianic pretenders to groups which withdrew into the desert to practice a strict religious discipline. On a religous level were varied renewal movements that sought a stricter interpretation of the Torah and an intensification of religious rules touching on circumcision, purification and dieting, rules that provided identifying norms of what it meant to be a Jew.

Jewish Response

Pious Jews, however, renewed their religious practices and intensified their religious norms and rules of behavior, for it was their religion that gave them their sense of identity as a people. Various renewal movements spread through Judaism, most of them emphasizing a stricter interpretation of the Torah, since it was the Torah which was at the center of Judaism. First let us look at the religious response—specifically the apocalyptic—of the Jews to the various threats they experienced.

Literary and Religious Response

This turbulent period between 167 B.C.E. and 70 C.E., sometimes called the inter-testamental period, witnessed a development and change in Judaism. From different pious circles within Judaism came an outpouring of new kinds of religious writing, of which apocalyptic and wisdom literature are the main examples. We shall attend only to apocalyptic literature and some of its ideas about the end of the world since later millenarian movements turn to this form of literature for their inspiration. Indeed, even though apocalyptic literature represents only a small part of the canon of the Bible, millenarian groups are especially drawn to the mysterious symbolism and predictions that are characteristic of apocalyptic literature.

Apocalyptic is derived from Greek word *apokalypsis* (a word used, for instance, in the title of the New Testament's Book of Revelation, 1:1) which means an uncovering or disclosure, a manifestation or revelation. Apocalyptic literature, a genre of religious literature with ties to the Maccabean revolt and to the Hasideans, became increasingly popular and widespread in Jewish circles in these last two pre-Christian centuries and continued to have a considerable vogue in Jewish and Christian circles through most of the first century or two of the Christian era.[5] Apocalyptic literature and apocalyptic eschatology were to inspire most, if not all, of the millenarian movements that we shall investigate. It was religious literature that appeared during trying times and again and again was to be turned to by pious believers for hope and comfort when they felt oppressed.

Some of the apocalyptic books or portions of books in the Bible are: Second Isaiah (chapters 40-55), Ezekiel, Isaiah 24-27, Daniel (2:13-45 and chapters 7-12); in the Christian Scriptures, Revelation, Mark 13 (with parallels in Matt. 24:1-44, Luke 21:5-36). Other apocalyptic books were not accepted into the canon of the Bible.

A typical apocalypse presented itself as a book of visions, written in the name of an ancient sage, that revealed the secrets of the heavens and the earth, including information about the end of days. Often the revealed secrets related to the purpose of God in history, and thus the apocalypses were to help the righteous to discern the signs of the

Jewish Origins

approaching end of the world which was to culminate in the Age to Come or the Messianic Kingdom. Apocalypses were not homogeneous in every respect, but works of this genre did contain some of the same general features or broad characteristics, such as a mysteriousness of form and symbolic visions, usually interpreted by a angel guide or mediator. Most, but not all, apocalypses convey the impression that the end of days was imminent. Literary devices like the use of numbers and esoteric symbols contribute to the sense of remote mystery of the revelation and suggest that revelation is not possible without supernatural help.[6]

The apocalyptic works, theological and conceptual innovations of the Second Temple period, were not produced by any single apocalyptic movement or circle and could be used by different groups or individuals. This type of literature, intended to exhort and console, characteristically arose to meet a pressing religious need of the day. The Book of Daniel, for example, seems to have provided support for believers in the face of foreign persecution, and the Book of Watchers provided reassurance in the face of a shock to Jewish culture. The constant factor is that the apocalyptic revelation of a transcendent world and an eschatological judgment puts a problem in perspective for readers of the book. To study apocalyptic literature in Greco-Roman Judaism raises a number of questions as its relationship to Persian influences and the move within monotheistic Judaism to the kind of dualism, good against evil, this world versus the next, that is found in apocalypses.[7]

Thus, Judaism's conflict with Hellenism, the growth of the Hasidean type of piety, the crisis engendered by the persecutions of Antiochus IV Epiphanes and the subsequent Maccabean revolt, all contributed to the emergence of the new phenomenon represented by apocalypses and apocalyptic ideas.[8] Out of the intolerable situation of the suffering and dying of the righteous, the apocalypses were born. At the heart of apocalyptic literature was a message of vindication for the suffering righteous, a message about the end times. The secret truth that was revealed was that God would enable his suffering faithful, his chosen ones, to triumph and have dominion over their enemies and the world.

Parts of the Book of Enoch are the oldest surviving apocalypses and they antedate the apocalyptic parts of the Book of Daniel by half a century at least. Apocalyptic literature such as the Assumption of Moses and the Book of Daniel was written in connection with the reform crisis and resistance to the Hellenistic persecution.[9] The Book of Daniel was composed about 165 B.C.E. when the spread of Hellenism exacerbated an "identity crisis" of, and essential threat to, the Jewish people. The Book of Daniel is composed of two parts: the stories in chapters 1-6 were written by the third century at the latest, while the apocalyptic visions of chapters 7-12 come from the time of the Maccabean Revolt after 168 B.C.E.

The Book of Daniel, the only apocalypse as a whole that was accepted into the Jewish Bible, was likely published within Hasidean circles as a form of resistance literature for a persecuted minority of the second century B.C.E. The book provided for those afflicted Jews consoling and encouraging answers to many questions. The edifying stories in the first part of Daniel are all concerned with some kind of ordeal that is envisioned by the pagans and that Daniel and his faithful companions become involved in. In each case the Jewish heroes win out at the climactic moments, thanks to the spectacular intervention of God. The Book of Daniel teaches unambiguously a religious—not historic—truth: that the God of Israel is Lord of History and King of all peoples, and his chosen people will have ultimate victory over the enemies of God.[10]

Chapter Seven is the core of Daniel. Daniel has a vision of four beasts, understood variously to represent the successive empires of the Babylonians, Medes and Persians or Assyrians, and Greece and Rome. The last beast had ten horns. After the destruction of this beast, the kingdom was given to the saints forever as the Fifth Monarchy. No dates are given but cryptic references in the twelfth chapter are made to a time of woe lasting 1290 days and then a fullness of joy beginning after 1335 days.[11]

> Daniel said, "I saw in my vision . . . four great beasts came up out of the sea. . . . I saw in the night visions, and behold, with the clouds of heaven there came one like a son of man, and he came to the Ancient of Days. . . . And to him was given dominion and glory and kingdom. . . . As for me, Daniel, my spirit within me was anxious and the visions of my head alarmed me. I approached one

Jewish Origins

> of those who stood there and asked him the truth concerning all this. So he told me, and made known to me the interpretation of the things. . . . Then I desired to know the truth concerning the fourth beast. . . . As I looked, this horn made war with the saints, and prevailed over them, until the Ancient of Days came, and judgment was given for the saints of the Most High, and the time came when the saints received the kingdom" (Dan. 7:2-22).

Many apocalyptic writings were very much concerned with eschatological matters, that is, the imminence of the end of time and the way people should act in this last period preceding that end. Moreover, the end of time was not just seen as a chance event but an event fixed in advance as was the whole course of history from creation. A strong impression is given of a dualistic opposition of the world to come versus this world of current pain and suffering. Apocalypses convey the suggestion that the course of history is predetermined for evil until the end of days. Only in the world to come will the true justice and righteousness of God be revealed, and only in it will the righteous be vindicated. In this world, by contrast, wickedness reigns, the powers and principalities control its course. Therefore the righteous who suffer unjustly in this world will find their vindication in the world to come.

Apocalyptic ideas played an important role in various Jewish resistance groups, in the early stages of Christianity and also in many of the millenarian groups that arose in later centuries. Because of its complexity, apocalyptic literature lends itself easily to partial interpretations and misreading. It is understandable that in difficult times many pious people turned to the Scriptures for comfort but read into the text their own hopes and needs.

Let us turn from the literature of apocalypticism to some of the movements and groups that emerged during this turbulent period.

Jewish Groups and Movements

Many groups, sects, movements and religious trends made up the richness and variety that was Judaism from the Defilement of the

Temple to its destruction. Responding to political and religious threats these groups varied considerably in nature, ranging from nonviolent retreat into the desert to the violence of armed insurrection to messianic pretenders that were harshly repressed by Roman military might. Religious passion and fervor animated many, if not most, of these movements. Judaism in this period was alive, agitated by controversies and so many divergent views. But all these sects or groups had one thing in common: they owed allegiance to the Torah. The Torah was the ground of Judaism and the foundation of nationhood.[12] Not all parties agreed on the significance of the Torah or its interpretation, but religion served a vital political function during this period. Religion seems to have functioned as one of the few channels in these early centuries to express political sentiment and political opposition and social discontent. The concerns of religion supplied the motivation and means of articulating a larger consciousness in a way that political parties and political ideology might serve in later centuries. Religion provided the sense of community and a vocabulary that later concepts and terms would articulate, such as nationhood, patriotism and identity as a people. Different religious interpretations and practices served, in part, some of the functions that in later centuries political parties or a nationalistic ideology might provide.

At this period in Palestine, there was a mood of imminent eschatological expectation in society in general, as apocalyptic literature and later the Christian Gospels demonstrate, even though there exists little direct evidence for an apocalyptic theology among any one particular movement. All the groups living in Palestine at this time, however, most likely operated broadly within the perspective of Jewish apocalypticism. We cannot say that all Jews at the time were apocalyptics, but their thoughts about God and his relationship to the Jews and the rest of the world made apocalypticism a live option. They shared the same range of assumptions about what did happen and what could happen. Their scriptures described a covenantal relationship between God and the people of Israel. They shared the belief that God revealed himself and his Torah to the Patriarchs and Moses, that God put the Jewish people under a set of obligations and made promises about the salvation of those who adhered to this covenant. From the earliest biblical sources we get a sense that Israel felt itself under obligation to this God who made them into a nation and who would

Jewish Origins

decisively intervene in the ongoing history of the world to save his chosen people.[13]

During the period of Jewish history about which we are speaking, the century or two before the time of Jesus, there existed a diversity of forms of social unrest among Palestinian Jews. Waves of religious renewal had brought about an almost fanatical seriousness about the practice of their religion. Some movements and leaders lasted for a brief period; others lasted for several years.

This period of Jewish history, when an apocalyptic spirit was widespread, witnessed the frequent fusion of patriotism and religion, and consequently political turmoil had an overlay of intense religious seriousness. The political message often expressed itself in the forms and language of religious apocalypticism. Virtually all of the Jewish opposition movements wanted to realize a rule of and by God. Believers often hoped God's rule would come in a miraculous fashion, and they expressed an imminent eschatology or belief about the end times. In this turbulent context the imminent end of the world usually meant the end of foreign rule or Roman rule or the rule by unbelieving men.

Only one of the groups we will consider is truly a millenarian group, but the various groups manifest how religion served as a political glue to motivate and hold people together in the absence of a political ideology and terminology.

The Maccabean revolt occurred in response to Antiochus and coincided with emergence of apocalyptic writings of importance to us for knowledge of the period. Part of what we know about the Maccabean revolt and the later war against the Romans in 66-70 C.E. comes from the two Books of Maccabees and the work of the ancient historian Josephus. The author of the First Book of Maccabees describes the Maccabean struggle with pagans and those Jews who were not faithful (1 Macc. 2:44-48). The author of this book fused religion and patriotism, a linkage that we shall see again and again, suggesting that the survival of the Jewish community depended on the survival of their belief and worship of the God of Israel. Despite his faith and fervent nationalism, however, the author of the First Book of Maccabees gives a reasonably reliable narrative of the Jewish struggle against cultural and military forces. The enemy are the Greeks and Hellenizing Jews; the heart of pious Judaism is represented by Mattathias whose third son Judas began the Jewish revolt against the Seleucids in 167 B.C.E. Various groups of Jews rallied to the Maccabee family, "the family through whom it was given to save Israel" (5:62), when Judas issued the call for action.

Israel's distinct identity and distinct religion would have been lost if it did not resist Hellenism by every means, politically and militarily as well as religiously. The author of First Book of Maccabees depicts the great pressure on Jews to adopt the Hellenistic cultural practices and surrender their own religious ways: "Then the king [Antiochus] wrote to his whole kingdom that all should be one people, and that each should give up his customs. All the Gentiles accepted the command of the king. Many even from Israel gladly adopted his religion; they sacrificed to idols and profaned the sabbath. And the king sent letters by messengers to Jerusalem and the cities of Judah; he directed them to follow customs strange to the land, to forbid burnt offerings and sacrifices and drink offerings in the sanctuary, to profane sabbaths and feasts . . . and to leave their sons uncircumcised" (1 Macc. 1:41-50). That precious symbol of Judaism, the Torah, was physically attacked: "The books of the law which they found they tore to pieces and burned with fire. Where the book of the covenant was found in the possession of any one, or if any one adhered to the law, the decree of the king condemned him to death" (1 Macc. 1:56-57).

Jewish resistance took different forms. Some Jews resisted by the sword. The Hasideans, "the pious," were scrupulously observant of the Law to the point of refusing to fight on the Sabbath (1 Macc. 2:29-38). "But many in Israel stood firm and were resolved in their hearts not to eat unclean food. They chose to die rather than to be defiled by food or to profane the holy covenant; and they did die" (1 Macc. 1:62-63). More and more Judaism identified with observance of the Law and the restoration and re-dedication of the Temple on Mount Zion (1 Macc. 4:36-37).

The author of the Second Book of Maccabees likewise interprets history theologically and gives emphasis to God's choice of Israel and his careful watch over his people (2 Macc. 1:25). The author stresses the importance of observing the Law of God, especially the Sabbath

Jewish Origins

(2 Macc. 8:27; 15:1-4). Religious fidelity took on a fervor and seriousness so that many Jews were ready to lay down life itself to preserve their faith (2 Macc. 6:18-7:42). This intensity and fervor is characteristic of all apocalyptic groups, especially those who face persecution or opposition to their beliefs.

The ancient historian Josephus further describes some of the Jewish sects of the time: the Pharisees, the Sadducees and Essenes, as well as the party founded by Judas and Zadduck, later called the Zealots (*JW* 2.119-166; *Ant* 18.11-22). In their response to the times these different groups and movements reflected the diversity of future millenarian groups as they attempted to read the signs of the times and to respond to them. Only the Essenes can properly be thought of as a millenarian group.

The Essenes

Josephus is one of the few sources of information about this Jewish sect that came into being in Palestine during these times of intense eschatological ferment. This group, the Essenes or the Community at Qumran, are of interest to us because of all the movements of this period, they most clearly had the qualities of a millenarian community. The name Essene probably covers a number of groups whose beliefs and practices, though perhaps not identical, were similar. Their eschatological asceticism was widely known in ancient times, even mentioned by the ancient Roman historian Pliny.[14] Perhaps the most outstanding characteristic of this unique group is their underlying eschatological tension, a sense of living in the final time before God's intervention (cf. 1 QpHab 7:1-8).[15] The Essenes as well as the primitive Christian Church believed that the last age was imminent. Indeed, they felt they were living in the last times; they were the last generation, and for them the new age had dawned.

The Qumran community apparently split off from the Judaism of Jerusalem some time in the course of or toward the end of the Maccabean revolt. Their origin seems tied up in a sense of deprivation, that is, they felt blocked from any control over the Jerusalem

Temple and its cult. They rejected the Pharisaic interpretation of the Torah, and they rejected the Temple priests as defiled. Believing themselves to be the true orthodox, they removed themselves from the Jewish society of the time.

The Qumran community took form under the leadership of a priest known as the Righteous Teacher who withdrew his followers to the desert to found a priestly community in the Qumran area near the western shore of the Dead Sea around 140-130 B.C.E. In preparation to be the new Israel the Qumran community took on a communal mode of life characterized by intense asceticism and self-control. They embraced celibacy and held goods in common, despising riches. They led a disciplined, simple life of prayer and work, organized by a rigorous code of behavior, especially in regard to sexual behavior. Admission to the community was a careful process lasting for several years. In fact, their communal lifestyle of discipline and celibacy anticipated the life style of Christian monastic groups that emerged in the early Middle Ages. The Qumran settlement, which archeological evidence shows to have been solid buildings and an elaborate cistern system, existed from the latter part of the second century until 68 C.E. when the Romans destroyed it.

The death of their leader, the Righteous Teacher, seems to have raised their messianic expectations. They expected at the end of days to be reestablished in the New Jerusalem. Their strong feeling of the imminence of the end led them to believe that their own community lived in a kind of anticipation of the end, a bridging as it were of the gap between this age and the age to come.[16]

Out of their concerns the Essenes fashioned a dualistic and deterministic theology. The dualism was between this world and the world to come as well as the utter opposition between good and evil. Opposed to the Righteous Teacher was the Wicked Priest, the archpersecutor of the sect. The angelic world was divided into two just as the world of men was—the righteous were led by an angel of light and the wicked by an angel of darkness. Men were predetermined to be in one or other of these groups. The times of the world were fixed and this age was to climax in a great battle between the forces of light and those of darkness. This battle was to take place both on a worldly level and on a cosmic level.[17]

Jewish Origins

The Essene literature, some of which is better known as the Dead Sea Scrolls, grows out of the assumptions of apocalypticism and expresses eschatological concerns. One of the scrolls, *The War of the Sons of Light against the Sons of Darkness*, depicts the messianic battle which will bring to an end the oppression of Israel, with the true Israelites (here the members of this sect) doing battle against the sons of darkness, be they Romans or Seleucids or some other enemy of Yahweh. This intensely apocalyptic scroll speaks of God crushing the power of evil and darkness in this world and how God will favor the forces of good or light.

The *Manual of Discipline*, which was composed approximately 150-125 B.C.E., depicts this community as representing the New Covenant between God and men. A person becomes a member of this covenant by entering this community. The *Manual* describes two opposing ways of life, that of the community dominated by the spirit of light and truth and the opposing way of life dominated by darkness. The *Rule of the Congregation* ends with a description of the Anointed Priest presiding over the celebrations of the eschatological banquet in the age of fulfillment (1QSa 2:11-22).

The Essenes never, however, developed into a widespread movement and, like the Pharisees, they did not espouse violence in pursuit of their eschatological expectations. Similar to other groups, their ritual and religious practices served to maintain their solidarity and separate identity in society, and they maintained an apocalyptic cohesiveness in the face of the enemy and the rest of the world. During the final war with Rome in 68 C.E., the Essenes were sorely tested and not found wanting: they underwent great tortures but did not violate their religion by blaspheming or eating forbidden foods. Although the Essenes did not directly survive, later millenarian groups and some Christian monastic communities have very similar qualities to the community at Qumran.

Other Groups: the Fourth Philosophy, the Sicarii and the Zealots

The harshness and insensitivity of the Romans and their client kings help explain the rise of various and often violent movements. For years there were insults to Jewish religious traditions, such as the incident when the Roman general Pompey along with his staff violated the sanctuary of the Temple where only the Jewish high priest was allowed to enter.[18] Ten years later, about 54-53 B.C.E., another Roman, Crassus, who was the governor of Syria, needed money for an expedition against the Parthians, and he plundered the Temple of its gold (*JW* 1.179; *Ant* 14.105-109). Herod, a client king of Rome, had come to power in 37 B.C.E. Herod initiated a variety of public works, such as public baths and the important restoration and rebuilding of the Temple, but he was not popular with the Jews. Although his reign provided some stability and prosperity, he represented a strong Hellenizing influence which the Jews felt diluted their religion and eroded their religious customs (*Ant* 15.380, 365). For example, Herod held lavish games where there were horse races and athletic contests in which the contestants competed nude in the Greek manner, a custom repugnant to the Jews. Herod also built temples to Caesar Augustus, and, although this was outside Jewish areas, this strongly affronted Jewish religious beliefs (*Ant* 15.267-276, 364).

Finally in 4 B.C.E., two rabbis, Judas and Matthias, who had a large youthful following, felt they should react to the most recent insult, a golden eagle which King Herod had erected in the Temple. Jewish religious law taught that any image or representation was a violation. The two rabbis taught their young followers that it was better to die than see the Law violated. Believing Herod to be dying some of these young men let themselves down from the roof of the Temple by ropes and began chopping off the golden eagle. About 40 of these students were arrested. Brought before the king, the young men were exultant in the face of death for they believed fervently that after they died they would enjoy greater happiness. All were executed (*JW* 1.648-655). Herod, towards end of his life when he was ill and declining, ordered to be executed several of his own sons and hundreds of their accomplices who plotted against him (*Ant* 16.394; 17.187).

Archelaus, succeeding Herod as ethnarch rather than as king, was unable to stem the resentment that erupted after Herod's death. The Jews wanted vengeance on those of Herod's administration who had abused them during Herod's life, and Archelaus's troops killed 3,000 Jews in this uprising (*Ant* 17.218). The Romans could not allow the increasing anarchy in Palestine; they removed Archelaus after nine

Jewish Origins

years (6 C.E.) and reduced his territory (Judea, Samaria and Idumea) to a province. The emperor Augustus sent Coponius, a Roman with imperial powers that included the death penalty, to administer the province (*JW* 2.117). The province was annexed to Syria, where P. Sulpicius Quirinius was legate, which meant the Judean Jews were directly subject to Rome and Roman ideas and policies (*Ant* 18.1-2). Roman administrative procedures followed, which involved a census and financial inventory. This effectively made the statement that Yahweh was not lord, but that the Romans were the true lords of Palestine. The shock of this immediately provoked an uprising led by Judas, a Galillean, who with a Pharisee named Saddock, inflamed the people by calling them cowards for consenting to pay tribute to the Romans and for tolerating the Romans rather than God as their lord (*JW* 2.118; *Ant* 18.4). The high priest Joazar urged moderation, but Judas and Saddock said that the Jews were now slaves, and they must seek their independence. They appealed to their religious idealism to strengthen them in face of probable bloodshed (*Ant* 18.5). The resistance party of Judas and Saddock is called the Fourth Philosophy.

The immediate cause of the founding of the Fourth Philosophy was the issue of paying tribute to Rome (which meant that God was no longer sovereign in Israel) (*JW* 2.118; *Ant* 18.1-2, 23). The driving motivation was that Yahweh was the sovereign of Israel and Yahweh's sovereignty required resistance to Israel's enemies as a religious duty.[19] These Jews had a passion for liberty and a fervor to resist the alien power of Rome. Their steadfastness in torture and violent death testifies, as it did with the later Christian martyrs, to their passionate commitment and faith. Their emotional intensity was such that often the word "madness" is used to describe their behavior, especially since the Romans and those in power were scarcely able to appreciate their wholehearted zeal.[20]

Judas's party or sect survived for a number of years and continued its opposition to the Romans. This group during the mid-fifties made itself notorious by a series of murders of distinguished individuals. These murders earned the perpetrators the name of Sicarii.[21] The name Sicarii comes from their daggers which were curved like the weapons called *sicae* by the Romans. The Sicarii murdered people in broad daylight in the middle of Jerusalem. They would mix with crowds, especially during the festivals, and conceal their daggers under their cloaks. They would stealthily stab their opponents and simply melt into the outraged crowds, undetected because of the naturalness of their presence. Acting as urban terrorists, they frequently assassinated establishment priests and other Jewish aristocrats who collaborated with the Romans during the fifties rather than any Roman soldiers or officials.

Other groups of Jews actively resisted or advocated armed violence for varying reasons. Many messianic and pietistic revolts of Herodian times were spontaneous and unconnected outbreaks, with little organization or leadership, the efforts of peasants and socially rootless people responding to the calls of different reform leaders and messianic pretenders.[22]

The historian Josephus, writing for Roman readers, could only view these men and their followers as brigands,[23] and the Roman occupiers could only see the appearance of these groups as highly dangerous and consequently often used force to keep passions under control. The Jewish extremists were for the most part deeply patriotic and motivated by an intense zeal for the Torah.[24] Jewish messianic expectations in the early Roman period were diverse and fluid, with no uniform expectation of a messiah until well after the destruction of Jerusalem in 70 C.E. The term messiah was not an essential element in Jewish eschatological expectation and its literary use is relatively rare prior to the time of Jesus. But at some level of Jewish society there was some anticipation of a kingly agent inspired by God to bring deliverance to his people.

The Fourth Philosophy differed from the Zealots who only made their appearance in 67-68 C.E. amid the violence of the Jewish revolt and Roman war. The Fourth Philosophy and the Sicarii (*Ant* 18.3-9, 23-25) were anti-Roman and anti-establishment and were prepared to suffer violence and death for their cause. Unlike the Zealots they were not peasant movements. The Fourth Philosophy and Sicarii, prepared to suffer violence and death for their cause, advocated resistance but probably not to the point of armed rebellion like the Zealots.[25]

Rather than lessening, the Roman disregard for Jewish religious sensitivities increased. Romans meddled in the appointment of the high priests. Pontius Pilate, appointed procurator about 26 C.E.,

Jewish Origins

offended Jewish religious scruples by bringing military standards into Jerusalem (cf. Ex. 20:4 and Deut. 4:16). Knowing this would offend the Jews, he acted covertly at night. When the Jews discovered this violation in the morning, they strongly protested. Pilate refused to yield on the grounds that it would be an offense to the emperor, but finally he relented when the Jews said they would rather die than transgress the Law. Pilate also used money belonging to the Temple to build an aqueduct which, of course, is secular. Pious Jews had contributed this money for the purchase of sacrificial animals. In response to the Jewish protest soldiers went beyond their order and killed many demonstrators (*Ant* 18.55-62; *JW* 2.169).

The violence was just part of the complex situation that continued to push Palestine toward the Revolt of 66-70. The revolt that flared up in 66 C.E. culminated in the Roman destruction of Jerusalem and the Temple in 70 C.E. In addition to the deteriorating economic conditions of the peasantry and the disintegrating social situation, there was a prolonged drought and serious famine in the late forties as well as renewed repressive measures by Roman forces. The Roman offenses against Jewish religious feelings and scruples, along with the political and economic oppression, increased the tension and bitterness in Palestine.

In 40 C.E. the Emperor Caligula, believing himself to be a god, ordered a large statue of himself erected in the Temple at Jerusalem (*JW* 2.185-187; *Ant* 18.261-262). Because of Jewish resistance, he sent Petronius with three legions and a large contingent of Syrian auxiliaries to carry out the order. Petronius held a series of meetings with the Jews and recognized their religion. He did return to Antioch without violence and reported to the emperor that to press on with this additional affront to Jewish religious customs would destroy the whole nation. Caligula threatened to kill Petronius if he did not carry through his orders, but fortunately Caligula was assassinated before this came about.

About the year 49 C.E. when Cumanus was procurator of Judea, another disturbance broke out that resulted in still another large loss of Jewish lives (*JW* 2.223-227; *Ant* 20.105-112). On one occasion a large crowd had gathered at Jerusalem for Passover, causing Cumanus to station soldiers in the Temple porticoes to prevent any violence.

One of the soldiers raised his robe in an indecent gesture that outraged Jews took as an insult to the Temple. Some picked up stones and hurled them at the soldiers. Cumanus, fearing loss of control that could spark a larger uprising, called for reinforcements. These armed troops pouring into the porticoes threw the crowd into panic. Trying to flee, people were trapped at the exits and trampled to death. Thousands of people perished in an appalling tragedy, triggered by one soldier in this time of tension.

Not long afterwards a Roman solider profaned a copy of the Torah and uttered blasphemies (*JW* 2.228-231; *Ant* 20.113-117). The sacrilege outraged the Jews and a large number protested to Cumanus. He backed down and beheaded the soldier and thus prevented still another outbreak of violence.

In addition to these religious and political tensions, over-population and over-taxation burdened the people, with the combined civil and religious taxation at a rate of approximately 40 percent.[26] Adding to the level of anxiety and social stress was a serous famine in 46 C.E. (*Ant* 20.101; 18.8; Acts 11.28-30).

Florus, around the time of the outbreak of open war between the Jews and Rome, 66 C.E., failed to deal reasonably with legitimate complaints. Further inflaming public feeling, he took money from the Temple treasury with still further rise in tension and outbursts (*JW* 2.293-296).

Once revolt had broken out, the Roman general Vespasian, having conquered Galilee, began to move south toward Jerusalem in the winter of 67-68. The conflict between Jews who advocated resistance and Jews who advocated surrender became acute. Advocates of resistance, mostly younger men, got the upper hand and began looting their neighbors and ravaging the countryside. They withdrew to Jerusalem where they merged into one group and eventually became strong enough to terrorize the city and to get control of the Temple. They called themselves Zealots (*JW* 4.161).

The name, *tous zelotas* (*JW* 2.444), means fanatical adherents. Possibly there were increasing numbers of individual fanatics. Jewish preachers had been praising zeal since Maccabean times. Roman oppression, brutality and taxation all were evoking much fanatical hatred which expressed itself as piety. Most probably the popularity of religious zeal that was inextricably linked to passionate patriotism may explain why a group would call itself *the* Zealots. It is likely that there were many individual zealots in the city and that they made up a large part of the following of Eleazar ben Simon, one of the Jewish leaders at this time (*JW* 2.564). The Zealots only came into existence in winter of 67-68, when the Jewish military position was growing desperate because of the Romans approach to the city. It is likely that various individual zealots and rural resistance groups who had taken refuge in Jerusalem formed a coalition against the Romans (*JW* 7.268-70; 4.135, 138). The Zealots were probably mostly Judean peasants, with a peasant piety, who were hostile to the Jewish establishment of the city as well as the foreigners. It was, however, a small but highly militant party which played an important part in the final defense of the city and its destruction. Their name has come to refer to those who are fanatically partisan for religious reasons.[27]

The Zealots were the spiritual children of the Maccabees. Although Josephus, writing for Roman readers, regarded the Zealots as brigands and robbers, they could equally well be described as fervent patriots, according to the point of view of the observer. Essentially they were a mixture of Jews, mostly patriotic and likely motivated by that fusion of religion and patriotism that seem to have been pervasive during this period. We may assume that part of their opposition to Rome was rooted in their religious zeal for the Torah.

The final period of the war and the siege of Jerusalem produced terrible horrors, the kind that apocalyptic passages associate with the end time. "But when you see Jerusalem surrounded by armies, then know that its desolation has come near. . . . For great distress shall be upon the earth and wrath upon this people; they will fall by the edge of the sword, and be led captive among all nations; and Jerusalem will be trodden down by the Gentiles. . . ." (Lk. 21:23-24); "Truly, I say to you, there will not be left here one stone upon another, that will not be thrown down. . . . For then there will be great tribulation, such as has not been from the beginning of the world until now, no, and never will be" (Matt. 24:2-28).[28]

Josephus described, possibly on the basis of eye-witness accounts, a catalogue of horrors, such as the crucifixion of prisoners (*JW* 5.451) and such uncompromising savagery as Arab and Syrian troops disemboweling deserters from besieged Jerusalem because the troops sought gold coins that people tried to smuggle out of the besieged city by swallowing them (*JW* 5.552). When the Temple was being destroyed, Jews could only question why God did not save his Temple. The End Time, the *eskaton*, surely must have arrived. Josephus described how one of the attacking soldiers hurled a fiery missile into the sanctuary. Jews with great wailing watched the sanctuary burn. While the Temple blazed, Roman soldiers plundered and slaughtered. The roar of flames, the battle cries of Roman legionnaires, the shrieks of the dying, the faces of victims emaciated from the siege, the heaps of corpses, the flow of blood, the scene must have indeed seemed like the final day, especially to those who had expected divine intervention (*JW* 6.253, 271-274, 286).

Conclusion

The two centuries before the destruction of the Temple was a troubled period during which different popular movements and groups arose in response to political, social and religious crises. Religious ferment had given birth to renewal movements that sought a stricter interpretation of the Torah and an intensification of religious rules touching on circumcision, purification and diet, rules that provided identifying norms of what it meant to be a Jew. When religious institutions and deeply rooted beliefs suffered attack, some believers saw their sufferings in terms of an apocalyptic portrait of the end time and the oppression of God's people. From the point of view of the Romans, some of the Jewish believers were fanatics and a nuisance that required frequent attention and troops to keep peace. From the viewpoint of fervent Jewish opponents to foreign occupiers, their religious identity and relationship with God were at stake. They ultimately perceived the Romans as depriving them of fulfilling their religious obligations and threatening the absolute sovereignty of Yahweh. Taken together with the other political and religious trends of the time, this partly explains the intensity of the movements that arose.[29]

Many of the diverse groups and movements in Palestine had an eschatological orientation, and the diversity of their response (ranging from the Essenes' withdrawal from society to the violence of the Zealots) to deteriorating conditions and oppression anticipates some of the diversity of later millenarian groups.

The last 70 years of this period, roughly from 4 B.C.E. to 70 C.E., coincides with the birth of Jesus, his public ministry and the early years of the Christian communities in Palestine. Let us now turn to these early Christian communities.

NOTES

1. D.S. Russell, *Apocalyptic: Ancient and Modern* (Philadelphia: Fortress Press, 1978), p. 8, and Norman Cohn, *The Pursuit of the Millennium* (New York: Oxford University Press, 1970), p. 21.

2. D.S. Russell, *From Early Judaism to Early Church* (Philadelphia: Fortress Press, 1986), pp. 9 and 58.

3. Michael Edward Stone, *Scriptures, Sects and Visions: A Profile of Judaism from Ezra to the Jewish Revolts* (Philadelphia: Fortress Press, 1980), pp. 15-16.

4. Josephus, *Jewish Antiquities* (Loeb Classical Library: Harvard University Press), hereafter cited as *Ant.*; Josephus, *The Jewish War* (Loeb Classical Library: G.P. Putnam), hereafter cited as *JW*. Josephus is a flawed source, being very hostile toward his own Jewish people as he writes for the Romans; he is, however, an essential source that must be used.

5. Michael Edward Stone, *Scriptures, Sects and Visions: A Profile of Judaism from Ezra to the Jewish Revolts* (Philadelphia: Fortress Press, 1980), p. 29.

6. Louis F. Hartman and Alexander A. DiLella, *The Anchor Bible: The Book of Daniel: A New Translation with Notes and Commentary* (Garden City: Doubleday, 1978), p. 62; John J. Collins, *The Apocalyptic Imagination: An Introduction to the Jewish Matrix of Christianity* (New York: Crossroad, 1984), pp. 4, 63; Michael Edward Stone, p. 29; D.S. Russell, *Between the Testaments* (Philadelphia: Fortress Press, 1972), p. 97.

7. Louis F. Hartman and Alexander A. DiLella, p. 2; Sheldon R. Isenberg, "Millenarism in Greco-Roman Palestine," *Religion* 4 (1974): 40, footnote #2.

8. Michael Edward Stone, pp. 29-30.

9. Richard A. Horsley and John S. Hanson, *Bandits, Prophets and Messiahs: Popular Movements in the Time of Jesus* (Minneapolis: Winston Press, 1985), p. 17.

10. Louis F. Hartman and Alexander A. DiLella, pp. 104, 108; Michael Edward Stone, p. 42.

11. John J. Collins, pp. 63, 208.

12. D.R. Russell, *Between the Testaments*, p. 49.

13. Horsley and Hanson, pp. 245-250; Sheldon R. Isenberg, pp. 30, 33.

14. Pliny, *Natural History* (Loeb Classical Library: G.P. Putnam), 5.17,73.

15. References to Dead Sea Scrolls, that is, documents found in the Qumran Caves, tend to be referred to by the number of the cave in which they were found, then the letter Q standing for Qumran and then sometimes the type of document, such as an interpretative commentary (p), and then the abbreviation of the Old Testament book of which they are a version. Thus the reference here is to a commentary on Habakuk, found in Cave 1, that adopts the thought of Habakuk to the community at Qumran.

16. Frank Moore Cross, *The Ancient Library of Qumran* (Garden City: Doubleday and Co., 1958), p. 96; Sheldon R. Isenberg, pp. 38-39; Michael Edward Stone, p. 67.

17. Michael Edward Stone, pp. 64-68; Frank Moore Cross, p. 82.

18. Tacitus, *The Histories* (Loeb Classical Library: Harvard University Press, 1956), 5.9; *JW* 1.152.

19. Cf. S.G.F. Brandon, *Jesus and the Zealots: A Study of the Political Factor in Primitive Christianity* (Manchester University Press; Charles Scribner's Sons, 1967), p. 48.

20. *deinotatos*, *Ant* 18.8; *anoia*, *Ant* 18.24; *aponoian*, *JW* 7.412

21. Morton Smith, "Zealots and Sicarii, Their Origins and Relation," *Harvard Theological Review* 64 (1971): 18; Richard A. Horsley and John S. Hanson, pp. 241, 200-205; cf. *Ant* 20.186; *JW* 2.254-56.

22. Morton Smith, p. 13; Sheldon R. Isenberg, p. 42, footnote #10; cf. L.D. Hankoff, "Religious Innovation in the Jewish Revolt Against Rome," in David A. Halperin, editor, *Psychodynamic Perspectives on Religion, Sect and Cult* (John Wright, 1983), pp. 1-30.

23. Josephus generally uses words like *lestes*, robber or brigand, and *lesterion*, band of robbers to describe these armed men. cf. *JW* 2.57.

24. Cf. William Reuben Farmer, *Maccabees, Zealots, and Josephus: An Inquiry into Jewish Nationalism in the Greco-Roman Period* (New York: Columbia University Press, 1956), pp. 82, 175.

25. Richard A. Horsley and John S. Hanson, pp. 89-93, 190-191, 198-199.

26. Fredrick C. Grant, *The Economic Background of the Gospels*, (New York: Russell and Russell, 1926, 1973), p. 105.

27. Morton Smith, pp. 16-19.

28. These Gospel passages seem to merge teachings about the destruction of the Temple at Jerusalem with details associated with the end of the world.

29. Cf. Charles S. Liebman, "Extremism as a Religious Norm," *Journal for the Scientific Study of Religion* 22 (1983): 75-86. Also Sheldon R. Isenberg, p. 29. The intensity and dedication was not unlike modern terrorist activity: cf. David C. Rapport, "Terror and the Messiah: An Ancient Experience and Some Modern Parallels," in David C. Rapport and Yonah Alexander, editors, *The Morality of Terrorism: Religious and Secular Justifications* (New York: Pergamon Press, 1982), pp. 13-42.

Chapter Two
Early Christianity
as a Millenarian Movement

Introduction

The previous chapter suggested some of the richness and complexity of Judaism in the two centuries before the destruction of the Temple in 70 C.E. Jews struggled to retain their religious identity amidst the commercial and cultural world of Hellenism with its tendency toward religious syncretism. To counter the drift towards assimilation by an alien culture and as a response to Roman occupation, different Jewish sects and leaders stirred up nationalistic feelings and revived native religous traditions.

The last 70 years of this period, roughly from 4 B.C.E. to 70 C.E., coincided with the birth of Jesus, his public ministry and the early years of the Christian communities in Palestine. The earliest Christian communities arose amidst the richness and diversity of Jewish apocalyptic thought and renewal movements. During these turbulent decades of the first century, Jesus's contemporaries might well have regarded him as just another religious leader whose followers established yet another sect in a time of religious ferment and sectarian movements. Within two or three centuries Christianity was to emerge conspicuously on the world stage, but the form of Christianity that emerged triumphant after the struggles of the first two centuries was but one among many varieties of Christianity known to have existed from the days of Jesus and his first followers.[1]

The principal source of information about the origins and early days of Christianity is the New Testament. Many of these writings, however, were gathered together during the tumultuous last part of the first century and present a complex mosaic. They offer little direct sociological data and interpretation is difficult. Further, many of the early Christian writers set down their thoughts at the time when Christianity was still involved in the task of self-definition and in a polemic with Judaism. Not only were there different traditions among the new Christian communities, many cultural and religious changes were taking place. For example, Jewish apocalyptic ideas and images influenced Christianity, even as Judaism itself began during this period to turn away from the apocalyptic tradition.

New religions, like Christianity, do not come into existence *ex nihilo* but in some sense begin as revitalization or even heretical movements in reaction to an established religion and, as such, are a tremendous threat to the old order.[2] The Jesus Movement, like other renewal movements, found initial success in the country areas, especially the areas of Galilee and Judea, for example. It was in the city of Jerusalem that Jesus was arrested and executed. But the authorities executed Jesus, however, not so much because he was a religious reformer but because they saw him as a political figure, like the leaders of other resistance movements, who seemed to threaten the overthrow of the established order. Later the Jewish authorities in the Sanhedrin, the supreme religious body and court of the Jews, took a principal part in the persecution of Jesus's followers, the early Christians (Acts 4:5, 5:17).

The Jewish officials of the Sanhedrin were not against this new Christian sect as such. But the Sadducees, who controlled the Sanhedrin at this time, feared offending the Roman occupiers and therefore saw in every messianic movement an endangering of their own existence (cf. Acts, chapters 4 and 5). Basically the followers of Jesus were tolerated as long as they kept the law, even though they were known to be Jesus's disciples. Only when Stephen declared that

Early Christianity

the Law and Temple were transitory was he persecuted. The Jesus Movement in Palestine made many concessions to Judaism and was allowed by the authorities to continue in its ways.

The study of early Christianity during the first century raises a number of problems not only of the methodology of approach but also because of faith and non-faith demands. Different scholarly and faith perspectives tend to see different facets of Christianity. Was Christianity a Jewish sect or Jewish heresy, a renewal movement within Judaism that had parallels with the other revival movements within Judaism, such as the Qumran community and some of the prophetic movements?[3] Or was Christianity a prophetic movement or a radical political movement similar to the Zealots?

Christianity as a Millenarian Movement

A number of scholars, especially anthropologists, see in early Christianity some of the qualities of a revitalization and millenarian movement and suggest that Christianity "derived its initial élan from radical millenarism."[4] This chapter will look at these aspects of early Christianity without precluding other perspectives. Millenarian groups, in general, tend to be marked by a) their beliefs about the imminent coming of the end of time, b) the release of great emotional energy, c) charismatic leadership, d) relatively loose organization, e) origins in a context of relative deprivation, and f) a membership with less status and power in society.[5]

Belief

The earliest Christian communities stood in the mainstream of Jewish apocalyptic thinking, and the earliest New Testament sources present a relatively unified picture: the Kingdom would come in the near future.[6] Soon, however, there did develop within the early Christian communities a more complex and ambiguous attitude toward the

Coming (*Parousia*) of the Son of Man and the imminent end of the world.

The earliest Christians thought that their world was soon to come to an end, even within their lifetimes. If Jesus was understood as the Messiah, his coming and his resurrection was the first act of the eschatological scenario.[7] Christians early began to interpret Jesus's words as predictions that had become realized. The earliest Church presented itself as an eschatological sect within Judaism that was different from other Jewish sects by the fact it awaited the crucified Jesus to return as Son of Man and by its consciousness of being already called and chosen as the congregation of the end of days. One scholar takes the view that "apocalyptic was the mother of all Christian theology."[8]

The earliest members of the Jesus Movement believed that the end of the present-world order was at hand. In Paul's earliest extant Epistle, to the Thessalonians, he uses the Greek term *Parousia* in the sense of he Lord's Second Coming several times (1 Thes. 2:19, 3:13, 4:15, 5:23). The earliest of the written Gospels, reflecting the concerns of the first generation of Christians, recalls Jesus as beginning his ministry with the urgent proclamation of the imminence of the end time and the coming of the Kingdom. The Gospel of Mark reflects the early community's sense of the imminent end of the present order: "The time is fulfilled, and the kingdom of God is at hand; repent, and believe in the gospel" (Mk. 1:15); "Truly, I say to you, this generation will not pass away before all these things take place," (Mk. 13:29). Passages from Mark's Gospel are starkly apocalyptic and depict Jesus in an eschatological struggle against evil (for example, Mk. 1:21-27). Even though Jesus' words were adapted and interpreted by the Gospel writers there is conveyed the urgency of the announcement of the coming of the Kingdom. Early Christians prayed for the coming of the Kingdom (Mt. 6:10; 1 Cor. 16:22). This sense of the looming end of the present order permeates the whole early Christian outlook prior to 70 C.E. and inspired intense fervor.

After the Easter experience in Galilee, the followers of Jesus went up to Jerusalem as the focus of the coming reign of God. They waited for the fulfillment of Jesus's promises as they understood them in the context of the time. Judaism had expected the End of Days to bring a gathering of the scattered tribes of Israel. By calling itself the congregation of God the earliest Church declared it fulfilled the hopes of Jewish apocalypticism.[9] The members of this early church were the chosen, the elect, the saints. The terms synagogue and *ekklesia* have this sense of a "gathering together."

The Apostle Paul, drawing upon early kerygma or preaching summaries, preached the message of Christ's death, resurrection and imminent return. His message implied an eschatological understanding of Christian life in this world, and he insisted that the law had come to an end and had no continuing theological significance for the growing Christian church. Paul's passages that are most vividly expectant of the return of Jesus, such as 1 Thes. 4:13-5:11, seem to serve the function of reinforcing Christian solidarity and instructing Christians how to behave until Jesus returns.[10]

Paul's message changed and developed. Like the first generation of the followers of Jesus, he expected the Lord's return soon (Phil. 4:5). Paul did not think the end had come yet but believed it would soon come. 1 Thes. 4:16-17 may be taken as typical expression of widely shared beliefs: "For the Lord himself will descend from heaven with a cry of command, with the archangel's call, and with the sound of the trumpet of God. And the dead in Christ will rise first; then we who are alive, who are left, shall be caught up together with them in the clouds to meet the Lord in the air."

The early tradition records Jesus using apocalyptic imagery: "The Son of man is to come with his angels in the glory of his Father, and then he will repay every man for what he has done" (Mt. 16:27); "And I tell you, every one who acknowledges me before men, the Son of Man also will acknowledge before the angels of God" (Lk. 12:8). The early communities recalled and interpreted the words of Jesus in the light of remembered events. For example, Mt. 24:1-25:46 refers to the fall of Jerusalem and the eschatological end even though the Romans had already destroyed Jerusalem by the time the Gospel was composed.

But like Paul the early communities also began to note the delay in the coming of the Kingdom. The Gospels contain passages that reflect the concern of the communities about the delay in the Lord's coming and the mysteriousness of the timing of the end: "But of that day or that hour no one knows, not even the angels in heaven, nor the Son, but only the Father. Take heed, watch; for you do not know when the time will come" (Mk. 13:32-33). There is encouragement to be alert in the face of the uncertainty: "You also must be ready; for the Son of Man is coming at an hour you do not expect" (Lk. 12:40; Mt. 24:44). "For you yourselves know well that the day of the Lord will come like a thief in the night" (1 Thes. 5:2). The Letter of James, writen probably late in the first century or even early in the second century, enjoins Christians to be both patient but hopeful because the Coming of the Lord is near: "Be patient, brethren, until the coming of the Lord. . . . You also be patient. Establish your hearts, for the coming of the Lord is near" (5:7-8).

The second and third generations of Christians had to confront the non-appearance of the Parousia. As those who had seen Jesus alive began to die off, the Christian communities became increasingly anxious about the delay of Jesus's return and the coming of the Kingdom.[11] Paul had confronted this issue of the delay of the Coming even in 1 Thes. 4:13-5:11 where there is reference to the concern that seems to have arisen when some believers died before the coming of the Kingdom. Apparently some had believed the kingdom was expected before any believers or those of the first generation would die.[12] The writer of the Second Letter of Peter, comparatively late (circa 125 C.E. or later), refers to "scoffers . . . saying 'Where is the promise of his coming?' " (2 Peter 3:3-4).

Gradually Paul seemed to reconcile himself to delay. In some passages he suggests a present aspect, that the End Time had already begun and that Christians had already been saved (2 Cor. 6:2). There seems to have been some adaptation of Christian belief to grapple with the unexpected delay. Some texts suggest a change in the timetable for the coming based on the conversion of the Gentiles: "And the gospel must first be preached to all nations" (Mk. 13:10).

Not only was the coming of the Kingdom delayed, Christians also had to come to terms with something totally unexpected, actual persecution. Consolation literature, like the Jewish apocalyptic literature, tries to deal with disappointment and despair at the delay of God's expected action as well as suffering endured by God's faithful. The prospect of the Lord's Coming was to provide hope and strength amidst

Early Christianity

present suffering and trials. Perhaps the most dramatic Christian response to persecution was the Book of Revelation. Its title in Greek, *apokalupsis* of Jesus Christ, not only links it explicitly with the Jewish apocalyptic tradition but also reaffirms Christian hope about the Coming, about "what must soon take place . . . for the time is near" (Rev. 1:1-3). The Book of Revelation uses strange symbols to evoke mystery like Jewish apocalyptic literature, although its Christocentric view of history also makes it different.

The book probably was written during the persecution at the end of the reign of Domitian, circa 90-96 C.E., and has among its purposes to strengthen and console the persecuted faithful by revealing the meaning of persecution. The author reveals that he, too, has shared his hearers' tribulations for the faith (1:9). He offers mysterious symbols, some of which he explains and some of which he does not. He also presents a series of visions which describe present situations and future eschatological events. He offers varying lengths of time that the persecution will last (11:3, 12:6, 12:14, but this may just be part of his mysterious use of numbers. He sees the cosmos, in particular, the Roman empire against the Christian churches, as a struggle between the forces of Satan against God. But final victory will come, along with the heavenly Jerusalem and a new creation. Satan will be bound for a thousand years; the saints will reign with Christ for a thousand years (20:1-6).

Emotion

The New Testament uses various words that suggest the intensity of the religious feelings of early Christians, although these feelings never approached the frenzied madness of some of the pagan cults.

Indeed Paul expected the first Christians to be different from the pagans, that they "must no longer live as the Gentiles do" (Eph. 4:17). Nevertheless Paul greets the readers of his epistles with an exhortation to rejoice, be filled with joy: *chairete* (Phil. 3:1; 1 Thes. 5:17). This word *chairo* is sometimes used in the New Testament writings in contexts of great religious joy (cf. Mt. 28:8; 5:12)

Whatever the Pentecost experience was, it was a faith experience that released intense emotions. Pentecost originally was a Jewish thanksgiving feast that concluded 50 days of grain harvest (Dt. 16:9-11; Lev. 23:15-21), and Jesus' disciples took the opportunity of this traditional feast to come up to Jerusalem. The Acts of the Apostles describes how the early Christian community was together in one place and was filled with the Holy Spirit and began to speak in tongues (2:1-4). The gift of speaking in tongues was an exhibition of great emotional excitement and religious exaltation (Acts 2:13).

The crowds drawn to witness the spectacle of the disciples speaking in tongues at first thought the enthusiasm of the Christians was possibly due to "new wine" (Acts 2:13), not unlike the celebrants of Bacchus. The author of Acts uses words that suggest the intense reaction of the crowd witnessing the disciples speaking in tongues: "amazed, bewildered," *existanto* (2:6, 13). (The words *existemi* and *extasis* suggest "be astonished," "be beside oneself," and are used of the ecstasies of Peter and Paul: Acts 10:10; 11:5; 22:17). Paul also refers to his own extraordinary ecstatic experiences, his visions and revelations (2 Cor. 12:1-8).

The author of Acts refers to the early community's "glad and generous hearts" (Acts 2:42-46). The gladness, *agalliasis*, of their meals together was probably a mood of eschatological joy.[13] The sense of being the community of the last time gives a sense of ecstacy. In his earliest extant writing Paul makes reference to the joy at the Lord's coming or the Parousia (1 Thes. 2:19). The expectation of the Lord's Coming and the time of the millennium gave a sense of fraternal equality, so that there are no distinctions (Rom. 3:22). "There is neither Jew nor Greek, there is neither slave nor free, there is neither male nor female" (Gal. 3:28).

Some Christians, expecting the imminent coming of the Lord, seem to have ceased working and were living on the generosity of others (2 Thes. 3:6-12). Perhaps they believed because of their election that all things were lawful for them (1 Cor. 6:12; 10:23). Later millenarian groups tend to be especially antinomian, that is, counter to traditional rules and customs.[14] Members of an elect group somehow feel that their membership gives them freedom to go beyond all previous rules and taboos, that established society is to be rejected. On the basis of

Early Christianity

their intense and supremely confident commitment and their sense that they are operating according to the divine plan, members can easily divide the world into good (us) and evil (them). An elated sense of freedom often can express itself in uninhibited aggression or sexual abberations, be it in extremes of asceticism or in sexual excesses.[15]

It is precisely this sense of freedom and unbounded enthusiasm that Paul tries to counter among the new converts in the first Hellenistic community at Corinth. Paul provides a dramatic glimpse into an enthusiastic early community when he writes to chide the Corinthian community for their excesses and abuses. Members of this oldest Hellenistic community experienced an unbounded sense of enthusiasm and ecstacy, along with a tremendous release of sexual energy—possibly believing that being among the elect with the End Time so near meant that they were freed from all former restraints and rules,[16] misunderstanding Paul's preaching on spirit and freedom. Their eucharistic banquets had become marred by divisions and even drunkenness (1 Cor. 11:17 ff.). Paul spoke to the new converts like children (1 Cor. 3:1; 4:14) and reminded them not to be divided, not to quarrel (1:10 ff.), not to be arrogant or sexually immoral (5:1-2).

Paul was especially concerned about new converts' spiritual gifts, those highly emotional orgiastic practices similar to pagan cults. Members of the first communities, assembled for the coming of the Lord (2 Thes. 2:1), believed that they themselves are caught up somehow in the divine and expressed this with intense emotion, feeling they have an integrity and experience that the hostile world cannot know.[17] Many of the new converts to Christianity experienced the emotional effects of conversion—ecstatic speaking in tongues—and regarded glossolalia, the gift of speaking in tongues, as an extraordinary manifestation of the Spirit's presence. Religious emotionalism under the impulse of the Spirit might make a Christian shout out praises of God in fervid improvisation. But mere ecstasy doesn't necessarily mean the Christian is one with the spirit. Paul urged appropriate limits on speaking of tongues, that it be used decently and for the building up of the church and balanced with other gifts, (1 Cor. 14:27 ff.). Unlike the pagans, the Christians should control these gifts. In this context of exerting some control, Paul says that women should keep silence in the churches. They should not go contrary to the customs of the primitive Palestinian communities, and so women are not to speak, (1 Cor. 14:34-35). Perhaps he has witnessed some of the excesses of the emotional excitement and religious enthusiasm of pagan Greek followers of Dionysus who were far more demonstrative than any Jewish Christians.

Christians interpreted such dramatic, visible signs as evidence that the Holy Spirit was present (cf. Acts 10:44-46). But Paul tried to dampen such enthusiasm and to interpret all significant functions in the community as gifts of the Spirit which enable those who receive them to perform some special function within the community; Paul enumerates among these gifts prophecy, teaching, service, and exhorting (Rom. 12:1-11).

Groups of charismatic persons, in the sense of those who under religious inspiration are given to intense emotional outbursts, have at times been a revolutionary force that is anti-organizational and foreign to everyday routine structures. In a pure form such charismatic groups are unstable and shortlived; as authority structures increase within a religious movement, charismatic qualities decline. Some writers even divide the early Christian Church into a primitive charismatic age that differs from a later, more organized hierarchic age.[18] The authorities of the institutional and routinized Church time and again faced up to members challenging their authority and wanting to return to the qualities of the primitive, charismatic Church.

Leadership

A religious movement usually begins under the powerful impetus of a prophetic figure. Jesus began the reform movement that became Christianity and Paul continued to build this growing movement. The New Testament literature testifies to Jesus's force and power with crowds who were amazed and astounded by his teaching (Mk. 1:22, 27; Lk. 4:32-36). Jesus acted with prophetic authority as he criticized the old and gave a vision of the new (Mt. 5:21-48; Mk. 1:22, 27; Mk. 2:25). Jesus was a charismatic, prophetic figure who astonished and excited crowds by his teaching. He sought to purify the established priestly aristocracy and temple cult—he overturned the tables in the temple and expelled the money-changers (Mk. 11:15-19; Lk. 19:45-48). Jesus formulated assumptions about the basic redemptive means of this time: the temple and the interpretation of the Torah. Millenarian movements are about moral regeneration.[19] Millenarian movements arise in a context of the challenge by new values to traditional assumptions. In brief, the Gospels depict Jesus in the way that many later millenarian leaders emulate.

The question of succession arises with the disappearance of the original charismatic leader.[20] Christianity had to resolve the problem crucial for the continuance of a movement which originated in a personally charismatic leader. The Gospels relate how Jesus transferred authority to his followers and how he commissioned his apostles to spread his message (Mt. 16:13 ff.). The different accounts of the resurrection serve to reinforce the authority of Peter (Mk. 16:7; Lk. 24:12; Jn. 21:2), but Luke's account provides the basis for the charismatic endowment of the apostles which was to occur at Pentecost.[21]

After the death of Jesus, during the early period of the Palestinian church, the decisive figures were wandering charismatic leaders and teachers, that is, traveling apostles and prophets and disciples who moved from place to place and could rely on small communities and groups of Jewish sympathizers without regard to organization. The sympathizers remained within the framework of Judaism and had no intention of forming a new church (cf. Acts 1:6). These wandering charismatics were homeless, lacking family and possessions. They preached ethical radicalism, and they delivered this message under extreme conditions. They were outsiders in their society with vivid eschatological expectations, who lived as though they expected the imminent end of the world.[22]

Gradually this teaching charism became institutionalized and bureaucratized in order to preserve the vision. Teaching authority had different sources of legitimacy: some leaders knew Jesus in his lifetime; others, like Paul, had charismatic gifts. Both Peter and Paul drew their authority from being apostles. The term "apostle" comes from the Greek word related to envoy, and so the sense is close to that of a messenger from God as in classical prophecy. Paul claims his authority comes from his acting as an ambassador and that he has the

Spirit of God (2 Cor. 5:20; 1 Cor. 7:40). Paul refers to his own personal experiences and, according to one scholar, Paul's innovations and style resemble "the model of a millenarian prophet."[23]

Among early Christians the tension between radical millenarian expectations and moderate institutional precepts gradually was resolved, and within a comparatively brief period Christians became more organized with non-charismatic leadership gradually emerging. Charismatic leadership initially is anti-institutional and breaks with traditional channels of authority, but if a movement is to survive it must consolidate and regulate how leadership and authority get bestowed. Despite freedom from the Law through Christ (Gal. 5:1; Rom. 7:4), the early Church faced increased structure and an ostensible decline in charism. The transition was from old rules (of behavior) to no rules to new rules.[24]

Organization

In the beginning of the Jesus Movement, shortly after the death of Jesus, the congregations had to differentiate themselves from the prevailing social environment. Thus they were intensely preoccupied with identity issues and with unity and stability. Their communities provided an identity for them and the only alternative as a life style to the frustrating confines of the social structures of the time. In the beginning all members of the community had the same status, and the communities had no fixed structures. Acts and the Pauline Letters make little if any mention of formal offices in the early congregations. Paul addressed his letters to the entire community and used familial terms such as "brothers and sisters." In Pauline communities there seems to have been no established officials, although hierarchies did arise later. Paul mentions a variety of gifts in a context of the common good (1 Cor. 12:8): "And God has appointed in the church first apostles, second prophets, third teachers, then workers of miracles. . . ." (1 Cor. 12:28). He proposes a community of equality and charity. He tells the Galatians that with Christ there is neither Jew nor Greek, neither slave nor free, neither male nor female (Gal. 3:28). Since possessions cause status distinctions, property was to be held in common, and wealth was to be abolished (Acts 4:32-5:11; Lk. 14:26; Mk. 3:31). To neutralize sexual subordination and possibly because of eschatological expectations, sexual continence is encouraged.

Most millenarian and revitalization movements seem to go through a stage of anti-structure in which they reject the normal social and status structures of society. Early Christians, because of their beliefs and sense of being unique, identified themselves as a special movement and gained a sense of social cohesion by means of these beliefs and practices that created a boundary between themselves and outsiders or "the world."[25]

Despite the failure of Jesus's second coming, Christians continued to re-define the mode of fulfillment of Jesus's words. As the primitive expectation of the end of the world was modified, so were modified the antinomian energies associated with the expectation of the imminent end. Consolidation and institutionalization during the second and third generation represented continued efforts to maintain the movement's values, symbols and norms, but institutionalization also caused changes. In addition to an increased moderation of emotional intensity, institutionalization involved the gradual concentration of power and authority in a distinct priestly hierarchy and an increased accommodation to the norms of the previously hostile society.[26] The early Church had been outside the system of power, but gradually became a highly visible establishment in society. The early Church had to make this transition from charismatic and amorphous forms of authority to traditional and bureaucratized forms of authority. The primitive expectations of the end time were to be modified and the energies were to be channelled into different directions, into martyrdom, asceticism, bureaucracy, antiheretical activities. The Church's necessary transitions gradually resulted in the routinization of primitive enthusiasm that characterizes all charismatic or millenarian movements in their second generation. Fervent Christians, however, repeatedly attempted to infuse new life into these necessary institutions by appealing to the memory of enthusiastic origins. The first generations of Christians formed a millenarian movement, but Christianity in later centuries was not characteristically millenarian.[27]

Social Context of Origin

Scholars suggest that millenarian groups emerge and thrive among groups of deprived people, people who do not have status, who are an oppressed and persecuted minority, who have suffered multiple deprivations or perceived deprivations.[28] These deprivations often include poverty, low status, and powerlessness. If these people have nothing, they are attracted to the idea of being an elect and can develop the fantasy of a total reversal of their lives and status. Hope then for the millennium flares up often when there is the cumulative deterioration of life conditions and awareness of prospects of further decline. Some crisis, such as plague or war, may act as precipitating events but the more regular causes seem to be deprivation, frustration and social and political isolation, situations where there is a discrepancy between expectation and harsh actuality.

These alone, however, are not sufficient causes. Expectation requires some vision of the means to satisfy expectation. Individuals have to find others who are in a similar circumstance and ready to take some remedial action to overcome the perceived deprivation. Those who respond to millenarian promises are cut off from the traditional sources of power and status and are unable to satisfy their hopes and needs in traditional ways. A void of hope rather than actual deprivation is the fuel for the millenarian flame. Also rapid social changes and encounters with radically different systems of values can result in cultural disintegration and disorientation that eagerly respond to millenarian hopes.

The renewal movements in Judaism likely drew recruits from those who had no roots in society and were critical of society. The Jesus movement was similar to these other movements and was within that tradition of apocalyptic Judaism where great expectations were followed by repeated disappointments. Christianity arose among those who were without political organization and who were restless and relatively deprived, whose hopes had been raised but not satisfied.[29]

Some scholars point to the protests of early Christianity, which reluctantly but increasingly rejected the view of the Jewish religious establishment.[30] Outside Palestine, the Church grew very rapidly,

Early Christianity

especially those congregations that did not keep the Mosaic law. In Antioch (cf. Acts 11:19 ff.) the Hellenists who fled Jerusalem baptized gentiles without circumcision, a declaration of their independence of Judaism. Even in Antioch, however, many congregations which were independent settled alongside the synagogues. They kept the central commandments but neglected the Mosaic ordinances. Paul's companion Titus was not circumcised, and it took an important apostolic meeting to resolve this issue (Gal. 2:3, 11; Acts 15:1). Increasingly early Jewish converts to Christianity surrendered their membership in synagogues to join small groups of Christian believers who worshiped in private homes.[31]

Later millenarian movements often sought to overthrow the existing social order. The first Christians tended to reject the Jewish religious community rather than the political order. As Christian communities spread, however, and encountered the Roman civil order, they increasingly saw the Roman Empire as the incarnation of evil. Rome embodied or symbolized the world and all that opposed God and his saints. The writer of the Book of Revelation portrays Rome as the beast (13:1), the great harlot (17:1), Babylon (17:5)—images that later millenarians would use against a variety of enemies. Rome was the great evil empire which persecuted the saints (17:6). But Rome will fall (18:2), and the ultimate triumph and glory belongs to the saints (19:1-9). After a terrible battle is fought (19:21), the Kingdom of Christ will triumph (11:15). A thousand years of happiness will be the reward for those who endure sufferings in the name of Jesus (20:4-6).

Nevertheless, the question as to precisely what conditions foster the emergence of new millenarian groups is a difficult one. Later chapters will continue to look at some of the historical and social issues that nurture new movements.

Members

Scholars, then, suggest that new sects tend to arise among those people who are marginal in society or experience some relative deprivation. The usual way of testing this hypothesis would be to examine the membership of the early Christian communities. The difficulty, of course, is that the ancient evidence was not gathered so as to conveniently confirm or deny modern theories and sociological categories.

The first Christian community stayed at Jerusalem, but as some of these Christians returned to the rural areas they established what became known as the Palestinian community. Even before Paul's conversion sometime in the 30's, Christians had left the Jerusalem area and even Palestine and had scattered. The rapid dissemination of Christians created the Hellenistic churches, at first on the western coast of Asia minor, then around the Aegean. In spite of its early roots in the countryside of Palestine, the new movement very quickly centered in cities. Increasingly the Palestinian Church contrasted with the developing missionary churches in such cities as Antioch, Ephesus, Corinth, and Rome. These cities and others were places where influential early Christian witnesses left their legacy of preaching, letters, and thriving communities of believers.[32] These groups, mostly small, consisted of Jews who had converted to Christian beliefs, and then increasing numbers of Gentiles joined these small communities. The public probably considered these small Christian communities or churches to be appendages of the various Diaspora synagogues.[33] That is, these communities tended to cluster close to the local Jewish communities and initially they were not easily distinguishable from these Jewish communities since they retained many Jewish practices.

Who were these early Christians? Because of their intense fervor and sometimes almost revolutionary spirit it might be expected that many were poor or slaves who were responding to the hope of gaining something more for themselves. Undoubtedly they were a diverse lot, a mixture of people from different levels of society.[34] Paul describes his flock: "not many were wise according to worldly standards, not many were powerful, not many were of noble birth" (1 Cor. 1:26). He also mentions the "poor among the saints at Jerusalem" (Rom. 15:26). Although sometimes "poor" in the Psalms has the meaning of pious or religious, these two Pauline passages seem to suggest a sociological meaning, and undoubtedly many early Christian converts came from the ranks of the disinherited and deprived whose situations were deteriorating.[35]

The early converts to Christianity probably did not represent the Jewish establishment, and the bitter controversies between Jesus and Pharisees likely resulted in there being no priests among the converted. Those who had no status or value now could apply to themselves Jesus's words, "Truly, I say to you, the tax collectors and the harlots go into the kingdom of God before you [the chief priests and Pharisees]" (Mt. 21:31) and "Blessed are you poor" (Lk. 6:20).

For more than two hundred years Christianity was essentially a movement among the lower classes in the urban areas of the empire.[36] There were occasional converts from among the upper ranks of society and from among the wealthy and the educated (although wealth and education do not seem to be the main criteria for social status at that time). Many lower-class Christians, however, regarded pagan culture with grave suspicion (the writing style of the early Christian sacred writings contrasts with the polished sophistication of the contemporary literature of the well educated, and there is little evidence for large numbers of well-educated Christian believers until well into the second century). When men of culture began to appear in Christian communities, they introduced a new and, for many, an unacceptable version of the faith. The highly educated Valentinus, Marcion, and even Clement and Origin had religious ideas that began to alarm their Christian contemporaries. The refusal of emergent orthodoxy to accept the Gnosticism of Valentinus serves to corroborate evidence which points to the fundamentally non-intellectual and non-aristocratic character of Christianity in this period.[37]

The aristocracy did not convert to Christianity in the early years, but the occasional convert from among the upper ranks of society or the occasional wealthy convert like Marcion presented a dilemma to the growing church. Since its inception Christianity had demonstrated a bias against the rich. Because the ideology of poverty in some ways had outlived the social conditions which spawned it and the ideology was too firmly embedded in the sacred writings to be discarded, it had to be adapted to meet a new set of social conditions, the situation of Christianity's growth among the rich and powerful.

Is there a correlation between the religious character of Christianity and its social constituency? Early Christian writers as well as pagan observers suggested some of the social factors that made Christianity attractive to its converts. Christianity's religious exclusivity offered a clear choice in an age of anxiety. Christianity made no social distinctions and was open to all social classes and nationalities: it accepted the manual worker, the slave, the outcast. Christianity, beyond its egalitarianism, offered a practical philanthropy, a warm sense of community. New sects commonly have an egalitarian spirit and provide the new converts with a community of love and acceptance.[38]

At a time when renewal groups of fervent Jews began to recognize that even an elect remnant within Israel could not satisfy intensified norms, the Jesus Movement in a radical breakthrough opened membership to foreigners and non-Jews. Christianity transformed traditional Jewish ethnocentrism into a claim of absolute universalism, that all people were called into the company of the elect.[39]

Challenges for Early Christianity

Emerging Christianity had to confront and overcome a number of challenges that compelled it to expand and open outward to become a world-wide religion. For example, Paul, like other early Jewish Christians, was involved in disputes over adherence to the Mosaic Law with its dietary and purification rules. Paul then began to puzzle over a broader concern, however, namely the lack of a faith response on the part of the Jews to the Christian message (Rom., chapters 9-11). Paul ultimately seems to have resolved this question by realizing the universality of salvation (cf. Rom. 2:9-10 and Eph. 2:13-22).

Another difficulty for the early Christian communities was persecution by both Jews and Gentiles (Mt. 10:17-18; cf. Acts, ch 4-5). The 65-70 C.E. period witnessed the religious persecutions of Nero, the deaths of the Apostles Peter and Paul and the catastrophe for Palestinian Judaism of the Jewish-Roman War. Then at the end of the reign of the Emperor Domitian, approximately 91-96 C.E., came another fierce persecution. The Christians believed they were chosen by God, so how could God allow them to suffer? The Book of Revelation seems to have been especially intended to reassure the churches amidst their trials and persecutions (cf. Rev. 12:1-20) and to reaffirm the expectation of Jesus' return—but somehow to push it off more vaguely into the future. Christians began to realize that suffering was another way to join with Christ, to gain spiritual liberation, to build up the Church, to realize that to suffer with Christ was to partake in Christ's glory (2 Tim. 2:11; Col. 1:24; 1 Peter 4:1-5:1). The idea began to grow that the blood of martyrs would be the seed for further converts to the Christian faith.

In addition to the various persecutions and the opposition of the Jews to the Christian message, the delay in Jesus's return and the non-appearance of the end of the world caused anxiety among Christians. Ultimately the non-fulfillment of their eschatological expectations created a sense of urgency and zeal among Christians. When people have sacrificed a great deal for their beliefs, disappointment must be fought by making an even greater effort to convince others—and themselves—of the validity of their position and the worthiness of their cause, as if to reassure themselves and prove to others that their hopes were not in vain.[40] Psychological discomfort (known as cognitive dissonance) seizes people when important beliefs on which they have made crucial decisions seem to be disconfirmed. The greater the investment and commitment based on the original belief, the greater is the anxiety and the need to allay it.

Would the lack of success in the expected conversion of the Jews, unexpected persecutions, and the non-appearance of Jesus disconfirm all that Jesus stood for and all that Christians believed in? One of the ways Christians dealt with their doubt and despair was to understand in a different manner how Jesus was already with them through his Holy Spirit. Also, intense proselytizing often seems to serve as a way of reconciling a group's hopes with the non-appearance of expected events, especially the expected end of the world. Later millenarian groups, rather than having their hopes shattered by the non-appearance of the Lord when they expected His return, often developed a new theological understanding to account for the Lord's delay and they intensified their proselytizing. Belief gets confirmed if more and more people share the same belief.

Historically the Palestinian Church declined in numbers and influence and was no longer the mother church for Gentile Christianity as it had been during the Pauline period. Peter, like Paul, had increasingly turned toward the Gentiles and had placed himself in service to the Hellenistic communities. Paul's missionary work gave impetus and importance to the new Hellenistic churches after 70 C.E. These Hellenistic churches gradually domesticated the prophetic and charismatic elements within Jewish Christianity as these churches became more established and less alienated from the established order of society. The Church, growing more democratic and less provincial, accommodated more to the surrounding culture and gave less emphasis to its initial eschatological concerns.[41]

Conclusion

The first generation of Christians constituted a millenarian group while later generations did not. With the passage of time and the continued delay of the fulfillment of the initial prophecies of the end time, Christianity had to adapt to changing conditions and modify its emphasis as it became a world religion, not just a minor sect within Palestine.

Over several generations, apostolic Christianity made the transition to early Catholicism, from the charismatic to the more institutional. Necessarily charismatic gifts gradually became domesticated and channeled into more bureaucratic structures. Doctrinal diversity and regional differences continued until about 120 C.E. when trends in the Church began to lead to greater unification, structure and accepted orthodoxy during the course of the second century.[42] The changes that came during the second century necessarily involved increased institutionalization.

If a radical millenarian group survives the early disappointment of its promises (the non-appearance of the end time), it must become moderate and institutionalized with more hierarchial authority. A sect, to follow conventional usages, is a minority religious group which rejects the whole spirit of the surrounding social environment. As a cult or sect compromises and accommodates to the demands of society, it gradually becomes a church. Wider acceptance and entrenchment within society means broadening its appeal and undergoing moderating changes. This seems to have been true of the Christian Church as it moderated its apocalyptic tradition and eschatological tension.[43]

A millenarian movement must fail if what it promises does not happen, that the end time will come on a specific date with all its rewards for the members. But some groups continue and become established as churches. The failure of prophecies does cause some members to leave, but most remain and come to find within the experience of the community a partial fulfillment of their millenarian dream. Opposition and suffering can also strengthen faith rather than weaken it. The fulfillment of millenarian expectations can take on the form of spiritual experiences as found in sacraments, meditation, ascetical practices, and mystical visions. In these new forms of fulfillment the attainment of millenarian bliss is largely individual. Other forms shape the experience of the entire community. Indeed, various elements in the emerging early Christian Church are best understood if they are seen as efforts to capture in the present those conditions of the ideal future: to be a loving and equal community in which each person is brother and sister, where distinctions between persons are abolished, and where material things and the demands of the flesh are unimportant (Rom. 12:1-8, Eph. 4:23-24).[44]

NOTES

1. Michael Edward Stone, *Scriptures, Sects and Visions: A Profile of Judaism from Ezra to the Jewish Revolts* (Philadelphia: Fortress Press,1980), p. 58; cf. Morton Smith, "Palestinian Judaism in the First Century," in *Israel: Its Role in Civilization*, ed. by Moshe Davis (New York: Harper & Row, 1956), p. 71.

2. John G. Gager, *Kingdom and Community: The Social World of Early Christianity* (Englewood Cliffs: Prentice-Hall, 1975), p. 12.

3. Gerd Theissen, *Sociology of Early Palestinian Christianity* trans. by John Bowden (Philadelphia: Fortress Press, 1977), p. 1 and 34; Robin Scroggs, "The Earliest Christian Communities as Sectarian Movement," in *Christianity, Judaism and Other Greco-Roman Cults* edited by Jacob Neusner (Leiden: E.J. Brill, 1975), pp. 1-23.

4. Yonina Talmon, "Millenarian Movements," *Archives Européennes de Sociologie* 7 (1966): 162.

5. Cf. Yonina Talmon, "Pursuit of the Millennium: The Relation Between Religion and Social Change," *Archives Européennes de Sociologie* 3 (1962): 125-148, also in *Readings in Comparative Religion: An Anthropological Approach* edited by W. Vessa and E. Vogt (New York: 1965, second edition), pp. 522-537; Anthony F.C. Wallace, "Revitalization Movements," *American Anthropologist* 58 (1954): 262-282; Weston La Barre, "Materials for a History of Studies of Crisis Cults: A Bibliographic Essay," *Current Anthropology* 12 (1971): 3-44; Norman Cohn, *The Pursuit of the Millennium* (New York: Oxford University Press, 1957, 1970), p 1-13; Robin Scroggs, "The Earliest Christian Communities as Sectarian Movement," in *Christianity, Judaism and Other Greco-Roman Cults* edited by Jacob Neusner (Leiden: E.J. Brill, 1975), pp. 1-23; John G. Gager, pp. 20-21.

6. Many passages from New Testament literature refer to the parousia of the Lord: 1 Thes. 2:19; 4:15; 2 Thes. 2:1; Mt. 24:3; 2 Peter 1:16; 3:4, 12; 1 Jn. 2:28. Other passages refer to the nearness of the parousia: Phil. 4:5; Heb. 10:25, 37; 1 Jn. 2:18; Rev. 22:10, 12, 20; cf. John G. Gager, p. 43.

7. Wayne A. Meeks, *First Urban Christians: The Social World of the Apostle Paul* (New Haven: Yale University Press, 1983), p. 171.

8. Ernst Kasemann, as quoted by Meeks, p. 171.

9. Cf. Rudolf Bultman, *The Theology of the New Testament*, trans. by Kendric Grobel (New York: Charles Scribner, 1951), p. 37; cf. Acts 7:38; 1 Cor. 12:28; Col. 1:18.

10. James M. Robinson and Helmut Koestler, *Trajectories Through Early Christianity* (Philadelphia: Fortress Press, 1971), p. 144; cf. Wayne A. Meeks, p. 175.

11. Cf. *1 Clement* 23:3-5 (written about 96 C.E.), *2 Peter* 3:3-9 (written about 125 C.E.), *1 Thes.* 4:13-5:11.

12. John G. Gager, p. 45.

13. Rudolf Bultman p. 40; cf. also *Theological Dictionary of the New Testament*, ed. by Gerhard Kittle, vol. 1, (Grand Rapids and London: William B. Eerdmans Pub., 1964), *agalliaomai*, p. 20.

14. Talmon, "Millenarian Movements," p. 168; Talmon, "Pursuit of the Millennium," p. 528; Scroggs, p. 4.

15. Cf. Talmon, "Pursuit of the Millennium," p. 529, and Michael Barkun, *Disaster and the Millennium* (New Haven: Yale University Press, 1974), p. 117.

16. Ronald Knox, *Enthusiasm: A Chapter in the History of Religion* (Oxford University Press and Galaxy Books, 1961), pp. 566-577.

17. Robin Scroggs, p. 6.

18. B. Holmberg, *Paul and Power: The Structure of Authority in the Primitive Church as Reflected in the Pauline Epistles* (Lund, 1978), p. 139.

19. John G. Gager, pp. 29-31; cf. Kennelm Burridge, *New Heaven, New Earth: A Study of Millenarian Activities* (Oxford: Basil Blackwell, 1980), p. 141.

20. John G. Gager p. 68.

21. Lk. 24:49; cf. John Howard Schutz, "Charisma and Social Reality in Primitive Christianity," *Journal of Religion* 54 (1974): 51-70; Tucker, "Theory of Charismatic Leadership," *Dædalus* 97 (1968): 731; Peter Berger, "Charism and Religious Innovation," *American Sociological Review* 28 (1963): 757; Max Weber, *On Charism and Institution Building: Selected Papers*, ed. by S. N. Eisenstadt (University of Chicago Press, 1968).

22. Gerd Theissen, pp. 7-11.

23. Wayne Meeks, p. 176.

24. John G Gager, p. 35; cf. Michael Hill, *A Sociology of Religion* (London: Heinemann Educational Books, 1973), p. 164.

25. Wayne Meeks, p. 85, 174; John G. Gager, pp. 33-34.

26. John G. Gager, pp. 49, 67, 69; Michael Hill, p. 143.

27. John G. Gager, pp. 32, 67-73.

28. Yonina Talmon, "Pursuit of the Millennium," p. 530; David Aberle, "A Note on Relative Deprivation Theory as Applied to Millenarian and Other Cult Movements," in *Millennial Dreams in Action*, edited by Sylvia Thrupp (The Hague: Mouton and Co., 1962), pp. 208-214.

29. David Aberle, pp. 209-217; Gerd Theissen, pp. 33; John G. Gager, p. 27.

30. Robin Scroggs, "The Sociological Interpretation of the New Testament: The Present State of Research," *New Testament Studies* 26 (1980): 164-179.

31. Leonhard Goppelt, *Apostolic and Post-Apostolic Times*, trans. by Robert Guelich (London: Adam and Charles Black, 1970), p. 61.

32. Goppelt, p. 123; cf. Wayne Meeks, chapter two on the urban environment of Pauline Christianity.

33. Goppelt, p. 105.

34. Wayne Meeks, p. 174.

35. Bultman, p. 39; John G. Gager, p. 22; Peter Worsley, *The Trumpet Shall Sound* (New York: Schocken Books, 1968), p. xlii.

36. John G. Gager, p. 114; also A.H.M. Jones, "The Social Background of the Struggle between Paganism and Christianity," in *The Conflict between Paganism and Christianity in the Fourth Century*, edited by Arnoldo Momigliano (Oxford: Clarendon Press, 1963), p. 17; Wayne Meeks, p. 72.

37. John G. Gager, p. 114; John G. Gager, "Religion and Social Class in the Early Roman Empire," in *The Catacombs and the Colosseum: The Roman Empire as the Setting of Primitive Christianity*, edited by Stephen Benko and John J. O'Rourke (Valley Forge: Judson Press, 1971), p. 113. Cf. also A.D. Nock, *Conversion* (Oxford: Clarendon Press, 1933, 1952), p. 187.

38. John G. Gager, "Religion and Social Class in the Early Roman Empire," p. 113; Robin Scroggs, p. 5; cf. also E.R. Dodds, *Pagan and Christian in an Age of Anxiety* (Cambridge: Cambridge University Press, 1965), p. 134.

39. Gerd Theissen, p. 57.

40. John G. Gager pp. 38-49. On cognitive dissonance, cf. Leon Festinger, Henry W. Riecken, and Stanley Schachter, *When Prophecy Fails* (Minneapolis: University of Minnesota Press, 1956). Cf. also Talmon, "Millenarian Movements," p. 171.

41. John Gagner, pp. 37-43.

42. John Howard Schutz, "Charisma and Social Reality in Early Christianity," *Journal of Religion* 54 (1974): 53.

43. Cf. Ernest Troelsch, *The Social Teaching of the Christian Churches* (New York: Macmillan, 1931); also, Thomas F. O'Dea, "Sects and Cults," *International Encyclopedia of the Social Sciences*, edited by David L. Sills (New York: Macmillan Co. and Free Press, 1968), vol. 14, pp. 130-135.

44. Goppelt, pp. 57-66.

Chapter Three
Continuing Millennial Hopes, Montanism, and Monasticism

Problems for Church Authorities

The Christian communities increased in number and size over the first few centuries. By the end of the second century Christianity was no longer an obscure eschatological sect, although it still was struggling for its existence in the face of scattered persecution. The effort of survival and expansion went hand in hand with efforts to further clarify and define orthodox beliefs and to defend against critics and rivals.

The rapid growth of the Church during the second and third centuries created problems for Christian leaders.[1] On the one hand expanding numbers may have diluted the fervor and sense of being a chosen elite that Christians had. New converts, many fresh from pagan cults, did not know the first generations of believers nor did they always hold strictly to the received Christian traditions. Church authorities had to face this new danger from within. Heretics and schismatics were looked upon as sowing weeds among the pure seed of the apostolic faith, and the bishops as shepherds of the Church had to drive off the "wild beasts from Christ's sheep."[2] On the other hand, increased hierarchical organization was felt necessary to protect the Church from these internal dangers. Increased regulation and control may have caused the bishops to seem impersonal, less charismatic, and mere administrators. Bishops, burdened with care for their flocks, felt compelled to take firmer control over charismatic gifts like prophecy, especially if prophets claimed unusual revelations or upset the communities by calling for the End Time.

Often non-religious factors, such as political and social unrest, prompted the rise of dissident religious movements since religious forms and experiences provided one of the few channels for dissent. Multiple levels of dissent serve as the background for the rise of Montanism during the second and third centuries when the Christian Church was still a minority, not yet the established religion of the Empire and not yet fully organized around the papacy.[3] A few bitter controversies broke out in which millenarian hopes occupied a central place and Church authorities found themselves confronted by millenarian groups in a fashion not unlike the way the growing Church itself had resisted the pagan establishment and secular authorities. Orthodox Christians were dealing with disappointment as they realized the Second Coming was being delayed into the uncertain future.

The focus in this chapter is briefly to look at some of the early subapostolic writings which spoke of the millennium and then focus on the dramatic millenarian movement of Montanus who sought to restore the enthusiastic expectation of the Lord's return.

The Millennium and Early Christian Writings

Early Christian writings are replete with ideas about the return of the Lord and the millennium. In the last chapter we addressed the apocalyptic and millenarian elements in the New Testament writings, especially the Book of Revelation, which was intended to comfort and strengthen the communities during time of persecution and pain. To the believers who were troubled as to why God was allowing His faithful to suffer, St. John revealed the hidden purposes of God: that

Christ would overcome Satan and the Roman Emperor in the final victory which would inaugurate the new Kingdom of God on earth.

A variety of subapostolic writings also circulated which the Church of the time seems not to have accepted as genuinely part of the New Testament canon. Writings like the *Epistle of Barnabas, 1-2 Clement,* the *Didache,* and *Hermas* were sometimes cited by the early Church Fathers as if they were Scripture. In addition there were the apologetical and catechetical writings of the early Church Fathers.

This early Christian literature continued to echo and amplify some of the New Testament concerns about the return of the Lord and the millennium. Two of the many issues of concern, in addition to when the Lord's return would be, were where his return would be and what the nature of the promised reign of the saints would be. We shall briefly consider how a few of these writings sought to flesh out the bald statements of Scripture and make the millennium more concrete.

The *Epistle of Barnabas,* probably compiled toward the end of the First Century, is charged with an air of eschatological expectancy. It regards the "present ages" as evil (2:1) and exhorts the reader to "carefully investigate the present situation and seek out that which can save us.... Let us hate the error of the present days so that we might be saved in the age to come.... The great scandal is at hand" (4:1,3). *Barnabas* uses a tradition that speaks of the eschatological consummation coming in six thousand years but also maintains an eschatological immediacy. "... In six thousand years the Lord will finish everything. For with him the 'day' signifies a thousand years."[4] After *Barnabas* the idea of a universal week of 7000 years was common, with the last "day" being a thousand years—the millennium period.

The *Didache* echoes the synoptic apocalypses of Mark 13, Matthew 24-25, and Luke 21 in that it urges watchfulness, expectancy, and uncertainty as to when the Lord is coming. The *Didache,* especially chapter 16, is premillenarian like so much of early Christian writing, holding that the Second Advent of Christ will bring the resurrection of only the righteous so that they can take part in the earthly rule of the saints. After the millennium would be the time of testing, the resurrection of the wicked, and the last Judgment.

Irenaus (140?-202?) suggests that the millennium will be a recapitulation of Paradise, with miracles and natural blessings, with peace and fruitfulness. The dominion that Adam once had over the beast would be restored, and the just and righteous would rule during the millennium, in this world, and the next and would receive a hundred fold what they gave up for Christ. They will sit at the Messianic banquet promised by Jesus (Mt. 8:11; 26:29). Jerusalem shall come down from heaven where those who survived the age of the Antichrist will reign.[5]

Justin (110?-165?) offers the orthodox belief that there would be a millennium and a resurrection of the body and that the scene of the millennium would be in a "rebuilt, embellished, and enlarged" earthly Jerusalem.[6] Justin seems to have given emphasis to the idea of an *earthly* happiness during the thousand years of the millennium, a point of contention for other early and later Christians.

The stern and zealous Tertullian converted to Christianity and became the first major apologist writing in Latin. Tertullian felt he had to defend the hope of the millennium against Marcion who denied that Christians could hope for a world which Marcion claimed was created by the Demiurge. Tertullian restated the eschatological hope that Christ was coming to this physical earth during the contemporary time.[7] Tertullian was concerned that Christians receive their reward on the very scene where they suffered and were tried. Writing at the end of the second century Tertullian regarded the Church as a community of saints waiting for the rapidly approaching end of the world. He scorned the pleasures of life since he expected the imminent arrival of the triumphant Christ.[8]

Tertullian grew ever more rigorous, in part, as a reflection of the spirit of Montanism. One small area of this enthusiasm was the great esteem for martyrs. Indeed, during the anxiety of persecution Christians in general at this time held martyrs in extraordinary esteem, seeing in the martyrs and prophetic figures assurance of the continued and dynamic presence of the Holy Spirit. Tertullian give central place to the Paraclete (Holy Spirit) who reveals that believers should not seek to die in "the marriage bed or in miscarriage or of gentle fevers"; rather they should seek to die as martyrs so that God may be glorified.[9] In fact, Christians should actively seek out martyrdom and even offer themselves to the magistrates. Tertullian, reflecting the burning enthusiasm of Montanism, even goes so far as to urge fervent Christians to go boldly into pagan assemblies in times of persecution and openly invite martyrdom or take their own lives. Some enthusiasts in the beginning of the third century did go to this extreme.[10]

In spite of or perhaps because of persecutions and the heroic witness of martyrs, converts streamed into the Church. But not all the new Christians had the same fervent faith and steadfastness. Not all were able to summon the courage necessary in times of persecution; not all were willing to die for their faith.

Montanus

One new convert to Christianity named Montanus brought very rigorous expectations to the practice of his new faith. In the face of a growing hierarchy and increased institutionalization of the Church, Montanus wanted to return to primitive Christian enthusiasm, to restore the primitive idealism and the charismatic gifts of the earliest period of the Church. Supported by the writings of the uncompromising Tertullian, Montanus vigorously sought to reawaken the militant expectation of the imminent coming of the Kingdom, an expectation that had grown increasingly less fervent with passage of time. Amidst the oppression of persecution, his prophecies aroused crowds to come and wait for that millenarian hour, so long delayed.[11] He exhorted his followers to revive a manner of thinking and feeling which was growing weaker. He placed a high value on the sacrifice of self and whipped up the faithful to martyrdom out of love for Christ.[12] It's probable that the Church was not so much threatened by Montanism's theology of the Second Coming and millennium as by his emphasis on ecstatic prophecy and voluntary martyrdom.[13]

Montanists

The origins of Montanism, the most important millenarian movement in the Eastern Church, are not clear. Information about Montanism is scarce, mostly drawn from orthodox Christian authors who described isolated elements of Montanism and provided extracts from Montanus's writings only for the sake of refuting them. These apologists, seeking to shield the Church and protect the faithful, have a special animosity towards any who threatened the well-being of the Church.[14]

Originally Montanus called his movement the New Prophecy, and Montanism only received its better-known name in the fourth century. It began in Phrygia (the north central section of what is modern Turkey) in Asia Minor, probably around 172 C.E. when Montanus had his visions.[15] In the eastern part of the Roman Empire, recurrent persecutions of Christians broke out, with the decade 170-180 C.E. being the high watermark of stress for Christians.

The towns of this area of Phrygia, Iconium, Pisidian Antioch, and Colossae had a mixed population containing some Jews who were attracted to Christianity as well as Jews who joined with pagan authorities to persecute Christians.[16] In the ancient world this area was known for its frenzied religious practices, and St. Jerome suggests that Montanus may have been a former eunuch-priest of Cybele before his conversion.[17] The pagan cult of Cybele, was still vital at this time and, like the orgiastic cult of Dionysus, stressed possession by the gods and a heaven sent madness (*mania*) that was frenzied and prophetic, excessive, and ecstatic.[18] St. Jerome may have based his speculation about Montanus on the kind of excessive and frenzied Christianity which Montanus practiced. Further, the cults of Cybele and Dionysus appealed to women, and women played prominent roles in the ceremonies of these cults. The prominence of women in Montanism in addition to Montanist religious practices that seemed out of control must have frightened some of the orthodox Christian witnesses of the time. Eyewitnesses commented on Montanus's ecstatic frenzy and prophetic madness. Witnesses were divided, some being scandalized and doubting that these religious experiences could be authentic and from the Spirit, while others became devoted followers. It should be noted that Christians of this period believed in the presence of the Holy Spirit and had a special reverence for those prophets through whom the Spirit communicated and those martyrs whose endurance was made possible by the presence of the Holy Spirit. Christians interpreted it as a sign of "the last days" when "the

Spirit was being poured out," and sons and daughters would prophesy and young men would see visions and old men would dream dreams because of the Holy Spirit (Acts 2:17). According to devout Christians, prophecy was among the apostolic gifts, and special rewards were granted to those who suffered for Christ—the guidance of the Spirit, visions, and a special relationship with the Lord.

Montanus's Apocalyptic Doctrine

Montanus's dominant belief seems based on the Apocalypse (or Book of Revelation) of St. John. Montanus opened the question of continuing revelation. He claimed God was with him, that the Holy Spirit was within him, and he even allowed himself to be called the Paraclete.[19] Like many millenarian cults Montanism gives central place to the Holy Spirit, and Montanus claimed it was the Spirit who spoke through him and his two female priestesses. Montanus voiced this vision: "It is I, the Lord God Almighty who dwells in this man," and "It is no angel that is here, or human messenger, but I the Lord God the Father has come."[20] Montanus did not claim to be God; the alien voice made that claim. Maximilla, a Montanist priestess and prophet, uttered her vision: "I am word and spirit and power,"[21] and she predicted wars and revolutions. Many were attracted by her predictions of social unrest. An opponent of Montanus, however, mocked these predictions and pointed out thirteen years later that this prophecy was not fulfilled and there had been no wars.[22]

Montanus was clear as to where he expected the Lord to return. Montanus gave the name of Jerusalem to Pepuza and Tymion, little insignificant towns in Phrygia, because he expected the Heavenly Jerusalem would descend to earth soon.[23]

The prophecies of Montanus and Priscilla and Maximilla were recorded and constituted a Third Testament after the Old and the New Testaments. Their followers regarded these revelations as a direct continuation of the prophetic mission of Christ and the Apostles and the last outpourings of the Paraclete, which were meant to complete any gaps in God's revelation. The principal revelation was that the

New Jerusalem would descend shortly and the thousand-year reign of Christ would soon begin.[24]

Because of his expectation of the Second Coming, Montanus lived an ascetic life and demanded that his followers also live a strict asceticism. To prepare for the End Time he dissolved marriage. His prophetesses Priscilla and Maximilla left their husbands from the moment they were filled with the Spirit, probably as part of the discipline of waiting for the last days and leaving behind the things of this world. Montanus also laid down strict laws on fasting. The fast involved eating dry food (*zerophagia*) and especially avoiding juices, moist foods, and wine. Some of these practices, including abstaining from bathing and fasting until sunset, resembled Jewish ascetical practices, and later Christian hermits would continue many of these forms of piety.

The Emotional Excesses of Montanism

Ecstacy and enthusiasm loomed as central and desirable traits of Montanus's Christianity. Eyewitnesses describe how he fell into frenzies and convulsions, how he became ecstatic and talked strangely, uttering prophecies. His hearers became moved, inflamed, and elevated by his prophetic gift. Maximilla and Priscilla, elevated by Montanus as priestesses, also spoke madly (*ekphronos*) in a prophetic way.[25] Followers such as Theodotus were known for their trances and mystical visions. Citizens of those times would not have regarded such dramatic and ecstatic religious behavior as unusual, except more orthodox Christians (such as St. Jerome, as we shall see) would have recoiled at the intensity and public display of the Montanists. Orthodox Christians noted with sarcasm and disapproval that some prophetic Montanists dyed their hair, penciled their eyelids, loved ornamentation, and took gifts of gold and silver.[26]

The Montanists, in their disputes with orthodox Christians, boasted of their martyrs as proof of the presence and power of the prophetic Spirit among them.[27] Some evidence indicates that both Montanus and Maximilla were even inspired in their enthusiastic fervor to commit suicide out of some yearning for martyrdom.

Leadership

Because his followers believed he possessed the Spirit and that the Spirit inspired him, Montanus had great authority. Christians in general, and the followers of Montanus especially, regarded prophecy as a special gift, and thus religious authority rested on the divine inspirations given to prophetic and charismatic persons of the community who received divine revelation. Montanists regarded the precepts of their revelation and tradition as obligatory because they came so directly from God. Montanists believed they formed a community of the elect with prophets as the chief figures of leadership and authority. Such charismatic authority differed considerably from the kind of authority taking shape in the Catholic Church where the bishops sought to safeguard the received traditions rather than add to them through prophetic communications. Inevitably tension would spring up between these contrasting forms of church authority. Prophets with a direct line to God would clash with bishops who held a hierarchical and structured view of the Church as they shepherded their flocks among the surrounding wolves of pagan mystery cults, Gnostic sects, and false prophets. Ultimately it was the enthusiastic process of Montanist prophecy that caused the orthodox Church authorities to turn away from Montanism.

Organization

Whatever organization Montanism had is not clear except that Montanus created a fund, which at first was administered by a man named Theodotus. Montanus organized the receiving of gifts under the name of offerings and provided salaries for those who preached his doctrine in established assemblies of believers who were awaiting the Second Coming.[28] This belief in the coming of the Millennium enabled the more ascetic and puritanical Christians to conceive of a Church encumbered with less organization than that demanded by fellow Christians who were more accommodating to the surrounding society. Thus no hierarchical structure seems to have been set up. When the expected End Time did not arrive and the prophecies of Maximilla were not realized, we do not know what happened to ascetic practices or what institutional structures had to be developed.

Social Context

The social seedbed of Montanism is not clear. Montanus strode onto history's stage at a time when the Church was experiencing an influx of converts and sporadic outbreaks of persecution. In spite of the security provided by the Pax Romana, late antiquity was an age of anxiety and change; one age was passing and a new world dawning. This period saw an intense ferment of new religious feelings.[29] There was great interest in the prophetic spirit, and even bishops encouraged their communities to go out into the desert to be ready for the coming of Christ.[30] Those who heard the prophetic utterances of Montanus and his followers believed in these promises and willingly made offerings of gold and silver and gave expensive gifts.[31] Prophecies about wars and strife found eager listeners who must have felt more secure in being among the elect and possessing a special knowledge of the future and the end of the world.

Some scholars suggest that eastern declarations of separateness were inchoate forms of political disengagement from the powerful and dominant Roman Empire.[32] In the ancient East religious differentiation and revolt may have been a subtler form of political revolt, but scholars do not know enough specifics to say confidently that was true in this situation. While Greek civilization valued rational and conscious control, it would be an overstatement to say that religions of enthusiasm would in part be a reaction against the hardened imperialism and the formalistic rituals of the Roman Empire. What can be stated more confidently is that in an oppressive atmosphere of persecution, the apocalyptic hope offered by fervent prophets and prophetesses with the absolute authority of God must have considerably influenced simple Christians.[33]

Membership

Followers of Montanus included rich as well as poor,[34] and women such as Maximilla and Priscilla held positions of prominence. Indeed, the prominent role of women underlines the protest of Montanism.[35] Evidence is scant as to who made up the followers of Montanus, but the ancient historian Eusebius relates the story of Alexander, a daring robber with whom Montanus lived for many years.[36] It is not clear, though, whether Eusebius from his orthodox Christian perspective was trying to damage Montanus's reputation by linking him with a criminal or whether the Montanist movement attracted outcasts from society. What is clear is the intensity with which the Montanists followed their prophets and defended them against the efforts of orthodox apologists who tried to refute and defame them.[37]

The Church Turns Against Millenarians

The Church in Asia Minor held synods or meetings where bishops and clergy discussed Montanism and judged it to be incompatible with the spirit of the Church. The synods excommunicated Montanists and at Rome Pope Zephyrinus condemned Montanism.[38] Montanism still spread to Syria, Egypt, Rome, Gaul, and North Africa by the year 200 C.E.[39] The Roman Empire's numerous commercial links and the great interest in religion in this period fostered the spread not only of Christianity but also of Christian heresies. Inner revelation, ecstatic prophecy, an emphasis on the Spirit, and private interpretation of prophecies appealed to the citizens of the second century. As Christian bishops combated some of these tendencies, they established several trends in Church discipline. Church authority continued to center on bishops and away from prophetic figures who claimed revelations from the Spirit. Montanism compelled the Church to form a more precise conception of the role of prophecy and ecstacy, which bishops regarded as increasingly suspect.

Early Christian literature like the *Didache* and *Hermas* warned the faithful against false prophets and those who claimed extraordinary gifts from the Holy Spirit. Orthodoxy required more control over religious sources of intense experiences, especially ecstatic prophecy, and orthodox writers increasingly declared demonic any prophetic furor such as that in the pagan Sibylline or Pythian tradition.[40]

The great Origen (185?-254?) opposed millenarianism primarily on the basis of its method of interpreting scripture. He opposed a literal reading of Scripture, the primary method by which millenarians interpreted Scripture and the basis on which they expected a future of bodily pleasures and luxuries and an earthly Jerusalem built of precious stones. The Gnostic Cerinthus, for example, had espoused such a sensual millenarianism; he stated that he was inspired by angels and claimed that there would be an earthly kingdom of Christ, in which men and women would have fleshly desires and the pleasures of the messianic feast, with a thousand years of celebrating nuptial festivals.[41] Origen, in contrast, believed that flesh and blood could not inherit the kingdom of God, and he emphasized the Pauline notion of the spiritual man with no worldly expectations.[42] For Origen, the hope of a Christian is heaven, and by contrast, the world is not worthy of a Christian's hope. Curiously Origen's ideas fostered a Greek dualism of above and below in place of the New Testament concept of time that compared this world with the world to come.

Eusebius (260?-340?) also criticized various early writers for their presentation of a millennium of sensual luxury. He criticized Papias' view of the material form of the millennial kingdom of Christ on this earth. Eusebius bluntly says that Papias was not a man of intelligence, that he should read the Scriptural promises mystically and symbolically.[43] Indeed millenarianism substantially disappeared from the Eastern Church because of its crude exegetical literalness and because of the fanaticism of millenarians like Montanus.

In the West, Commodianus, less sophisticated than Eastern writers, described the millennium as a return to the golden age, a time after the age of Antichrist, a time of marrying and having children, with all the good things of earth at hand. He even links the return of the lost tribes of Israel to the Antichrist tradition.[44] Another Western writer, Lactantius, also described in a literalistic way the golden age of the millennium by reaching out to such other prophetic traditions as the pagan poet Virgil's Fourth Eclogue and the Sibylline Oracles.[45]

St. Jerome, however, finally turned away from the literal understanding of Scripture so commonly found among millenarians and orthodox writers who fleshed out Scriptural ideas on the millennium. He believed St. John's Apocalypse should be interpreted in a spiritual way, a way that would actually undermine any earthly millennium. St. Jerome simply does not believe in a millennial kingdom or a physical restoration of Jerusalem but he cannot condemn such notions since many "other church writers had held these things."[46]

But the most powerful voice against a literalistic view of the millennium was St. Augustine. Essentially Augustine says the millennium is now, the time of the Church, the time of the first resurrection from sin to the life of grace. The second resurrection is still to come. The 1000 years of Rev 20:1-6 refers to the finite time that the Church will last until the end of the world. Christ rules now in the Church. Satan is bound now but will be released at the end of this age to test the Church.[47] Augustine's voice proved decisive in the West for over five hundred years, effectively suppressing the millenarian impulse as too literal, exaggerated, and crude an interpretation of Scripture.

Thus Montanism, a fervent and enthusiastic kind of millenarianism, prompted the Church and spiritual writers to move to a more mystical and allegorical interpretation of Scripture. Orthodox Christians and Church writers moved away from a concern with eschatology, the parousia, and the millennium. As expectations of an imminent Second Coming receded, Christians turned their attention to other areas of life and other forms of spirituality.

Hermits, Holy Men, and Monasticism

The Christian Church, especially the African Church, for the first three or four centuries continued to hold in high esteem martyrs and prophets and a rigorist asceticism. In the third and fourth centuries African Christians such as the Donatists flourished and revered in a special way the direct communication of God's will to the believer by means of the Holy Spirit, and they continued to emphasize asceticism and the importance of prophecy.[48]

The Churches of Asia Minor, where Montanus's Phrygia was located, and the Churches of North Africa tended to develop similar forms of Christianity, a Christianity characterized by a strong ascetical and dissenting streak. Desert areas and outlying areas at the periphery of the Roman Empire, such as North Africa, Phrygia, and Egypt evolved a Christianity more rigorist and extremist than the Christianity of the great cities. Urban areas, more cosmopolitan because of enforced contact with other forms of culture and religious practice, tended to be more moderate and accommodating. Often dissenting and especially enthusiastic religious groups originate in remote country areas. For example, the Circumcellions were rural North African peasants and workers who became religious fanatics and glorified martyrdom. They dressed like monks and carried clubs and the relics of martyrs, which they also sold.[49] A Donatist theology that was literalistic, apocalyptic, and martyr-dominated inspired them, and they served as agrarian revolutionaries.[50] These peasants were similar to the monks of Egypt who protested against taxes, the rich, and moneylenders. To some degree they resembled the Taborite peasants of 1415 and the German peasants of 1525 whose revolutionary aspirations were raised by Luther's Reformation.

When Constantine converted to Christianity in 312 C.E. he brought the weight of the central government of the Roman Empire to the support of Christianity. This ended the persecution and martyrdom of orthodox Christians. The Emperors supported the mission of the Church, and Church and Empire began to have overlapping interests of order and organization. The Emperor's concern for the unity of his Empire often spilled over into his concern for Church unity. The Roman Church declared schismatic and heterodox local religious traditions and groups which threatened Church unity, and the state vigorously persecuted these dissident groups.[51] In fact, St. Augustine himself petitioned the Emperor to impose religious unity on North Africa, by force, if necessary.

The millenarian elements in Christianity, the hope for the imminent return of Jesus, were prominent as long as Christians were a persecuted minority, but once Christianity became the established religion of the Roman Empire during the fourth century, millenarian yearning declined—or, more correctly, took complex new forms for several centuries before reasserting itself in the early Middle Ages. As a sense of the imminence of the millennium faded, many devout Christians channeled their fervor first into a hermetical lifestyle and then into the more organized monastic form of life. Holy people, ascetics, hermits, and later the monks replaced the martyrs in an age when martyrdom of blood no long existed.

During the second and third centuries a substantial hermetical movement grew in Egypt and the wilderness areas of Palestine and Syria. By the fifth and sixth centuries the holy man played an important role in society.[52] These hermits cultivated a spirituality based primarily on Scripture and only remotely on millenarian expectations: to live in the world as though they were not of the world at all. And if they could not be martyrs for their faith, they could be spiritually martyred, live a life of austerity so as to prepare for the Heavenly Kingdom, and torment the body so as to be spiritually more prepared for the Kingdom. It might be offered that the Jewish Essenes were the forerunners of the desert hermits, but the Christian ascetics and hermits performed different ascetic practices. The main form that religious discipline took was abstention from food, drink, and other necessities of life. The ascetics prized self-torment in the forms of various repressions and deprivations to make the body uncomfortable. Some of these men and women performed spectacular feats of mortification, occasionally going to such excesses that some have referred to it as a form of spiritual madness.[53] The motivation of these spiritual athletes rested on their belief in the essential dichotomy between this world and the heavenly world. They followed Pauline notions that flesh and blood could not posses immortality (1 Cor. 15:50).

In the West, the papacy was becoming the focus of Church authority and organization, and gradually monasteries began to eclipse individual holy men. For the sake of the unity of the Church and the protection of the faithful, the hierarchy carefully regulated the sources of spiritual experience.[54] The development of monasticism accelerated during and after the fourth century when the threat of persecution and martyrdom ceased. The monks were bloodless martyrs, and ascetic excesses were regulated by monastic rule. As the world became Christian, Christians could not so easily break with the world, and the end of the world did not seem so imminent. Millenarian expectations were reinterpreted and relegated to secondary importance.

Monasticism provided a way of life for those Christians who did not want to be of the world while they waited either for the coming of Christ for or their own departure from this world by death. St. Martin, bishop of Tours in France, founded a monastery near Potiers about 362, John Cassian founded a monastery at Marseilles. St. Benedict, who died in 550, founded Monte Cassino in about the third decade of the sixth century and wrote his influential Rule, which, because of its moderation and common sense, spread rapidly in the West. In contrast to the East where monks and hermits often formed an anti-institutional protest and counterbalance to established Christianity and the clergy, Western monasticism from the fourth century onward was a vehicle for reform and was incorporated within the Church's institutional authority. Authority and institutional structures were sufficiently flexible, and for several centuries new forms of Christian life style and reform movements did not take on the heterodox or anti-institutional appearance that later reform efforts did. Holy and charismatic figures attracted followers to a particular form of the Christian life. Later reformers such as St. Francis and St. Dominic, responding to deeply felt frustrations and problems which routine methods were not coping with, would transmit to their followers a way of life and rules, but these reforming energies for the most part remained within the boundaries of the Church and did not become rival, dissident sects.

There was a price to the Church's fight against movements like Montanism. Eschatological concerns and prophetic ecstacy became less central and more suspect. A negative consequence of Montanism on Church practices was the determination to exclude women from any priestly or teaching office. Church leaders regarded women as often too impulsive and too emotional.[55] Despite other early traditions of Christian women who prophesied (cf. Acts 21:9), the Pauline tradition was reaffirmed: that women must keep silence in the churches, and be subordinate (1 Cor. 14:33-35). "I permit no woman to teach or to have authority over men; she is to keep silent" (Tim. 2:12).

The early Church was never a monolithic reality, even though later movements, including millenarian movements, looked back toward the early communities as if they were a unitary and primitive ideal. Increasingly, as the Church expanded and itself became part of the establishment, it periodically had to face the prospect of heterodox sects reacting against it in a way similar to those early Christian communities that had mobilized a radical apocalypticism and radical preparedness for the end of the world.

NOTES

1. Cf. W.H.C. Frend, *The Donatist Church* (Oxford: Clarendon Press, 1952, 1985), p. 116.

2. Eusebius, *Historia Ecclesiastica*, v.iii.3; hereafter cited as *H.E.*).

3. Cf. A.H.M. Jones, "Were Ancient Heresies National or Social Movements in Disguise?" *Journal of Theological Studies, N.S.* 10 (1959): 280-298; W.H.C. Frend, "Heresy and Schism as Social and National Movements," *Studies in Church History* 9 (1972): 37-56.

4. *Barnabas* 5.4; cf. Hans Bietenhard, "The Millennial Hope in the Early Church," *Scottish Journal of Theology* 6 (1956): 13.

5. Irenaeus, *Haereses* V.28, 3; 32, 2; 36, 3. Cf. Hans Bietenhard, "The Millennial Hope in the Early Church," *Scottish Journal of Theology* 6 (1956): 13-14.

6. Justin, *Dial. cum Trypho*, 80-81.

7. Tertullian, *Adversus Marcionem*, iii.24; iv.31; cf. Hans Bietenhard, p. 15.

8. Tertullian, *De Oratione*, xxix; *De Spectaculis*, xxx.

9. Tertullian, *De Fuga in Persecutione* ix.4. Cf. Frederick C. Klawiter, "The Role of Martyrdom and Persecution in Developing the Priestly Authority of Women in Early Christianity: A Case Study of Montanism," *Church History* 40 (1980): 253.

10. Tertullian, *Ad Scapulam*, v.1-5.

11. Cf. Pierre de Labriolle, *La Crise Montaniste*, Paris: Ernest Laroux, 1913, pp. 108, 129; Michael Hill, *A Sociology of Religion* (London: Heinemann Educational Books, 1973), p. 176.

12. Cf. Tertullian, *De Fuga in Persecutione*, xi.

13. Cf. Frederick C. Klawiter, p. 254.

14. Pierre de Labriolle, *Les Sources de L'histoire du Montanisme* (Paris: Ernest Leroux, 1913), p. xiii; de Labriolle's work gathers together some of the key original sources on Montanism.

15. de Labriolle, *La Crise Montaniste*, p. 12; cf. Ronald A. Knox, *Enthusiasm* (Oxford University Press, 1950), ch. 3, pp. 25-49; Timothy D. Barnes, "The Chronology of Montanism," *Journal of Theological Studies* 21 (1970): 403-408.

16. J. Massingberd Ford, "Was Montanism a Jewish-Christian Heresy?" *Journal of Ecclesiastical History* 7 (1966): 146.

17. St. Jerome, *Letters*, 41.4.

18. Cf. Walter Burkert, *Greek Religion* trans. by John Raffan (Cambridge: Harvard University Press, 1985), pp. 110-111; Erwin Rhode, *Psyche: The Cult of Souls and Belief in Immortality among the Greeks* (New York: Harcourt Brace and Co., 1925), pp. 255-259.

19. Eusebius, *H.E.* V.xviii.14.

20. Epiphanius, *Panarion* 48.11. Cf. de Labriolle, *La Crise Montaniste*, pp. 37-38.

21. Eusebius, *H.E.*, V.xvi.17.

22. Eusebius, *H.E.*, V.xvi.19. Much of our information about Montanus comes from this contemporary anonymous account which Eusebius quotes, cf. *H.E.* V.xvi.1.

23. Eusebius, *H.E.*, V.xviii.2.

24. E.R. Dodds, *Pagan and Christian in an Age of Anxiety* (Cambridge: Cambridge University Press, 1965), p. 64.

25. Eusebius, *H.E.*, V.xvi.6-10.

26. Eusebius, *H.E.*, V.xviii.11.

27. Eusebius, *H.E.*, V.xvi.20.

28. Eusebius, *H.E.*, V.xvi.2; de Labriolle, *La Crise Montaniste*, p. 26.

29. E.R. Dodds, p. 3.

30. Hippolytus, *In Daniel*, III.xviii-xix.

31. Eusebius, *H.E.*, V.xvi.9; V.xviii.11.

32. Cf. Mary Douglas, "Social Preconditions of Enthusiasm and Heterodoxy," in *Forms of Symbolic Action* edited by R.F. Spencer (Seattle: University of Washington Press, 1969), p. 70.

33. Frederick C. Klawiter, p. 253.

34. Eusebius, *H.E.*, V.xviii.11.

35. Cf. I.M. Lewis, *Ecstatic Religion* (London: Harmondsworth, 1971), p. 31.

36. Eusebius, *H.E.*, V.xviii.9.

37. Eusebius, *H.E.*, V.xviii.13.

38. Eusebius, *H.E.*, V.xvi.10; de Labriolle, *La Crise Montaniste*, p. 30; cf. Jules Lebreton, *History of the Primitive Church* (New York: Macmillan and Co., 1949), p. 660.

39. de Labriolle, *La Crise Montaniste*, p. 207.

40. de Labriolle, *La Crise Montaniste*, p. 558.

41. Eusebius, *H.E.*, III.28, and Hans Bietenhard, pp. 17, 26.

42. Origen, *De Principiis*, II.11.

43. Eusebius, *H.E.*, III.29 and VII.24.

44. Commodianus, *Carmen apologeticum*, 791-6, 941-946; *Instructionum*, I.29.

45. Lactantius, *Divinarum Institutionum*, VIII.24.

46. Jerome, *Commentar. In Jeremiam Prophetam*, lib. IV, cap. xx.

47. St. Augustine, *De Civitate Dei*, XX. 7.

48. W.H.C. Frend, p. 114.

49. Isidor, *De Officiis Ecclesiasticis*, ii.15.

50. W.H.C. Frend, "Circumcellions and Monks," *The Journal of Theological Studies* N.S. 20 (1969): 549.

51. Peter Brown, "Religious Dissent in the Later Roman Empire: The Case of North Africa," in *Religion and Society in the Age of St. Augustine* (New York: Harper and Row, 1972): 243, 256.

52. Peter Brown, "The Rise and Function of the Holy Man in Late Antiquity," *Religion and Society in the Age of Augustine* (New York: Harper and Row, 1972), p. 138.

53. Cf. E.R. Dodds, *Pagan and Christian*, p. 4; Stevan L. Davies, "Ascetic Madness," in *Pagan and Christian Anxiety: A Response to E. R. Dodds*, ed. by Robert C. Smith and John Lounibos (New York: University Press of America, 1984), pp. 12, 19.

54. Cf. Philip H. Ennis, "Ecstacy and Everyday Life," *Journal for the Scientific Study of Religion* 6 (1967): 40.

55. de Labriolle, *La Crise Montaniste*, p. 555.

Chapter Four
Reformers and the Revival of Prophetic Prophecy

Introduction

As the year 1000, the end of the first millennium of Christianity, approached one would have expected to find across Europe reports of widespread apprehension, even terror, of the Imminent End.[1] But the year passed relatively quietly, probably because St. Augustine's influence had long muted apocalyptic and millenarian impulses, and the Catholic Church, as the dominant religious institution, maintained control over spiritual innovations.[2] Some medieval Europeans did expect that Christ would return when the year 999 ended, and there were those who were convinced that when the eve of the millennium came that the Day of Wrath would dawn. But no specific millenarian group arose, and the fears of the year 1000 were no greater than when some comet, eclipse or other wonder appeared and terrorized those who had few means but religion to explain unusual natural phenomenon.

The two or three centuries following the year 1000 saw complex social and intellectual changes that led ultimately to the Reformation. As the religious and political unity of Christendom started the extended process of breaking up, social tensions increased, and there was an upsurge of apocalyptic expectations and radical eschatological or millenarian movements, especially in the later Middle Ages. Various enthusiastic and heretical groups emerged but were for the most part reformist rather than revolutionary.

Ecclesiastical authorities often did not know how to deal with reforming zeal and energy. The ordinary reaction of those in charge was to try to keep control, and the social institutions did indeed keep multiform zealous energies in check for some time. The control of the Church and its preservation of orthodoxy very likely served to keep down the rise of fringe groups and particularly any millenarian groups. But once the religious and political unity of Christendom began breaking up, with a rise in social tensions and an increase in apocalyptic writing, there was an upsurge of radical reform and eschatological or millenarian movements.

Above all else the eleventh and twelfth centuries were reformist, and Europe began to experience a great religious awakening. The eleventh century witnessed the Cluniac reforms, the foundation of the Cistercian and Carthusian Orders, the first Great Crusade, and the building of many of the great cathedrals. Reforming ideas from Cluny and other monastic centers spread rapidly, and although these reforms gained a momentum the originators could not have foreseen, they did not directly respond to lay needs nor exhaust spiritual hungers. People sought new means by which their aspirations and expectations could be met. A revival in the study of the Gospels brought about a changing spirituality and a search for new spiritual forms.[3] A new spirituality placed a renewed emphasis on living according to the precepts of the Gospels, specifically imitating the life of Christ and his apostles, with a devotion to evangelical poverty. Common people manifested a great enthusiasm for the pure simplicity of the apostolic life and a reliance on the inspiration of the Holy Spirit.[4] Throughout Europe a sense of individualism was on the rise, and this along with the emphasis on simplicity and the Holy Spirit stressed individual experiences that often led to the rejection of the institutional Church as mediator and Church authorities and priests as intermediaries. These protests were the harbingers of forces that culminated in the Reformation.

Reformers and Prophetic Prophecy

The Crusades, beginning in 1095 under Pope Urban II, were not so much the result of apocalypticism as they were a stimulus to the revival of apocalyptic themes. Jerusalem became a concrete historical place as well as an apocalyptic ideal and apocalyptic city par excellence.[5]

In 1073 Hildebrand was elected as Pope Gregory VII (d. 1085), and he struggled against the Emperor Henry IV. This struggle was resolved in the Concordat of Worms in 1122 and confirmed the following year in the First Lateran Council. With the papacy looming as the preeminent authority in the West, came a reconsideration of eschatological and apocalyptic themes. Some contemporary writers, for instance, began to reflect on what role the popes would play in the End Times. Gregory VII himself made frequent uses of Antichrist images in his reforming efforts. While not suggesting that the end was near, Gregory did highlight the difference between the followers of Christ and the servants of the Antichrist as he sought to free the Church from the influence of secular rulers.[6]

Some enthusiastic movements, because they were not accepted by the official Church, grew outside Church boundaries with great energy and inevitably in opposition to the Church. The founding of the Mendicant Orders (the Franciscans, for instance) would keep some of the spiritual ferment within the institutional Church, but authorities tended to view as heretical, and were quick to condemn, many enthusiastic believers who wanted to use the Gospel as a rule of life and did not wish a monastic rule approved by the hierarchy. Consequently the Church at times had difficulty in channeling religious energies and alienation. Many of the spiritual aspirations and reformist energies did not have a cohesive or organized form. Church authorities simply did not always know how to respond to and incorporate reformist urges and religious impulses. Many of the changes brought a growing sense of apocalypticism, as some reformers linked the pope with the Antichrist. Opposition and persecution, disasters and periodic upheavals, such as the Black Death in 1348, gave rise to an apocalyptic outlook and a search for security and a sense of election among sects which considered themselves "God's chosen."

In a world of orthodoxy, protest and dissent often appeared to be heresy. To step outside the accepted framework was to be opposed to authority, and so heresy began to seem endemic. The Church was the major institution in most people's lives, and to disagree or dissent or criticize meant to walk a narrow path between reforming piety and heresy. Many of the enthusiastic reformers were probably not deviant in doctrine, but because the authorities did not always know how to respond, they sometimes tarred dissidents with the brush of deviancy.[7] Many of the spiritual aspirations and reformist energies did not have a cohesive or organized form. These energies often appeared in small groups of only local importance which developed along their own lines, often outside the Church and often bitterly in opposition to it.[8] Authorities sometimes confused sincere reformers with those who were genuinely heterodox. Some reformers, like Peter Valdes, began as orthodox, but after confrontations with the hostility and ignorance of the hierarchy, became more extreme and heterodox. Only the width of a hair separates Peter Valdes from Francis of Assisi, but one was condemned and the other canonized.[9] Church authorities simply did not always know how to respond to and incorporate reformist urges and religious impulses.

Between 1199 and 1215 a number of religious groups of a pious or charitable character proliferated, with many urging a return to an idealized view of the early Church, that is, a life style characterized by simplicity and voluntary poverty. St. Augustine's theology still continued to shape the flow of Christian thinking, with his pessimistic view of the world. For Augustine, time was static, with the Church on earth merely waiting for the Last Judgment; human earthly existence was malignant. Since the Fall, according to Augustine, this world was a "life of misery, a kind of hell on earth."[10] Augustine had ridiculed the idea that the thousand-year kingdom of Christ in Revelation 20:1-6 would be a glorious earthly kingdom; on the contrary, he affirmed that the kingdom was an image for the life of the Church in the present.[11] Augustine's view allowed no place for millenarianism, and no significant millenarian groups emerged during these centuries. Christians, however, were not sure whether the interim period between the first and second coming of Christ was one of mere stagnantion or one of growth.

Joachim of Fiore

Joachim of Fiore then burst upon the medieval scene and became the most important apocalyptic writer of the Middle Ages. Rather than seeing the interim period between the First and Second Coming of Christ, the Incarnation, and the Last Judgment, as a stagnant waiting period, Joachim saw the gap between the two great divine interventions into time as a period of expectancy, of progression, of growth. Joachim's electric theology of human history dealt with this gap in time and inadvertently provided legitimation for all kinds of millenarian hopes and dreams for the next several centuries.[12]

Joachim of Fiore (c.1135-1202), a biblical scholar, was more than a simplistic millenarian prophet of approaching climax. He was born in Calabria and went on a pilgrimage to the Holy Land where he underwent a dramatic conversion. He gave away all his money and rich clothing, and he entered the Benedictine monastery of Corazzo about 1171. Soon becoming the abbot, he sought a perfect realization of monastic life and wanted to have Corazzo incorporated into the reforming Cistercian order. On this work in about 1183 he travelled to Casamari near Rome. Here he had the visions that launched his writings on apocalypticism.[13] He met with popes who encouraged his research, and he became an international figure who made a dramatic impact upon his contemporaries. In 1184 he appeared before Pope Lucius III to interpret Sibylline prophecies about the future. In the winter of 1190/1 at Messina an English courier left an account of the meeting between the famous Abbot and Richard the Lion Hearted, who was on his way to the Third Crusade. The Crusaders hoped for a prophecy about the fate of Jerusalem. Ever scholarly, Joachim would not have given a snap prophecy but would have commented on the present times since he felt an imminent and deepening crisis in history. He found contemporary happenings illuminated Scripture, and Scripture gave clues to the last events which were soon to happen. In 1191 he deeply impressed Emperor Henry VI by his interpretations of events. During this period he became dissatisfied with the Cistercian order; by 1190 he started a new convent of his own at Fiore in Calabria and in 1196 received papal approval for his own Order.[14]

All his work was grounded in Sacred Scripture, and he sought like many medieval thinkers to break through the literal meaning to find the inner spiritual meaning. Through personal spiritual experiences and reflection, he saw the mystery of the Trinity as the key. In the history of the human race the mystery of the Trinity's inner relations were expressed within time itself. All history is in three successive stages: the Age of the Father, the Age of the Son, and the Age of the Holy Spirit. The Age of the Holy Spirit would be the final epoch, a time when men would be filled with understanding of the Scriptures, the sacraments would be done away with, and faith would be changed to love. The new age would begin after the destruction of the Antichrist and would be prepared for by an order of barefoot monks. Of special importance is Joachim's concept of the meaning of history. His *Book of Figures* dealt with the patterns of history, and dividing history into three overlapping states, respectively ascribed to the Father, the Son and the Holy Ghost. In true apocalyptic fashion he saw his own age as being in crisis. In current events he saw signs of the Antichrist and the pope of the last days. He stressed the domination of the spiritual and charismatic over the institutional, rational, and Scholastic logic. His dissent from Augustine's view of history and his critique of the Church had a radical, quasi-revolutionary influence which was to last for several centuries. His critique of the Church, in which he hoped for a new and better Church, would be used by proto-revolutionary ideologies of later centuries and by groups who found themselves described in his writings and who justified their own importance by his writings.[15]

Joachim died in 1202, and in 1215 the Fourth Lateran Council condemned particular points of Joachim's theology while stressing his submission to the papacy in his lifetime. Joachim's reputation, however, spread as a herald of the coming Age of the Holy Spirit, as a prophet of the Antichrist, and as a seer who understood the patterns of history. By the 1240s the evolutionary possibilities of his patterns of history began to be recognized. Joachim had believed that history would come to fruition by entering the third age and that human agencies would contribute to bringing the Church through the transition. Two orders of spiritual men must lead the Church of the second age into the coming third age. Joachim found these two orders prefigured in the many twos in the Scriptures, such as the raven and dove of Noah, the two angels who rescued Lot from Sodom, Paul and

Barnabas, Moses and Aaron. In the 1240s many from the two great Mendicant Orders, the Dominicans and Franciscans, believed that they were the barefoot spiritual men prophesied by Joachim. Not unexpectedly many Dominicans and Franciscans appreciated this prophetic role in saving the world, and as many Dominicans and Franciscans fervently espoused his ideas, Joachim's reputation soared. One group from among the Franciscans, the Franciscan Spirituals, especially came to appreciate the implications of Joachim's doctrines for themselves. Joachim also interpreted the Book of Revelation's Dragon with seven heads and the seven seals and openings. The seven heads were the great persecutors of the Church, with the Antichrist as the last persecutor. Crusaders fastened onto his comments that Saladin, the Islamic leader, was a possible Antichrist. Other writers used Joachim's name to spread what became a popular belief that identified Emperor Frederick II with Antichrist, while others identified the Antichrist with Alfonso of Castille.[16]

The Franciscan Spirituals (or Zealots)

By the time Francis of Assisi began his mission, Church authorities were more receptive to the new spirituality that he offered. Francis of Assisi had been born in 1182, the son of a wealthy merchant. His charm still attracts across the centuries, even as other medieval personages chill by their austerity and self-abnegation. In 1208 Francis's small band of followers took pledges of humble service and poverty. This ideal of a simple life style expressed powerfully the mood and longings of the time and helps explain the explosive growth—like enthusiastic sects— of the two mendicant Orders, the Franciscans and Dominicans. The ideal for these Orders was a poor itinerant preacher who embraced a life combining poverty, love, and wandering proselytism. They represent a turning away from the purely ascetic ideal of early monasticism and a turning toward a spirituality which emphasized the humanity of Christ.[17]

Francis came to Innocent III in 1210 seeking approval for an unconventional way of life with a rigorist, even harsh, standard of poverty. Having struggled with others who sought approval for a poor way of life, the hierarchy was initially hostile, and again Innocent was faced with the challenge of how to incorporate into the Church another enthusiastic band of Christians. A papal ban in 1184 on new religious ways of life had forced some groups into heresy and opposition to the Church. A crucial condition which finally won over the pope was Francis' promise to be obedient to the Holy See. Although the Lateran Council would in 1215 reconfirm rules against the establishment of new religious orders, popes granted recognition to new religious ways of life to keep within Church control some of the fervor of the new movements. In 1210 by giving oral recognition to Francis' small band, Innocent III attempted to harness Franciscan zeal for evangelical poverty. The Franciscans and Dominicans quickly transformed from unstructured wandering bands of preachers into highly organized orders which would perform important services for the Church, not the least of which was the Inquisition.[18]

Francis' utter lack of concern for the morrow and lack of interest in education, while possible with a small band, was not practical in a great religious organization. Housing, organization, the bare necessities of life were required for a religious order. Even before his death in 1226 the Franciscan Order had attracted great numbers of men, men whose learning and eloquence sometimes caused them to be restless when tending the sick and preaching to country folk, tasks that Francis' early companions were content with. By 1260 Francis probably would not have been able to enter his own order since by then Franciscans were an educated, clerical order with possessions and involved in universities.

Even during Francis's lifetime two parties were growing up among the Franciscans. A friar named Elias and a few of the other superiors of the Order sought mitigation of the strictness of the rule of poverty and placed more emphasis on learning and oratory. The other party, many of Francis' own intimate companions, were drawn to the contemplative life and wished to adhere to the strictness and simplicity of the original way of life. These two bodies were the forerunners of the two later parties, the Conventionals and the Spirituals, whose conflicts over poverty would divide the Franciscans from 1220 to 1260. The Conventionals allowed modifications of the ideal of absolute poverty and tolerated the necessary institutionalization of Francis's charism by setting up houses, libraries, churches for the sake of their ministries of preaching and education. Once again routinization, which enabled the Franciscans to provide great service to society, was gained at the seeming loss of the original freshness and spontaneity of the first years. The Spirituals, on the other hand, maintained a rigid adherence to St. Francis's Rule and ideal of poverty.

It is not clear how Francis felt towards developments in the organization he founded. He did feel antipathy toward Elias, a Franciscan superior, and Francis had been concerned that his Order would decline from its original purity and zeal. In his dying wishes, dictated in the last few days of his life, he urged his followers to observe the Rule strictly and not seek modifications. The original Rule forbade friars to receive money either personally or through agents. Four years after Francis's death, Gregory IX began a series of papal decrees which built upon the original Rule and mitigated the strictness of Franciscan poverty. Learning was encouraged, and convents often were removed from country districts into towns.[19]

The Spirituals believed Francis was so unique that he indeed represented a turning point in history. The Spirituals found specially attractive Joachim's concept of a transition from a second to a third age in history; this idea offered an eschatological basis for clinging rigidly to Francis' Rule and ideals. The Franciscan Spirituals, also called Zealots—a term which echoes back to earlier ages of passion—greeted the election in 1247 of John of Parma as General with joy, expecting him to exert special leadership to preserve the purity of Franciscan poverty. John strove to follow St. Francis's example in style of life and in his travels was accompanied by only one friar. He was friend and adviser to St. Louis, King of France, to the pope, and various cardinals. John fostered a fusion of Spiritualist fervor with Joachim prophecy. It was his companion, the "fanatical" Gerard of Borgo San Donnion who pushed to extremes Joachim's work, which he regarded as the new Gospel of the Age of the Holy Ghost. Gerard dramatically announced the arrival of the third age and exaggerated the vital role of his Order.

By the middle of the century Joachim's ideas were the focus of attention. The year 1260, according to Joachim, was the year when dramatic signs of transition to the third age were to take place. Frederick II died peacefully in his bed, however, and the year passed quietly, except for outbursts of the Flagellant movement. Moderate Franciscans sought to read the signs of the times but not look for sudden changes, while the Spiritualists increasingly diverged from the Order by their fervent expectation of calamity and by a passionate assumption of an eschatological role in ushering in the new age. In 1257 John of Parma was forced to resign from his leadership of the Franciscans, and Bonaventure became new head of Franciscan order. He had to suppress the lunatic fringe of Joachites within the Franciscans. Gerard was confined in a cell for 18 years during which time he still nourished his expectations about the Antichrist. Bonaventure himself was apocalyptic in outlook and himself deeply influenced by the Joachite tradition, and in many ways was the ancestor of such later Spirituals as Peter Olivi. Bonaventure gave an apocalyptic interpretation of the person of St. Francis, seeing Francis as the Angel of the Sixth Seal and the harbinger of the coming seventh age of the Church, the dawning of the contemplative age. In the continuing struggle over the meaning of poverty between the Spirituals and Conventionals, Bonaventure was caught between the two parties. The stricter Spirituals as a group led holy and ascetical lives, but their burning zeal for poverty often went to excess, while the Conventionals were more moderate and felt the Order needed to bring its learning to the service of the Church and the poor. The Conventuals, however, under the leadership of St. Bonaventure, convinced pope Nicholas III in 1279 to declare permanent the various mitigations of the Rule that had crept in, specifically the use of worldly goods.[20]

The influence of Joachim continued to exert a fatal attraction over the minds of Franciscan Zealots, enthusiasts with patched habits and passionate mysticism. They were not a homogenous movement, and they attached different meanings to Joachim's ideas. They plunged into apocalyptic speculations and vividly described the coming age of peace and love as well as coming conflicts with the Antichrist. They delivered tirades against popes who opposed them and often identified these popes as the Antichrist. The Spiritual Franciscans or Zealots believed they were caught up in a cosmic conflict, that a crisis of evil would accelerate in a crescendo before the Church could pass over the Jordan into the age of the Holy Spirit. Their special role was to safeguard for the future the spiritual treasure of Francis's rule and ideals of poverty. Their passionate expectation in the coming cataclysmic struggle was the driving force that bolstered their bitter opposition

Reformers and Prophetic Prophecy

to the acceptance by the Order of gifts of money and property. The Spirituals criticized such Franciscan "abuses" as the building of churches, the richness of vestments used in services, stained glass windows, the excessive number of habits possessed by friars, and the unnecessary fineness of the cloth. The Spirituals were devoted to their patched and skimpy habits as symbols of pure poverty. Increasingly these poor but enthusiastic friars were harried, alienated from the bulk of the Order as extremists, exiled, and persecuted. Their opponents frequently were able to raise the cry of heresy against them because of their Joachite ideas. Traditionally such persecution only entrenches and confirms for the believers the belief that the terrible times have come. Their conviction of the ultimate triumph of their ideals and fervent belief that they were the chosen elite who should reform the world enabled them to endure harsh persecutions.

Peter Olivi, a Franciscan leader of the Spirituals in Provence in southern France, was considered by his enemies to be a heretic or even the Antichrist—increasingly part of the vocabulary of abuse of medieval religious enemies. He was born about 1248 in Languedoc and spent his student days at the University of Paris. During this period, after the first generation of Franciscans had died, disputes about poverty became more intense, with great arguments over such questions as whether Christ and his apostles owned anything, even their clothes. He gradually gained fame in his Order for his theological learning and holiness. In 1279 when Pope Nicholas III held a celebrated inquiry into questions of poverty, Olivi was invited to participate. Olivi thought of poverty as the highest mode of existence, and he taught that the only path to perfection lay in complete renunciation of possessions, following the example of Christ and the apostles. For Olivi the Franciscan rule embodied the means for leading such a holy life. Olivi took from Joachim the idea that history, with its three epochs, would flower after the defeat of the Antichrist, whoever that might prove to be. The coming of St. Francis marked a turning point in history, the beginning of the final epoch and a time of combat with the forces of the Antichrist. Francis was the Messiah of the new age, with the mission of renewing the following of Christ rather than introducing any new doctrines. The Franciscan Rule had cosmic significance and possessed the same sanctity as the Gospel. He fervently believed the Roman Church should authenticate this new revelation of the Spirit. Olivi and the Spirituals could only see a wealthy Church as carnal and corrupt, persecuting them and rejecting poverty just as Christ's teachings were rejected. For Olivi the Church of his day was Babylon, the great harlot, and the crime of the Church was the denial of poverty.[21]

When Boniface VIII became pope in 1295 he more strictly repressed the Spirituals, whose hopes soared again with Boniface's death in 1304. The next pope Clement V moved the Holy See to Avignon, and the scattered Spirituals adopted a hermetical life of waiting for the final crisis of history—their ascetic zeal calls to mind the Montanists. Olivi died in 1298 and in 1299 the Chapter General at Lyons condemned his writings, but a fanatical Olivist group, mostly simple-minded enthusiasts, refused to compromise or give up their ragged and patched habits. Olivi's followers were persecuted and some burned in 1318 by the authorities, but they continued to hold Olivi sacred, and his ideas passed into the vernacular texts of a growing lay religious movement known as the Beguins who regarded Olivi as their founder and venerated him even more than St. Francis. The fanatical millenarianism and anti-papal attitudes of the Spirituals touched some but not all of the religious and semi-religious associations which Franciscan spirituality inspired.[22]

The Spirituals survived in quite diverse forms as the Beguines and Beghards in France—especially Provence—Belgium and the Rhineland, while the heirs of the Spirituals in Italy were the Fraticelli. Beguines and Beghards were groups of lay men (Beghards) and women (Beguines) who sought to follow the new spirituality of a simple life according to apostolic principles. These lay associations expanded rapidly, and their lack of uniform rules and their relative freedom from ecclesiastical regulation stirred the suspicion of Church authorities who were quick to see heterodoxy and who accused some associations of preaching the advent of the Antichrist and the approaching end of the world. In Germany Beghards more commonly came from lower classes and consequently tended to be guilty of doctrinal deviations because of lack of training. The Council of Lyons in 1274 ordered those Beguine communities dissolved which had been formed after 1215 and which had not been recognized by the Church.[23]

The Fraticelli

Italian Spirituals became the Fraticelli, and the Fraticelli fractured into at least three different bodies, remote scions of the Provencal Zealots and of Olivi. As the Fraticelli became more fanatical and more heterodox, revolutionary hopefuls found it hard to wait patiently, and these impetuous spirits split off from the Franciscan Order. Late in the 1300s they declared themselves separated from the Church and fiercely attacked the papacy. Carrying Joachim's thought to its logical extreme, they declared heretical any who denied the poverty of Christ. In their extremism they declared Pope John XXII a heretic and the Antichrist, and they denied that the bishop and clergy who followed John had power to administer sacraments. The disturbances caused by the Great Schism, which rendered the Papacy powerless to combat heterodox movements, greatly aided the diffusion of these sects. If the hierarchy of the Church opposed the perfection of the future age entrusted to a select few, themselves, they did not believe the Church to be the true Church of Christ but rather the expected Antichrist who was associated with the troubles of the end time and the persecution of God's people.

These Fraticelli caused headaches for the Holy Office and the Inquisition because often members of the nobility interfered with Church officials who attempted to restrain the Fraticelli. It is not always easy to trace the evolution of these movements into exclusive sects whose members believe themselves to be the faithful of Christ persecuted by evil ones. In Italy, social unrest created a ready audience for heresy and prophecy. Attacks on the rich struck a receptive cord among workers, and the shopkeepers and artisans followed Fraticellian ideas. The later converts to the Fraticelli were very different from the original founders. These new converts included humble members of society such as winesellers and artisans and were influenced rather by a general discontent with conditions of the Church and in society rather than by intellectual or theological convictions. The sect continued to be active in Italy, with martyrs such as Michael da Calci, an itinerant preacher martyred in 1389 in Florence. The last important appearance of the Fraticelli was before the Inquisition in 1466. Of all the groups that we have discussed so far they were the most fervently millenarian, except for an occasional and radical flagellant group.[24]

The Flagellants

The flagellants were fervent groups of lay people which evolved spasmodically into more radical and heterodox movements. Flagellant processions first appeared in Italian cities in November 1260, the year that pseudo-Joachite prophecies suggested would usher in the third age and people expected dramatic happenings. In Italy at this time, warfare between the Guelphs and Ghibellines in the aftermath of the struggles between Frederick II and the papacy caused widespread conditions of insecurity. The flagellant movement lessened in Italy when the expected end time or transition did not arrive, but in 1261-2 the movement crossed the Alps and appeared in Germany, where the flagellants were more organized in their rituals, songs, and even costumes. In the beginning of the movement in 1260, chroniclers describe people from all levels of society as joining the movement, rich and poor, nobles and merchants, soldiers and civilians, old as well as young, to whom religious men of the monastic and mendicant orders as well as the secular clergy ministered. After the initial appearances, the flagellants soon seemed to number mostly the poor, peasants and weavers, smithies and cobblers, just as the later and more radical groups were mostly society's marginal people.[25]

Flagellant processions, bands ranging variously in size from 20 to 300 and often led by priests, snaked from town to town, day and night, with banners and crosses and flickering candles. In each town, they would process two by two and would group in the marketplace or in front of the church where they would divest themselves of their outer garments and whip themselves, usually until the blood came. Sometimes pious onlookers would catch the blood on cloths and daub it on themselves saying it was miraculous blood. The penitents would sing mournful hymns about the nativity and passion of Christ and would cry out in loud voices, "Holy Virgin, please take pity on us! Beg your son Jesus Christ to spare us! Mercy, Mercy, Peace, peace."[26] Hurling themselves to the ground they would stretch out their arms in the form of a cross, and then rising again they would make a general confession. Many followed this pattern for thirty-three days and then would return to the towns, villages, or castles from which they had come. This public display of penance and dramatic self-scourging would cause great emotional response and sobbing outcries in the onlookers who ran to see them. In fact, emotions were so intense that one contemporary witness records that even hearts of stone would be moved and no eye could hold back the tears.[27]

The initial movement flickered and died—or went underground—within a few years, and only occasionally were there appearances, such as Strassbourg in 1296, Bergamo in 1334, Cremona in 1340. In 1349 came the explosion. In 1347 the Black Plague first appeared in Sicily, and in three months it crossed over to the mainland of Italy where it caused great panic. A few years previously earthquakes had caused damage in Naples, Rome, Pisa, and Venice, and from 1345 through 1348 rain and bad crops caused serious food shortages. By 1346 a number of wealthy Florentine financial houses had declared bankruptcy, and the Guelphs continued fighting the Ghibellines.[28] These calamities were as nothing when the Black Plague struck. Boccaccio, writing about Florence, described the symptoms of a plague victim, as "certain swellings in the groin or the armpit . . . an infallible sign that he would die. . . ."[29]

Driven by terrible sights as well as fantasies, people fled from cities and abandoned possessions. In Florence there was insufficient ground to bury the dead. In Venice as many as 600 people a day were dying, and in Vienna 500 a day were dying from the pestilence. The governments of cities tried to maintain operation and order. But precautions were in vain because they did not directly attack the cause of the disease. The plague seemed an overwhelming and inexplicable disaster; it truly seemed that the end of the world was approaching. Driven by terror of the plague and fear of God's punishment, processions of flagellants reappeared and scourged themselves to seek forgiveness and ward off the wrath of God. For a few months during 1348-9 their processions and ritualistic scourgings generated enormous fervor. Throughout most of 1348, the flagellants remained organized and relatively straightforward in their penitential goals, and authorities did not challenge them. By the end of 1349 and the following year, when the plague did not go away, some groups were spurred towards greater millenarianism. In fact millenarians interpreted the disastrous events as signs that the demise of the world was at hand. The flagellants initially performed their bloody scourgings as penance in the hope of appeasing God's wrath and thereby warding off crises like plague and war. but what began as a form of penance lurched into a way of salvation that threatened the authority of the Church. Flagellants increasingly got out of hand and challenged lay authorities by their bloody rites.[30]

One key apocalyptic element for the flagellants was a "heavenly letter" read out during their services. This message from God, a letter supposedly written by God and delivered by an angel at Jerusalem had a simple and apocalyptic message. This letter, put forward repeatedly in different versions throughout the Middle Ages, told of the miseries and abominations which were to precede the Second Coming. If people would do penance and amend their ways, God would be merciful. The letter heightened the flagellants' sense of urgency. By their penitence they would purge themselves of their sins.[31]

Some flagellants began to view their scourgings as more powerful than the Church's sacraments. The flagellants' hysterical power over ordinary people threatened to get out of control, and their challenge of the effectiveness of the sacraments galvanized Church authorities. The University of Paris condemned the flagellants in March 1349, and in October 1349, Clement VI issued a bull, *Inter sollicitudines*, which reproved the flagellants on two grounds: for attacking the Church by denying it could forgive sins and for taking a habit (black with crosses on front and back). The flagellants, in their terror and in the belief they were in a holy war, turned upon and slaughtered Jews whom they believed to have poisoned drinking water. Many flagellants, however, heeded the warnings of ecclesiastical authorities, left the movement and received penance and absolution from prelates and the pope's representatives. In addition to the response of ecclesiastical authorities were the actions of political authorities. For example, the King of France simply banned the flagellants. But in Germany where central authority was weak, flagellants were more common, more influential, and radical. Stronger central authorities in England, France, and the Iberian kingdoms restricted the activities of flagellant groups and kept them within bounds. The peak passed and by 1350 the movement had subsided, for by its nature it could not be long sustained.[32]

It was in Thuringia that occurred the most formidable and radical flagellant outbreak. Schmidt claimed for himself a messianic faith and those prophecies of Isaiah which foretold the coming of Christ. Schmidt became the leader of the only true religion—a sect which denied the real presence and the power of the Church's sacraments—and he took the title of King of Thuringia. His followers had to confess to Schmidt, be whipped by him, and swear obedience to him. After this their only obligation was total submission to Schmidt the messiah. The reward for the followers of Schmidt was the certain knowledge that in and through them human history was attaining its end. The flagellants of 1349 were to them as John the Baptist was to Christ, and they believed even Christ was just their predecessor. Christ pointed the true way to salvation by enduring flagellation, but now they beat themselves and would gain salvation in this way: they replaced baptism of water with baptism of blood. Their bloody skins were to be the robes of innocence. They expected the millennial kingdom in which they would be grouped around their emperor-god and they would be called on to be princes. Many members of the sect sold their possessions and refused to work in the expectation that the end was near. Small outbreaks of the plague kept their fervor high. It may have been the epidemic of 1368 which inspired Schmidt to announce that the Last Judgement was approaching and the millennium would begin in 1369. Authorities, however, finally got control of the group and burned Schmidt with a number of followers in Nordhausen in 1369. He had inspired an apocalyptic blend of Waldensianism, Joachism, and a cult of blood.[33]

In 1370 the Bishop of Wurtzburg forbade flagellation in his diocese, but the flagellants did not vanish completely. A variation of them appeared, called Dancers, which appeared in North Germany and Flanders between 1373 and 1375. Dancers, a transitory phenomenon, were groups of men and women who entered towns and villages and danced and sang themselves into a frenzy until they collapsed. They stressed intense spiritual excitement and believed their penances were a substitute for the sacraments. Their hostility to Church doctrines and discipline aroused Church authorities sufficiently so that the Dancers disappeared rapidly. In 1391-2 new groups of flagellants were found among the peasants and artisans near Heidelberg and near Erfurt. Civil authorities by now acted quickly and burned the leaders. The first major inquisition against flagellants came in 1414 when Henry

Schoneveld, the Dominican inquisitor, entered Thuringia and surrounding areas to hunt out remnants of Schmidt's flagellant sect. In 1414, the secular authorities, proceeding more swiftly and harshly than Church authorities, quickly burned the leaders. It would thus seem that even before the Hussites appeared in Bohemia that radical religious ideology could threaten established powers, and civil authorities were beginning to recognized how unmanageable a religious force like the flagellants could be. What had begun as a genuine religious impulse was taken too far and radicalized, so that it imperilled not only doctrinal orthodoxy but social structures as well.[34]

Savonarola and Florence

Apocalyptic and millenarian sentiment did not disappear in Italy but persisted through the efforts of prophetic preachers, who predicted woes, war and death. As the Turkish menace approached from the East during the middle of the fifteenth century, predictions also increased of the end time and the appearance of the Antichrist. The last decade of the century belonged to that extraordinary millenarian prophet, Savonarola of Florence. Fra Girolamo Savonarola elicited millenarian excitement in Florence in the waning years of the 1400s, although no organized or formal millenarian group arose. The civic tradition of business-oriented Florence and popular tradition created an environment in which Savonarola's millenarian message was keenly attended to. Amidst social and political crisis, the charismatic Savonarola viewed the world as a battleground between good and evil forces and offered to the chosen people of Florence an apocalyptic vision of ultimate redemption in an earthly paradise.[35]

Savonarola was a fiery Dominican preacher who was one of the most flamboyant in the line of popular Italian prophets. He began preaching in 1482 at the priory of San Marco in Florence. Driven by a sense of a mission to reform the Church and society, his sermons took on the apocalyptic tone of prophetic preacher. He increasingly focused on the sinfulness of the time but did not neglect political issues. The scourge of God would devastate all of Italy, he predicted, and a new Cyrus would bring the sword of God's wrath. Savonarola foretold disaster for Florence and Italy: the Last Days were approaching. The world would soon enter the fifth age when the Antichrist would appear, Christians would vanquish the Antichrist, and the Turks and pagans would be baptized. Florence would have a special role as the new Zion, the center of Christian reforms which would spread over the whole world. But Florentines must renew themselves, he insisted and make Florence worthy to be the city of God. All of this had been revealed to the angelic prophet—Savonarola himself, of course.

In a worldly city of hard-headed business men and sophisticated artists and craftsmen, Savonarola created a sensation and drew an enthusiastic response. His vision of civic glory and religious reform, a golden millennium, seemed very near. Florence would be a paradise on earth. The city had long anticipated becoming a New Jerusalem and a new Rome in the dual mission of spiritual and political leadership, a city whose destiny was shaped by God.[36]

When the patricians expelled the Medici, Savonarola began to be more optimistic that the French King Charles VIII might indeed be the fulfillment of prophecies of the coming of a new Charlemagne who would reform Christianity and bring in the new flowering of religion. The coming of the French was to open the fifth age, the time of the Antichrist and the conversion of the world to Christianity. Savonarola was certain that Florence would play a glorious role in the new golden age.

However, the Medicis began to recover their control and influence. Accused of heresy, Savonarola was executed by the secular authorities on May 23, 1498. Prophetic preachers continued their warnings of the approach of Judgement Day but in a distinctly more subdued manner after the Fifth Lateran Council in 1516 put restrictions on those who preached of "terrors, threats, imminent catastrophes."[37] In spite of his death and restrictions, the memory and influence of Savonarola continued to burn brightly for a hundred years.

Conclusion

"Why are these fools awaiting the end of the world?" remarked Boniface VIII in what may have been a common reaction of thirteenth-century observers to the eschatological groups of the time.[38] The upsurge of eschatological groups in the thirteenth century is worth noting, especially after a relatively quiescent period of hundreds of years. It is not that there were more crises during this period, but rather the resurgence of groups, as if brought about by rain after a long drought, depended on several important variables. Joachim of Fiore broke the theological hold that Augustine had on the notion of history and reopened the question of the timing of the Second Coming. Further, the world was getting more complex, with multiple sources of power and influence emerging, while the Church's monolithic control over people's lives was loosened. The medieval order was growing diverse as many forces were released, political and economic and social.

Few of the groups were heretical, although the rigidity of the Church at times drove sincere, orthodox reformers to more radical and heretical positions. The flexibility of an Innocent III kept within the Church various spontaneous movements, including the Franciscans, that could easily have been lost by repressive rigidity. Some movements were pushed by authoritarian opposition to radical stances. But none of these factors can explain precisely why some groups became millenarian and others didn't. The Beguines had Joachite ideas but did not have the radical passion of Schmidt's followers. The Waldensians were serious in their pursuit of holiness and poverty, but they did not have the millenarian concerns that some of the Fraticelli manifested in their pursuit of Franciscan ideals.

Why some groups take on millenarian hopes and others don't cannot be as easily noted as the fact that those which do become millenarian have characteristics in common with other millenarian groups. Many of the movements looked at in this chapter seem to have cut across class lines, at least in the initial stages, and women seem well represented. These movements, such as the Fraticelli, manifest the intense passion that earlier millenarian groups displayed, which motivate them to great lengths in the holding firm to their convictions, whether it be the absolute ideal of poverty or that the third age was soon to come.

Savonarola followed in the Italian tradition of prophets, apocalyptic preachers, and religious visionaries whose themes were similar to those developed by Joachim of Fiore. Savonarola was a unique link between prophecy and politics, although he did not gather around himself a millenarian movement. It was possible to be millenarian in the sense of expecting the imminent, radical betterment on earth before the Last Judgment, without being oriented towards revolutionary action, but some millenarian groups could indeed be revolutionary.

In the next chapter the focus is on the Hussite Movement and the two extremist millenarian offshoots of that movement. For these movements and groups political opposition becomes a greater part of their religious stance. Twentieth-century hindsight can see more clearly the adumbrations of the Reformation. As unity and the authority of the Church changed, as new theologies appeared, as the lay and middle classes gained power, as some groups openly defied the Church, the number of extremist and eschatological groups would grow. The Reformation would bring in major changes to society and release a richer flowering of millenarian groups.

NOTES

1. Cf. Henri Foucillon, *The Year 1000* (New York: Harper and Row, 1971).

2. Bernard McGinn, *Visions of the End: Apocalyptic Traditions in the Middle Ages* (New York: Columbia University Press, 1979), pp. 29, 88.

3. Brenda Boulton, *The Medieval Reformation* (Baltimore: Edward Arnold, 1983), pp. 14, 17.

4. Gordon Leff, *Heresy in the Later Middle Ages* (Manchester University Press, 1967), Vol. 1, p. 31; cf. Jeffrey Burton Russell, *Dissent and Reform in the Early Middle Ages* (University of California Press, 1965).

5. Bernard McGinn, pp. 89, 94-5.

6. Bernard McGinn, pp. 94-95.

7. Gordon Leff, p. 47. For a contemporary view of one such group of pious enthusiasts, the Humiliati, see Jacques de Vitry, *Historia Occidentalis* edited by John Hinnebusch (University of Fribourg Press, 1972), ch. 28, *"De religione et regula humiliatorum,"* pp. 144-46.

8. Cf. Milan Loos, *Dualist Heresy in the Middle Ages*, translated by Iris Lewitova (Prague: Academia, 1974), p. 110.

9. Gordon Leff, p. 1; cf Brenda Boulton, "Tradition and Temerity: Papal Attitudes to Deviants, 1159-1216," in *Schism, Heresy and Religious Protest* edited by Derek Baker (Cambridge University Press, 1972), pp. 79-80.

10. *De Civitate Dei*, 22.22

11. *De Civitate Dei*, 20.7

12. Marjorie Reeves, *Joachim of Fiore and the Prophetic Future* (Harper Torchbooks, 1977), p. 1; cf. also Marjorie Reeves, *The Influence of Prophecy in the Later Middle Ages: A Study in Joachism* (Oxford: Clarendon Press, 1969); and Morton W. Bloomfield, "Joachim of Flora: A Critical Survey of His Canon, Teachings, Sources, Biography and Influence," *Traditio* 8 (1957), pp. 260-311.

13. His three major treatises are: *Concordia Novi et Veteris Testamenti, Expositio in Apocalypsim*, and *Psalerium Decem Chordarum*.

14. Bernard McGinn, pp. 126-127; Marjorie Reeves, *Joachim of Fiore*, pp. 22-23.

15. Marjorie Reeves, *Joachim of Fiore*, pp. 5-6; Decima L. Douie, *The Nature and the Effect of the Heresy of the Fraticelli* (Manchester University Press, 1932; New York: AMS Press, 1978), p. 209; Bernard McGinn, pp. 128-129, 146-147.

16. Marjorie Reeves, *Joachim of Fiore*, pp. 13, 27-29; Decima L. Douie, pp. 6, 31.

17. Brenda Boulton, *Medieval Reformation*, p. 67; Milan Loos, p. 187; cf. Jacques de Vitry on the Franciscans, ch. 32, *"De ordine et predicatione fratrum minorum,"* pp. 158-163; cf. also M.D. Lambert, *Franciscan Poverty: The Doctrine of the Absolute Poverty of Christ and the Apostles in the Franciscan Order 1210-1323* (London: S.P.C.K., 1961).

18. Brenda Boulton, *Medieval Reformation*, pp. 69-73; Gordon Leff, p. 41.

19. Decima L. Douie, pp. 1-3.

20. Marjorie Reeves, *Joachim of Fiore*, pp. 32-35; Decima L. Douie, pp. 5-10; cf. Bernard Gui, *Manuel de L'Inquisiteur* Latin and French text edited by G. Mollat (Paris, 1926), IV, "*De Secta Bequinorum*," pp. 109-193.

21. Cf. David Burr, *Olivi and Franciscan Poverty* (Philadelphia: University of Pennsylvania Press, 1989); Christopher Hill, *Antichrist in Seventeenth-Century England* (Oxford University Press, 1971), p. 7; Decima L. Douie, pp. 37-38, 83-84, 97, 114-115.

22. Marjorie Reeves, *Joachim of Fiore*, pp. 38-43; Decima L. Douie, pp.10, 92-3.

23. Cf. Ernest W. McDonnell, *The Beguines and Beghards in Medieval Culture* (New York: Octagon Books, 1969).

24. Decima L. Douie, pp. 212, 215, 226; Marjorie Reeves, *Joachim of Fiore*, p. 40.

25. "Gesta abbatum Trudonensium" in *Monumenta Germaniae Historica, Scriptores* edited by Georgius Heinricus Pertz (Hanover: Kraus Reprint, 1963), vol. X, p. 432: "multitudo hominum nobilium. . . ." Also, Herman of Altaha, "Annales" in *MGHS* vol. XVII, p.402: ". . . in primis . . ." Also Justin of Patavia, "Annales," in *MGHS*, vol. XIX, p. 179, "nobiles pariter. . . ." And "Annales Mellicenses," in *MGHS*, vol. IX, p. 509: "divites quam pauperes. . . ." See also Norman Cohn, *The Pursuit of the Millennium* (New York: Oxford University Press, 1970), pp. 129-130.

26. Jean Froissart, *Chronicles* ed. by Geoffrey Brereton (Baltimore: Penguin Books, 1968), pp. 111-112.

27. "Gesta abbatum Trudonensium," in *MGHS*, vol. X, pp. 431-432; also Jean de Venette, *The Chronicle of Jean de Venette* edited by Richard A. Newhall (New York: Columbia University Press, 1953), p. 52; Matthew of Newburg, "Chronica," *MGHS, Nova Series* IV, edited by Adolf Hofmeister (Berlin, 1955), ch. 117, p. 271; Justin of Patavia, "Annales," *MGHS*, vol. XIX, p. 179: "ad cuius flebilem. . . ."

28. Philip Ziegler, *The Black Death* (Penguin Books, 1984), pp. 40-45; also, Robert Gottfried, *The Black Death* (New York: The Free Press, 1983), p. 72.

29. Boccaccio, *The Decameron*, trans. by G. H. McWilliam (Penguin Books, 1981), p. 50.

30. "Kalendarium Zwetlense," *MGHS*, vol. XIX, p. 692; Matthew of Newburg, "Chronica," p. 271; Robert E. Lerner, "The Black Death and Western European Eschatological Mentalities," *American Historical Review* 86 (1981): 537.

31. Robert E. Lerner, "The Black Death," p. 537.

32. Jean de Venette, p. 52; Robert Gottfried, pp. 71-2; Gordon Leff, pp. 487-491.

33. Norman Cohn, pp. 142-144.

34. Gordon Leff, pp. 491, 567; Norman Cohn, p. 146; cf. also, Richard Kieckhefer, *Repression of Heresy in Medieval Germany* (Liverpool University Press, 1979), pp. 96, 97; Richard Kieckhefer, "Radical Tendencies in the Flagellant Movement of the Mid-Fourteenth Century," *Journal of Medieval and Renaissance Studies* 4 (1974): 157-176.

35. Donald Weinstein, *Savonarola and Florence: Prophecy and Patriotism in the Renaissance* (Princeton, N. J.: Princeton University Press, 1970), p. 33; Ottavia Niccoli, *Prophecy and People in Renaissance Italy*, trans. by Lydia G. Cochrain (Princeton, N.J.: Princeton University Press, 1990), pp. 93-98.

36. Donald Weinstein, pp. 98-111; cf. Donald Weinstein, "Savonarola, Florence, and the Millenarian Tradition," *Church History* 27 (1958): 3-17.

37. Ottavia Niccoli, p. 104.

38. Cited by Bernard McGinn, "The Abbot and the Doctors: Scholastic Reactions to the Radical Eschatology of Joachim of Fiore," *Church History* 4 (1971): 30-31.

Chapter Five
The Taborites and Adamites of Czechoslovakia

This chapter focuses on the mass movement of the Taborites and its extraordinary fringe group, the Adamites. Both were millenarian, and both went to such extremes that one can only regard them with a mixture of awe, horror, and headshaking at the lengths to which humans can go in the pursuit of their beliefs.

The Taborites and Adamites were radical offshoots of a larger religious reform movement in medieval Czechoslovakia known as the Hussite movement. More accurately, the Hussite movement included other issues than just religion. It was a religious reform movement wrapped in nationalistic feelings that became a revolution. Hussitism, like so many other religious movements, began as a movement for reform which went beyond anything its founders intended. It became a revolt and finally a revolution in the name of Christianity. A jumble of Czech nationalism, aspirations for religious reform, and social tensions all came together and produced a violent movement. The movement was a forerunner of the Reformation and an early manifestation of nationalism.[1] It also was a revolution which generated a radical branch of fanatical millenarianism.

Reformist Efforts in Czechoslovakia

In 1378 Charles the IV, King of Bohemia, and the Holy Roman Emperor, died. His strong central direction had given eastern Europe and Bohemia stability and order. Succeeding to the throne was Charles' seventeen-year-old son Wenceslas IV, inexperienced and incompetent, a man whose passion was hunting for bear and wild boar. The inconsistency and weakness of Wenceslas allowed the social frictions and strife to increase which Charles's strong hand suppressed.

To counteract clerical corruption and troubles, Charles had begun in 1358 to invite to Prague a series of great reform preachers who called for moral reform and religious revival in Bohemia. Reformers like Thomas of Stitny and Matthew of Janov tried to open up the sources of full religious experience to the masses and encouraged the use of the Czech language in preaching and writing. Matthew of Janov insisted on the frequent and even daily reception of Communion. In addition to the emphasis on religious reform, these great preachers also planted the early apocalyptic seeds that were to result in later excesses. For example, Matthew warned his hearers that history was a struggle between Christ and the Antichrist. Matthew opposed the formalism and ceremonies of the Church as mere human traditions. He sought to protect the faithful from the Antichrist by removing human ceremonies from the Church and making room for Christ in a reformed Church. Jan Milic of Kromeriz, a fiercely ascetic reformer whose refusal of meat and wine was reminiscent of wandering preachers of the twelfth century, also manifested an obsessive interest in the coming of the Antichrist. Indeed, he readily found evidence of the Antichrist in the simony and corruption of the Church, the oppression of the poor, and even though he was a court preacher he believed that kings and the powerful were instruments of the Antichrist.[2]

The Czech reformers believed passionately that the path of reformation lay in a return to the principles of the early Church. They issued the familiar call to return to the simplicity and fervor of the early Christians. The reformers emphasized the Scriptures, vernacular preaching, and moral purity. The evil and injustice of the world, they said, manifested the Antichrist, and the remedy was a concern for the practice of religion and personal piety rather than dogma.

Hus was not a revolutionary, but the mantle of leadership of the broad reform movement fell on him because of circumstance. Hus became president or rector of the University of Prague in 1409, and his position shielded those more radical—or even heretical—than himself. As Prague University became the spiritual center of the Czech nation, it became a highly visible platform for the reform movement. As the university grew into a national institution, the religious reform movement became a national movement.

From the radical circles in Prague came most of the ideas and priests who were to lead the provincial radical movement that was to become the Taborite movement. Two Prague reformers stand out as early leaders of Hussitism—Jakoubek of Stříbro and Nicholas of Dresden, who based many of their ideas on Matthew of Janov, Wycliffe, Waldensianism, and even some vague notions of Joachimism. Like Hus and other reformers Jakoubek and Nicholas protested current conditions in the Church; they hated simony and ecclesiastical corruption. They believed that the Antichrist, in the form of the pope, was corrupting the Church by allowing the acquisition of wealth and power. They urged, as a remedy, a return to the simplicity and purity of the early Church, a Church stripped of wealth.

The most remarkable—even radical—feature of Hussitism was the repudiation of close control by the papacy in doctrinal matters and the establishment of some measure of religious toleration. Of all the controversies Hus was involved in, the most crucial occurred in 1412 when he protested against indulgences being sold by Thiem, indulgences which Pope John XXIII had ordered sold for the purposes of raising money for a war against King Ladislas of Naples. Not only did Hus protest this, but he went so far as to declare that Christians did not have to obey the pope if his commands went against the Law of Christ. Archbishop Zbyněk excommunicated Hus, and the excommunication was upheld by the pope. Hus's reforming efforts became a national issue when Catholic prelates, assembled at Constance for a Church Council, summoned him to justify himself. Although the Roman Emperor Sigismund, as protector of the Council, assured him of a safe conduct, Hus was put on trial for heresy in November 1414.

Hus insisted on the Bible as the supreme authority of religious truth—a challenge to the Church's authority. When the sentence of death was pronounced, Hus, the story goes, looked at Sigismund, and Sigismund blushed, unable to justify the breach of his safe conduct. Hus died at the stake on July 6, 1415.[3]

Hussitism and Utraquism 1415-1419

When news arrived in Bohemia of Hus's death it inflamed the Czech people and sparked a chain of complicated, intoxicating events. His death, regarded by the people as a martyrdom, accelerated the spread of the reform movement, and a Diet of the nobles of Bohemia and Moravia showed their support for the movement when they vigorously protested on September 2, 1415, to the Council of Constance. Their letter, blending religious sentiment with patriotic feelings, was a thunderclap: a national rejection of an ecclesiastical decision on a matter of doctrine—an astounding and unprecedented move for pre-Reformation Europe.[4]

Several days later, on September 5, many nobles formed the Hussite League to defend Hussitism against threats and its enemies, that is, the Roman Church and the defender of the Church, the Emperor Sigismund. This Hussite League shielded the spreading practice of Communion under the two forms of bread and wine and tried to keep the decrees of the Council of Constance from being carried out in Bohemia through the period of 1415-1416. The majority of the 58 nobles at the Diet, under the leadership of Čeněk of Wartenberg, swore to defend the freedom of preaching in all their estates, to obey the bishops only as long as they acted according to the Scriptures, and to acknowledge the University of Prague as the highest authority in any disputes about the faith.[5]

Many of the common people of Moravia, Bohemia, and Prague began to feel more defiant in the face of the threats of the Roman Catholic prelates at Constance, and they also began to have greater enthusiasm for the new reform ritual of receiving Communion under two forms. Even though the Scriptures recount the institution of the Eucharist under both forms,[6] ancient Church tradition had restricted the chalice to the priest alone. Hussitism became something more than mere reform aspirations when Hus's friend and associate Master Jakoubek of Stříbro first began to dispense Holy Communion in both forms to laymen at Prague University, basing his demand of the chalice for the laity on historical studies. Jakoubek implied that the contemporary Church had deviated from the truth of the New Testament and the practices of the primitive Church. In reality the ritual of Communion under both forms represented only a minor issue of Eucharistic theology, but the Council of Constance in June 1415 solemnly condemned this innovative practice of granting the chalice to the laity, and a number of Czech masters at Prague University also opposed it.

The practice of Communion under both forms spread rapidly. The custom, however, further separated those who practiced it from the Roman Church. The practice now became enormously popular and such a crucial reform touchstone for common men and women that in many places priests who were not offering the chalice were driven from their churches. The chalice summarized the Bohemian reform movement in one clear-cut gesture and symbol—more powerfully than abstruse theological doctrines such as the limits of the Church's authority over Scriptural precedents—and the red emblem of the chalice was later to appear on black Hussite battle flags. Priests widely gave the Body and Blood of Christ under the forms of bread and wine to the common people. Those who practiced this custom became known as Utraquists (from the Latin *sub utraque parte*, under both forms) or Calixtines (from the Latin word *calix* for chalice). Utraquism was the epitome of Hussitism, and some decried it as heretical, even though the movement at this stage was nothing but a branch of the Catholic Church cut off from the main trunk of authority.[7]

In addition to the support of the nobles, the reform movement gained further support among the masses of people when the Catholic hierarch put Prague under an ecclesiastical interdict in October 1415. This resulted in the Hussites gaining control over most of Prague's churches. Reform enthusiasm, anger at Hus's death and the protection of powerful lords and magistrates all fostered the spread of Hussitism, with its Utraquist services. In October 1415, a Catholic League was formed to counter the Hussite League. In late 1415 the struggle continued, although the Hussite movement had by now spread into all classes of Czech society, both in Prague and in the rural provinces.

The Two Wings of Hussitism

But the shape of the Hussite reform was changing. Loyal Roman Catholics in 1415 tended to lump together all Hussites as dangerous radicals, even heretics. Within the Hussite movement itself, however, two major parties or wings continued a troubled co-existence. The conservative branch of Hussites or Utraquists was perhaps closest to Hus in his reforming ideas. They drew back, however, from religious revolt and social and economic change. Even though they sought the chalice for the laity and discarded those parts of the liturgy which seemed to them incompatible with Scripture, they were not willing to leave the Roman Church. They held on to Church traditions and did not rely solely on Scripture as an ultimate religious authority. Although they did not develop their ideas beyond the stage reached by Hus, they wavered between moving back toward Rome or in a direction ever more radical. To this party belonged mostly the nobles, wealthy citizens, and university masters.

The other party, the radical wing of the Hussites, was ready to venture considerably beyond any position that Hus could have imagined. These activists became known as the Taborites, taking their name from the Biblical Mount Tabor, and they would constitute the bulk of this radical group. They turned increasingly to extremism and revolution. They were evangelical and discarded everything that did not stand on a biblical base. The Taborites became millenarians who expected the coming of Christ at an early date. They made drastic changes in the mass, stripping away ceremony, and substituting Czech for liturgical Latin. They destroyed statues of the saints and rejected purgatory and opposed confession.

To this radical wing belonged most of the peasants, many of the artisans and working people, and some members of the middle class. The spiritual leader of this party initially was the successor of Hus in the Bethlehem Chapel, Jakoubek of Stříbro, but when the external military threats increased he reverted to the conservative party, and his place was taken by the radical clerics Húska, Želivský, and Koranda, who increasingly urged the use of physical violence to further the Hussite reforms. The greatest and perhaps the most interesting of these radical clerics and agitators was John Želivský, a gifted orator and former monk of the Premonstratensian monastery of Želiv.[8]

Events Leading to the Establishment of Tabor

As the Hussite reform movement spread into all classes, both in Prague and in the provinces, despite opposition from reactionary nobles and clergy in the rich monasteries, radical anti-Roman Catholic outbursts began to emerge in certain areas, especially around Plzeň and the south Bohemian region of Ústí-nad-Lužnicí where Tabor was later to be founded. Out from Prague had come priests and ideas which introduced Utraquism to the country areas. In 1416 began the so-called "going to the mountains" movement. That is, country Hussites began to make pilgrimages to agreed-upon-places for large open-air liturgical gatherings. In the rural district of Bechyne in southern Bohemia, even as far back as 1412, religious assemblies in open fields and on hills had occasionally replaced services in the narrower halls of churches. To gather in open areas was now the regular practice for rural Hussites. Large open air gatherings took place at Mt. Tabor, Oreb, and Beranek and other mountains.[9] At these hilltop assemblies Taborite radicalism took birth, a movement which Hus personally would not have welcomed, even though his sermons and ideas had played the role of midwife.

The eruption of this provincial extremism of the Taborites is noteworthy for being so rapid and widespread. It is not so easy to explain. Rural and radical Hussitism differed considerably from the spirit of Hus and the university masters whose criticism of the Church never broke out of an essentially Catholic and scholastic frame of reference. Perhaps extremism spread so quickly in rural, southern Bohemia because social and economic conditions were worse there than elsewhere. Or perhaps it was because the rural areas were so far from the University which was serving as the moderating force of orthodox authority.

Whatever the reason for its rapid growth, the form of provincial Hussitism known as Utraquism became the radical Taborite movement. The rural Taborite priests simplified drastically the elaborate trappings of the late medieval Church as they destroyed images and celebrated a simpler Czech liturgy in barns and stables. These radical Hussites or Taborites claimed that the whole system of vestments, altars, statues, and other equipment had been invented by humans. They gradually transformed the mass into a new and radically simplified Communion service that was aggressively Utraquist, and their attitude was anti-ecclesiastical. They distinguished between good and bad priests, the bad being those who did not agree with Hus, Jakoubek, and other reformers. Sometimes laymen assumed priestly functions, particularly preaching and the hearing of confessions. These extremists baptized in streams and ponds, held services in Czech, and rejected such traditions as pilgrimages and the cult of the saints.[10]

The difference in views increased between the urban Utraquist Hussites of the University of Prague and the radical groups in the rural areas, especially in the south of Bohemia. The moderate Hussite masters at Prague University had begun to wonder whether Jakoubek of Stříbro and his rural followers were not going too far, for example, in demanding Communion under both forms, even for children right after baptism.

In 1417 the masters at the University of Prague still sought to maintain and develope Hussitism as a unified and national reform movement and to prevent a split from developing. Their concern was to keep a university reform program from decaying into a popular sectarian heresy. They took steps to assert religious authority over the whole Hussite movement. The university masters had been giving fraternal admonitions to those Hussites who were radical reformers, that is, those in the provinces (such as Wenceslas Koranda, who was from Prague but who then went to Plzeň) and those in Prague gathered around Jakoubek and Dresden. Jakoubek's and Dresden's reform experiments and anarchic propagation of novelties not only made rapprochement with the Catholic Church increasingly difficult but also threatened the authority of the university over the movement

Taborites and Adamites

as a whole. On the end of the spectrum opposite the extreme reformers, the Hussite nobles despised new and novel doctrines.

On January 25, 1417, the university masters and the conservative Hussite nobles met at St. Michael's Church in the Old Town of Prague and issued an official declaration which reaffirmed many Church traditions and condemned the radicals' rejection of purgatory and the mass and the cult of the saints. The university masters were more liberal on March 10, 1417, when they officially sanctioned Communion under both forms as beneficial to salvation. This compelled even the anti-Hussites in Prague to outward conformity. By giving with one hand and pruning with the other, the masters tried to bring the provincial extremists back into the national movement. This effort by university masters to yoke the forces of the university to the radical barn priests was an invitation to the radicals to seek change within the national movement and within the university's world of ideas.[11]

All during 1416 and 1417 the situation remained somewhat ambiguous and confused. Hussite priests were installed, at the expense of orthodox Catholic incumbents, in parishes by Hussite nobles. At the same time, the growing Taborite radicalism was worrying the masters at Prague University, the majority of whom were Hussites with a strong tendency towards orthodoxy, differing little from Rome. King Wenceslas himself was by now succumbing to pressure and had begun to take active steps toward a policy of Catholic restoration. The masters had issued a declaration of fraternal warning to the more radical country Hussites in February 1418. In September 1418, a Hussite synod assembled at Prague and attempted to fashion unity among the different Hussite factions. The synod, on the one hand, basically accepted Catholicism but on the other hand violently attacked Church abuses. The synod did sanction Communion under both kinds even for infants and granted its official permission for the use of Czech in the mass.

If any unity was achieved, it did not last. The events of 1419 forced Hussitism onto paths of inner disintegration as the radical Taborite movement continued to develop apart from the conservative wing of Hussites, resulting in the foundation of Tabor in early 1420 as the capital of one part of a national movement that had finally split asunder.[12]

A brief snapshot of Taborite beliefs is in order here to help differentiate them from the more conservative wing of the Hussite reform movement which never substantially went beyond the ideas of Hus or the doctrines of the Catholic Church.

Taborite Beliefs: A Radical Millenarianism

Taboritism, the country version of Hussite reform, evolved into a radical millenarianism never dreamed of by Hus. Taboritism, as largely a rural movement, flourished most vigorously in the south-central region of Bohemia, especially around Bechyne and Sezimovo Ústí at the lower course of the Lužnicí River. The crucial formation period was from early 1419 to February 1420, with the millenarian period from November 1419 to February 1420, and the period from 1420 to 1421 marks Tabor's ascendancy when militant Hussitism consolidated and got defined. Taborite beliefs continued to develop and change during the 1420s. In fact, later Taborites had to deal with doctrinal differences among themselves such as with issues of pantheism and whether Communion contained the real presence of Christ.

The radical Taborites were essentially fundamentalists and evangelicals who confined their belief to what was contained explicitly and literally in the Bible. They felt that the Latin Bible had hidden the message of Christ, and now Czech translations unveiled the very sources of Christianity. Since Christ and the Scriptures are the authority for religious truth, the main task for priests was to preach the Gospel in the vernacular. The reformers also urged a return to the practices of the original, primitive church revealed in the New Testament, a kind of restorationism. Taborite reformers sought to sweep away most of the accumulated outward ceremonies of the Church such as masses, prayers, confession, ceremonial pomp, vestments, images, saints days, vigils, and pilgrimages, all of which they regarded as human inventions. Furthermore, in order to return to the principles and actual experience of the early Church, Taborites felt they should share "all things in common" according to the spirit of Acts 20:44-45. In many ways, especially through their joyful hymns, the Taborites sought to have and believed they were living an extraordinary experience, that of the revived primitive Church. God was near and they were living and defending His Law.[13]

Most Taborite priests had been highly educated, but early in the movement sermons attacked book learning and any reading except Scripture. The only learning fostered among the Taborites was education in the Bible, a practice unique among the common people of that time, and even young women were versed in the Old and New Testaments. Nothing religious was or could be true unless it was found in the pages of the Bible. Perhaps this was the most revolutionary of all Taborite innovations, this supposed freeing of the mind from all theological tradition and offering the possibility of an entirely new, fresh approach to all religious problems, the offer to individuals to find for themselves the presence and essence of God. All too soon this theological tenet was to be tested when self-appointed prophets arose. Taborites did not tolerate doctrinal deviancies among their ranks, especially on the issue of the true presence of Christ in Communion, Communion which held such a central place for Taborites.

Another revolution was the break in priestly ordination. Here the Taborites differed dramatically from moderate Utraquists. Utraquists maintained the strict boundary between priest and laymen and the importance of bishops for ordination. Taborites felt that the function of priests was one of ministry, of service to the community. Priests could elect their own bishop who then could ordain as priests those considered worthy of the office, except that the Taborites allowed their priests to marry. Taborites also abolished traditional confession to a priest in favor of confessing to God who alone could absolve from sin. The leveling of status between priest and laymen, along with the expectation of the coming Kingdom of Christ as a state in which there were no rulers or nobles and Christ alone as King, produced a kind of primitive socialism.[14]

The message of religious equality (that laity and clergy were equal) coupled with vague expectations for a better life in the coming Kingdom of Christ served as a magnet for the least privileged Czech people. Further, the use of their own language in worship fostered a sense of community among the common people. The coming end of the world and everyday needs soon required the sharing of physical and material resources. As long as the sense of being the elect in a special time remained strong, all were equal and social distinctions did not solidify. As a result women enjoyed remarkable equality with men. Women also fought side by side with men—extraordinary for any age, much less the Middle Ages.

Basic to Hussitism was the insistence on a pure life, a life without sin. But Taborites put such emphasis on a blameless life that they developed a puritanism which even Calvin would have approved. Ostentatious and ceremonial clothing was a sin for Taborites. Taborites insisted on a strict interpretation of the Second Commandment, that no one but God in each form of His trinitarian appearance was a legitimate object for worship, and so any form of veneration of the saints was idolatry.[15]

At the end of 1419 the Taborites embraced a most militant form of millenarianism. At first, the country radicals found hope in passively awaiting Christ's intervention and the establishment of his kingdom. They believed that the Day of Judgment and the end of the world were to come in the immediate future and a new age would follow. They established five cities as places of refuge. This passive faith reached a pitch in February 1420, when the radical preachers Húska and Koranda predicted the Day of Wrath would come and that Babylon and the enemies of God's law would be destroyed and the elect would be saved. Once February passed and these millenarian expectations proved false, a second stage of millenarian faith developed under pressure of persecution with the establishment of Tabor as a fortress, as the seat of the warriors of God. This was the stage of active chiliasm that exhorted the people to prepare for Christ's coming by force.

This active, militant millenarianism shaped Tabor into a unique religious brotherhood and military community. This assembly of people was not a stable society but a new social congregation with no ties to the rest of society and gathered out of fear of persecution and religious conviction that the end was at hand. The radicals' religious beliefs combined with the armed threats of their extinction brought about this potent combination: they were prepared to fight for God and their own salvation. Fifty years of native reform sermons by Hus's predecessors had portrayed history as a struggle between Christ and Antichrist, with simony and Church corruption as the activity of the Antichrist. Now the enemies of God appeared in the persecutions and threats of the king, the Catholic nobles and the Emperor Sigismund. The radicals developed a theology differing from that of Wycliffe and Hus: the necessity of struggling against the Antichrist as active spiritual warriors of God to wage a holy war of self protection and to destroy the enemies of God by fire and sword.[16]

The Taborite communities had a sense of living in an extraordinary time. Soon the death of King Wenceslas, astrological prophecies, physical threats and violence, the apocalyptic preaching, would all fan their religious zeal and the conviction that early in 1420 Christ would return to earth to establish His Kingdom. For those who looked, there were abundant signs that would indicate the end of things. They believed that Christ would return to earth amidst fires, storms, wars, and convulsions of nature. "For nation will rise against nation, and kingdom against kingdom, and there will be famines and earthquakes in various places. . . ." (Mt. 24:7). It was not to be a time of Christian love but of Old Testament vengeance, a time when the elect were filled with the Holy Spirit and kill and destroy all who were outside the community of the saved.

Outbreak of Revolution

Three years after the death of John Hus, international Catholic opposition to Hussitism appeared about to crush the native Czech reform movement. The Council of Constance finally resolved the Great Schism over who was the legitimate pope and elected Cardinal Colonna Pope Martin V, to whom fell the task of dealing with the Bohemian experiments. The Council tended to see every expression of dissent as a sign of heresy, and this rigid attitude towards the Czechs fostered a temporary unity among Hussites and allowed Czech moderates no maneuvering room. In early 1419 the Catholic reaction to the Hussite experiments increased tension to the breaking point.

The Emperor Sigismund was determined to suppress by an armed crusade the Hussites who were now openly labeled heretics.

The tremendous pressure from the international Catholic world and the influence of his Hussite advisors made King Wenceslas and his wife Queen Sophia who had been defenders of Hus start to yield to outside threats and seek a Catholic restoration. Even though King Wenceslas in June 1418 issued an order forbidding his subjects to follow any summons before an ecclesiastical court outside the Kingdom of Bohemia, in February 1419 the King restricted permission for holding Hussite services to only three Prague churches, too few for the large Hussite community. The Prague Hussites, now confronting the problem which the rural Hussites partly solved by their open air assemblies, held worship services in squares in front of churches. Some Hussite priests left Prague to join the rural Taborite movement. The intransigent radicals in Prague led by Želivský refused to give up their religious demands, and in the streets of Prague turbulence and agitation against the king's constricting policy increased.

The radicals gathered a huge crowd on July 22, 1419, for an open-air meeting on a hill called Tabor near the town of Bechyne. In the Old Testament (Judges 4:6 ff.), Tabor was the mountain where Deborah gathered an army of 10,000 to prepare them for the decisive battle with the Canaanite king. In the Gospels (Mt. 28:16-20) Mt. Tabor was the hill on which Jesus was transfigured, a special place of refuge for chosen disciples and a special place of revelation in the Judeo-Christian tradition. The country Hussites had for years held these large outdoor assemblies, but the July 22 gathering was perhaps the greatest of all, with possibly as many as 40,000 attending. This meeting was ostensibly a religious occasion, with a sense of brotherhood and a concern to imitate the early church.[17]

But such a large gathering becomes a political force by its very existence, and all these worshippers assembled without the permission of the government could only appear ominous to the established powers. The nobility and substantial burgers of Prague and university masters shrunk back from any extreme gestures. After each of the large meetings the rural contingents returned to their scattered homes, but this religious congregation was taking on a new social existence, a mass movement. Events were inching towards revolution.

But revolutions are usually cityborn, and the final spark for the Hussite Revolution was indeed supplied by the radicals in the city of Prague itself. King Wenceslas felt he could not let the fanatical Hussites in the New Town section of Prague get out of hand. To stop the growing street violence and anarchy, the King had ordered on July 6 the replacement of the New Town government by anti-Hussites. The reaction was immediate. John Želivský quickly lumped the King with other enemies of God and the Czech people. Eight days after the huge gathering in the provinces, on July 30, 1419, in the Church of Our Lady of St. Mary in the Snow, John Želivský's sermon fiercely attacked the new City Council, and he called upon his hearers to follow him. The crowd, preceded by Želivský carrying a monstrance with a consecrated host, marched to the Church of St. Stephen, where Želivský preached about the war between Christ and Antichrist. A service was held and Communion under both forms distributed. The procession then started back to the New Town but stopped in front of the town hall, a large building at the northern end of Prague's wide Cattle Market. Members of the Council tried to reason with the crowd from the windows. The crowd on the street below the windows grew more and more excited. Suddenly shouts went up that a stone was thrown at the priest carrying the host. Enraged at the enemies of God in the town hall, the crowd forced the locked doors and rushed up the stairs. A few members of the Council rushed out rear doors to escape. The crowd seized the others and hurled them out the windows to the street below. Furious demonstrators killed the survivors, as armed men occupied the building. This was the First Prague Defenestration, the first outbreak of violence, and the first overt act of revolution, the first use of force by Hussites in the defense of truth and God's Kingdom.[18]

Events moved rapidly. Reliable Hussites quickly formed a new city council. A large number of citizens mobilized and gathered weapons, and Captain John Zizka who was to become so essential to Taborism made his first appearance on history's stage. News of the revolt caused tremendous excitement at the royal court where King Wenceslas became so enraged he suffered a stroke. He rallied sufficiently to send for help from Sigismund who was then in Hungry. On August 16 the King suffered a second stroke and died. The death of the King encouraged the radical Hussites even more, especially since he had intended to block them and since his death fitted perfectly into the prophetic millenarianism of the radical priests. With the King out of the way inhibitions to open revolution lessened.

Sigismund, as brother of the king, was now the presumptive heir and new king. He was, however, at Buda in Hungry and preoccupied with preparing for war against the Turks. The radical Hussites distrusted Sigismund and believed that if he were to gain power over Bohemia the survival of their religious movement was doomed. Sigismund as the protector of the Church was the swordbearer for the Roman Church and thus combined military and religious power. Sigismund would not intervene with the papacy on behalf of the Hussite way of worship. John Želivský preached that Sigismund was really the Great Red Dragon cast out of heaven according to St. John's Book of Revelations (12:3 ff.).[19]

On August 17, the day after Wenceslas death, riots broke out in Prague. Catholic monasteries were attacked, and the great chapter house of the Carthusian order at Smichov was burned. German inhabitants of Prague began to flee the city. The puritan character of the radical wing of the Hussite movement manifested itself in attacks on Prague's brothels, many of which were put to the torch. Similar violence occurred in Písek, and Pilsen, Hradec, Kralove, Zatec, and Louny.

Pressure on the radical movement increased as the nobility grew inclined to try to stop by force the congregations from meeting, and royalist and Catholic nobles were already rounding up and even killing Hussites. The radicals held theological discussions whether war could be waged with swords or if war should remain on a spiritual level. They also discussed the probability that the nobles would no longer defend God's truth and that the burden would fall on the common people. Jakoubek backed away from his previous radicalism and, together with the masters of the university, he recommended that Christians tolerate evil patiently while doing everything possible to prevent war. Želivský and his adherents opposed this cautiousness. The Prague radicals and country Taborites sought an alliance with each other and organized themselves so as to be capable of military activites against the reactionary nobles, the more orthodox citizens of Prague and the distant but ominous threat of Sigismund.[20]

Taborites and Adamites

In the western Bohemian district of Plzeň, Wenceslas Koranda, the fervent and evangelical radical from Prague, took a more active leadership role among the country people. On September 17, another great open-air meeting was held, this time on a hill called Bzi, near Plzeň, a meeting dominated by Koranda. The serious situation in Prague and the seemingly hopeless struggle of the radicals heightened their millenarianism. The radicals felt the necessity of fighting on behalf of God's truth, and the violent character of the movement fully emerged. Koranda preached that no one could save the Taborites but the Taborites themselves. Koranda warned his hearers to prepare with weapons for the day of Christ and to be ready to defend their faith by force against the servants of Antichrist. Koranda stirred up millenarian and revolutionary hopes among the peasants, an urgency to restore ancient religious practices along with an awareness of being the direct successors of the people of Israel. His hearers believed that all cities would be destroyed and that all the faithful would be saved only in the mountains and in certain cities. The millenarian ideas led to the conviction that the faithful should move into five towns in order to escape the punishment which God was to send on towns and cities. Since Isaiah (19:18) said five cities would escape, five towns were named as places of refuge: Plzeň, Klatovy, Louny, Zatec, Slany. After the revolution, Koranda promised, there would be no more evil men.[21]

The millenarian ideas of Koranda and other wandering radical priests gave poor and oppressed farmers the opportunity to become warriors for God. The end of the sinful age was going to be a time of punishment by sword and fire for those who opposed the law of God. The task of the faithful was to destroy corruption, destroy sin, and increase the glory of God. The preachers created an expectancy of God's judgment over evil that inflamed their listeners to fanaticism and a war-like attitude. In short, reacting to the threat of religious persecution and annihilation, Taborites felt they were in a desperate eschatological crisis, that the time of great suffering had begun about which Christ and his prophets had warned.

Meanwhile, Queen Sophia was named regent after the death of Wenceslas, and the nobles sought an accommodation with Sigismund that could only be dangerous for radical Hussites. With the Queen's consent, the High Burgrave of Prague, Čeněk of Wartenberg, called a general diet which sought to open negotiations. The majority of Prague's clergy and nobles were essentially ready to surrender all but the most essential Hussite principles, such as Communion under both forms, reading the Gospel in Czech, and honoring Hus. In short, the conservative faction did not seek to go an inch beyond a basic Utraquism at this point. Rather tamely the conservatives sought to solve the problem of Hussite security by getting a hearing before the pope to plead for these few principles, while the radical program was by now intertwined with doctrines that could not co-exist with conservative Hussitism.

Much depended on Sigismund's reaction. Because of his preoccupation, however, with a crusade against the Turks, he put off coming to Bohemia for several months. This delay weakened even further those moderates who were seeking to uphold law and the social order and strengthened the radicals who sought a new society based on the Hussite creed. Sigismund had lost an opportunity by not responding at once to the Bohemian problem. Meanwhile, Želivský's Prague radicals remained intransigent and prepared for confrontation.

Queen Sophia and her government of Czech nobles headed by Čeněk of Wartenberg, in fear of anarchy and dreading renewed unrest, banned public gatherings and ordered the royal army to occupy the left bank of the Moldau and to prevent Hussite pilgrims from entering Prague. Čeněk fortified the Hradcany Castle, increased guards, and hired German mercenaries. The Taborite, John Zizka, energetically countered these measures by capturing the fortress of Vysehrad, the other royal castle, on October 2. Violence and fighting flared up. Royalists throughout Bohemia had armed and were determined to prevent Hussite radicals from the provinces from entering Prague. (After the great September gathering country Taborites had planned to meet with radical Prague Hussites on November 10 for the sake of mutual assistance.) Some country radicals under Koranda got through to Prague, while the first real battle of the Hussite revolution was fought when a small group of Taborite pilgrims from Sezimovo Ústí were ambushed and killed near Živhošť by a Catholic noble Lord Peter of Sternberg. Bloody fighting broke out in Prague for days between radical Hussites and orthodox royalists, but no conclusive results were achieved since Čeněk of Wartenberg remained in firm control of Hradcany. This revolutionary violence ended with a truce,

Taborites and Adamites

and the Queen and the government fled Prague. For radical Hussites the threat of extermination had become brutally real.[22]

The country Hussites, or Taborites, did not accept the truce and left Prague. John Zizka accompanied them and journeyed to Plzeň, which was the natural center of western Bohemia. Sigismund wrote to the prelates and nobility and town magistrates to declare his determination to restore religious order and to threaten death and confiscation of property for those who refused to obey legitimate authorities. He emphasized that Hussites and Utraquists were to be persecuted and exterminated. Koranda and Zizka and other radical leaders took control of Plzeň and expelled the royalists. The radicals organized the defense of that city and destroyed its monasteries and churches. They also began to prepare defenses for Písek and other southern cities.

It was during this winter of 1419-1420 that the final shift occurred in the Taborite mood—from pious withdrawal and non-violence to militarism and intense adventist expectation. All 26 of the Taborite priests, along with Húska and Koranda, had predicted the coming of Christ to be during February 1420. Taborites felt it was a special time and the Day of Wrath was imminent. Preachers were telling people to leave their homes. There were mass withdrawals from towns and villages, a leaving of land and burning of homes in order to flee to Tabor or one of the five chosen cities—for the sake of saving their souls. Masses of people now concentrated in fortified Taborite towns, cut off from the stabilizing routine of everyday life, increasingly imbued with the conviction that the entire world outside their communities was foredoomed to destruction. Communities organized themselves like the primitive church. Such a situation of vulnerability and fear could only generate violence of an intense and fanatical kind.[23]

Sigismund now began to realize just how serious the situation in Bohemia was and how inadequate was the royal army to crush the Hussite heretics. Preparing to lead an armed crusade against the Hussites, Sigismund had arrived in Brno in December 15, 1419, and summoned the Czech government and nobles. Sigismund was able to come to terms with those who declared fealty to him. It soon began to be clear, however, that he was going to proceed in force against not just the Taborites but all Hussites. His unbending attitude soon unleashed a fanatic opposition to Hussites, and mercenaries and royalists started attacks upon the hated heretics in widely separated parts of the country. The city of Kutná Hora was especially brutal in its efforts at the annihilation of Hussites. German national feeling and religious sentiment in this city combined to create a fanatical hatred for any Hussite. The town's hangman was so overworked, it is said, that those Hussites he was not able to hang were thrown into abandoned mineshafts to die from either the plunge or starvation. Within a short period over 1600 Hussites were killed.

Country Hussites prepared for war, while moderate Prague Hussites realized they could never expect from Sigismund even the minimum concession of Communion under both forms, and even these moderate Hussites realized they would have to fight for their religious beliefs. Country Hussites under Zizka began small-scale raids against the enemies of the chalice within southern Bohemia's castles, small towns, and monasteries. Zizka was an implacable destroyer of those whom he felt were enemies of God. He did not prevent his peasant soldiers from cutting captured soldiers' feet off, throwing people into fires, and even making one captive by the name of Pynta kill other captives. He did insist, however, on sparing the lives of women and children. He kept only arms and horses and burned all other spoils, including rich clothing and jewelry, chalices, and gold. No earthly riches should tempt the soldiers of Tabor away from their task of defending the Law of God.

Taborites led by Zizka attacked Ústí on Ash Wednesday night, February 20, 1420. Most of the citizens of Ústí were sound asleep and drunk from the customary pre-lenten celebrations. Once Ústí was captured, the Taborites abandoned it since they could not easily defend it and they decided to settle on a nearby mountain, Hradiste, where there was an abandoned fortress. From February onward the fortress Hradiste was known as Tabor.

Tabor, now established as an actual place, became the gathering place for radical Hussites from far and wide. It was a rough, ascetic encampment devoid of any luxury or nicety. It also came to mean the spiritual union of communities or congregations gathered for armed defense and organized for waging holy war, communities consciously set up as antitheses to established society which Taborites referred to as Babylon. Tabor became the capital city of the federation of the

Taborite towns, towns that had either been captured or joined the Taborite union voluntarily.

Up to this point Tabor had been a spiritual movement with ill-defined aims and little organization, with priests like Húska and Koranda initially in leadership positions. Things underwent a dramatic change with Zizka's arrival in Tabor on March 26, 1420. All revolutions have sooner or later to settle down and get organized: Zizka decisively gave focus and military organization to the movement. He assembled the men available to him, primarily peasants and townsmen and artisans, into a remarkable army. Even though they were armed simply, even primitively, with farm implements, flails, some pikes or swords, their religious fervor made up for all else that they lacked. The fight was for the Law of God, not for riches, but to destroy evil and to renew the face of the Czech land and to prepare the way for the coming of Christ. Millenarian preachers had promised that those who fought for the Law of God would acquire eternal salvation and be rid of earthly burdens.

Zizka's army of the poor and peasants became transformed into warriors of God that were to prove superior to the great international crusades sent against them. Zizka, a professional soldier, changed nothing theologically but had a simple soldier's faith that he was fighting God's own fight and that God would supply all that was needed for the defense of his Holy Law. The religious and social revolution had become a holy war. By March 1420, it had become fearfully clear that Sigismund, by his actions and decrees, was determined to exterminate Hussitism.[24]

On April 1, 1420, the Pope published a bull encouraging all faithful Christians to crusade against the Hussites. He promised forgiveness of sins to all who would fight against the heretics. Sigismund, as king of the Holy Roman Empire, was the temporal head of Christendom and by leading the Crusade acted as the sword bearer of the Church of Rome. The approach of Sigismund with his German mercenaries and armed crusaders filled Prague Hussites with panic. Prague Hussites held a mass meeting in front of the Town Hall on April 3, 1420, swearing readiness to defend the use of the chalice at the Lord's supper. The university masters and some of the nobles urged Praguers and all Czech Hussites to fight for the cause of God. A revolutionary assembly on April 20, 1420, issued a manifesto with 4 articles that called for Communion under both kinds and freedom to practice their religion.

Fearful Hussite nobles tried to negotiate with Sigismund, now only 40 miles from Prague with his large army. The last chance for a peaceful solution passed as Sigismund asked for too much. He wanted unconditional surrender, even if the whole Czech kingdom would have to be destroyed. Sigismund's obduracy forced a drastic rethinking among the people of Prague who now realized submission was impossible, and so a new spirit of resistance pervaded the city. As the common danger became clear, all Hussites felt the need to forget their doctrinal differences and establish a unity for the purpose of defending themselves. John Želivský attacked Sigismund as the apocalyptic dragon and rallied the people to new efforts. Čeněk of Wartenberg, although dismayed by the realities of revolution and disheartened by the atrocities committed by Zizka's peasant soldiers, resolved his own indecisiveness and felt compelled to join the revolution. He rallied a large part of the Hussite nobility against Sigismund in defense of the Chalice. The people of Prague, in turn, realized the very fate of Hussitism was at stake, and in order to renew the alliance with the radicals of Tabor, they sent urgent messengers to the Taborite towns in the west and south of the country. The community of Tabor answered promptly. Zizka left Tabor on May 18 at the head of a strong army in support of Prague. All parties of Hussites united now militarily under one flag, black with a red chalice, in defense of the Chalice.[25]

Entering Prague on May 20 the puritanical Taborites soldiers were horrified by the urban luxury. To the ascetic peasant soldiers, the well-to-do Praguers appeared terribly sinful with their sumptuous fashions, jewelry, even the well-cut beards on the men. Some of the stern country Taborites became so outraged with the seeming dissolution of the urbanites that they began to rip off and cut off whatever offended their moral sensitivities. Resentful, angry Praguers complained to Taborite commanders who forbad further reforming molestations of the citizenry of Prague. Discipline was tightened and daily religious services explained the need to fight for the Law of God. Taborite leaders themselves were dissatisfied with the lack of military preparedness and the lack of reformatory zeal shown by the city. Complaints from both urban and country Hussites led to meetings. The growing danger from without led to agreements as to the common religious aims of the movement which were expressed in Four Articles in a May 20th Manifesto. These four articles which emphasized communion under both forms and the punishment of serious sin became a central statement of Hussite doctrine during the long years of Hussite wars.[26]

On July 14, 1420, the Battle of Vitkov was fought between Sigismund and the Hussites. Sigismund's mercenaries shouted and mocked the Czechs: "Ha, ha! Hus, Hus! Heretic, heretic!" The frightful word heretic could only motivate these first Protestants even more, since they were convinced that they, the followers of Hus, were the true followers of Christ who were defending the Law of God. Out of a deep resentment and passionate religious conviction came the determination not to surrender or yield but to fight against all odds. Hussite women, to the horror of the outside world and as one indicator of the radical social changes among the Hussites, took an active part in this and later battles and were not considered inferior to men. Lawrence of Brezova describes, on the basis of an eyewitness account, women who fought "like men." One woman, he describes, fought savagely and, as she refused to yield ground to enemy soldiers, cried out that "a true Christian must never retreat before the Antichrist."[27]

The typical battle deployment of Taborite troops positioned the priest in front carrying the Host, then the bowmen, then the peasant soldiers with their flails and pikes and pitchforks. The Taborites felt that God would not abandon those fighting for His Law, that God Almighty was entering this battle and they were His warriors. Battle hymns and prayers filled the air, along with cries and shouts. At least one battle hymn promised "the one who gives his life for Christ, will gain heaven."[28] Flapping in the smoke and breeze were black battle flags with the emblem of the red chalice, the visible symbol of religious conviction and the Hussite belief that before God all men were equal.

But it was not just religious fervor, however, that added to Taborite and Hussite intensity and desperation, but hatred and fear and a thirst for vengeance. They hated anything Roman Catholic and anything which opposed the law of God and reform of the Church. They feared Sigismund's German mercenaries who had previously shown little restraint in butchering Czechs. The German mercenaries' atrocities against 40 young boys and the Royalist troops who murdered all the Hussites at Chotebor inflamed a desire for merciless vengeance. Paradoxically, the very same religious passion which demanded the Taborites to be disciplined and good Christians also encouraged them to use any savage means to kill the enemies of God. Their fanaticism and the conviction that God was on their side in a Holy War drove the Taborite armies to unparalleled efforts, time and again, against superior armies of crusaders and mercenaries. Resistance and any behavior which seemed blasphemous led Zizka and his soldiers to burn and slaughter and kill as savagely as any godless mercenary. Ordinarily the Hussites spared women and children, but after the victory at Chomutov, for instance, Taborite women led the captured women of Chomutov outside the walls of the town, stripped them and killed them all, even the pregnant women.

At Vitkov the Hussites prevailed, thanks to the ferocity of Zizka and his Taborite fighters. Hussites believed it was not their prowess but a miracle of God that gave victory over Sigismund's huge army. They knelt on the field of battle, raised their eyes to the sky, and sang the *Te Deum*. Sigismund's withdrawal ended the siege of Prague, but the greater part of the country was still dominated by his castles and those of the royalist nobles. Nevertheless, Zizka's and the Taborites' victory at Vitkov blunted for the time being the efforts of Hussite enemies.[29]

Hussite Disunity Continues

As soon as Sigismund withdrew and the external threat to Prague ended, the frictions and divisions between the two main Hussite parties erupted once more. Doctrinal differences exacerbated differences in values. The Taborite peasants demanded that the citizens of Prague change their social ways and worship in the Taborite manner. The Taborites wanted simplicity in worship, the removal of statues and other idolatries from churches, simplicity of life and the expulsion of all drunkards, prostitutes, and thieves from the city. Although the presence of Taborites in Prague strengthened the radical Prague Hussites led by Želivský, it further deepened the gulf between Tabor and the more conservative Hussites of Prague, especially among the university masters. The Taborites, exalting the common man, despised higher learning and especially despised the professional theologians and university masters.

The unbending puritanical attitudes of the Taborites alarmed the sophisticated Praguers. The Taborites clung to notions of the poverty of the primitive church, the elaborate beauty of Prague's churches and the sumptuousness of liturgical vessels and vestments scandalized the Taborite peasants. Moderate Hussites and Catholic Praguers—those who still remained in the city—took pride in the rich beauty of the great city's architecture and joined the monks in fear of the hostility of the country Hussites. Indeed the Taborites burned three monasteries in the New Town before Prague's butchers' guild finally offered resistance. The city council of the Old Town tried to warn off further fanatic destruction by designating St. James Monastery and several other religious buildings essential warehouses for food and weapons.

An explanation for the Taborite zeal for destroying splendid churches possibly lies in their genuine aversion to any hint of idolatry, but their destructiveness might also have sprung from the restless nervousness of an uprooted people far from their homes and amidst alien surroundings. Whatever their reasons and motives, on August 6, 1420, a Taborite crowd burned one of Prague's most beautiful monasteries, that of the Knights of the Cross on the Zderaz. Taborite priests, having encouraged their people to this religious vandalism, issued to Prague's government an ultimatum in which they threatened to leave the city unless the authorities close all remaining public drinking houses and brothels, forbid the wearing of costly or showy clothing, and punish anyone caught stealing. But most shocking was their demand for the destruction of all monasteries and churches not needed for the service of the faithful as well as the destruction of all ornate religious objects and gold liturgical vessels. After a Taborite mob led by Koranda burned the great Cistercian monastery at Zbraslav, Prague could only believe that the men and women of Tabor were reckless and demented terrorists.[30]

The Taborite Communion service further dismayed the Praguers and caused disagreement. Since the Taborites emulated the early Christians, they did not think that church buildings or altars or vestments or costly liturgical vessels were necessary for their liturgy. Accustomed to mass celebrated in barns or fields, on a table instead of an altar, they simplified their mass to a Scriptural reading, the words of institution, then the Lord's Prayer and the passing of the bread and wine to the communicants. They sang joyful Czech hymns and psalms, and the whole ceremony ended with a sermon. On one occasion in Prague, the Taborites entered the church of St. John, and their priest in everyday clothes simply bowed his head and said the Lord's prayer with his people. He then said the words of consecration over the bread and cups filled with wine, which he then passed to the congregation. This scandalized the Praguers, who murmured that these were truly heretics. For their part the Taborites ardently rejected the ritual of the Roman Church, with its elaborate vestments and precious vessels, as human inventions not based on Scripture. In fact, the extremist Taborite priest Koranda said in his opposition to the Roman mass that it would be proper to follow the ritual of the Old Testament and even sacrifice animals, since such a ritual would be based on the Scriptures and not on mere human invention.[31]

Calmer heads realized that to prolong the stay of the Taborite army within Prague would only exasperate wounded sensibilities among the Hussite factions, so on August 22, 1420, the whole Taborite host with its leaders and priests, its women and children, its wagons and weapons, left Prague. More mundanely, the harvest season was approaching, and survival depended on the gathering of food.

After the Taborites returned to Tabor, Zizka led some of his soldiers on a harassing guerrilla war against Sigismund's supporters in southwestern Bohemia and soon had domination of most of the countryside in the south by November of 1420. Thus, within a period of eight months Tabor had become powerful and feared throughout Bohemia.

Sometime in September 1420 the Taborites at Hradiste (Tabor) elected Nicholas of Pelhřimov, a priest, to be their spiritual leader and bishop. The election of this brilliant man, who undertook to formulate a theology consonant with Tabor's biblical idealism, issued an open declaration of independence from the Roman Church and was the first of its kind in the history of Protestantism. Although the Taborites did not consider themselves bound to any tradition of episcopal succession or ordination, they needed someone to formulate an official theology and to set some curbs on those among them who were preaching ideas and beliefs far beyond what Hus's followers could accept. The Taborite episcopacy and the implication of an emerging institutional structure did not survive, but the election of bishops was resumed after Tabor's fall by its spiritual successor, the Church of the Brethren.[32]

Doctrinal differences and controversies among the Taborites grew during the fall and winter of 1420 with the appearance of the Pikarts (or Picards). Although the Prague masters and the Taborites' disagreements about doctrine led to the Taborite exit from Prague in August, at least these two parties shared a similar theological platform. These two parties could agree on their opposition to Pikartism. The Pikarts existed in Tabor as an extreme left-wing party, and even Tabor warned them of their heretical excesses. In July 1421 a Hussite synod was held in Prague, partly in an effort to organize and administer a Hussite Church and partly to defend Hussitism against the danger of Pikartism, but no solution was yet reached.

Adamite Heresy Within Taborism

In relation to Prague Hussites, Taborites were radical. Yet within Tabor the Pikarts were even more radical, and in turn the most extreme of the Pikarts were to become known as the Adamites. The existence and growth of the Pikarts seems to have moved the Taborite community to elect Nicholas of Pelhřimov as a means to control peculiar beliefs. The word Pikart may have come from a variation on the word Beghard or even Picardy where a variety of unconventional religious groups flourished.

The Pikarts at Tabor held vaguely pantheistic notions about God being in everything, especially themselves. They denied the existence of the Devil and original sin, and believed they were fully redeemed and good, even if their impulses resulted in sexual excess. Totally foreign to the spirit of Tabor and the Hussite reform movement was the Pikart denial of Christ in the Eucharist. Martin Húska and Peter

Kániš, the two of the leaders of Pikartism, anticipated Luther's Eucharistic doctrine in considering the bread and wine as merely symbols. Húska, asserting that Christ had come and His body was in heaven, denied that Christ was present in the host. In many ways this Eucharistic doctrine reflected a radical new age, the third age, similar to that of Joachim of Fiore. In the third age Christ's passion need not be memorialized but simply commemorated, and Húska's commemorative doctrine of the Eucharist encouraged the congregation to pass around the bread and break and divide the bread among themselves. To the majority of Hussites and Taborites who believed that the words of consecration resulted in the transubstantiation of the bread and wine into the real presence of Christ, the Pikart doctrine was an outrageous heresy. What were the Hussites fighting and dying for, if Communion was a mere gesture rather than a powerful reality? On January 29, Zizka had Húska arrested for heresy and executed in August.[33]

The doctrines and licentious behavior of the Pikarts, increasingly depraved and intolerable in the eyes of Tabor, led to their expulsion from Tabor. The 300 exiled Pikarts settled in the woods near the town of Přiběnice, and it was the extremism of Kániš that led to the fanaticism of the Adamites. They considered themselves the sons of God and the friends of Christ. All human impulses, they believed, came from God and were manifestations of God. All men had all women in common, and marriage was prohibited. To curb or inhibit one's sexual desire would be wrong, and there would be no sin if a brother were attracted to one of the sisters of the community and had sex with her. If she should refuse, she would sin. If she should conceive, her pregnancy was the result of the Holy Spirit. The Adamites engaged in group dances which would end in what ordinarily would be described as orgies. The Adamites sought to live as if the Millennium had indeed come and all prophecies fulfilled, that they were like Christ and that there was no original sin, and that they themselves were as innocent as Adam and Eve in Paradise. Since Adam and Eve wore no clothing, clothing must be sinful and so the Adamites discarded all clothing. They went naked at all times, supposedly not minding the cold and believing their nakedness symbolized sinlessness.[34]

Taborites and Adamites

The Adamites believed they were already immortal, the only humans who truly had God in themselves. All others outside the elect were worth nothing, were as beasts who could be destroyed, especially if they stood in the way of Christ and His elect. Accordingly, the Adamites went out at night and surprised neighboring villages, taking food and mercilessly killing all inhabitants. They ravaged two small towns and a number of villages. They fought with fanatic and reckless bravery, believing that anyone trying to attack them would be blinded and that no one could hurt them.

The Adamites' lewdness and savagery deeply shocked their contemporaries, especially Zizka. Zizka led troops against them and massacred most of them in a fierce battle at the Nezarka River on October 21, 1421. Zizka pressured the survivors to repent and change. Peter Kániš with 50 followers steadfastly refused to recant. Zizka ordered them to be burned. The victims, believing they were martyrs for Christ, mounted the stake smiling and crying out that this very day they would rule with Christ in heaven. The Adamite sect, however, seems to have survived in very small groups in parts of southern Bohemia up to the eighteenth century.[35]

Continued Hussite Wars

Zizka led the Hussite armies to victory during the great battles of the winter of 1421-1422 which enabled the Hussite movement to survive and continue. No single event marked the end of the movement, not the murder of Želivský in 1422 nor the death of Zizka in 1424, nor the defeat of Tabor at the Battle of Lipany May 30, 1434. The Hussite struggle against German mercenaries and other foreign crusaders taught Czechs to think of themselves as a nation in almost a modern sense.

The Hussite movement was one of the first upheavals which toppled the social structures of the Middle Ages and liberated the individual from the embrace and burden and security of the Catholic Church and moved Europe in the direction of religious tolerance. The Hussite Movement, with its radical and fragmenting Taborite and Adamite groups, was a social and religious milestone in which passionate believers broke off from the Church to seek a new path. Like the distant sound of thunder heralding an approaching storm, the Hussite Movement sought reform and anticipated the Protestant Reformation a hundred years before Luther and Calvin. In fact, it prepared the religious atmosphere for the Reformation by being the first reform movement (or, from the perspective of the Catholic Church, heresy) that successfully resisted the efforts of the Catholic Church to suppress it. Charles V did not try to do to Luther what Sigismund did to Hus and tried to do to Hus's followers.

Conclusion

The extraordinary achievement of Tabor was to form a society which was founded upon and animated by millenarianism. Even though the millenarian period of Tabor was brief, the society of Tabor lasted for years and supplied its adherents with the basic human needs. Tabor seems to have been able to achieve such social organization and temporary stability because of the number of middle-class people in the movement and because the movement existed within the larger Hussite movement that represented a cross-section of Czech society. Tabor's strenuous efforts were made under the threat of persecution and extermination—powerful motivators, indeed.[36]

Tabor differed from other millenarian movements in its leaders, most of whom, despite their charism, never claimed they were prophets or messiahs or had any special revelation. Zizka excelled as a military leader but had simplistic theological notions, while Koranda and Želivský had good theological training. Possibly the larger context of Hussitism, with its core of trained theologians, kept the theology of Tabor and the Adamites from being trivial and irrational, although religious passion vitalized the Taborite and Adamite movements.

Indeed, modern students can look back with astonishment at the energy, single-mindedness, and belief of the Taborite armies as they time and again faced superior crusading armies and defeated them. But even more provocative is the mental image of perhaps hundreds of Adamites urgently carried along by the passion of their belief, their unshackled sexuality and their savage aggressiveness. They lived in the belief that they and the times were extraordinary, that God was in them and they were the elect. Although the Adamites were just a small fringe group that eventually vanished from history's stage, their fanatic living out of their radical theology leaves much to ponder.

Bohemia and Moravia, exhausted by the Hussite wars, settled into a precarious religious equilibrium by the middle of the 1400s. Decisively defeated at Lipany in 1434, the Taborites disintegrated as a military power but transformed themselves into a new form of Hussitism. Believers drawn from evangelical Taborites, Waldensians, and others organized themselves apart from the majority Utraquists and the minority Catholics. These new, socially egalitarian and pacifistic Hussites called themselves the Unity of the Brethren. Members of the Unity of Brethren sought the ideal of the primitive, apostolic church. In 1478, however, the Brethren's unity began to crack, as one branch was willing to accommodate to civic life, but the rural party was still strictly adhering to the rigorist ideals that caused the Brethren to set themselves apart from towns and the world. In 1500, on the very eve of the Reformation, the two parties broke apart into separate communities, with the rigorist party known as the Amosites.

When Martin Luther first heard of the Brethren and their search for the ideal apostolic church, he failed to distinguish them from Waldensians. Orthodox Germans in general regarded the Czechs as "pestiferous heretics and defamers of the Catholic faith, or crass, uncouth, and ridiculous barbarians." Like his orthodox German colleagues Luther expressed his hostility for the Czech heretics and the Unity of the Brethren. But in 1519, however, Luther changed his opinion toward the Czechs and the majority party of the Brethren at the Leipzig disputation. By 1520 Luther had read Hus's De ecclesia and confessed his complete change of mind toward the formerly hated Hussites: "In short, we are all Hussites without knowing it. . . ." Indeed, the Hussites could be regarded as the first Protestants.

NOTES

1. Howard Kaminsky, *A History of the Hussite Revolution* (Berkeley and Los Angeles: University of California Press, 1967), pp. 1-2; F.G. Heymann, *John Zizka and the Hussite Revolution* (Princeton, N.J.: Princeton University Press, 1955), p. 49. Kaminsky and Heymann are invaluable on this period and on these groups, and I have followed them closely.

2. Zdenek Bednar, *The Sociological Development of the Taborite Movement* (unpublished Ph.D. dissertation, Boston University, 1954), p. 56; Malcolm Lambert, *Medieval Heresy: Popular Movements from the Bogomils to Hus* (New York: Holmes and Meier Publications, 1976), pp. 276-7.

3. F.G. Heymann, pp. 55-57.

4. Malcolm Lambert, p. 300.

5. Howard Kaminsky, "Hussite Radicalism and the Origins of Tabor 1515-1418," *Medievalia et Humanistica* 10 (1965): 107; F.G. Heymann, p. 58; Malcolm Lambert, p. 306.

6. Mt. 26:26-29; Mk. 14:22-24; Lk. 22:17-20.

7. F.G. Heymann, pp. 58-59; Malcolm Lambert, p. 304; Howard Kaminsky, "Hussite Radicalism," pp. 103-104; Howard Kaminsky, *History*, p. 268.

8. Zdenek Bednar, p. 113; Malcolm Lambert, p. 308; F. G. Heymann, p. 59; cf. R.R. Betts, "The Social Revolution in Bohemia and Moravia in the Later Middle Ages," *Past and Present* 2 (1952): 27; Ernest Werner, "Popular Ideologies in Late Medieval Europe: Taborite Chiliasm and Its Antecedents," *Comparative Studies in Society and History* 2 (1960): 344.

9. Lawrence of Brezova, "Hussite Chronicle" (*Vavrince z Brezove kronika husitska*), in Jaroslav Goll, editor, *Fontes Rerum Bohemicarum* (Prague, 1893), vol. V, pp. 456-465; hereafter cited as Lawrence of Brezova. This source is probably the most reliable of contemporary sources for this complex period. Cf. also, Malcolm Lambert, pp. 305-308.

10. Howard Kaminsky, "Hussite Radicalism," pp. 109-112; Malcolm Lambert, pp. 295, 305, 307-308.

11. Lawrence of Brezova, p. 389; Howard Kaminsky, "Hussite Radicalism," pp. 118-120.

Taborites and Adamites 151

12. Howard Kaminsky, "Hussite Radicalism," pp. 122-128.

13. Lawrence of Brezova, pp. 397, 414, 456-465; F.G. Heymann, pp. 193-196; Howard Kaminsky, *History*, pp. 288, 342-343; Gordon Leff, *Heresy in the Later Middle Ages* (Manchester University Press, 1967), Vol. II, pp. 691-692.

14. Howard Kaminsky, "The Religion of Hussite Tabor," in *The Czechoslovak Contribution to World Culture*, edited by Miloslav Rechcigl, Jr. (The Hague: Mouton & Co., 1964), pp. 210-223; F. G. Heymann, p. 79.

15. F.G. Heymann, pp. 77-78; Zdenek Bednar, p. 201.

16. Lawrence of Brezova, p. 403; Zdenek Bednar, pp. 176-177; 183-184; Howard Kaminsky, *History*, pp. 340, 345.

17. Lawrence of Brezova, p. 403; F.G. Heymann, pp. 59-62, 79-80; Howard Kaminsky, *History*, pp. 281-286.

18. Lawrence of Brezova, pp. 345-346; Howard Kaminsky, "Hussite Radicalism," pp. 102-103; F.G. Heymann, p. 66.

19. Lawrence of Brezova, p. 347; F.G. Heymann, pp. 66-67.

20. Lawrence of Brezova, p. 347; Zdenek Bednar, pp. 143-146, 150; Gordon Leff, p. 690; Howard Kaminsky, "Hussite Radicalism," pp. 129-130.

21. Howard Kaminsky, *History*, pp. 311, 320; F.G. Heymann, pp. 70, 80.

22. Lawrence of Brezova, p. 355; Howard Kaminsky, *History* pp. 299, 307, 312, 332.

23. Lawrence of Brezova, p. 356; F.G. Heymann, pp. 82-85; Zdenek Bednar, pp. 153-154; Howard Kaminsky, *History*, pp. 309, 318; 323, 330.

24. Lawrence of Brezova, pp. 353, 362-365; F.G. Heymann, pp. 86-88, 102, 108-111; Zdenek Bednar, pp. 155-156, 195-198.

25. Lawrence of Brezova, p. 362; F.G. Heymann, pp. 91, 94, 112-113, 121, 281; Zdenek Bednar, pp. 161, 191-194; Howard Kaminsky, *History*, pp. 336-337.

26. Lawrence of Brezova, p. 371; F.G. Heymann, pp. 125, 129.

27. Lawrence of Brezova, pp. 383-387; F.G. Heymann, p. 11.

28. See "Zizka's Battle Hymn," in F.G. Heymann, p. 497.

29. Lawrence of Brezova, pp. 444, 477-478; F.G. Heymann, p. 207.

30. F.G. Heymann, pp. 139, 167-168; Lawrence of Brezova, pp. 388, 397-399; 491, 513.

31. Lawrence of Brezova, pp. 529-530; Zdenek Bednar, pp. 187, 204-208.

32. F.G. Heymann, p. 173; cf. also, John Martin Klassen, *The Nobility and the Making of the Hussite Revolution* (East European Monographs: Columbia University Press, 1978), p. 66.

33. F.G. Heymann, p. 211, 265; Zdenek Bednar, p. 209; Howard Kaminsky, *History*, p. 347.

34. Lawrence of Brezova, pp. 275, 493-495; F.G. Heymann, pp. 211-213.

35. Lawrence of Brezova, pp. 517-520; F.G. Heymann, pp. 263-265.

36. F.G. Heymann, pp. 12-13; Howard Kaminsky, *History*, p. 360.

Chapter Six
Thomas Müntzer and the Millenarian Anabaptists

The Context of Anabaptism

On January 3, 1521, the papal bull *Dicet Romanum pontificem* excommunicated Martin Luther, and five months later the Emperor Charles reinforced that excommunication with an imperial ban. But not even Luther himself was able to stop the changes that his reforming teachings unleased. Luther's writings and preaching unintentionally opened the door for the more radical reformers who called for social and political changes that went far beyond anything Luther had envisioned.

From the very beginning of the reform movement, Luther and other reformers like Zwingli and Calvin found themselves in controversy on two flanks at once. On the right flank the reformers struggled with the pope and Roman authorities who were resistant to change. But it was the left or radical wing of the reform movement that threatened in Luther's eyes an orderly and comprehensive reform of Christendom. Luther and the Protestant leaders thought of their radical foes on the left as monstrous fanatics and libertines.[1] Some of these radical reformers, becoming known as Anabaptists because they sought rebaptism as a special sign of faith and repentance, sought to reform the reformers.

Several factors contributed to the radical and sour reputation that the Anabaptists earned among their contemporaries. All the reformers, mainstream and radical alike, gave emphasis to the Bible. Once people began to read the Bible, however, they began to interpret it for themselves and claim divine promptings which ran counter to both old and new orthodoxies. The Anabaptists, for example, divested Baptism and the Eucharist of the traditional awe-inspiring supernatural power and shifted emphasis to the direct encounter with God through the presence and working of the Holy Spirit. They believed salvation required a deliberate act of faith, and faith, a gift of the Spirit, was attested by an emotional experience, after which the newly regenerated believer would receive the believer's baptism. This radical Anabaptist message rested on a literal interpretation of Scripture, an emotional subjectivism, and the authority of direct inner revelation from God. They along with the Spiritualists emphasized subjective and mystical experiences that contained a radical tendency to oppose external authority. These various tendencies inclined the Anabaptists and the Spiritualists toward extremism and excess in some of their individual communities.[2] These radical reformers were to provide unending headaches for the German princes and the emerging Protestant religious establishment.

For their part, the Anabaptists were profoundly disappointed with the Reformers. The Anabaptists emphasized the baptismal experience of regeneration and the possession of the gifts of the Holy Spirit. Baptism gave believers a missionary role, and laymen began to have a new role and prominence as leaders. This sense of a new being in Christ made the Anabaptists and Spritualists dissatisfied with Lutheran, Zwinglian, and Calvinist formulations on original sin and justification which seemed to undercut personal religious experience and efforts to imitate the original apostolic community. The Lutheran doctrine of *sola fides* or faith alone soon allowed formalism to stifle official Lutheranism. Not only because of his doctrine of salvation but also because of his alliance with established secular powers who initially sheltered him, Luther failed to hold large numbers of the common people, who often sought the emotional religious experiences offered by the Anabaptists and the Spiritualists.[3]

Thomas Müntzer and the Anabaptists

Anabaptism was not a homogenous movement but a collection of sects that usually grouped around a leader who claimed to be a divinely inspired prophet or apostle. Most of the recruits to these movements were from the ranks of artisans and peasants, who had no theology except a limited knowledge of the Bible interpreted in the light of direct inspiration. Authorities tended to be afraid of them and were quick to smother them. In reaction to the hostility with which they were met and also because of increasing social and economic difficulties, Anabaptist suspiciousness (just as paranoia tends to create the very state it fears) increasingly interpreted suffering in apocalyptic terms as the last great onslaught of Satan and the Antichrist against the Saints. The majority of Anabaptists continued a tradition of peaceful and austere dissent, similar to that of Waldensians, but some branches of the Anabaptist movement developed a passionate and apocalyptic millenarianism.

These millenarian Anabaptist groups represented not merely a theological irritant to the Protestant establishment but a social danger to civil authorities as well. Their religious beliefs provided a social agenda. Their increasingly drastic eschatology and their interpretation of the Book of Daniel and the Book of Revelation led them to propose radical changes in society. They sought to clear away old religious abuses and urged the more radical idea of reassembling or restoring the apostolic church as it existed in the age of the martyrs. The church, according to them, consisted of the elect alone and was to be strictly severed from the ungodly pagan world. Central among these extremists, Thomas Müntzer and the Münster Anabaptists denied all external, social authority. They were the spiritual heirs of the Taborites whom they resembled in their eschatological intensity and their reintroduction of the Old Testament idea of warrior saints. They believed themselves to be the chosen remnant of the Lord, and they sought to reform not merely the church but the whole of society.[4]

It was the intensity of the Anabaptists that scared their contemporaries. Not only did some Anabaptists predict the Last Day, but even Luther and Calvin were convinced that the Day of the Lord was near. While Luther and Calvin waited for the coming of the Lord in hope and confidence, the Anabaptists predicted a day of retribution when unbelievers would be exterminated mercilessly. The harshness of this vision may have been related to the harshness with which they were treated but also related to the ecstatic characteristics of Anabaptists which stressed the inner working of the Holy Spirit. The strong stress on the spirit as opposed to the letter of Scripture often produced intense emotional and ecstatic states.[5]

Not surprisingly, the Anabaptists received a harsh response from 1529 onwards, but these harsh attacks only increased their fanaticism and sense of being special. That glittering and glorious mantle that comes from single-minded devotion seemed to settle on those believers ready to suffer great hardships for their convictions.

One individual who especially stands out is Thomas Müntzer, a prophetic and charismatic Spiritualist, whose theology and agitation of the peasants earned him a violent Lutheran response. After his initial Lutheran discipleship Müntzer traded insults with Luther, calling Luther a false prophet, and Luther in turn called him the "archdevil of Allstedt." Müntzer and his followers gained among Lutherans the sobriquet of "die Schwarmer," or fanatic enthusiasts.[6] The Anabaptists forced Luther to back off on his early doctrine of freedom of conscience to a position which allowed religious freedom to exist only within strictly defined limits.

Lutheran Spiritualist: Thomas Müntzer

For some of the German people, Luther's revolution triggered a sense of liberation as well as disorientation amidst a changing social and religious landscape. Luther and Melanchthon, for example, looked on Thomas Müntzer as the personification of the social and religious unrest to which the new evangelical ideas could lead. Luther emphasized faith and the Bible, while Müntzer gave emphasis to spirit and transformation. But Luther and Melanchthon[7] also saw Müntzer as a demonic spirit who would only bring discredit to the reforming movement by rebelling against the civil authority. Müntzer based his revolutionary theology on the Bible in such a way that it bound together inner mysticism and outer activism. His revolutionary attitude to society involved a rejection of human laws and commands which represented the "dead" world, a world which Müntzer urged be replaced by individual communication with God. Müntzer's mystical theology is grounded in the biblical apocalyptic tradition. Müntzer was not, however, merely a dreamy, speculative theologian; he wanted to rip out the godless by direct revolutionary action. He involved himself in popular rebellion and he espoused the use of violence. He was a principal spokesman of Revolutionary Spiritualism, holding the superiority of Spirit over Scripture itself—radical ideas that led to violent excesses and ultimately to the millenarian experiment in the city of Münster.[8]

Müntzer's Background and Theology

Müntzer was born in Stolberg, about 50 miles from where Luther was born, in the Harz Mountains in Thuringia in December 1488 or 89. He received a good education in classical languages and Scripture. Müntzer attended the University at Leipzig and at Frankfort on Oder and received training as a secular priest. In addition to sharing a Thuringian background with Luther, he also shared some of Luther's inquiring doubts and troubled searchings. Luther's influence enabled Müntzer to break away from Catholic orthodoxy, but not long afterwards he abandoned Luther and worked out his own doctrine. He gradually evolved an aggressive, militant millenarianism.

In 1520 he took up ministry in town of Zwickau where he became the preacher in St. Catherine's Church and came into contact with Niklas Storch. Storch, a weaver and a layman, who was also known as one of the Zwickau prophets, energized Müntzer's theology. Storch opposed the established government and society. He proclaimed that God communicated directly with the Chosen because the Last Days were at hand. Storch revived old Taborite doctrines and was advocating a war of extermination in which the Chosen were to rise up and annihilate the godless so that the Second Coming could take place and the Millennium could begin.[9]

Under the influence of Storch Müntzer seems to have passed through a form of conversion experience, and he grew increasingly radical and activist. He jettisoned Lutheran ideas and called for a return to spiritual illumination to overcome the learning of the Lutheran theologians. Unlike Luther, who associated faith with belief in Scripture, Müntzer stressed the vital connection between faith and personal religious experience. For him, external baptism was unnecessary because it was inner baptism that made a person a member of the church of the faithful. He used the first chapters of John's Gospel and interpreted the references to water as the movement of the Spirit.[10]

In his evolving theology Müntzer gave a radical emphasis to subjective religious experiences that would enable the common people to set up a social revolution. Müntzer believed that the elect are granted direct instruction from the Holy Spirit in the form of visions, dreams, and ecstatic utterance. The preacher is the one to awaken this visitation of the Spirit among the hearers.

Before the Elect are ready for such an awakening and the coming of the Holy Spirit, they must be prepared by fear. In his pamphlet of 1523 *Von dem gedichteten Glauben*, Müntzer acknowledges his debt to Joachim of Fiore and says the elect must first be purged by spiritual misery and despair and abandon all pleasure in the world. The second stage of salvation is the bestowal of the cross. Personal suffering was the necessary prelude to salvation. The poor, the suffering, and the downtrodden were specially chosen. Christ on the cross gave an example of this kind of preparation. It is then that the Spirit comes, and then the elect possess the key of David and unlock the meaning of Scripture.[11]

At Zwichau Müntzer preached a revolutionary Biblicism. Drawing on the Book of Revelation and passages of the Old Testament, he recalled Elijah's slaughter of the priests of Baal, Jehu's slaying of the sons of Ahab and Jael's assassination of the sleeping Sisera. He developed a theological basis for his revolutionary activism. His theology emphasized direct revelation through visions and dreams, possession by the Holy Spirit, and the coming of the Millennium which would be preceded by the Turk as Antichrist. Müntzer preached the elect must prepare the way for the Millennium by force of arms. Needless to say this was a revival, conscious or not, of Taborite ideas.

Müntzer emphasized the elect were those who had received and were possessed by the Spirit, and he increasingly separated the Spirit from any necessary tie to the Bible.[12]

Soon Müntzer's sermons were full of impending doom and fierce anticlericalism; he denounced the opulence of the local Franciscans who promptly appealed to the bishop. Müntzer by his blood-thirsty sermons, before the end of 1520, had established something like a reign of terror in Zwickau, and no cleric was able to stand up against him. At least one priest was driven out, pelted with stones and dung, and barely escaped with his life. Soon, however, the danger of civil unrest and the recklessness of Müntzer's teaching aroused attention and opposition. In April 1521, (the same month that Luther faced his accusers at the Imperial Diet of Worms), the Council expelled Müntzer. Storch, the leader of a gang of sectaries, also had to flee Zwickau after authorities made arrests.[13]

Because of his involvement with the revolutionary Zwickau movement, Müntzer was obliged to flee to Prague in June 1521. Prague at this period was largely Utraquist and welcomed him, believing he was a Lutheran reformer. But his concepts of reform and renewal were more radical than those of the Utraquists, and he would have awakened among the Amosites the memory of the millenarian Taborite eschatology of the heroic days.[14] He wanted political power to be transferred to the common people from the nobility and those in power. He spoke to Hussite radicals, and building on the local Taborite expectations, he expressed his confidence in the imminent gathering of God's people. His Prague Manifesto appeared in November 1521. In language that was often violent, he used the poverty of the people to denounce their oppressors, whom he identified as the learned and the priests. These clerics and priests had spiritually impoverished all people, he said, by distorting or obscuring the Gospel. He called for an uprising of the predestined saints, a revolutionary restoration of the common people who should elect their leaders. Borrowing from Eusebius the apocalyptic view of a Fall of the Church in the sub-apostolic age, Müntzer asserted in the land of John Hus that a new church and a new age would begin of which he, Thomas Müntzer, was the dedicated prophet. He was the preacher who was announcing the foundation of new church, which was to consist solely of the elect and was guided directly by God. He said the time was "now," and "I am ready to offer my life." Further, *he* was the preacher who should awaken the call of God in his hearers' hearts. "Oho, how ripe are the rotten apples. Oho, how soft are the Elect. The harvest is here and God has called us to it. I have made my sickle sharp and my lips, hands, skin, body ... are a curse to unbelievers ... in your land the new apostolic church will start ...."[15] In the end Müntzer openly avowed millenarianism to justify the violence of the elect, that is, to prepare for the End Times the elect must use the sword.

On January 22, 1522, Prague authorities expelled Müntzer who then returned to Germany. He seems to have wandered from place to place in extreme poverty, almost as if in preparation for some new mission to which he felt called. He continued to hold an unshakable sense of his prophetic mission and began to refer to himself as "Christ's messenger." In 1523 he took up duties as the parish priest of the small and isolated Saxon town of Allstedt. He married a former nun, Ottilie von Gersen, and soon he dominated the town. His preaching attracted peasant audiences from miles around. With a series of liturgical innovations he developed a vernacular liturgy. When Duke Ernest of Mansfield and Duke George of Saxon forbade their subjects to attend these novel liturgies because they were contrary to a recent Imperial Mandate, Müntzer violently denounced them, addressing the Duke Ernest as a "miserable bag of worms," "a heretical rogue and oppressor of the people." When challenged, Müntzer defended himself by saying that the zeal of the Lord had eaten him up and that he had become a reproach to the wicked. Civil magistrates who act contrary to Christian belief should be killed like dogs, he furiously maintained.[16]

As he came into conflict with the civil authorities, Müntzer organized his followers into what were essentially revolutionary Christian bands, "the Christian League," ready to take up arms for the defense of the gospel. In May 1524, some of his followers vandalized a shrine of the Virgin. Luther had repeatedly warned the rulers of Saxony against such radical preachers like Müntzer, and in July 1524, Duke John ordered Müntzer to preach before him in Allstedt so that he might see and hear for himself.

Thomas Müntzer and the Anabaptists

Müntzer's Sermon to the Saxon Princes

On July 13, 1524, before the Duke who was the brother of the Elector Frederick, the Duke's son John Frederick, and various officials, Müntzer preached one of the most extraordinary sermons of the Reformation on the topic of the second chapter of Daniel. This was Müntzer's last chance to enlist authorities in Saxony to his program of anticlerical war on behalf of the Gospels. He knew the importance of the situation and he pulled out all the stops. The Duke listened without immediate protest as Müntzer made a fiery appeal for Christian revolution. All earthly rule must be abolished under the dominion of the Spirit, he said. Blasting Luther's notion of faith, Müntzer urged a theology of the Spirit. Müntzer passionately asserted that revelation has not stopped, but that it is instead the authentic sign of the last days. He gave to the princes his credentials as a true prophet and as the priest who should be at the head of their armies. He outlined a bold theology of history, not unlike that of Joachim of Fiore. He made an impassioned plea to the princes to yank out and cut off unbelief and godlessness by means of the sword.[17]

Müntzer urged his royal hearers to be daily conscious of the fresh revelations of God. Through his Holy Spirit God reveals to his elect wonderful things about the eschatological transformation of the world. The time is now. The time is now for the priesthood of the common man to break the last of the evil kingdoms, the imperial-papal monarchy. A sign of the Last Days is God's pouring out of his Holy Spirit on his sons and daughters who will prophesy and dream dreams and have visions. Many of the elect are now receiving a decisive revelation. The end of the fifth kingdom is now. The poor laity and the peasants see it clearly. You, the esteemed princes of Saxony, must take up the cause of the Gospel. A new prophet Daniel must rise up and interpret for the princes the vision and go before the army. If you princes correctly see the corruption of Christendom and the deception of the false clerics and vicious reprobates (Luther and his followers), then you will become enraged and eliminate all those who hinder the Gospel—unless you princes want to be ministers of the devil. The sword is necessary to wipe out the godless, and God will strike to pieces all adversaries who oppose his Elect. You princes must see your predestined role and join the elect to punish the godless reprobates under the Antichrist. You princes are the executors of God's wrath against the godless. If you princes don't do it, the sword will pass from you to the people. The Church must come back to its origin by plucking out of the vineyard of God the weeds in the time of harvest. The godless rulers should be killed, especially the priests and monks who revile the gospel as heresy.[18]

In his sermon Müntzer interpreted chapter 13 of Paul's Letter to the Romans in a revolutionary way, saying that the princes were the protectors of the revolutionary elect. In Müntzer's realized eschatology the sword was to be used to wipe out the ungodly and nonbelievers. If the princes failed their duty the sword would pass from them to the people. Like the Taborites he saw the poor as potentially the elect and whose mission was to inaugurate the Millennium. Müntzer believed that the end of the world should be brought about as soon as possible for the returning Christ. Müntzer's program was nothing less than an eschatological and righteous revolution, of equality of possessions. He believed that God wanted the primitive church to be imitated, with the saints being equal and in common possession of the gifts of the Spirit and the goods of life. In such an escathological armed revolt, mere mortal death is nothing in comparison to eternal damnation imposed by God.

As Luther had used apocalyptic imagery to depict the pope as the Antichirst, Müntzer was now portraying Luther as an eschatolgical figure, the Beast of the Apocalypse, because Luther was energetically countering Müntzer's efforts. Previously Müntzer had merely maligned Luther; in his pamphlet *Hochverursachte Schutzrede* he referred to Luther as the "unspiritual soft-living flesh at Wittenberg," as "Dr. Liar," as an "archscoundrel," and as a "deceptive fox."[19] He had broken completely with Luther and now the stakes were different. Müntzer envisioned not only a religious revolution which would allow freedom for the preaching of God's word and the preparation for the End Time but also a social revolution. He saw Luther's close involvement with the princes as opposing both social and religious revolutions. Müntzer unambiguously committed himself to the common people, to social and religious revolution, to the transfer of power from the nobles to the people. All who oppose this process of the last days must be violently annihilated.[20]

Duke John reflected on the radical character of Müntzer's reform and summoned him for a hearing on the first of August 1524. Luther's vitriolic tract on theological radicalism *A Letter to the Saxon Princes*, appearing in late 1524, alerted Duke John to the danger of revolution.[21] Luther supported princely authority in church and state and did not wish to hand power over to the masses. Luther did not support any attack on lawfully constituted authority and was frightened of any movement that would jeopardize the cause of the Reform movement. Increasingly authorities imposed restraints on Müntzer because they feared he would make trouble. His apocalyptic and anticlerical fervor ruined any positive work he had accomplished. His fervent followers expected much and he left Allstedt on the night of 7/8 August 1524 to join the peasant armies in their revolt.[22]

The Peasants' War

Among the German and Swiss peasants, social ferment and economic unrest comparable to that of the English Lollards and the Bohemian Taborites caused sporadic outbursts of violence in the years 1291-1517. Generally the unrest occurred in areas where the peasants had been relatively prosperous and free but where a multitude of petty civil and ecclesiastical lords were attempting to expand their own jurisdiction at the expense of the peasants. The Great Peasants' War of 1524-1525 saw the unrest and violence spread wider, supported this time by an appeal for evangelical freedom. A final spasm of uprisings would occur ten years later with the revolt in Münster and similar uprisings in Amsterdam and elsewhere.

The focus here is on the Great Peasants' War which broke out in June 1524 near Schaffhausen. In the many fiefdoms and regions that made up Germany at this time, the peasants carried a wide variety of economic burdens, social tensions, and political expectations. Some peasants actually seem to have been doing well and were impatient at obstacles standing in the way of further social and economic improvements. The move by local princes to create absolutist principalities increased frictions between feudal authorities. In addition to the economic and social uneasiness that many felt, the year 1524 had opened with a sense of great excitement and foreboding because a

Tubingen mathematician in 1499 had predicated an extraordinary conjunction of planets with a consequent flood that would engulf the earth in February 1524. Not everyone agreed with his prophecy, but all agreed that some terrible evil impended as the year 1524 began. Regional differences, however, make it hard to point to any hierarchy of causes for the outbreak of peasant violence that started in May 1524. These rebellious movements, by early 1525, had increased and began to spread in Upper Swabia and then into other parts of Germany. The peasant uprisings in general were unopposed and sporadic and terrorized the whole countryside. When confronted, however, by professional troops, the peasants offered but slight resistance and were usually slaughtered.

Müntzer provided for the peasants of Thuringia a leadership of articulated ideology. Essentially he made the poor the elect. He offset the coming reign of the poor and downtrodden with the extermination of the rich and powerful. Müntzer believed Christians should all be equals, and that any who opposed the gospel should be exterminated. He had begun to make a transition from spiritual needs to economic needs. On a material side now, he believed that everyone—especially the poor—should receive what he needs. Anyone, especially princes or nobles who opposed this, should be hanged or have his head chopped off.[23]

But Müntzer, despite his fame, was not especially influential nor effective in any practical way. He had fled from Allstedt which had been safer because of its remoteness. He had to avoid the grasp of the Catholic Princes, especially Count Ernest of Mansfield and Duke George of Saxony, and he had to avoid the orbit of Wittenberg where Luther was influential. So Müntzer fled to the Imperial Free City of Mühlhausen, 45 miles south-west of Allstedt.

At Mühlhausen the reform efforts and anticlericalism of a former Cistercian monk Henry Pfeiffer had caused turmoil for at least a year. Pfeiffer's efforts to gain a larger representation of poorer citizens and guild members in the town council had caused social and religious unrest and had excited Müntzer's eschatological expectations. The tinder-box political situation and revolutionary spirit suited his mood and seemed to confirm his sense of the fullness of time. Because of his fame as an antagonist of Luther and because of his writings, he overshadows Pfeiffer in historical hindsight. The reality is that Müntzer was active in the Peasants' War for only several weeks, and the people accepted him because he was a famous man and because he spoke their inflammatory language. But he failed to win them to his eschatological strategy. The people of Mülhausen were more familiar with the locally-born Pfeiffer and preferred his more practical efforts. Getting swept along, Müntzer allied himself with Pfeiffer, however, and regarded himself as a Biblical warrior-priest, and referred to himself as "Thomas Müntzer with the sword of Gideon," or "a servant of God against the godless," or "Thomas Müntzer with the hammer."[24] Acting quickly, local authorities and princes expelled the two prophets on September 27, 1524.

In November and December 1524, Müntzer was in the area of Waldshut in Griessen, capital of the county of Stühlingen. He saw the revolt and violence of the peasants through an apocalyptic lens. He believed the revolt was the end of the fifth monarchy as Daniel had prophesied and which he himself had predicted in his Allstedt sermon before the princes. He saw himself as "a prophet in front of the army."

Müntzer and Pfeiffer, on the run in south Germany, although they were in considerable danger from civil authorities, did establish a link of sorts between the Thuringian and south German revolutions. In February 1525, Müntzer and Pfeiffer returned to Mühlhausen, where the two revolutionaries were more successful than they were the previous autumn. Müntzer began to preach, although without official permission. He foresaw the onset of victory, and exuberantly—almost gleefully—exhorted the peasants that the swords of the saints should not grow cold. By May 17 Müntzer and Pfeiffer were able to get the city council replaced by an "eternal" or eschatological council. They told the people that they must give up their valuables if the Spirit was to dwell among them. Their theocracy, however brief, did have a communist-like style to it. No longer did Müntzer have any expectation that he might win the princes to his cause, and his concern for the spiritually impoverished turned toward the economically impoverished.[25]

But consistent revolutionary programs and principles did not particularly appeal to the peasants. Ideas that would have abolished social and political traditions did not gain acceptance, and the peasant armies could not agree on any guiding ideas and principles. Müntzer was one of the few who tried to articulate a larger vision. He clearly articulated the demands of God and Scripture, but he would not accommodate revolutionary ideals to existing social and political institutions. He was a fiery prophet, not a pragmatic politician. In fact, his idealistic agitation, based on Ezekiel 34, Matthew 24, and Revelations 6, while it seems to have encouraged some of the unorganized peasant bands of Thuringia to loot and burn monasteries, probably confused the peasants more than inspired them.

On April 25th a revolt broke out at Langensalza, and Müntzer mobilized his band of Mühlhausen followers. A force of 400-600 left Mühlhausen on April 26th under Müntzer's flag, a rainbow on a white flag that symbolized the new covenant. On reaching Langensalza the peasant army found the gates shut against them. Pfeiffer led off a detachment on what was essentially a looting expedition. Although these men had no special grievance nor did they have the same fervor of peasants in other parts of Germany, they plundered the monasteries of Homburg and Volkenroda. On the following day they sacked the nunnery of Schlottheim and on the 29th, two castles and the nunnery of Marksustra. On May 6th or 7th the men from Mühlhausen returned to their city.[26]

By May the revolt had spread over the whole of Thuringia. The movement lacked cohesion, however. The peasants pillaged in their districts in small detachments. On May 4th a large detachment had concentrated at Frankenhausen, most likely with the intention of attacking the castle of Ernst of Mansfield.

Müntzer and Pfeiffer seem to have had a falling out, with Pfeiffer becoming established as military commander of the peasants. Müntzer was more the preacher who lent his famous name. He was known as a famous, learned, pious man who had thrown in his lot with them; he had no military ability, which is what the peasants needed. Pfeiffer, by contrast, had been born in a Mühlhausen, whereas Müntzer had been there only for a few months. On May 10th Müntzer left Mühlhausen with only about 300 men, and it can be wondered if he intentionally, like Gideon, wanted to show his faith that the elect, no matter how few, would put to flight the ungodly. He even gave a homily saying that he would catch enemy cannon balls in his sleeves; he declared God spoke to him and promised victory.

On May 12th, Müntzer reached Frankenhausen. He wrote threatening letters to Counts Albrecht and Ernst signed "Thomas Müntzer mit dem schwert Gedeonis," that is, with the sword of Gideon. On the 13th he seems to have passed the sentence of death on three men who were believed to be spies for the princes. He sent a letter to the people of Erfurt to beg for men and weapons. He prophesied on the authority of Ezekiel and Daniel that the wild beasts would be driven from the land and power would be given to the people.[27]

On the morning of the 14th Philip of Hesse, by energetic marching and with no concern about this flanks, arrived with about 5000 soldiers at Frankenhausen. The Protestant Philip, cooperating with the Catholic Duke George of Saxony, assembled his forces on the high ground over looking Frankenhausen. The princes offered to spare the peasants if the trouble-maker Müntzer and his followers would be handed over. The princes regarded him as the leader, but this was most likely due to his fame rather than any military expertise. When Philip brought up his artillery, the peasants panicked and fled when the first shots fell among them and they realized that God was not protecting them. More than 4000 perished in a bloody rout. The disaster at Frankenhausen ended the war in Thuringia as other small bands of peasants quickly dissolved.

Müntzer also fled, but a knight, Otto von Eppe, found him in bed in Frankenhausen and captured him. His captors took him to Heldrungen where Duke Ernest had him tortured and extracted a signed recantation from him. On May 27, 1525, Müntzer was beheaded at Gormar and his head placed on a pole. Pfeiffer was executed the same day with 26 others.[28]

Summing Up Müntzer

By November 1525 the Peasants' War had flickered out, mostly because it had no universally recognized leader and only an improvised organization. The evangelical counsel of a few prophetic clerics and the miliary skills of a few disaffected knights were insufficient to sustain it. In a real sense the peasants and artisans worsened their economic and political situation by their violent actions, and their enthusiasm for Luther's religious reforms also declined. Luther had consistently felt the peasants were endangering his reform program, and he was right. Those who gained from the civil unrest and violence were the princes who centralized their control in areas of civil and religious jurisdiction.

Although Müntzer left behind only a half dozen tracts and a few dozen letters, he was one of those figures in history that evokes highly varying interpretations, depending on the bias or theoretical stance of the observer. Communist historians, for example, tend to see him in a friendly light as a Lenin-like figure. On the other hand, Müntzer's opponent Luther seems to have believed him to be either "mad or drunk," as he says in an August 3, 1523, letter to Spalatin.[29]

Müntzer may well have been unstable mentally, with some proneness toward a paranoid view of his enemies. But he also was gifted, especially as an agitator. What was especially explosive about him was his combination of mysticism and apocalyptic. He emphasized the "hurricane of the Spirit" and the revelations through dreams and visions, just as in the Apostolic Church. He saw in the revolt of the peasants the unfolding of his apocalyptic and violent vision, a confirmation that the new age was at hand and that the Elect must wipe out the ungodly. The Old Testament dominated his thinking and provoked his unrestrained and militant millenarianism. Müntzer believed that too much of Christendom had been perverted by knavish persons. His apocalyptic vision became the basis for a violent revolution, an Old Testament war against the "Canaanite" ungodly, that calls to mind the violence of the Taborites.[30]

The Anabaptist Movement

The Peasants' War had been a political revolution against a background of religious reform. The dismal end of the War did not resolve existing social, political, and religious stresses. Emerging Anabaptist groups channeled reform hopes into efforts to establish an eschatological kingdom in various cities, such as at Münster, Amsterdam, and Strasborg.

Several segments made up the Anabaptist movement. One segment had its origins in lay Bible study groups in Zurich, Switzerland. Laymen close to Zwingli grew impatient with his vacillating interpretations of the sacraments and his changing attitude toward political authority. On January 21, 1525, the layman Conrad Grebel baptized a former priest George Blaurock, and this marks the formal beginnings of this New Testament-oriented pacifist branch of the Anabaptist movement. We have already seen something of the Old Testament-oriented revolutionary branch, which Nicholas Storch had originated in Zwickau in Saxony about 1520. Thomas Müntzer had joined Stroch and had become the spokesman for this wing of the movement.[31] All the branches of Anabaptism, whether pacifist or promoting revolution, encountered persecution.

The revolutionary violence of the Peasants' War and reform efforts had fallen short. During this period the cloth industry of Flanders was collapsing, and larger numbers of workers were unemployed, insecure, and harassed. Many of these urban workers and artisans were Anabaptists and were soon to be forced from their homes and cities by persecution. One of these was a bookbinder, Hans Hut, who had been a follower and disciple of Thomas Müntzer.

Hut believed Müntzer's apocalyptic expectation that the end of the world was drawing near and that wars and strife were foreshadowing the new era. He differed from Müntzer by opposing the sword and violence. In the spring of 1526 Hut was baptized and became a "new Man." He claimed he was a prophet of God whose mission it was to announce that at Whitsuntide in 1528 Christ would return to earth. Rebaptized saints with swords of justice would persecute priests and kings and nobles in preparation for Christ's establishing the Millennium. Hut spread Müntzer-like Anabaptism throughout South Germany, continuing Müntzer's apocalyptic hopes but without open violence. Hut brought Anabaptism to several areas, but when 1528 passed without Christ's coming, Hut's millenarian hopes failed also, with the result that former advocates of Müntzer's naked sword also abandoned hopes for Hut's sheathed sword. Hut was captured in 1527 and imprisoned at Augsburg and died soon after.

From 1524 to 1525 Lower Germany and the Netherlands had been largely uninvolved in the Peasants War because these areas enjoyed better economic conditions and more legal rights. But soon, Westphalia and its chief city Münster would become the center of eschatological and social aspirations for many local and refugee artisans and peasants who were sustained by the apocalyptic vision of Melchior Hoffmann. Ironically the experiment inspired by the nonviolent Hoffmann led to an uprising that was to get out of hand and had to be stamped out by force.[32]

Melchior Hoffman

It was the lay preacher Melchior Hoffmann who carried Anabaptism into North Germany and the Netherlands. Hoffmann, born in 1495 in Swabia, had been a furrier by trade. In 1523 the religious reform movement drew him in and he was soon preaching. In 1525 he journeyed to Wittenberg where he received Luther's enthusiastic approbation. In 1530 he published a book in which he divided church history into 3 periods: the first extended from apostolic times to the reign of the popes, the second was the period of the unlimited power of the popes, and the third began with the Reformation when the papacy was to be deprived of power. Soon, however, the established Lutheran clergy accused him of heresy, and he began to have doubts about whether the Lutheran church was the true Christian church.

The Anabaptist movement, with its piety and simple biblical faith, attracted him and he joined the Anabaptists in 1530 by getting baptized. He organized and shepherded an increasing number of Anabaptist congregations. The civil and religious authorities of Flanders continued in their loyalty to Rome and so executed and burned a number of Anabaptists. Hoffmann rejected any use of force and the bearing of arms.

Thomas Müntzer and the Anabaptists

As persecution increased, Hoffmann's uninformed theology began to drift toward millenarianism. He confidently believed that the Bible taught that man's fallen history was about to be consummated in a new age. He considered himself a prophet called to testify to the imminence of the final judgment. He repeatedly referred to Enoch and Elijah, the two witnesses of Christ's return. He actually began to believe that he was one or the other of the two. He tirelessly journeyed from city to city, and his followers, called Melchiorites, increased in numbers. He developed his own peculiar allegorical doctrine, and more experienced theologians advised him to return to his furrier's craft. The book of Daniel and the Last Things began to preoccupy him more and more, and he began to predict that the end of the world was to come in 1533 when Christ would appear. Hoffmann's confidence increased in his mission and its approaching climax. With an assurance not unlike that of Müntzer and Hans Hut, he announced that Strasbourg had been chosen as the New Jerusalem. In May 1533 he sent a letter to the Strasbourg City Council, explaining that the kingdom of Christ would begin in Strasbourg after a terrible slaughter of unbelievers. The authorities arrested Hoffmann, probably injustly since insurrection and revolt were not to be feared from this non-violent prophet. Hoffmann several times had to push back the date when Christ would come at the head of the 144,000. Several times the appointed day came with great expectation but passed uneventfully and disappointingly. After 10 years in prison, Hoffmann died in 1543.[33] His confinement in prison, however, did not quiet the excited expectations he had aroused. His speculations only set the stage for the excitement which culminated in the Münster uprising, an outbreak of revolutionary millenarianism in the spirit of the Pikarti and Thomas Müntzer.

Many Anabaptists believed the final culmination of the world was near. Anabaptists in Esslingen on the Necker were planning in 1528 to set up the Kingdom of God by force of arms. Civil authorities, however, alerted to these plans, intervened and crushed this movement by 1530. Authorities in various cities took stern efforts to keep control of their citizens. An imperial decree declared that any who rebaptized others were to be burned. Anabaptists tried to seize control of Deventer, Leyden, and Amsterdam but failed. In Amsterdam seven men and five women stripped off their clothes as a sign, they said, of the naked truth that they spoke, and they ran through the streets of

Amsterdam crying out "Woe, woe, woe, the wrath of God." They were set upon and killed. Rising to a new crescendo, religious persecution fanned believers' fanaticism, only confirming for them that the times were extraordinary. Most of the victims were simple and devout believers who sought refuge from persecution. As word spread that the city of Münster was open to religious ideas, swarms of poor and homeless people were attracted by the prospect of a haven. Anabaptists chartered thirty ships to sail to that refuge.[34] Münster was to succeed Hoffmann's Strasbourg as the new Jerusalem.

The Millenarian Experiment in Münster

Münster, a major city in northwestern Germany, had a population of about 15,000. The city was in 1532-1535 to become a center of radical Anabaptism and of social and religious revolution. Certain political and social conditions in the city led to Münster's vulnerability to rapid and radical change. The city enjoyed a large measure of self-government under the sovereignty of the bishop of Münster, Franz of Waldeck, who had his own civil court. He along with a city council ruled the city. Because the city was a member of the Hanseatic League, the 17 craft and merchant guilds were active in government, and no important measure could be passed without their approval. When Luther began his religious reformation, traveling merchants soon brought his ideas into the city.[35]

The excitement of the times prompted rapid changes. In 1531 a young priest of Münster, Bernard Rothmann stimulated further religious unrest in the city when he began to deviate from traditional Catholic doctrine. After a visit to Wittenberg, the center of Lutheranism, he returned to Münster and began to preach the Lutheran message. He was a very eloquent preacher, and his church of St. Maurice, just outside the city gates, was too small to accommodate the throngs that desired to hear him. Early in 1532 the city council strictly ordered him to preach only in his own church and the bishop wanted to outlaw him, but the guilds supported and protected him. Rothmann disregarded the city council and the bishop and began to preach in the open outside of St. Lambert's Church within the city walls. In

February a crowd that included Bernt Knipperdolling, a rich cloth merchant, supported Rothmann's defiance and took over St. Lambert's Church. During a series of July meetings the guilds agreed to continue to protect Rothmann, and by August of that year the guilds had forced the town Council to install Lutheran preachers in all churches. By 1533 Münster was officially a Lutheran town.[36]

The bishop tried to restore Catholicism to the city, and he blockaded roads leading to Münster. Between August 1532 and February 1533 a number of evangelical preachers had come to Münster and were given positions in the city churches. In 1533 conflict continued, and Rothmann continued his rapid theological evolution and soon abandoned his Lutheran faith to embrace evangelical Anabaptist ideas.

The Council was in the hands of those who favored Rothmann and his party. During 1533 the division increased between those with Lutheran sympathies and those who supported Rothmann and the evangelical preachers. Rothmann continued provocatively to put forth his views on baptism in his sermons, and his behavior only widened the breach between himself and the Lutheran party. Münster's Catholics and Lutherans tried to close ranks against Rothmann and the growing number of desperate Anabaptist fugitives who sought refuge in the city for both religious and economic reasons. The city Council attempted to silence him and expel him. Rothmann exerted his considerable power and his followers prepared to resist. Rothmann became not merely a religious leader but the head of a radical party which essentially controlled the situation at Münster by January 1534.[37]

Jan Matthys

Melchior Hoffmann, languishing in prison in Strasbourg, had earlier baptized a follower named Jan Matthys upon whom his prophetic mantle now fell. Hoffmann was a man of peace who taught his followers to await the coming of the Millennium in quiet confidence, avoiding all violence. Matthys did not follow the way of love and peace preached by Hoffmann. Nor did he follow Hoffmann's command to wait for two years before he began his own ministry. Matthys, a tall, gaunt man with a long, black beard, had been born in 1509. He had limited education and had been originally been a baker in Haarlem in North Holland.[38] He was soon to become a revolutionary leader and a fanatic, with his behavior becoming more and more erratic. The excitement and his intoxicating power over people seems to have affected his ability to function appropriately and to control his impulses.

Matthys quickly proclaimed himself a prophet sent by God to establish the kingdom by force. It had, he announced, been revealed to him that he and his followers were called to cleanse the earth of the ungodly. Matthys taught that the righteous must take up the sword and actively prepare the way for the Millennium.

In 1533 Matthys acquired followers in Amsterdam, and he sent them out two by two as apostles to proclaim that Enoch had appeared and the Millennium was near its fulfillment. In each town they visited they baptized great numbers of adults. Two of Matthys' representatives, Bartholomeus Boeckbinder and Willem de Cuyper, arrived at Münster in January 1534, with Jan van Leyden arriving soon after. These heralds of the Millennium caused great excitement in the city. Rothmann and other Anabaptists were rebaptized along with many nuns and well-to-do laymen and a large part of the population. Leyden, also known as Jan Bockelson, a man of twenty-five who had been converted and baptized by Matthys only a few months previously, informed Matthys that toleration of all creeds prevailed in Münster. Matthys quickly concluded that the new era predicted by Hoffmann had arrived, and that persecuted people would find refuge in Münster.[39] It seemed to Anabaptists as if the time had finally come when God's commands could be kept without danger of persecution or death, that baptisms could be performed without fear.

Events in Münster moved rapidly during February, 1534. The power of the Anabaptist party, principally through Rothmann's efforts, increased. Leyden established relations with the guilds and with the patron of the Anabaptists, the cloth merchant Knipperdolling, whose daughter he was soon to marry. On February 8 Leyden and Knipperdolling ran wildly through the streets, summoning all the people to repent of their sins. The Anabaptist leaders unleashed a flood of hysteria, especially among women, some of whom began to see apocalyptic visions of such intensity that they would throw themselves to the ground, screaming, writhing, and foaming at the mouth. The atmosphere of the city became charged with supernatural expectations. The city Council feebly tried to check the Anabaptist movement. The Anabaptists made their first armed move and occupied the Town Hall and marketplace on February 9, 1534. The Anabaptists, however, were still a minority, and Lutherans could have dispersed them if they had been willing to use force. In mid-February the prophet Matthys arrived. Rothmann and other local Anabaptists preachers could not compete for popular support with the Dutch prophets and were soon carried along on a wild movement which the locals no longer had any power to influence. On February 23 Bernard Knipperdolling was elected mayor or burgomaster. On following days the Anabaptists looted monasteries and churches, and in a nocturnal orgy of iconoclasm they destroyed the sculptures and paintings in the cathedral.

Jan Matthys quickly dominated Münster, and the Council soon was no longer effective. On February 25, in order to create an unsullied New Jerusalem, Matthys disclosed his plan to put to death any of the godless who were in the city. He declared that any wicked person, any who failed to acknowledge him as God's prophet, should be destroyed. Needless to say, this alarmed the Lutherans and Catholics who might have still been in the city. Knipperdolling intervened and Matthys decided merely to expel any of the "wicked" who refused to be baptized in the Anabaptist fashion. On the morning of February 27, armed men, urged on by Matthys in a prophetic frenzy, rushed through the streets calling: "Get out, you godless ones, and never come back, you enemies of the Father!" In the marketplace preachers stood ready to baptize any Lutherans and Catholics who stayed behind. On February 28, the day after the expulsions, the bishop started to assemble an armed force outside the city in preparation for retaking the city he once ruled. By March only the "Children of God" remained in the city, and they called each other brother and sister. They believed they could live without sin in a community of love.[40]

The Münster Anabaptists sent out messengers to urge Anabaptists elsewhere to come and assemble with their families in Münster. The earth was doomed to be destroyed before Easter. Münster alone was to be saved as the New Jerusalem, the New Zion. Many Dutch Anabaptists who had suffered severely under Catholic authorities considered this a God-sent message and sailed from Amsterdam and other cities across the Zuiderzee. The leaders in Münster sent messages that a social revolution was taking place and that the poor and homeless should come to Münster. Civil authorities in Germany and the Netherlands were very concerned. Anabaptism was made a capital offense, not only in the diocese of Münster but in neighboring principalities and the archbishopric of Cologne. Soldiers now patrolled the roads leading to Münster and arrested many fugitives. Some refugees were lucky enough to be allowed to return to their homes, while authorities imprisoned or killed others. Nevertheless large numbers of fugitives did succeed in reaching the New Jerusalem.[41]

Many of the newcomers adhered to the New Testament beliefs of the Swiss Anabaptist movement. Matthys and Leyden, however, transformed the peaceful vision of Swiss Anabaptism into a fierce, Old Testament militancy. Matthys seems to have appealed to the semi-literate and was uncompromisingly anti-intellectual himself. The Anabaptist leaders of Münster boasted of their lack of learning and declared that it was the unlearned whom God chose to redeem the world. When the Anabaptists had sacked the cathedral, they tore up and burned the books and manuscripts of its old library. In the middle of March, Matthys banned outright all books except the Bible. The literal Old Testament thinking and anti-intellectualism of the Münster Anabaptists cut them off from any other theological tradition. By the end of March Matthys had established himself absolutely in control of thought and behavior in the heavenly city.

Matthys created an atmosphere of terror in which to work out his millennial vision. A blacksmith from Münster challenged the foreigner Matthys. Surrounded by his bodyguards, Matthys declared to the assembled crowd that the Lord was outraged at this slandering of a prophet and would take vengeance on the community unless the godless smith was dealt with. Matthys himself then stabbed and shot the man. He had Rothmann and the other preachers announce that all possessions were to be in common. He collected together those who had recently been baptized out of convenience rather than belief at the time of expulsions. He told them that unless God forgave them they must perish by the sword. He terrified them by having them locked in a church. Matthys entered the church with a band of armed men. Many of the imprisoned crawled to him, imploring that he intercede with God for them. He intimidated the terrified people before assuring them that he had indeed won their pardon and God would receive them into the community of the saved.[42]

By now the seige army of Münster's former bishop, Franz of Waldeck, had the city surrounded. The original Anabaptist principle of non-resistance had been weakened by the fanatical view that the "children of Jacob" must actively help God punish and annihilate the "children of Esau." On April 4, 1534, Jan Matthys received what he took to be a divine inspiration to go outside the city walls with just a few followers to disperse the besieging army as in the days of ancient Israel. Matthys believed himself to be a miracle working prophet, and he believed a small band could drive off the besieging army with the God's aid. With a small band he charged out from the city and was promptly killed on April 5. A young woman, Hille Feicken, also succumbed to a foolhardy inspiration when she tried to kill the bishop just as Judith had beheaded Holofernes in ancient Israel. She was captured and quickly put to death.[43]

John of Leyden

After Matthys's death John of Leyden (also known as Jan Bockelson) quickly seized control of the hapless city. The youthful former tailor was handsome and eloquent, and he appears to have been an excellent organizer. On the dark side, however, he seems to have been what contemporary chroniclers refer to as "demon-possessed," an apparent reference to his ability to fall into a trance at will and to prophesy. Certainly his frequent revelations came at opportune times, and he used them shrewdly to maintain control over the Anabaptists of Münster. He claimed, for instance, to have received a revelation that Matthys was soon to die. Other commentators say he was a megalomaniac whose behavior can't be adequately interpreted either as sincere fanaticism or as calculating hypocrisy. What glimpses of Leyden that come down through history seem to suggest he was similar to such contemporary cult leaders as Jim Jones. At any rate, the excitement and extreme conditions of religious expectations, biblical literalism, and the threatening siege fostered extreme practices within the city.

Early in May 1534, Leyden ran naked through the city in a frenzy and fell into a trance which lasted 3 days. He then called the people together and announced that God had instructed him to dissolve the City Council and to appoint twelve men as elders, to rule like the elders of the twelve tribes of ancient Israel.[44] Leyden announced that the burgomeister Knipperdolling should become the sword-bearer and his office should punish wrongdoers. Death was the punishment for every kind of insubordination, of young against parents, of wife against husband, of anyone against God's representatives who ruled the city.

The bible-centered Anabaptists wanted to return to the practices of the early Christian church. Whether it was for biblical or military reasons, they began to practice a form of community of goods. Soon the surrender of money and goods was to be the touch-stone of true Christianity. They gathered food and clothing into central areas. Men on duty dined together while someone read from the Old Testament. Exclusive possession of anything began to be regarded as sinful, and the doors of houses had to be left open. All things were to be in common, with no private property. Anabaptist propaganda let the world know of the Münster ideal of community of goods. This ideal attracted many poor refugees, who had their own goods confiscated on their arrival in Münster.

Most of the Anabaptists were surprised to find themselves at war, but Leyden and Knipperdolling vigorously exerted leadership. Despite their fanaticism they transformed the Anabaptists into an effective military organization. The leaders selected officers, assigned tasks, organized day and night watches on the city walls, and prepared fortifications. Often at night Leyden himself went to inspect the walls and the guards. The Anabaptists had less than two thousand men able to bear arms, but they so effectively organized these to meet the siege that when a major attack came on May 25, 1534, the attacking soldiers of the bishop, supported by the rulers of Cleve and the electorate of Cologne, failed miserably.[45] Anabaptist defenders of Münster lost only a few men, and Leyden's position as absolute leader was entrenched. His success enabled him to dare to put into effect another of his plans.

Anabaptists tended to have a strict code of sexual morality, but Leyden now decreed a new regulation of behavior. He assembled the people of the city and explained how God had revealed to him that the biblical precept to "increase and multiply" was a divine commandment. Justifying his decree from the pages of the Old Testament, Leyden proposed that the new Jerusalem of Münster must emulate the example of the Patriarchs of Israel and that men were to take more than one wife. The citizens of Muünster balked at this proposal far more than they had resisted the idea of community of goods. For eight days in the city hall Leyden debated the question with the preachers and elders, but finally he announced that any who opposed this law were considered sinners and sinners were to be put to death. Rothmann appears weakly to have gone along with Leyden and preached on three successive days that plural marriage was the divine plan for the new Israel. The Münster preachers rationalized the practice of polygamy in terms of the war between the "children of light" and the "children of darkness." More practically, polygamy probably served as a form of social welfare, with men decreasing because of fighting and constituting only one third of the adult population in the city. As of July 1534, there were only about 1700 men but almost 7000 women and several thousand children in the city. At any rate, now unmarried women had to accept the first man who asked for their hand. All adults of marriageable age had to marry. Conditions became tense.

On July 29, 1534, Heinrich Mollenhecke and 200 armed followers demanded an end to the practice of polygamy. They seized Leyden, Knipperdolling and Rothmann in the city's market place. While Mollenhecke and his companions considered what to do next, supporters of Leyden overpowered the rebellious men. Leyden ended this challenge by having Mollenhecke and 48 of his followers executed. By August, polygamy was firmly established, although social tensions continued. Leyden himself took 15 wives, including the daughter of Knipperdolling and the young widow of Matthys, Dieuwertgen by name. Because of the influx of new women into the households of established wives, there was turmoil and conflict. Some women who resisted the new policy were executed. On at least one occasion when

Leyden heard a Münsterite condemn the practice as debauchery, he drew his sword and killed the man. Divorce had to be tolerated. Although some residents maintained a vigorous puritanism, others contracted and dissolved marriages promiscuously. An observer might have believed the sexual behavior of some in the Kingdom of the Saints began to look like a latter day version of the Adamites.[46] Polygamy above all else has darkened history's view of the Münsterite uprising.

Leyden continued to concentrate on the siege, and he kept the garrison vigilant as a disciplined force. His prestige was at its highest when at the end of August 1534, a major attack was beaten off very effectively. Leyden used the occasion to have himself proclaimed Messiah of the Last Days. One of his supporters, a goldsmith and prophet named Johann Dusentschur, declared that God the Father revealed to him that Leyden was to be named King of the New Zion and that he should surpass in authority all the kings on the earth. He was to inherit the scepter and throne of his forefather King David and to keep them until God would reclaim the kingdom from him. Dusentschur anointed Leyden and proclaimed him King of the New Jerusalem. For the next few days the preachers delivered sermons explaining that the Messiah proclaimed by the prophets of the Old Testament was indeed Leyden.

Leyden had an elaborate throne erected in the market square where he held court. Leyden, the former tailor, had priestly vestments from the days of the Catholics converted into royal robes. He wore a royal insignia with a gold chain which supported a ball representing the earth and bearing the inscription "a king of righteousness everywhere." He named his chief wife, the widow of Matthys, Queen Divara. He made people fall on their knees before him. Anybody opposing him was to be killed.

King Leyden gave new names to things and used various rituals to proclaim the millennial fantasy. Sundays and feast days were abolished, with days of the week being renamed in an alphabetical system. Dressed in his royal robes, King Leyden wore rings and ornaments and spurs made from precious metal by city craftsmen. Whenever the king appeared in public, a fanfare would herald his arrival. A train of splendidly dressed retainers and court officers would appear and then the king would ride up on horseback, with his crown on his head and scepter in hand. Knipperdolling marched behind, having been named chief minister. Rothmann was now the royal orator. A well-armed royal bodyguard always accompanied the king and protected the procession. In contrast to the magnificent style of life for the king and his court, Leyden imposed rigorous austerity on the population. The prophet Dusentschur announced that God the Father had revealed to him that He abominated all superfluity in clothing—except in the king, of course—so clothing and bedding were severely rationed. All surplus had to be handed over on pain of death. Leyden explained that pomp and luxury were permissible to him since he was wholly dead to the world and flesh. He promised the common people that they, too, would soon sit on silver chairs, eating at silver tables.

The Final Agony of Münster

The governments of several provinces agreed to aid the bishop in the siege of the city. The ring of soldiers around Münster effectively cut off any who sought to reach or leave the besieged city. The inhabitants, however, continued to defend the city with enthusiasm, although life was becoming very difficult for them. During the fall famine increased. King Leyden prophesied that the city would be relieved by Easter, but when time came he had to change his prophecy to refer to spiritual aid. He allowed old men, women, and children to leave. Although the besiegers allowed some of the fugitives to pass through, they executed hundreds.[47]

Millennial prophecies and promises continued to motivate and hold the town in excitement. On October 13, 1534, the prophet Dusentschur came forward with another divine revelation. Apostles should be sent out to spread the message of the new Zion. Leyden sent out 27 apostles, most of whom were caught and put to death. Aside from these representatives, another form of millenarian propaganda existed in the form of the writings of Rothmann. In October Rothmann produced his pamphlet *Restitution* and in December his booklet *On Revenge*. Rothmann encouraged the inhabitants of Münster by saying that the day of revenge over the wicked was at hand. He also invited those who would have a part in the Kingdom of God to come to

Münster where the throne of David was already set up and that Leyden now occupied that throne. Cloaking the idea of the three ages in a new form, Rothmann said the first age, an age of sin, lasted until the Flood; the second age was an age of persecution that lasted until the present; the third age, an age of vengeance and triumph for the saints, was now: the time of tribulation was at an end and Christ was about to return. Indeed, the Kingdom was already set up in Munster, and from this Kingdom the people of God must sally forth to wield the sword of Justice and enlarge the Kingdom. To them falls the duty of purifying the whole world of evil in preparation for the Second Coming. The saints should take revenge without mercy against all those not marked with the Sign. Once this great killing was accomplished, Christ would come. Then a new heaven and earth would appear in which the saints would live without weeping.[48]

These dramatic promises were kept fresh and the inhabitants kept on edge by the spectacular stunts of Leyden and those who served him. For example, in October, the prophet Dusentschur announced that the Trumpet of the Lord would sound three times and that all inhabitants should gather in the cathedral square. As soon as they heard the sound of the trumpet, all should arm themselves and rush to the square in order to surge out in attack against the enemy armies. They would be endowed with supernatural strength so that 5 from Münster could kill 100 enemies, and 10 from Münster could kill 1,000. It was actually Dusentschur himself who blew the trumpet, but apparently it would have been suicidal not to follow the command of the prophet so everyone—men, women and children—rushed to the square. The king appeared on his horse and at the last minute called off the expedition; he had merely wished to test the loyalty of his people, he announced. Being satisfied, he invited the populace to a banquet. After a communion and some dinner, the king, acting on a sudden illumination, sent for a captured soldier from the prison and beheaded him.

Leyden intensified the terror within the city. A few days after he proclaimed Leyden as king, Dusentschur announced a new revelation that all who persisted in sinning should be brought before the king and sentenced to death. Within a few days executions began. One woman was beheaded for denying her husband marital rights; another woman was executed for practicing bigamy—it seems that polygamy was a male right and not sinful for men. A third woman was killed for insulting a preacher and mocking his doctrine. Whatever his reasons, Leyden increased his sadistic domination over the female saints and thoroughly cowed the population. In his exercise of control, Leyden used immigrants to form his bodyguard. These newcomers to the city had nothing and so stood to rise or fall with him. Leyden armed these men and supplied them with rich clothes, food, and good horses. The people discerned that Leyden might as easily turn these armed men against them as against the enemy outside the walls.[49]

Thousands of copies of Rothmann's pamphlets were smuggled out and distributed in Holland and Frisia. This propaganda had an inflammatory effect on Anabaptists elsewhere. Conditions of unemployment and famine elsewhere, especially in Holland, led to mass uprisings of Anabaptists. Many of the followers of Melchior Hoffmann had their eager hopes dashed when the expected Kingdom of God did not appear. This disappointment, in addition to persecution and economic adversity, led them to abandon their peaceful views. In January 1535, a thousand armed Anabaptists assembled in the province of Groningen under a prophet who called himself Christ, the Son of God. These men intended to march toward Münster in the belief that King Leyden would meet them and make their enemies melt away. The Duke of Gelderland scattered them. In March 800 Anabaptists captured a monastery in West Frisia and held it until they were exterminated. Fighting broke out in Oldeklooster. An attempt at Minden was made to establish a new Jerusalem like Münster. In May, an uprising at Amsterdam was put down. The aim of these uprisings was similar to other millenarian movements: to kill all earthly rulers since there was only one rightful ruler who was soon to come. Anabaptists planned attacks on Leiden, Woerden, The Hague, Oudewater, and other cities. The New Jerusalem called forth great hope and devotion among Anabaptists and common people in Northwest Germany and the Netherlands. Civil authorities were very upset and usually responded with savagery to put down the outbursts.[50]

The bishop intensified efforts to reduce Münster. The officials of the states of Upper and Lower Rhine and at Koblenz agreed to supply troops and equipment. With the city completely cut off from the outside world and with food shortages severe, the inhabitants were killing horses for food and by late spring of 1535 people ate anything: dogs, rats, grass, even bodies of the dead. They realized that the city could not hold out much longer. Leyden continued as unchallenged king of this nightmare kingdom. He promised people that God the Father would change the cobblestones to bread, and many believers wept to find the stones continued to be stones. Leyden, in late spring, summoned the starving population to take part in three days of dancing, racing, and sport, because it was God's will. The many deaths from starvation required communal graves. In May 1535, Leyden relented and allowed any who wished to flee the city, but he cursed the fugitives, saying that the reward of their infidelity would be damnation. The besiegers usually caught and killed these fugitives.

The siege of Münster ended abruptly. Two men, Hans Eck and Heinrich Gresbeck, escaped to the camp of the besiegers and revealed the weaknesses in the defenses. On the night of June 24, 1535, a surprise attack by the bishop's soldiers penetrated the city. The hours of desperate night fighting recall the fall of Jerusalem. Several hundreds of the surviving Anabaptist defenders accepted an offer to lay down their arms and they dispersed to their homes. But over the next few days victorious soldiers massacred many in the city. Rothmann seems to have died fighting. Queen Divara refused to renounce her faith and was beheaded. The victors were able to capture Leyden, and the bishop ordered that he be led about by a chain and exhibited. Leyden, during his imprisonment, at first defended his doctrines, then tried to bargain for his life by offering to persuade Anabaptists to conform and have their infants baptized. He said he was guilty of teaching great errors, especially on polygamy and on divine kingship. On January, 1536, he and Knipperdolling were tortured to death with red-hot irons. Afterwards, their bodies were suspended in cages from St. Lambert's Churchtower in the middle of Münster. Those who had fled from the Anabaptists returned, and the city again became officially Catholic.[51]

Consequences

Münster and Münsterism caused untold harm to the cause of millenarianism and Anabaptism. Tales about the Anabaptist Kingdom

Thomas Müntzer and the Anabaptists

at Münster caused waves of horror through Europe, and no one would trust even those Anabaptists who were innocent and peaceful. Both Protestants and Catholics distrusted advocates of millenarianism and sought to stamp out Anabaptism. The Catholic Counter Reformation used the story of Münster not only against all Anabaptists but also all reformers. In the ten years after Münster about 30,000 Anabaptists were put to death in Holland and Friesland alone. Some small Anabaptist congregations continued at Dortmund, Osnabruck, Soest, Minden, Lemgo, but they gradually died out. The harsh measures of the Counter Reformation drove many Anabaptist to emigrate. Surviving Anabaptist groups were absorbed into the New Testament-oriented, pacifist congregations under the leadership of Mennon Simmons. Peaceful Anabaptists, known as *Stabler*, men of the staff rather than the sword, survive in some contemporary denominations, such as the Mennonites, the Bretheran, and the Hutterian Bretheran. Separatist traditions of withdrawing from the world into self-contained communities prevailed among most of these groups in reaction to the disaster at Münster. Mennonites are the main surviving group of German, Swiss, and Dutch Anabaptists. The teachings of the Anabaptists influenced the Amish and the Quakers as well as the Baptists.

A few Old Testament-oriented Anabaptist revolutions flicked, but the disaster at Münster had a lasting effect. Johann Batenburg, seemingly a new Matthys and Leyden, was quickly executed in 1537. In 1567 a cobbler named Jan Willemsen gathered 300 militants and set up another New Jerusalem in Westphalia in the area around Wesel and Cleves. These saints practiced polygamy, and Willemsen as messiah had 21 wives. They used Rothmann's *Restitution* to justify some of their practices. Claiming that all things belonged to them, they turned into a robber band which attacked the residences of nobles and priests. Messiah Willemsen and his followers were captured and burned at Cleves in 1580.[52]

Speaking broadly, neither the reformers nor the revolutionaries achieved what they hoped. Luther's actions, so revolutionary in the spiritual field, had led masses of people in town and country to expect that he would also support a fight for liberty in other than purely religious terms. He had harshly criticized the exploitation of the peasants and had advocated changes. But Luther turned against the peasants and, fearing for his own reform efforts, violently condemned any social revolution; in fact, he proclaimed that supporters of revolution should be killed off like made dogs. Luther's turning away from the peasants weakened the democratic element in Lutheranism, and the Lutheran Church ceased to be the great popular religious movement he hoped. Lutheranism, under the vigorous supervision of the princes became in its own way as conservative as the Catholic Church.[53]

NOTES

1. George Huntson Williams, *The Radical Reformation* (Philadelphia: The Westminster Press, 1962), pp. xxviii-xxx.

2. Claus-Peter Clasen, *Anabaptism: A Social History, 1525-1618* Ithaca & London: Cornell University Press, 1972, p. 121, and R. N. Carew Hunt, "Thomas Muentzer," *Church Quarterly Review* 126 (1938): 213; cf. George Williams, pp. 27, 43, 208.

3. George Williams, pp. xxiii-xxv; Norman Cohn, *The Pursuit of the Millennium* (Oxford University Press, 1970), pp. 252-3; R. N. Carew Hunt, p. 231.

4. George Williams, pp. xxvi-xxviii; R. N. Carew Hunt, p. 214.

5. Claus-Peter Clasen, pp. 120-121.

6. E. Gordon Rupp, "Thomas Müntzer: Prophet of Radical Christianity," *Bulletin of John Rylands Library* 48 (1966): 467. Luther made several attacks on Anabaptist Schwärmer in his *Wider die Himmlischen Propheten*, in J.K.F. Knaake, G. Kawerau, E. Thiele, et al., eds. *D. Martin Luthers Werke. Kritische Gesamtausgabe* (Weimar, Harmann Bohlaus Nachfolger, 1883-), vol. XVIII, pp. 37 ff. (hereafter abbreviated as *WA*) and in *Von den Scleichern und Winkelpredigern* in *WA*, XXX, p. 510ff. For further on Müntzer, cf. Franz Gunther, ed. *Thomas Müntzer: Schriften und Briefe. Quellen und Forschungen zur Reformationsgeschichte*, XXXIII (Gutersloh, 1968), and Eric W. Gritsch, *Reformer without a Church: The Life and Thought of Thomas Müntzer, 1488[?]-1525* (Philadelphia, 1967); Gordon Rupp, *Patterns of Reformation* (London: Epworth Press, 1969), pp. 157-356.

7. Cf. Melanchthon's contemporary life of Muntzer, although it is biased: Philipp Melanchthon, "Die Histori Thome Müntzers," in Ludwig Fischer, ed., *Die lutherischen Pamphlete gegen Thomas Müntzer* (Tubingen: Max Niemeyer, 1976), pp. 27-42.

8. George Williams, p. 44; Norman Cohn, p. 252; cf. Otto Brandt, *Thomas Müntzer: Sein Leben und Seine Schriften* (Jena, 1933), p. 38.

9. James M. Stayer, "Thomas Müntzer's Theology and Revolution in Recent Non-Marxist Interpretation," *Mennonite Quarterly Review* 43 (1969): 143.

10. George Williams, p. 52.; Carew Hunt, p. 219, 232.

11. George Williams, p. 51; cf. Otto Brandt, p. 132.

12. George Williams, pp. 45-46; Norman Cohn, pp. 235-236; James M. Stayer, p. 150-151; cf. Eric W. Gritsch, "Thomas Muentzer and the Origins of Protestant Spiritualism," *Mennonite Quarterly Review* 37 (1963): 188.

13. Carew Hunt, p. 221-222; Gordon Rupp, *Patterns of Reformation*, p. 167.

14. George Williams, p. 217; cf. Reinhard Schwarz, *Die apokalyptische Theologie Thomas Müntzers und der Taboriten* (Tubingen: J.C.B. Mohr, 1977).

15. Gordon Rupp, *Patterns of Reformation*, p. 179; Williams, pp. 47-49; and James Strayer, pp. 147; E. Gordon Rupp, "Thomas Müntzer," pp. 468-470; Carew Hunt, pp. 224-226. There is a translation of the shorter version of "The Prague Manifesto" in Lowell H. Zuck, *Christianity and Revolution: Radical Christian Testimonies 1520-1650* (Philadelphia: Temple University Press, 1975), pp. 32-35.

16. E. Gordon Rupp, "Thomas Müntzer," p. 470; Norman Cohn, p. 238; Carew Hunt, pp. 227, 233, 238.

17. Cf. George Huntston Williams and Angel M. Mergal, "Introduction," *Spiritual and Anabaptist Writers* (Library of Christian Classics, vol. XXV, Philadelphia: The Westminster Press, 1957), pp. 47-48; Gordon Rupp, *Patterns of Reformation*, p. 201.

18. *Spiritual and Anabaptist Writers*, pp. 49-70.

19. Thomas Müntzer, "A Highly Provoked Defense," in Lowell H. Zuck, *Christianity and Revolution*, pp. 39-44; cf. George Williams, pp. 53-55; Norman Cohn, pp. 242-243; Carew Hunt, p. 239.

20. Peter Blickle, *The Revolution of 1525: The German Peasants' War from a New Perspective* trans. by Thomas A. Brady and H.C. Erik Midelfort (Baltimore and London: The Johns Hopkins University Press, 1981), p. 150.

21. Martin Luther, "Brief an die Fursten zu Sachsen von dem," "Letter to the Princes of Saxony," *Luther's Works* (American Edition: Philadelphia and St. Louis, 1958), vol. 40, pp. 49-59; in *WA*, XVI, pp. 210-221; also in *Die lutherischen Pamphlete gegen Thomas Müntzer*, edited by Ludwig Fisher (Tubingen: Max Niemeyer, 1976), pp. 1-12.

22. George Williams, p. 57; Carew Hunt, p. 237, 243.

23. George Williams, pp. 59-60, 64; Peter Blickle, pp. 88-89; Norman Cohn, p. 245.

24. Peter Blickle, p. 148; George Williams, pp. 75-76; Gordon Rupp, *Patterns of Reformation*, pp. 221-225.

25. Carew Hunt, pp. 246-7; Peter James Klassen, *The Economics of Anabaptism, 1525-1560* (The Hauge: Mouton & Co., 1960), p. 26.

26. Carew Hunt, pp. 227, 247-250.

27. Norman Cohn, pp. 246-250; Carew Hunt, p. 252-254.

28. Carew Hunt, pp. 257-259; Peter Blickle, pp. xvii-xviii.

29. George Williams, pp. 82-83; Gordon Rupp, *Patterns of Reformation*, p. 187; Carew Hunt, pp. 264-6.

30. E. Gordon Rupp, "Thomas Müntzer," pp. 475, 477.

31. Lowell Zuck, "The Beginnings of the Anabaptist Movement," *Christianity and Revolution: Radical Testimonies 1520-1650* (Philadelphia: Temple University Press, 1975) p. 67; George Williams, p. 120.

32. Norman Cohn, pp. 254-255; Lowell Zuck, pp. 76-77; George Williams, p. 83.

33. "Melchior Hoffmann," *Mennonite Encyclopedia* (Scottdale, Penn.: Mennonite Publishing House, 1956), vol. 3, pp. 778-787; Lowell Zuck, p. 83.

34. "Münster Anabaptists in the Netherlands," *Mennonite Encyclopedia*, vol. 3, p. 782.

35. John Horsch, "The Rise and Fall of the Anabaptists of Muenster," *Mennonite Quarterly Review* 9 (1935): 92; "Muenster Anabaptists," *Mennonite Encyclopedia*, vol. 3, pp. 777. My account of Münster closely follows Norman Cohn and John Horsch. Basic sources are the Latin account of Hermann von Kersenbroch, *Anabaptistici furoris Monasterium inclitam Westphaliae metropolim evertentis historica narratio* in Heinrich Detmer, editor, *Geschichtsquellen des Bistums Munster*, Vol. v & vi; and H. Gresbeck, *Summarische Ertzelungk und Bericht der Wiederdope und wat sich binnen der Stat Monster in Westphalen zugetragen im Iair MDXXXV*, in C.A. Cornelius, editor, *Berichte der Augenzeugen uber das munsterishche Wiedertauffeich* (Munster, 1852), pp. 3-212.35.

36. "Münster Anabaptists," p. 777; Norman Cohn, p. 259; John Horsch, pp. 92-3.

37. John Horsch, pp. 9-103; Norman Cohn, p. 259.

38. "Jan Matthijsz van Haarlem," *Mennonite Encyclopedia*, Vol. 2, p. 79; Norman Cohn, p. 262.

39. John Horsch, p. 129; Norman Cohn, p. 260; "Jan van Leyden," *Mennonite Encyclopedia*, Vol. 2, pp. 77-78.

40. Norman Cohn, p. 261; John Horsch, p. 131.

41. "Münster Anabaptists," p. 778; John Horsch, p. 131; Norman Cohn, p. 267.

42. Norman Cohn, pp. 264-267.

43. "Münster Anabaptists," p. 778.

44. John Horsch, pp. 135-136; Norman Cohn, pp. 268-9.

45. Norman Cohn, pp. 263-265; John Horsch, p. 136.

46. Norman Cohn, p. 270; John Horsch, pp. 138-9.

47. Norman Cohn, pp. 271-273; John Horsch, p. 140-142.

48. Bernard Rothmann, "A Restitution...of Christian Teaching," in Lowell Zuck, pp. 99-101; Bernard Rothmann, "Concerning Revenge," in Lowell Zuck, pp. 102-104; "Bernard Rothmann," *Mennonite Encyclopedia*, pp. 367-369; Norman Cohn, p. 274.

49. Norman Cohn, pp. 275-276.

50. "Münster Anabaptists in the Netherlands," *Mennonite Encyclopedia*, vol.3, p. 782; Norman Cohn, p. 277.

51. "Münster Anabaptists," p. 779; Norman Cohn, pp. 278-280; John Horsch, pp. 142-143.

52. Norman Cohn, p. 280; "Münster Anabaptists in the Netherlands," p. 783.

53. Frederick G Heymann, "The Hussite Revolution and the German Peasants' War: A Historical Comparison," *Medievala et Humanisitica* NS 1 (1970): 154-155.

Chapter Seven
England's Fifth Monarchy Men

The Münster episode served to discredit millenarianism on the Continent as something bloodthirsty and subversive of the political and social order. At Münster millenarianism had, in part, been able to flourish because of the breakdown of political order. In England, although millenarian sentiment had been endemic in society since the fifteen century, the intactness of the social order and prompt government intervention prevented any millenarian explosions until the Civil War.[1] The intense efforts on the Continent to search out and execute Anabaptists in the spring of 1535 were not happening in England even though English authorities apprehensively followed the rise and fall of Münster. Anabaptist refugees generally found in England an accepting climate. A rare exception occurred in the November 1538 trial, condemnation, and burning at Smithfield of Jan Mathijsz van Middleburg, ironically an Anabaptist spokesman *against* revolt and violence.[2]

At the end of the sixteenth and early in the seventeenth century, the political and religious situation in England, rather than any economic crisis, caused a wave of general millenarian excitement to wash over the country, touching people of all classes. Indeed, it is likely that during the period of the English Revolution, millenarian ideas were more widely circulated than in any other period or place. People seriously considered the prospect of the imminent end of the world, and increasingly interpreted biblical prophecies about calamities and the Second Coming as referring to the contemporary situation.

Specifically, it was English Puritans who regarded themselves as the saints and the Papacy as the Antichrist and expected the imminent end of the world. The Puritanism of the 1630s evolved into the revolutionary Puritanism of the 1640s. The extraordinary political convulsions of the Civil War period and the absence of normal restraints made the 1640s remarkable for the extent, variety, and intensity of millenarian ideas and activity.

The execution of King Charles, the breakdown of censorship during the interregnum, and the collapse of traditional social controls gave people a sense that they were living in an unprecedented time, a time without parallel in earlier English history. Political, religious, and social conditions during these middle decades of the seventeenth century allowed the explosive emergence of widespread millenarianism and various new sects such as the Ranters and Muggletonians.

If the zenith of millenarianism was reached during the late 1640s, then the 1650s tended toward the erosion of the millenarian tradition. It was only when the wave of millenarian excitement and expectation had begun to recede that the most radical of English millenarians, known as the Fifth Monarchy Men, emerged in a desperate attempt to revive declining millenarian hopes. They aroused great fear during the 1650s and came perilously close to seizing absolute political power. To their contemporaries the Fifth Monarchy Men seemed violent revolutionaries, behind a facade of saintliness. Cromwell is said to have remarked that "they had tongues like Angels, but had cloven feet."[3]

The Fifth Monarchy Men was a minor but glamorous and radical sect which took shape shortly after the execution of Charles I in 1649 and survived until the mid-1680s. The name of the movement was derived from the vision recounted in the seventh chapter of the Book of Daniel. In that vision, the four beasts represent the great empires of Babylon, Persia, Greece and Rome, which would be destroyed at the end time and replaced by the reign of God and the saints, the so-called Fifth and last Monarchy. More than any other movement of this period the Fifth Monarchy Men represented the total fusion of

England's Fifth Monarchy Men

millenarian theology and political extremism. They saw the millennium in political and social terms rather than in the largely theological and passive terms of earlier English millenarians. Like the millenarians of Münster, Fifth Monarchy Men felt it was a divine duty to establish the millennium by action and by force if necessary. Their political vision and their professed readiness to use violence deterred academics and gentry from supporting the movement, which consisted largely of artisans, journeymen and apprentices.[4]

The Fifth Monarchy Men became organized amid the complex political and social turmoil of the late 1640s and the 1650s. This chapter focuses on this specific group, rather than attempting to deal with the complex issue of the Puritan apocalyptic vision. To understand how the Fifth Monarchy Men arose and differed from other radical English groups and continental millenarian groups, it is necessary to review briefly some of the historical, political and religious events that made the middle years of the seventeenth century in England so tumultuous.

Historical Background to the Civil Wars

Around the time of Luther, England's King Henry VIII had relied on Protestant support to throw off Catholic influence and papal authority. Henry's successor, Queen Elizabeth I, continued as head of the established church to resist any religious doctrines that she thought undermined royal authority. She resisted adopting the Presbyterian system and supported efforts to stamp out Protestant extremism such as the Calvinist demand for the abolition of bishops. The Protestant extremists who denounced bishops, crucifixes, and vestments became known as Puritans, because they wished to purify the Church from any Catholic remnants. Puritans, however, and Protestants in general gave political support to Queen Elizabeth against Catholic Spain and the pope.

Elizabeth's successor was James VI from Scotland who continued Elizabeth's vigilance against Calvinism and Presbyterianism as threats to royal authority. His resolution to keep the Church of England free from Presbyterian and Calvinist influences brought James increasingly into political and religious conflict with Protestants, both moderates and the more radical Protestants such as the Puritans. When James VI died in 1625 his twenty-four-year-old son Charles I succeeded him.

Charles I stirred up widespread dissatisfaction not only because of the extravagance of his court but also for his economic policies and the perception that he had Catholic sympathies in his religious policies. Charles had chronic problems in raising money, and his conspicuous lack of concern for the Protestant cause in the Thirty Years War aroused resentments. In ecclesiastical policy Charles relied on William Laud, Archbishop of Canterbury. Laud retained for the Established Church of England such Catholic remnants as bishops, liturgical vestments, and crucifixes that English Protestants began to see in the Laudian Church thinly disguised popery and Catholic idolatry.

Charles dissolved Parliament in 1629, and he ruled without Parliament for 11 years. In 1637 Charles inadvisedly tried to extend Archbishop Laud's High Church rituals onto his Scottish subjects by replacing the Book of Common Order which John Knox had established in 1560. Scottish Presbyterians felt Charles was out to destroy them and to impose Catholic-like rituals on them; they accordingly rebelled. In 1639 Charles sent an army to invade Scotland. Soundly whipped by the Scots, Charles and his army returned to London, defeated and desperate for money. Charles had no choice but to summon Parliament.

This Parliament, now in a strong political position, met on November 3, 1640, and came to be known as the Long Parliament. It continued in existence in truncated form until 1660 when it dissolved itself. Under the leadership of John Pym, this Parliament in 1641 began to act in a revolutionary manner. Parliament ordered the release of the king's political prisoners and attacked through impeachment the king's chief minister and Archbishop Laud, both of whom were eventually executed. But Parliament itself was divided into religious factions, with the Puritan faction demanding that papal residues in the Church of England be abolished "root and branch" and that the Church be transformed into a Presbyterian Church. Puritan preachers began to use apocalyptic imagery, identifying the royalist cause with the papal Antichrist, and they urged their hearers in Parliament and the army to throw down Babylon and prepare the way for the Kingdom of Christ. When 30,000 Protestants were massacred in Ulster in 1641, civil war became inevitable.

The English Civil War had begun in earnest in August 1641, and although mostly secular causes started the war, immediately Protestant millenarians began interpreting the war as the decisive apocalyptic or millenarian struggle. For the next four years Royalists battled against Parliamentarians all across England. The supporters of the king came to be known as Cavaliers from Spanish word *caballeros*, with the implication that the Royalists were somehow foreign, Spanish, and Catholic. Parliamentarians came to be known as Roundheads, since many were from the ranks of apprentices whose hair was typically cropped short. In general, Catholics supported the king while the more extremist Protestants supported the Parliamentary cause.

Initially things went badly for Pym and the Parliamentarians, and they appealed to Scotland for help. The price for Scottish support, however, was that the Church of England must be made into the Presbyterian Church. Even though this would alienate moderate Anglicans who supported Parliament, Pym had no choice but reluctantly to go along. Accordingly in September 1643, Parliament passed an act making the Church of England Presbyterian. Thereupon a Scottish army crossed the English border to join forces with Cromwell.

Cromwell led his Roundhead army of pious Puritans and Independent church men to victory over the Cavalier forces of Charles I in June 1645. The war ended in 1646, and the King became a prisoner of Parliament. But now a different conflict emerged, the conflict between the Parliamentarians and Presbyterians on one side and on the other side the Independents and extremist Protestant sects.

During the 1640s England had seen a rise in Independent churches. These churches abolished the distinction between clergy and laity so that they were nonhierarchial. They also were essentially without ritual. The Independent Churches believed that any group of Protestants should be free to meet for worship without permission from the established Church or Presbyterians or any other authority. Cromwell, brought up as a Puritan, was a deeply religious Calvinist who joined the Independents in demanding religious toleration for all Protestants and opposing any kind of Catholic-like rituals.[5]

Presbyterianism, which for a hundred years had been a revolutionary creed, now became a counter-revolutionary one. Presbyterians opposed any religious worship outside the organization of the Presbyterian Church. Anglican noblemen and High Churchmen became Presbyterians, since they were afraid that the religious toleration demanded by the sects and Independents would lead to political anarchy. As so often happens in revolutions, the moderate leaders of a movement in the early stages become alarmed at the forces which they had unleashed.

Presbyterians controlled Parliament, while Cromwell's victorious Roundhead army was made up largely of Independent or Congregational believers. Parliament wanted the army disbanded now that war over but was delaying to pay the soldiers because of financial problems. Cromwell refused to release any soldiers.

In the summer of 1647, believing that Presbyterian leaders in Parliament were organizing a military force for a coup against Independents, Cromwell ordered the army to march on London and sent officers to seize the King, who was being held prisoner by Parliament. Charles now became a prisoner of Cromwell. Cromwell tried to bargain with Charles and offered to restore Charles on the throne if he would allow religious toleration. Charles tried to play off Parliament against the army, and he refused to become either a Presbyterian or to grant religious toleration. For his part, Cromwell had to face the more extreme members of his army. Many of his soldiers demanded not only religious freedom but also political democracy. Committees of agitators formed in every regiment. These agitators pressured Cromwell to act vigorously against the King and the Presbyterian Parliament. Some of these agitators were influenced by a man named Lilburne and his followers who were known as Levellers. Levellers (and some groups that shall be mentioned below) sought political democracy and the right for all males except wage earners to vote. During October and November 1647, discussions were held between groups of agitators and Cromwell and other leaders. Cromwell and most of his officers opposed these reforms, essentially holding out for a society that had clear class distinctions between nobleman, gentleman, and yeoman, while the Levellers sought reforms that would put more political power into the hands of the small independent yeomen and farmers and craftsmen.

In November 1647, Charles escaped from Hampton Court while the leaders of the army and Parliament were debating what terms to offer. Charles fled to Carlsbrook Castle on the Isle of Wight and reopened negotiations with the Scots. In May 1648, the Second Civil War broke out as a result of negotiations between Charles, the Scots, and Presbyterian leaders in Parliament. The Scots and Parliament offered to restore Charles as king, and in return Charles agreed to establish Presbyterianism as the official established religion, with no toleration for the Independent sects. Cromwell's army and the Independents, although outnumbered, successfully regained control.

In a period of extraordinary events, the army leaders and Independents purged any Presbyterians from what remained of the Long Parliament, and the resulting truncated Parliament, with Independent and neutral members, was called the Rump Parliament. This small, unrepresentative body abolished the monarchy and resolved on Jan 1, 1649, to establish a republic and constituted itself the supreme governing body. The Rump appointed a Council of State to govern the country. Charles was beheaded on January 30, 1649. The millenarians interpreted the beheading as clearing away the last obstacle to the reign of King Jesus, and they justified the execution as God's work according to Ezekiel 21.26: ". . . take off the crown; things shall not remain as they are."[6]

Millenarianism and Religious Radicalism

The period of these unprecedented events probably represented the zenith of millenarian excitement and expectation. Earlier English history offered no parallel to the Civil War and the execution of a king. Englishmen during the 1640s and 1650s had a sense of living in a time of unprecedented political change, a time that somehow was the climax of human history. With the long Puritan tradition of interpreting political events in a millenarian sense, many of the

Puritans and Independents depicted the Civil War as a battle in which the saints themselves sought to establish Christ's Kingdom against the forces of the Antichrist. It was as a part of this larger current of millenarian excitement and expectation that the Fifth Monarchy Men came into existence.[7]

The Protestant Reformers had made the Scriptures more generally accessible and fostered the belief that the Bible spoke directly to individuals. People turned to the Bible to extract a message about their times. The Reformation had confronted Protestants with the problem of why God had allowed the Roman Church to persecute the truth for a thousand years. An interpretation of biblical prophecies suggested that the whole of history was a working out of the divine plan. The prophecies also seemed to explain the chaos following the Reformation which seemed without parallel in the history of the church. John Foxe, whose *Acts and Monuments* gave English apocalyptic ideas their greatest impetus, reinterpreted church history to show that in all ages true Christians had recognized the pope as the Antichrist.[8]

A careful reading of the Bible raises thoughts about the end of the world and describes the last days as a time of war, woe, and decay. As far back as the reign of Elizabeth, learned men, looking into the Scriptures for answers to current problems, had agreed that the world was most likely drawing to its end. Apocalyptic interpretations were given to prominent events of the times, and commentators began to claim that each political event such as the defeat of the Spanish Armada could be identified with complete confidence in the Book of Daniel and in St. John's Revelations. Thus one commentator identified the first vial of wrath, mentioned in Rev 16.2, with the venereal disease which struck the French army during the Italian wars at the end of the fifteenth century. There were similar contemporary interpretations of what the third vial of divine wrath (Rev. 16:14), namely, Elizabeth's legislation against the Jesuits or the English fleet's defeat of the Spanish Armada in 1588 or the English army's opposition to the popish Charles I in 1642. One famous pious prophet, John Napier of Merchistoun, the Scottish inventor of logarithms, reconciled for the first time all the prophetic numbers and identified all the seals, trumpets, woes, and vials. Napier concluded that Rome and her allies would fall by 1639, and that the world would end about 1688.[9]

During the early years of the seventeenth century, there was growing agreement that Christ's Second Coming was imminent. Individuals coming to the Bible with no historical sense but with high expectations to find the key to events of their own time easily found the message that Christ's Second Coming and the dissolution of all things were at hand. Interpreters pointed out that current turmoil, disputes, and destruction seemed to betoken the end of the world. Some argued that the millennium had already begun, others thought it was imminent and sought to determine the date for the end of the world and the spectacular events that would precede the end. One writer in 1597 fixed on 1666 as the date when the anti-Christian Rome would fall, a prophecy which found widespread support and even anxiety as that date approached. 1666 was popular because the number of the Beast who first had to be overthrown was 666, according to Rev 13.18. An alternative date was 1656 since this was the supposed number of years to have elapsed between Creation and the Flood.[10]

Prophets and pseudo-Messiahs had came forth at various times with dramatic public prophecies, and some of them attracted followings. In 1586 the minister Ralph Durden was imprisoned for predicting the downfall of the Tudor monarchy, which he identified as the Beast of Rev 17. He prophesied that he would lead the Jews and all the saints to rebuild Jerusalem and would defeat all the kings of the earth. He pointed to a birthmark on his thigh as final proof that he was the messianic king of Rev 19.16. Another prophet was William Hacket who claimed that God had commanded him to prepare for Christ's Second Coming. In 1590 Hacket had gone to London as a messenger of the Second Coming to proclaim to the city that Christ Jesus had come. Other figures like Traske, Farnham, and Bull had founded sects, which prompt government action kept from developing into problems. The growing number and variety of these prophecies and religious leaders suggest the widespread lay concern and preoccupation over the world's end.[11]

In 1642 Henry Archer published his *Personal Reign of Christ Upon Earth . . .*, a tract filled with millenarian details. Quoting freely from the Book of Daniel, Archer described the four pagan monarchies that had already existed: the Babylonian/Assyrian, the Mede/Persian, the Greek, and the Roman. After the downfall of the Roman monarchy, a fifth would arise, that of Christ. Then the Savior would come forth from heaven to set up his monarchy and kingdom. Christ would withdraw back to heaven again and leave to his saints the governance of his kingdom until his third coming after a thousand years, when the day of Judgment would begin and all the wicked would be destroyed. Archer, like others of his time, was very much concerned about the precise date when the Fifth Monarchy would be established. Archer confidently predicted that Christ's coming from Heaven and raising the dead and the beginning of his thousand-year kingdom would be in 1700, in about 45 or 50 years.[12]

The wave of millenarian expectation is reflected in the preaching and writing during the Civil War period. Printing presses spewed forth a flood of eschatological prophecies and tracts. The London bookseller George Thomason issued works by 112 ministers during the period of 1640-1653. About 70 percent of these works, a total of 78 books, were millenarian.[13] Presbyterian, Independent, Baptist and Puritan preachers disseminated millenarian ideas to their hearers. Thomas Goodwin's notable sermon *A Glimpse of Syons Glory*, preached in 1641, proclaimed clearly that Christ's reign would begin in 1650 and by 1695 would be completed. "God is beginning the pouring of the fifth vial, namely upon the beast . . . then comes in Jesus Christ reigning gloriously." This sermon represents the Puritan vision of a glorious millennium on earth, a vision that was a central theme in Puritanism during the course of the Puritan Revolution. When civil war broke out, many preachers joined the army as chaplains and spread millenarian views in the New Model Army and urged soldiers to destroy their enemies and establish the New Jerusalem. The most striking characteristic of the formal preaching to the Long Parliament was the millenarian tone and content. Puritan preachers who spoke before Parliament called for the zealous prosecution of the war: the millennium, the war, and the cause of God were presented as one and the same struggle. With confident energy and utopian enthusiasm preachers called on the common man to fight the Lord's battles against the Antichrist.[14]

The Civil War with its unprecedented political and social turmoil made calculations about the coming end time to be of intense concern for the general population and not just the learned and scholarly. In the highly charged atmosphere of the 1640s millennial expectations and enthusiasm existed at all levels of society. The belief that

Doomsday or the millennium would arrive "on such a day in such a week" was the common talk about London and throughout England. Many of the leading politicians and officers seem to have accepted these millenarian views. The stern Oliver Cromwell and Sir Henry Vane certainly did. Figures like Sir Walter Raleigh and John Milton spoke of Christ as "the shortly-expected King." In March 1643 Parliamentarian troops in the Wallingford area seriously considered a rumor that Christ was coming to destroy Charles I.[15]

However it was arrived at, there was a consensus in England in the middle of the seventeenth century that remarkable events were taking place or would soon take place: the fall of the Antichrist, the Second Coming and the millennium. The Puritan saints fervently believed that the predicted millennium was very close, and they explained the Civil War as its precursor. Ordinary people shared in this strong millenarian excitement and expectation that probably reached its peak in the late 1640s.[16]

Radical Groups

One other area needs to be looked at before focusing on the Fifth Monarchy Movement. During the 1640s various extremist political and religious groups and sects appeared, seeking solutions to the problems of the time. Society was changing, and a discontented common people bitterly distrusted the gentry and nobility. The financial hardships of 1620 to 1640 had only increased class antagonism. The 1640s worsened as a series of disastrous harvests followed the disruption of the civil war. There was a large surplus of casual labor. Much of the population lived very close to the poverty line if not below it. Between 1647 and 1650 food prices rose steeply and wages lagged behind. Taxes were unusually burdensome. Pym's new excise tax felt especially severe as it came on articles of popular consumption like tobacco and beer. The disastrous harvest of 1648 led to widespread hunger and unemployment, especially among disbanded soldiers. Mutinies broke out in the army when men who refused to volunteer for service in Ireland were demobilized without pay, and in May more serious revolts broke out among troops in Oxfordshire, Wiltshire, and

Buckinghamshire. The king had been tried and executed in January. Thus the economic and political situation in 1649 was explosive.[17]

The new radical groups and strange sects with descriptive names sought to create an egalitarian utopia and to restore freedom; they opposed tithes and the state church. The Levellers, for example, wanted to level society; that is, they wanted a wide extension of the franchise beyond the narrow ruling class and wanted to overthrow what was for many a holy notion, private property. The Diggers made up a smaller movement and earned their name from digging in and planting common lands in a symbolic gesture of ownership. Another group, the Quakers, earned an early reputation for their religious frenzies, but they had to disassociate themselves from the drinking, swearing, and womanizing sect called the Ranters.[18]

The Ranters, probably the most peculiar and radical sect of the Cromwell Interregnum, were an incarnation of the Hobbesian nightmare of the masses running wild in the streets. In this period of the 1640s when everything English was being questioned, overturned and revalued, the Ranters were rowdy and coarse, they joked and drank, they cursed and blasphemed. They aimed their message at the lowest level of English society, and they found a large following among London's poor, the rural poor, among landless people, among criminals and prostitutes, among rogues and thieves. Their message was essentially anarchistic: that religion was a sham and God was within; that there was no heaven nor hell, so there was no need to live as if there were.[19]

Most of these radical groups disappeared, with only a few groups like the Baptists and Quakers surviving as religious sects. But the most troublesome of all these radical groups was the Fifth Monarchy men. They fused together millenarian theology with political extremism. They interpreted political events in millenarian terms and felt they were actively engaged in a millenarian struggle. Their fusion of nationalistic hopes and apocalyptic enthusiasm and their readiness to use force attracted artisans, apprentices, and soldiers. They emerged shortly after the execution of Charles I in 1649 when the millenarian wave in England was ebbing because regicide for the socially conservative seemed a herald not of the New Jerusalem but a new Münster.[20]

Emergence of Fifth Monarchy Movement

Filled with enthusiasm and millenarian hopes, Puritan saints in 1649 were confident that the Rump Parliament would finally set up Christ's kingdom in England. The saints and various radical groups called on the Rump Parliament for drastic social reforms that would invert the social order. They wanted to transfer government from "carnal men" to godly men, that is, the saints, and to destroy altogether the national established church. They wanted to impose strict morality, reform the law, purge the clergy and abolish tithes, reduce taxes and remove the privileges of the riches. The legal system with its feudal remnants, its lack of equality, its harsh punishments did cry out for reform. Tithes still pressed heavily, and many felt it wrong to pay into a church system that was ungodly. A truly large order and revolutionary. As high as the hopes were of the Diggers and Levellers and Puritan saints in the spring of 1649, it was a terrifying time for men of property and wealth and the established clergy as they faced a revolution.[21]

But by 1651 it was beginning to appear that the Rump was no more likely than the Long Parliament had been to establish the reign of the saints, to adopt the Mosaic laws, or to remove the remnant of the State Church. Moderates and Presbyterian clergy felt that chaos and overturnings had proceeded far enough, and millenarians perceived that the Rump was not a gathering of saints but a cautious, worldly body. Activist millenarians like John Canne, John Spittlehouse, Peter Chamberlen, and John Rogers turned to their last hope for the establishment of Christ's Kingdom: Cromwell. 1651 seems to have been the year when the Fifth Monarchy was set up as a pressure group to campaign in favor of millenarian ideas that political leaders were abandoning. Christopher Feake, John Simpson, and several Independent and Baptist ministers as well as men from the army visited Cromwell to urge him to do something for Christ's cause, but after several meetings with Cromwell, they realized that Cromwell's vision of the future differed from theirs. Accordingly they began to see themselves as the only remaining instrument loyal to Christ. At the end of 1651 they inaugurated regular meetings at All Hallows the Great, Thames Street, where they agreed on a six-point program.[22]

The chief objectives of their plan were: to have regular meetings to pray and preach against the government as an obstacle to Christ's kingdom, to seek the removal of ungodly magistrates and ministers, to further Christ's Kingdom at home and abroad. At a meeting at Fleetwood's lodgings in Somerset House, these Fifth Monarchy ideas were presented to some of the leaders of government and army and leading Independent churchmen like Owen, Thomas Goodwin, Philip Nye, and Sidrach Simpson, all of whom responded with hostility. Feake and other Fifth Monarchists, however, began again and called supporters to London House and later to Blackfriars, probably at St. Anne's where Feake held a lectureship. The Fifth Monarchy meetings continued, with the saints reviling the Rump and even demanding a religious crusade abroad, namely the Dutch war.[23]

The disillusionment of the saints grew as the Rump and Cromwell failed to inaugurate a new era, and the saints began to feel an urgency to act for themselves. Unless they formed their own active organization to remove the apostate regime by propaganda or even violence, the saints realized, the millennium would not arrive. The Fifth Monarchy movement thus emerged as a reaction to fading, not rising millenarian expectations. In many ways it was a desperate attempt to realize whatever was possible from the millenarian hopes of the 1640s. Their willingness to justify violence marked the key difference between the Fifth Monarchy Men and earlier English millenarians like John Foxe, Napier, Brightman, Alsted, and Mede. While holding on to earlier apocalyptic ideas like the concept of England as an elect nation, the Fifth Monarchy vision gave emphasis to the destruction of kings and rich merchants, of seas of blood and torments of fire and brimstone.[24]

The Fifth Monarchist Men developed into a political and religious sect that expected the imminent Kingdom of Christ on earth, a theocratic regime in which they would establish a godly discipline over the unregenerate masses to prepare for the Second Coming. Fifth Monarchists expected King Jesus to directly intervene in English politics to bring about the effects which various political groups and methods failed to accomplish. Although the Fifth Monarchy Men had some political objectives in common with the Diggers, Ranters, and Quakers (such as abolishing class distinctions, abolition of tithes and a state church, and reform of the law), they differed profoundly in their ideology and in the means that they advocated to achieve these ends. Millenarianism formed the core of their ideology, and they claimed it as their duty to take up arms to overthrow any obstacles to the establishment of Christ's Kingdom. The Fifth Monarchists, mostly preachers, soldiers, and members of the urban lower classes, were eager to resort to political action and violence, if necessary, to attain the millennium. They firmly embraced the belief that God would use human instruments to established his kingdom on earth. A characteristic objective, for example, as expressed by some soldiers and junior officers, mostly sectarians of humble origins, was the destruction of Antichrist and the advancement of the Kingdom of Jesus Christ. Their contemporaries began to view them as dangerous, violent revolutionaries who hid behind the appearance of saintliness.[25]

The Fifth Monarchist's active vision differed from the rather passive ideas of earlier English millenarians. The Fifth Monarchists believed that the saints themselves must clear the way for the millennium and not leave this to God alone. The Fifth Monarchy petition, the *Certain Quaeres*, was published on the 19th of February 1649 and expressed the hope that the army would never be anything but God's instrument for bringing about the Kingdom. Fifth Monarchists perceived England as the first of God's nations and his unique instrument for carrying the godly revolution to all lands. Wars were to be millenarian crusades, and the Dutch War of 1652-4 was viewed in this perspective. In other pamphlets and declarations they described the political, social, and economic structure that they expected when the millennium came. The millenarian rule of the Saints was to be marked by the abolition of tithes, the reestablishment of the Mosaic laws and a rigid moral code, the raising of the humble, and the pulling down of the great. The Fifth Monarchists's elitist belief in the rule of the elect over the ungodly differed from the egalitarian tendencies of the Levellers and other disappointed radicals.[26]

Leadership

No one individual consistently exerted leadership in the Fifth Monarchy Movement. The Movement initially attracted a number of men who were close to Cromwell. Cromwell himself had been sympathetic to Fifth Monarchist ideas until about 1653. His sometime deputy, Major-General Harrison was an enthusiastic supporter and continued to be so for several years. Harrison, an implacable foe of royalist cause had come from a middle-class family in Newcastle-under-Lyme, Staffordshire. He rose to the rank of colonel in the army by 1645. Harrison early converted to the ideas of English millenarians and was one of the army leaders who brought Charles to Windsor Castle, and he wanted to execute the king as a way of preparing for the millennium and the rule of saints. Harrison was the most prominent of Fifth Monarchy men but not the leader.[27]

Another prominent Fifth Monarchist who had Cromwell's ear was John Rogers. Born in 1627 at Messing in Essex, son of a parish vicar, young John was converted to religion at ten years of age by listening to scary Puritan sermons that threatened hell-fire and damnation. Rogers may also have had psychological problems, as he had raging fits for which he was bound hand and foot until the attack was over. After a period of hardship, he had a mysterious dream which he took as a revelation. He began to preach in Huntingdonshire and by 1647 was able to return to his native Essex as Presbyterian minister of Purleigh. He decided to come to London, dropped his Presbyterian affiliation, and accepted the position as preacher at the Independent church of St. Thomas Apostle in London. After his break with Cromwell, Rogers' eloquence and persistence made him one of the prominent Fifth Monarchy men.[28]

Another prominent figure in the Movement was Christopher Feake, a well educated minister who had begun to publish his millenarian views in 1649. He was minister of Christ Church at Newgate, a lecturer at St. Anne's, Blackfriars, and head of the gathered church in Swan Alley and Warwick Lane. He was probably the most important Fifth Monarchy leader in London during the most active decade of the Fifth Monarchy Men and was very active in their formative meetings in 1651.[29]

John Spencer was a Baptist and a Fifth Monarchist minister who attained the rank of Major in the Parliamentarian army. From 1652 onward he was a prominent Fifth Monarchist but after being jailed by the government began to moderate his views and resist violence. He appears to have had some mental instability and began to lose influence with the saints. Captain John Spencer was a Baptist preacher who wrote a millenarian defense of the civil war early in the 1640s. He was among the early Fifth Monarchy Men but, unlike others, did not split with Cromwell during the Protectorate. John Spittlehouse served in the army during this turbulent period but finally seems to have been dismissed for his activities as Fifth Monarchist. A capable writer, he published some of the Fifth Monarchy tracts. Vavasor Powell was a chaplain in the Parliamentarian army and had a major influence on Harrison becoming a millenarian and Fifth Monarchist. Powell was a supporter of the Barebones Parliament and became a fierce critic of Cromwell and the Protectorate.[30]

Barebones Parliament

In 1651 Fifth Monarchy Men and discontented officers in the army began to attack the Rump Parliament because of its sterile debates and posturings. By the spring of 1653 these attacks on the government had reached such a level that they could not be ignored. These attacks by means of pamphlet, sermon, and tract brought notoriety to the Fifth Monarchists and further discredited the Rump, already unpopular. Harrison and believers like him had become disillusioned with the government and urged Cromwell to inaugurate a new regime in which government would be carried on exclusively by men chosen for their moral and religious qualifications. Cromwell, like the army as a whole, was impatient with the posturings of the Rump ministers and did not see the Rump accomplishing any reforms.

Cromwell was in a difficult position. He did not want to embrace the extremist positions of Feake and other Fifth Monarchists, but he was still a millenarian and had theological ideas similar to many Fifth Monarchists. Influenced by Fifth Monarchy ideas, Cromwell decided to see if government by the saints was possible. He decided to replace the Rump and he acted suddenly. On April 20, 1653, Cromwell staged a coup by having Harrison bring in soldiers under Lt-Col. Worsley to dissolve the Rump by force.[31]

Cromwell, pressured by Fifth Monarchist advice from Harrison, Rogers and others, adopted a plan for a Parliament of Saints, based on the model of the Jewish Sanhedrin. Many Fifth Monarchists, such as Rogers, Spittlehouse and Aspinwall were so convinced that Cromwell was the instrument of God that they were ready to grant him absolute powers and hailed him as the latter-day Moses. Amidst the euphoria of the saints between April and July 1653, only Feake and his church, whom Cromwell tried to silence, retained their suspicion of Cromwell.

The Parliament of Saints first assembled on July 4, 1653, amid the enthusiasm of many Fifth Monarchists that the long-awaited reign of saints was finally to begin. From the beginning of the Puritan Revolution, Independent divines and radicals had preached their eschatological sermons, and now the Puritan millenarianism was to be triumphantly embodied. Cromwell himself, in his opening address before handing over power, believed that England was now on the verge of a new and auspicious era. This so-called Barebones Parliament, after Praise-God Barbone, a member who was a leather-seller but better known as a lay preacher, consisted of men chosen by Cromwell and his officers. It ranged from the future Earls of Sandwich and Shaftesbury to a group of twelve Fifth Monarchists among whom was Major-General Harrison who had been the violent critic of the Rump and had sponsored several men who became leading Fifth Monarchists.[32]

Members of Barebones wanted to make England the New Jerusalem, and various Fifth Monarchists published books and pamphlets in confident expectation that the beginning of Christ's Kingdom was now at hand. William Aspinwall's pamphlet on the seventh chapter of Daniel traced the downfall of the four monarchies and tried to prove that Charles I was the little horn and Cromwell was the choice instrument of God to execute the biblical judgement on the little horn. John Spittlehouse, another prolific Fifth Monarchist pamphleteer, expressed his conviction as to how near at hand the millennium was. In his tract of July 5, 1653, Spittlehouse hoped that the Lord would lead Cromwell over the Jordan into the land of the Canaanites, that is, over the narrow seas to Holland and France and Rome, so that he could crush the anti-Christian powers who opposed Jesus Christ.[33]

The Barebones Parliament, however, quickly disappointed everyone, because no clear majority was able to emerge, in spite of a large number of members with a radical outlook. The total membership was 144. Among the twelve Fifth Monarchists were Harrison and the regicide John Carew; of the twelve, six were justices of the peace, two had been sheriffs and nine held army or militia commissions. These Fifth Monarchists caucused among themselves, consulted with the Blackfriars preachers and in general acted together as a group. They were able to play a significant role in two important proposals that they felt were necessary steps to prepare the way for the millennium and which also were objectives for other radicals. These two measures concerned a massive reform of the law and the abolition of the remnants of the state church.[34]

But other members of Parliament could not accept the extremism of these radical proposals which, if implemented, would be an attack on property (by destroying tithes and ecclesiastical patronage) and on order itself (by destroying the law). These deep divisions among the members prevented Parliament from acting. Thus the Mosaic law did not become English law, and the two key resolutions that millenarians hoped for did not get implemented. All groups were dissatisfied, and Fifth Monarchy Men both in and outside Parliament were discontented and disillusioned. In the autumn of 1653, Harrison and other Fifth Monarchists were suspected of plotting disruptions. At Blackfriars on November 28 Feake and his colleagues attacked Cromwell as the man of sin and the old dragon. Chamberlen and Spittlehouse, who had previously admired and supported Cromwell, turned violently against him and finally were arrested for sedition. When a moderate bill to reshape the Church while preserving tithes was defeated, the conservatives and moderates, confusing the small group of Fifth Monarchists with a larger group of radicals, felt they could not control Parliament. They called on Cromwell and resigned their power on December 12, 1653. Cromwell sent soldiers into Parliament and expelled Harrison and any other radical members still present. Cromwell took the reins of power into his own hands and set up the Protectorate. The new regime abandoned all radical reforms and any preparation for the millennium.[35]

The fall of the Barebones Parliament caused dismay among the extremist Fifth Monarchists and irrevocably split them, not only from the government and Cromwell but also from other radicals and millenarians. General and Particular Baptists and Independents, for example, all accepted the Protectorate and urged their followers to wait patiently and passively for God to bring in the millennium. Fifth Monarchy Men, on the other hand, ferociously opposed the government and Cromwell; indeed, they saw Cromwell as an apostate and his government as part of the Anti-christian Fourth Monarchy. The Fifth Monarchist conviction that it was their duty to act as God's instruments in preparing for God's Kingdom could only alienate other millenarians who were afraid of anarchy or revolution.[36]

The government reacted quickly to the Fifth Monarchist dismay at the fall of Barebones. The government, worried about maintaining order, first focused on the army, since there was a possibility of an army mutiny led by Fifth Monarchist officers. The regiments most likely to be disloyal were those of Fifth Monarchists like Harrison, Overton, and Rich. Within a few days of the fall of Barebones Harrison was relieved of his commission and eventually arrested. Major General Overton promised not to act against the government. Major Wigan and others like Rich either resigned from the army or were removed from command.

But it was the London preachers Feake and Powell who reacted most violently to Cromwell's coup and were the loudest in protest. Feake turned his apocalyptic imagery against Cromwell and implied that the little horn in Daniel 7.8 was not Charles I but rather Cromwell. Powell prophesied the imminent fall of Cromwell's government. Simpson announced a vision that Cromwell would soon fall. On the following day, the government arrested all three and banned all meetings at Blackfriars. Feake and Simpson were moved to the prison at Windsor where they proved to be troublesome. They tried to continue to lead the opposition movement from there. Jailers had to beat drums to drown out Feake's efforts to preach through his jail window.[37]

With the main critics of the government in jail or silenced, lesser figures carried on attacks against Cromwell's government through sermons and pamphlets and visions. But none of this shook the government, which claimed that it was arresting people like Feake and Rogers not for religious reasons but for sedition and political activities. By the end of 1654 the government's actions had consider-

England's Fifth Monarchy Men

ably set back the Fifth Monarchy Movement. The leading critics were substantially silenced, and worrisome army leaders who might have subverted the government's control over the army had been removed.

The government's next concern was to prevent a conspiracy among the different radical groups. During 1654 and 1655 there were rumors of a massive conspiracy of the Levellers, Commonwealthsmen, Royalists, and Fifth Monarchists. In February 1655, an informer told the government that Harrison, Feake, and Rogers were involved in a plot. When Cromwell summoned a Fifth Monarchist delegation to answer this charge of plotting sedition, the saints ignored the summons on the grounds that an illegal government had no authority to issue orders, but they were finally brought before Cromwell. They argued that arms indeed could be taken up against the government. The government imprisoned Harrison, Carew, and others. The government energetically circulated propaganda to counter the pamphlets and tracts of John Sturgeon and John Spittlehouse which attacked Cromwell. By arrests and confinement the government removed the leading saints from a means to propaganda and sow further discord. Crowds of 250 to 500 assembled but the removal of the ablest leaders and the failure of the saints' expectations sapped enthusiasm. On December 3, 1655 there was a mass meeting of 500 at All Hallows and there were arrests. During the winter of 1655-1656 the Fifth Monarchy Men held secret meetings in London and arranged to have contact with other groups and sects. There seems to have been discontent throughout the country, but in spite of rumors of all sorts of plots and conspiracies, nothing much actually happened.[38]

Venner's Plots

More plots were hatched than actual insurrections. For example, members of a group called the Commonwealthsmen met with a group of Fifth Monarchy Men that included Thomas Venner, Arthur Squibb, and John Portman, a former high navy official, but the government arrested these plotters in the summer of 1656. Fifth Monarchy Men, nevertheless, continued their efforts at plots and printed attacks. Fifth Monarchy Men, by 1657, organized a national network, with contacts all around the country. In London, Thomas Venner and his followers had created a secret network with five groups of 25 men and they began to plan physical violence against the government. But internal divisions between moderates and militants were weakening the movement.

A small group of militant saints in Venner's congregation continued with plans for an armed uprising. But leading saints such as Harrison, Rich, and John Rogers refused to have anything to do with the plotters, being unwilling to stir up violence unless providence clearly showed that this was God's will. Despite this disagreement and friction within the movement, Venner's men gathered weapons, maps, and telescopes, produced a manifesto called *A Standard Set Up*, and planned to assemble in Shoreditch and march to East Anglia, where they expected more enthusiastic support. But the government had learned of the insurgents two or three hours prior to the uprising. On April 9, 1657, at about 7 PM at Whitehall a troop of government horsemen captured and arrested about 25 men who were assembling, with arms and ammunition. Also seized was a declaration in which the plotters set forth a new government. They proclaimed that they were encouraged by the "wonderful, undeniable signs of the times," that they were motivated by the "love of Christ," and that they were acting under "the Standard of our Lord, King Jesus."[39]

Their manifesto declared that it was an honor for them "to girt on a sword for Christ . . . [&] to become soldiers in the Lambs Army . . . to destroy the Beast and Whore. . . ."[40] Harrison and Rich were arrested again, but it was soon clear that they had not been involved. Venner and two of his lieutenants were kept in the Tower until 1659 with the other plotters being released.[41]

The dismal failure of this episode and the apparent likelihood that the monarchy would be reestablished in the person of King Cromwell rather than King Jesus caused further discouragement and uncertainty among Fifth Monarchists. Many dropped away from the movement, convinced that there would be no millennium or that it would be established elsewhere or that it was still in the far distant future because none of vials of wrath were yet poured out. A few Fifth Monarchists stubbornly clung to hope by re-interpreting and re-calculating dates in the Book of Revelations, calculations many previous millenarians had to make when the expected day of wrath did not arrive. The remainder of 1657 passed without great commotion in heaven or on earth and Fifth Monarchist Men remained inactive and the movement seemed in eclipse.

The death of Oliver Cromwell in September 1658, temporarily revived the hopes of Fifth Monarchy Men and other dissident groups. Cromwell's son Richard succeeded him as the new Protector, but he lacked his father's power and effectiveness. Several prominent Fifth Monarchy Men like Overton, Courtney, and Portman were released from prison, and Fifth Monarchist men agitated during this turbulent period but the English revolution was unraveling. The saints's vociferous demands for political, social, and religious revolution brought discredit to any republican governments which tried to accommodate them. Their machinations, along with rumors of imminent massacres and conspiracies, helped bring about the general belief by 1659 that there could be no order until the king returned. In April 1659, army leaders forced Richard Cromwell to dissolve Parliament and the Protectorate collapsed.[42]

The Rump reassembled in December 1659, but few believed it could provide a permanent government. By February 1660, General Monk had marched down from Scotland and recalled the Long Parliament. When Presbyterians who had been excluded from the Long Parliament in 1648 were recalled for the February reassembly, the Restoration became inevitable. The members of the reassembled Parliament voted for the return of Charles Stuart as the only way to secure a settlement. Fifth Monarchists like Rich and Overton tried to organize resistance to Monk, but their efforts were in vain.

Charles II entered London in May 1660, a day of gloom for Fifth Monarchy Men. Their millenarian hopes had been created and sustained by the extraordinary events of the previous twenty years, and all now seemed to come to an end. Many Fifth Monarchy Men seem to have moved towards quietism and were re-absorbed gradually into the ranks of the Baptists and Congregationalists. But one small group still persisted in plotting. They gathered around Thomas Venner. In January 1661, he led about 50 followers through the streets of London in one more attempt to set up God's Kingdom by force.

Contemporary accounts describe the suppression of the rebels by government forces. These accounts refer to the Fifth Monarchy Men as "rebells" and "traytors" and "phannatick parties." Samuel Pepys in his diary under 9 and 10 January, 1661, refers to the commotion and the "Fanatiques" in the city.[43] Government troops killed 26 of the saints and captured another 20. Venner received 19 wounds before he was captured. The government tried Venner within two weeks. He was drawn and quartered on January 19, two days after the trial. A dozen others were executed, and their heads were put on London Bridge. Even though the Fifth Monarchy Men were implicated in plots for the next three or four years, they all led to nothing.[44]

The Decline of the Fifth Monarchy

After the Restoration of the monarchy in 1660 the Fifth Monarchy lingered as a fading movement over the next quarter of a century. Little in English social and political events encouraged the hopes of Fifth Monarchy members. Some members on the fringe of the movement seem to have turned towards groups like the Quakers. Nevertheless, millenarians had to explain why their expectations of Christ's Coming had not been fulfilled, and some Fifth Monarchists suggested that the sins and apostasy of Englishmen had forced God to turn away in horror. The Great Plague and Great Fire of 1665-6, a few thought, could be interpreted as divine retribution for the sins of the nation.

Harrison and Carew were eventually arrested and executed as regicides, and several important leaders, such as Rich, Overton, Portman, and Powell, were imprisoned. Rogers and Feake still occupied pulpits but tried to avoid notice. Tillam of Colchester and Pooley of North Walsham, despairing of England, led a group to the Palatinate to await the millennium there. They adopted all the religious rites of the Jews and hoped to rebuild the temple.[45]

Conclusion

The Fifth Monarchy was a heterogeneous movement, with membership roughly falling into three distinct groups. First, there were a number of army officers, some from the gentry and some risen from the ranks. Second, there were a number of clergy, some from the universities, many having connections with the army. These first two groups were small in number but produced most of the pamphlets and provided what leadership there was. Although all the members of the Fifth Monarchy expected the imminence of the millennium, the first two groups often disagreed with the mass of members. The leaders tended to falter at key moments with regard to using violence and anarchy in seeking to establish Christ's kingdom, although they did articulate attacks on the rich, the covetous, and the great merchants.[46]

The third group was numerically the largest and came mostly from the lower class of society, many of whom dwelt in social and economic insecurity. Contemporaries described the saints as "the worst of men, the Scum, and very froth of baseness . . . the very raf of Billingsgate . . . a company of illiterate men, and silly women . . . poor, obscure, illiterate."[47] In short, most of the Fifth Monarchy members were in occupations with a high level of insecurity; many were young male apprentices who, because they had little to lose, were prone to militancy. Indeed, the Fifth Monarchy's vision of the millennium, calling for a social revolution and the confiscation of the lands of the ungodly, attracted those with the most to gain.

The actual number of Fifth Monarchists was difficult to gauge. The saints wished to impress and their enemies were alarmist, so both give inflated figures. The foremost Fifth Monarchist scholar, however, finds it reasonable to conclude that their number never exceeded 10,000.[48] In terms of a national movement, 10,000 is not a large number and is probably in line with other movements like the Levelers and Commonwealthsmen.

The Fifth Monarchy Movement had appeared at a time of intense upheaval, flux and excitement. The 1640s and '50s were an especially tumultuous time, a time of great overturning, questioning, revaluing of everything in England. Reform was much needed in the legal, political, economic, and religious spheres. In addition to Parliament's struggle against the king and the disruption of the civil war there was significant financial hardship for the common people and a series of disastrous harvests. These years witnessed an enormous popular upheaval, a florescence of radical ideas of all kinds, a fantastic outburst of energy. For a short time ordinary people were freer from the authority of church and social superiors than they had ever been before. The shakeup of the civil wars increased social mobility and allowed for the emergence of various radical groups in a burst of exhilaration and energy. Various groups of common people attempted to impose political and social solutions to problems of their times. Groups like the Levellers, Diggers, and Fifth Monarchists and the various sects such as Baptists, Quakers, and Muggletonians emerged. Some groups like the Baptists and Quakers survive as religious sects but most of others disappear.[49]

For a while anything seemed possible, and only gradually was control re-established during the Protectorate of Cromwell which lead to the restoration of the rule of the gentry and the king in 1660. The revolutionary decades had been a period of intense strain, but England, to the relief of some and the disillusionment of others, returned to the old familiar forms. England and its king, bishops and social system survived. The English experiment in republican democracy was tried and failed.[50]

By its very nature, the Fifth Monarchy movement could only be a minority movement and ultimately a failure. They were part of the pervasive millenarianism of an age in which people took the Bible seriously. Differing interpretations of the Bible offered a multitude of possibilities as to the nature of the millennium, and the saints selected those possibilities which were in accord with their own aspirations, just as other millenarians were equally selective. Many political actions took place against a background of millenarian thinking, and it was not always easy to differentiate between political and religious issues. However, not only did Christ's Kingdom fail to materialize, but the revolutionary political, social, and economic implications of the Fifth Monarchy views alienated almost all the gentry, merchants and mainline clergy. As primarily an artisan movement the Fifth Monarchy were effectively cut off from genuine power. As an elitist movement of extreme religious zeal, they could only hope to attract a minority even from the lower social classes.[51]

It was not the economic crises alone which produced the pervasive millenarian wave of the 1640s. Rather the millenarianism of the period sprang from broad political and religious upheavals. A rather full record of sermons, pamphlets, and other writings provide a pretty full record of what people thought and discussed. They speculated about the end of the world and the coming of the millennium. They found new sects to express these new ideas. The Fifth Monarchy movement only came at the end of this millenarian wave. The Fifth Monarchy was not the zenith of Puritan millenarianism, but rather a desperate attempt in the 1650s to revive an impulse that was already wasting away. Revolutions cannot be perpetuated for very long—it was as if the energy were somehow spent. After 1653 the evidence from the period shows the decrease in sermons on eschatological themes from Independent ministers, with only the Fifth Monarchy preachers fanning the millenarian flame. Ultimately they too lost the millenarian excitement, and the flame flickered but did not die out, as Puritan traditions at least continued into the next century.[52]

Perhaps the Fifth Monarchists used rhetoric that was overheated, but many of their social and political aspirations were very worthwhile. Their political skills did not match their aspirations, however, and they were frustrated with the compromises demanded by democratic processes. In comparison with continental millenarian movements, the Fifth Monarchy movement was more diffuse and lacking in the kind of charismatic leadership that could mobilize the membership to uninhibited feats of arms. The Fifth Monarchy Men did not manifest the excesses of the Münsterites, nor were they so alien from their own social institutions. Under the threats of the Fifth Monarchy the English social order bent but did not give way. While Feake and Rogers were gifted preachers, they were not military men. The military men, in turn, lacked charismatic leadership abilities. Ultimately the Fifth Monarchy Men did not have a great impact on English society and faded from English history. But millenarian concerns did not leave England.

NOTES

1. B.S. Capp, *The Fifth Monarchy Men: A Study in Seventeenth-century English Millenarianism* (London: Faber and Faber, 1972), p. 228. Hereafter, *The Fifth Monarchy Men*. I have relied heavily on Capp, the single most reliable expert on the Fifth Monarchy Movement. Capp seems to have an encyclopedic knowledge of the innumerable tracts and pamphlets from this period.

2. Irvin Buckwalter Horst, *The Radical Brethren: Anabaptism and the English Reformation to 1588* (Niewkoop: B. De Graaf, 1972), pp. 77-79).

3. Cited by B.S. Capp, *The Fifth Monarchy Men*, p. 14. Cf. also William M. Lamont, "Puritanism as History and Historiography," *Past and Present* 44 (1969): 145.

4. B.S. Capp, "Extreme Millenarianism," in Peter Toon, editor, *Puritans, the Millennium and the Future of Israel: Puritan Eschatology 1600 to 1660* (Cambridge: James Clark & Co., 1970), p. 66. This article (pp. 66-90) is a succinct summary of the movement. Cf. Alfred Cohen, "Prophecy and Madness: Women Visionaries During the Puritan Revolution," *Journal of Psychohistory* 11 (1984): 411-430.

5. Jasper Ridley, *The History of England* (Routledge & Kegan Paul, 1981), pp. 169-175; cf. Christopher Hill, *The World Turned Upside Down* (London, 1972), p. 80. See also Tai Liu, *Puritan London: A Study of Religion and Society in the City Parishes* (Newark: University of Delaware Press, 1986); William M. Lamont, *Godly Rule: Politics and Religion 1603-1660* (London, 1969); Paul Christianson, *Reformers and Babylon: English Apocalyptic Visions from the Reformation to the Eve of the Civil War* (University of Toronto Press, 1978); Katherine R. Firth, *The Apocalyptic Tradition in Reformation Britain 1530-1645* (Oxford University Press, 1979).

6. Jasper Ridley, pp. 176-184; P. G. Rogers, *The Fifth Monarchy Men* (London: Oxford University Press, 1966), pp. 14-18; cf. B.S. Capp, "Extreme Millenarianism," p. 50.

7. Keith Thomas, *Religion and the Decline of Magic* (New York: Charles Scribner's Sons, 1971), p. 143.

8. John Foxe, *The Acts and Monuments*, edited by J. Pratt (1877); Christopher Hill, pp. 74-76; B.S. Capp, *The Fifth Monarchy Men*, p. 25; cf. Katherine R. Firth, *The Apocalyptic Tradition in Reformation Britain 1530-1645* (Oxford: Oxford University Press, 1979).

9. B.S. Capp, *The Fifth Monarchy Men*, pp. 26-27; B.S. Capp. "Extreme Millenarianism," p. 77; Peter Toon, "The Later-Day Glory," in Peter Toon, editor, *Puritans, the*

Millennium and the Future of Israel: Puritan Eschatology 1600 to 1660 (Cambridge: James Clark & Co., 1970), p. 25.

10. Keith Thomas, p. 141; cf. Robert G. Clouse, "Johann Heinrich Alsted and English Millennialism," *Harvard Theological Review* 62 (1969): 189-207.

11. B.S. Capp, *The Fifth Monarchy Men*, pp. 29-32; Keith Thomas, p. 144; P.G. Rogers, p. 11.

12. Cf. P.G. Rogers, pp. 8-13.

13. B.S. Capp, p. 38; Keith Thomas, p. 142.

14. John F. Wilson, *Pulpit in Parliament: Puritanism during the English Civil Wars, 1640-1648* (Princeton, N.J.: Princeton University Press, 1969), p. 195; Tai Liu *Discord in Zion: The Puritan Divines and the Puritan Revolution 1640-1660* (The Hague: Martinus Nijhoff, 1973), pp. 1-3; an excerpt from Thomas Goodwin's sermon, "A Glimpse of Syons Glory" is quoted by Lowell H. Zuck, *Christianity and Revolution: Radical Christian Testimonies 1520-1650* (Philadelphia: Temple University Press, 1975), pp. 214-221.

15. B.S. Capp, *The Fifth Monarchy Men*, pp. 40, 43; Keith Thomas, p. 142; Christopher Hill, p. 77.

16. Christopher Hill, p. 77.

17. Christopher Hill, pp. 17, 32-3, 86-87.

18. Chyrsostom Kim, "The Diggers, the Ranters and the Early Quakers," *The American Benedictine Review* 25 (1974): 461-465.

19. Jerome Friedman, *Blasphemy, Immorality, and Anarchy: The Ranters and the English Revolution* (Athens, Ohio: Ohio University Press, 1987), p. xi.

20. B.S. Capp, *The Fifth Monarchy Men*, pp. 35, 37, 45, 228; B.S. Capp, "Extreme Millenarianism," p. 66.

21. B.S. Capp, *The Fifth Monarchy Men*, pp. 55-56; Christopher Hill, p. 88; P.G. Rogers, p. 29.

22. B.S. Capp, "Extreme Millenarianism," p.79; B.S. Capp, *The Fifth Monarchy Men*, p. 59. A number of publications from the civil war period record the beginnings of the Fifth Monarchist Movement, among them C. Feake, *A Beam of Light* (1659), pp. 39-45; and W. Erbery, *The Bishop of London* (1653).

23. B. S. Capp, "Extreme Millenarianism," p. 79; B.S. Capp, *The Fifth Monarchy Men*, p. 59.

24. B.S. Capp, *The Fifth Monarchy Men*, p. 58; Christopher Hill, p. 77; Keith Thomas, p. 143; B.S. Capp, "Extreme Millenarianism," p. 77.

25. B.S. Capp, *The Fifth Monarchy Men*, p. 14; Keith Thomas, p. 142; Christopher Hill, p. 58; B.S. Capp, "Extreme Millenarianism," p. 78.

26. B.S. Capp, "Extreme Millenarianism," p. 68, 78; B.S. Capp, *The Fifth Monarchy Men*, pp. 52-54, 90, 230.

27. P.G. Rogers, pp. 15, 17; B.S. Capp, *The Fifth Monarchy Men*, p. 251.

28. P.G. Rogers, pp. 22-23.

29. B.S. Capp, *The Fifth Monarchy Men*, pp. 58, 248-9.

30. B.S. Capp, *The Fifth Monarchy Men*, pp. 259, 262, 263.

31. P.G. Rogers, pp. 27, 19; Austin Woolrych, *Commonwealth to Protectorate* (Oxford: Clarendon Press, 1982), p. 103.

32. Tai Liu, *Discord in Zion*, p. 86; Austin Woolrych, p. 166; P.G. Rogers, p. 24; B.S. Capp, *The Fifth Monarchy Men*, pp. 61, 64; B.S. Capp, "Extreme Millenarianism," p. 80.

33. P.G. Rogers, pp. 24, 28, 29.

34. Cf. Austin Woolrych, pp. 165-233 on the make-up of Parlement and members' differences; B.S. Capp, *The Fifth Monarchy Men*, pp. 68-70.

35. B.S. Capp, "Extreme Millenarianism," pp. 81, 88; B.S. Capp, *The Fifth Monarchy Men*, pp. 73-75.

36. B.S. Capp, "Extreme Millenarianism," p. 81.

37. B.S. Capp, *The Fifth Monarchy Men*, pp. 99-105, 108; B.S. Capp, "Extreme Millenarianism," p. 82.

38. B.S. Capp, *The Fifth Monarchy Men*, pp. 102-105.

39. Champlin Burrage, "The Fifth Monarchy Insurrections," *English Historical Review* 25 (1910): 740.

40. *A Door of Hope. Or, A Call and Declaration for the gathering together of the first ripe Fruits unto the Standard of our Lord, King Jesus* (London, 1660-1), p. 16, cited by Champlin Burrage, p. 740.

41. Champlin Burrage, p. 724; B.S. Capp, "Extreme Millenarianism," pp. 83-84, 88.

42. B.S. Capp, "Extreme Millenarianism," p. 84; B.S. Capp, *The Fifth Monarchy Men*, p. 130.

43. Champlin Burrage, pp. 741-744.

44. B.S. Capp, *The Fifth Monarchy Men*, pp. 118; B.S. Capp, "Extreme Millenarianism," p. 88.

45. B.S. Capp, "Extreme Millenarianism," pp. 83, 88.

46. B.S. Capp, *The Fifth Monarchy Men*, pp. 135, 231.

47. Cf. B.S. Capp, *The Fifth Monarchy Men*, pp. 82, 86.

48. B.S. Capp, *The Fifth Monarchy Men*, pp. 81-82.

49. Christopher Hill, pp. 11-12, 17, 32-33, 68-69, 86-88.

50. Christopher Hill, pp. 11-12, 57.

51. B.S. Capp, "Extreme Millenarianism," p. 89.

52. Peter Toon, "Conclusion," in Peter Toon, editor, *Puritans, the Millennium and the Future of Israel: Puritan Eschatology 1600 to 1660* (Cambridge: James Clark & Co., 1970), p. 128; Christopher Hill, p. 292; for the persistence of Puritan millenarian traditions, cf. William M. Lamont, "Puritanism as History and Historiography: Some Further Thoughts," *Past and Present* 44 (1969): 132-146, and William M. Lamont, "Richard Baxter, The Apocalypse and the Mad Major," *Past and Present* 55 (1969): 68-90.

Chapter Eight
France from the Seventeenth to the Nineteenth Century

The millenarian impulse did not slacken in France, but millenarian ideas episodically provided for believers a seemingly rational explanation of events in periods of social and political ferment. During the seventeenth and eighteenth centuries millenarianism was part of the general religious excitement, and several currents of millennial faith are discernable. The lesser current, more characteristic of England, was the scholarly, respectable study of biblical prophecy by learned individuals who sought to puzzle out the signs and date of the world's end. The other current of millenarianism, more common in France, was a popular and prophetic millenarianism that stressed the coming of a new age and the return of Christ. French millenarianism tended to derive from a wider variety of sources, such as popular piety and popular prophecy. A precise division, however, between these two currents, one more scholarly, the other more popular and prophetic, is not always possible. What is noteworthy is the way the prophetic millenarianism of France was exported to England and revitalized English millenarianism.

Several millenarian movements existed in France, differing from each other in geographical location, social level, and style. This chapter will first consider the Camisards and then turn to several other groups that would flourished around the time of the Revolution and after.

France's Camisards or the "French Prophets"

When Reformation ideas entered France, the peasants of the Cévennes, a mountainous region in northern Languedoc embraced Protestantism deeply and made it an encompassing part of their everyday life. These Protestants, known as Huguenots, sought from the Catholic King of France tolerance for their Protestant culture and religious practices. After considerable hostility and violence, in 1598, the Edict of Nantes granted these Huguenots religious liberty and legal equality. After 1660, however, King Louis XIV renewed the religious persecution of the Huguenots. By 1681 royal troops were quartered in Huguenot homes and were encouraged to harass the people. They boarded up Huguenot schools and pulled churches down. The King revoked the Edict of Nantes in October 1685. Despite harassment, surveillance, and persecution by Catholic authorities, Huguenots attempted to preserve their religious tradition, a tradition that began to include millenarian and even fanatical elements.[1]

In Languedoc and neighboring Dauphiné arose lay preachers who gathered the Huguenot faithful in illicit assemblies for a simple service of psalms, scriptural exegesis, and a sermon. Deprived of trained Protestant ministers and tormented by guilt for having accepted the Revocation and the temporary repudiation of their faith, these Huguenots of southeastern France began to believe that their sufferings were part of God's plan for the coming of the millennium.

A Huguenot pastor, Pierre Jurieu, exiled in Rotterdam, perhaps best expressed these millennial themes in his *Apologie pour l'accomplissement des prophéties*, which was published in Rotterdam in 1687, and in his famous *Pastoral Letters* of 1686-88, which circulated clandestinely in Languedoc. Jurieu predicted that the Day of Judgment would come in the year 1689 and noted that already there were extraordinary storms and fires falling from heaven, the signs which would accompany the downfall of the Beast of the Book of Revelation (19:20) or the

Antichrist. Jurieu's prophecies of the coming revolution, the persecution of the righteous, and the final regeneration of humanity eventually led to a rebellion in Languedoc.[2]

A flowering of lay prophets appeared among the people of the Cévennes in 1688, which gave them much hope and encouragement. Great attention was paid to biblical passages that spoke of prophecy, such as: "And in the last days it shall be, God declares, that I will pour out my Spirit upon all flesh, and your sons and your daughters shall prophesy. . . ." (Acts 2:17). The people began to look for these prophets. They hoped persecution would not last long, the last days would be near, and the world would bloom once again after their ordeal was over just as Jurieu had predicted.

Somewhat unexpectedly the prophetic messengers turned out to be children who prophesied while they were asleep. The first noteworthy prophet was Isabeau Vincent, a sixteen-year old shepherdess, who suddenly cried out and began to sing the Ten Commandments while she was asleep. Each night thereafter, believers sat in her room, and she sang, preached, and prayed while asleep. Men sat nearby carefully copying down the words by which she exhorted all to repent as their persecution would last just 42 months longer, and the faithful would have eternal life.

Other prophets, young and old, became inspired and gave forth utterances, such as the world would end for the wicked in three months while the faithful would reign on earth with Jesus for one thousand years. Many of these prophets manifested physical symptoms of shaking, falling, choking, and convulsions, which suggests the intensity of the emotional period that the Huguenots were living through. Thus a Languedoc farmer's sleeping wife might flail her arms and legs and shout "Mercy, mercy" and predict that only a few months remained of their suffering. In 1688 many children were prophesying throughout Dauphiné. In the village near the home of Isabeau Vincent supposedly more than 600 prophets had received the Holy Spirit by the year's end. By January 1689, the fateful year began with more intense, public, and violent prophecies. As April and the expected Judgment Day approached, prophecies and visions continued. Some thought that the flight of England's James II and his replacement by the Protestant William of Orange—just three and a half years after the Revocation of the Edict of Nantes—fulfilled Isabeau's and Jurieu's prophesies of deliverance.³

French royal officials, however, in the spring of 1689 brought a harsh touch of reality to Huguenot areas when they hunted down the prophets, confining younger ones to convents or prisons and condemning others to death. The prophets had expected that a short but cruel peak of persecution would herald the final deliverance. April of 1689 arrived, but Judgment Day did not. Accordingly Pierre Jurieu in Rotterdam revised his prophetic chronology and put forward alternate dates for the end of the reign of the Beast of the Apocalypse, one of which was 1690. Gradually the blaze of messianism and prophetic millenarianism flickered and went underground. Huguenot prophets remained silent for a time, while refugees preserved the spirit and hopes of the intense period of 1688-89.

By the autumn of 1701, prophets reappeared and prophecies abounded. Again prophets made millenarian utterances and again people pointed out signs and miracles, such as a newborn infant speaking out in refusal of Catholic baptism, a Marie Boiteuse weeping tears of blood, a man walking barefoot but unharmed over burning coals. Early in 1702 an itinerant band of prophets and their companions renewed guerila warfare against royal troops. These Huguenots of Cévennes came to be known as Camisards, a word that seems to derive either from the word for "night attack" (the obsolete French word *camisade*) or from the patois for a white shirt (camisole).⁴

The revolt, born of misery and persecution, lasted for two years. Camisard leaders made it known that their people only wanted the restoration of the religious liberties they had under the Edict of Nantes. Scrupulously following divine orders given by inspired young prophets the Camisards gained a series of small victories in 1703. By 1704, however, 20,000 royal troops outnumbered their Camisard opponents by ten to one, although the Camisard guerillas believed themselves to be divinely warned against traitors, to be guided to their camps at night by celestial lights, and protected from ambush by guardian angels. Some of the visionaries of the Vivarias region believed themselves protected by angels white as snow and no bigger than one's finger, a belief that recalls Thomas Münster stopping cannon balls with his sleeve. Believers burned more than 200 Catholic churches in Cévennes, destroyed Catholic images they thought idolatrous, and murdered priests they thought hostile to themselves.[5]

Prophecy was central to the Camisard religion and culture and not just a symbol or symptom of socioeconomic deprivation. Even though most Camisard prophets were poor peasants and village artisans and small landowners (some were wool combers, bakers, one was a pig castrator, another a weaver or a mason), they seem not to have been from the poorest homes nor most depressed regions. Unlike the Fifth Monarchy Men and the Levellers in England 50 years before, the Camisards did not seek radical equality or social change. The English tended to be pacifistic and nonviolent whereas the Camisards were heralds of war. They fought more for purification, to cleanse the world before the millennium. The young prophets after 1700 had been reared secretly in the Protestant faith and had known little but persecution, bitterness, and despair over forced conversion to Catholicism. These child prophets, by their prophetic utterances, confirmed for their elders that a new generation of believers had survived to carry on the Huguenot traditions. New waves of prophets promised redemption for the year 1705, then 1706, then 1708, just as their predecessors had done for 1689.[6]

Up to the time of the Camisard revolt in 1702, the majority of prophets had been female. It was almost as if the Huguenots had found an ingenious way to sidestep the biblical injunctions against women preaching (". . . The women should keep silence in the churches," I Cor. 14:34). Although Huguenot society had some rough sense of equality between male and female, seventeenth century society was not accustomed to female leadership, and Huguenot guerilla leaders were men and male hands held the reins of leadership. As for the Catholics, religious leadership was entirely male as was government and military leadership. But the presence of women in some leadership role seems to have contributed to the venomousness of the Catholic response against female prophets and the Huguenot society that would allow such an aberration.[7]

A few French Prophets went to England and reinvigorated the English millenarian movement. The next chapter will consider these missionaries.

Jansenist Convulsionaries

Other kinds of millenarian movements were active in France during the time of the Camisards. Jansenism, that severe form of seventeenth-century French Catholicism,[8] had a millenarian streak which manifested itself in cells of believers scattered throughout France who prayed for the Second Coming. These believers sheltered the expectation that France was destined to perform a divinely appointed mission, such as reuniting the world in a single, purified Church. Jansenism began to disintegrate into a number of divergent movements, however, with perhaps the most notorious being the Convulsionaries—mostly women—whose religious excesses disgusted their more orthodox confreres. The Convulsionaries depicted the Last Days in ways more apocalyptic than millenarian when they emphasized God's wrath and doom far more than the joys of the heavenly kingdom. They undertook grotesque and extreme forms of penances, including the endurance of a form of crucifixion for several hours.[9]

Jacques-Joseph Duguet, who died in 1733, was a millenarian Jansenist who set the date for the Second Coming in the year 2000. He believed that many developments must occur before the Second Advent of Christ, perhaps the most important being the conversion of the Jews. During the earlier period when Duguet was writing, the Huguenot Pierre Jurieu, advanced similar ideas. While Duguet, however, placed the millennium in the comparatively distant future of 2000 C.E., Jurieu taught that it was at hand.

After the first great outbreak of Convulsionary activity, different individuals came forth to declare themselves to be Elijah, the prophetic figure whose return would supposedly signal the end of the world. One was a priest from Troyes named Pierre Vaillant who preached the coming of Elijah to various Convulsionary assemblies in the early 1730s. Another individual, a renegade priest, called himself Brother Augustin, and he taught that he was Elijah's precursor who would die for men's sins and be born again. He gathered around himself a group of Convulsionaries, one of whom, Sister Restant, claimed she was the woman of Chapter Twelve of the Book of Revelation who would "crush the head of the dragon," a claim that later women like Ann Lee, Catherine Théot and Joanna Southcott would later make. Throughout the rest of the 1700s Convulsionaries continued to spread reports that Elijah had arrived, that he was coming to Paris, that he was in Paris.[10]

At Lyons in 1773 a group of pious Catholics formed a group called the *Amis de la vérité* which was sympathetic to the efforts of the Convulsionaries. A similar group existed at Grenoble who believed that Elijah had come, that the Jews were returning imminently, and that the thousand year reign of Jesus Christ was about to begin.

The most famous of the French millenarian sects of the eighteenth century was the Fareinists, a group linked with both the Convulsionaries and the *Amis de la vérité*. The Fareinists formed in the village of Fareins, near Lyons, in the 1780s around two brothers, Claude Bonjour, a vicar, and his younger brother Francois, a curate. Francois preached a form of Jansenist millenarianism: the apostasy of the gentiles, the conversion of the Jews, the coming of Elijah as a precursor of the reign of Jesus Christ. These millenarian ideas spread through the area, with priests and prophetesses taking them up.[11]

The spread of these ideas in a poor and overpopulated region caused some concern and embarrassment for ecclesiastical authorities, specifically Archbishop Montazet of Lyons. The archbishop and royal authorities began to repress the movement before it might get out of control. Francois Bonjour fled to Paris where he made contact with the sect of Brother Augustin during the onset of the Revolution. Francois also became involved with one of his female followers, Claudine Dauphan, who announced she was to give birth to the prophet Elijah.

Soon after the fall of the monarchy in August 1792, Bonjour announced that Claudine, now his wife, had given birth to a boy, the new Elijah. Bonjour, like other millenarians on both sides of the English Channel, saw the Revolutionary excesses in France as preceding the Second Coming. The baby boy would not only be Elijah but also the incarnation of the Holy Spirit. The Fareinists lasted through the Revolution until 1805 when Napoleon's police scattered the group. Some belief, however, in the Fareinists' doctrines and in the coming of Elijah continued in the Fareins region until well into the nineteenth century.[12]

Millenarians During the Time of the French Revolution

The French Revolution brought no sizable millenarian movement but instead an assortment of individuals in England and in France who interpreted contemporary political events in eschatological terms. What is worth comment is that they began no longer to fit the tradition of learned, respectable figures but were often uneducated and from the lower socio-economic class, exemplars of popular religion.

Ever more noticeable is the presence of women in leadership roles. Women had long been active in millenarian movements but usually in the role of follower or prophet. With the approach of the nineteenth century, more women were to take on more conspicuous and authoritative positions.

Two French woman emerged as prophets, Suzette Labousse and Catherine Théot. Although neither established a coherent body of followers or ever formed a sect, they shaped public opinion during the anxious period in which revolutionary change was especially intense.

In the initial stages of the French Revolution in 1789 and early in 1790, many believed that religion and revolution would triumph together. French citizens expected regeneration and progress; they envisioned a golden age. During the months of 1790 when the National Assembly worked on the reorganization of the French Church and clergy, tension increased as some revolutionaries asked if revolution was compatible with religion. In the sharp wrenching of religion from the life of the state, France was nearly torn apart. During these six anxious months of 1790, interest in the prophecies of Suzette Labrousse was at its peak.[13]

When the Revolution erupted in 1789, Suzette Labrousse, forty-two years of age, had been living a solitary life of prayer and good works in the village of Vauxains, in Perigord, for nearly 20 years. Because her rather vague message of universal spiritual regeneration sounded like prophecy, she attracted considerable attention during the early years of the Revolution. Her prophecies seemed to endow the Revolution with a profound eschatological significance. She piously believed the revolutionary events were a prelude to God's regeneration of the entire world.

Actually, her prophecies were rather vague and diffuse, promising the regeneration of France and the Catholic Church. Nevertheless, she expressed her prophecies in conventional Catholic terms, untrammeled with the philosophical jargon of the Enlightenment. She maintained that the third age of the Spirit has arrived with the Revolution, and she endowed the Revolution with a religious and eschatological significance. During the anxious time of late 1789 and early 1790, Labrousse's pious notions seemed to explain and justify the Revolution in a such a way that a group of priests from Perigord and Guyenne began to discuss them seriously. Selecting those ideas that confirmed what they wanted to believe, the priests found comfort that all would be well, that the ordeal would be brief and followed by regeneration.[14]

The month of May 1790, however, came and went without the miraculous sign in the heavens she had more or less predicted. She was unconcerned and simply postponed the time of its occurrence. Her speeches and writings predicted that the contemporary calamities would climax in 1791, which, of course, they didn't. Her *Discorsi*, written in vague, sometimes incoherent and ungrammatical French, show her to be eccentric and unlearned but probably not mad, as some had believed.[15] Her moment in history's spotlight passed, with no millenarian movement and no disciples to carry on her thoughts.

Catherine Théot never achieved the public prominence as a prophet that Suzette Labrousse did in 1790 but Théot did start a minor millenarian movement.

Théot was born at Barenton, near Avranches, in Normandy, in May 1716. For many years she worked as a domestic servant in a convent in Paris. Although uneducated, she nevertheless came to believe that she alone could understand Scripture, and she began to preach against the preachers. She had had millenarian ideas since at least the 1770s. She promised that the age of the Reign of God would come very soon, although she expressed little interest in the nature of the world after the Second Coming. Her notion that the third age was the culmination of human history recalls Joachim of Fiore, and she assured her followers that the Revolution was part of a divine plan. Morality and the true Church would triumph and prepare the way for Christ's return. She regarded herself as the New Eve, and as a "virgin who would receive the little Jesus, who would come from heaven to earth."[16]

From the records of the Paris police it is known that most of her followers were artisans, petty shopkeepers, and servants from the neighborhoods of the Left Bank, although the circle of the Duchess de Bourbon was also interested in the movement. Women made up the majority of Théot's disciples, whose number probably never exceeded a hundred. These followers claimed Théot as the Mother of God, the Mother of the Word, and the New Eve. In 1794 her followers introduced a ceremony of ritual kisses. This rite consisted of making the sign of the cross on the believer's forehead and kissing the believer on both eyes, both cheeks, and on the forehead and the chin. This ceremony of kisses seems intended to assure the faithful followers that they would be protected at the time of Christ's Second Coming and offered personal immortality—at a time when hopes for the millennium were also accompanied by an increased fear of death.

The authorities arrested Théot and some of her disciples at various times, but essentially her movement was regarded at the time as a fringe group, being vilified even at the National Convention in 1794 as a school of fanaticism. Théot and her small movement represented a movement of popular piety quite different from the tradition of learned theological speculation about the End Time. Hers was a melange of beliefs, some popular millenarian beliefs and some beliefs that connect her with the heresies of the Middle Ages, such as her anticlericalism, her denial of the efficacy of the sacraments, and her notion, similar to that of the Spiritual Franciscans, that God's elect must break with the sinful Church. Théot's movement never gained a sufficiently critical mass to become influential during the excitement of the Revolution.[17]

French millenarianism characteristically drew from a wide variety of sources, from popular piety and a popular prophecy and from the eighteenth-century search for spiritual enlightenment in such areas as occultism and mesmerism. Various records and accounts survive of fringe movements and even millenarian charlatans—almost more than

France

can easily be assimilated and integrated. For example, a man by the name of Marie-Daniel Bourrée de Corberon, left a manuscript, now in the Calvet Museum in Avignon, which records his spiritual pilgrimage through the lush spiritual undergrowth of fringe religion of the late eighteenth century: the ideas of Swedenborg, mystical Masonry, mesmerism, alchemy, sweepings left over from the Great Awakening and the revival of religion—some of which promised regeneration or a new age and had millenarian implications.[18]

Corberon records dealing with a probable charlatan prophet whose ideas and actions anticipated those of later, more sincere millenarians. In 1784 Corberon met Jean-Baptiste Ruer a fifty-year old Parisian who claimed to have received heavenly communications each night. Jesus Christ was to return to earth and initiate the third age. Ruer predicted great events were to occur: kingdoms would fall, revolutions would break out, the Jews would return to the Holy Land, and the world would be renewed and take the form it had at creation. Ruer described the services that would be performed in the rebuilt Temple at Jerusalem where Ruer himself would be king since he was an offspring of David. Ruer also expected that God would dictate to him five hundred volumes on science, including all that King Solomon knew. Ruer predicted the end of the world would come in 1786. His followers prepared themselves. They procured a house and stocked it with food for the year of disaster. As the year of doom passed with no sign of the predicted events, the small band and Corberon became restive. Ruer's constant demands for money from Corbon and others on how to survive the Time of Disaster and be saved make Ruer's integrity suspect.[19]

Nineteenth-Century France and the Marian Age

Eighteenth- and nineteenth-century religious prophecy in France suggested that the Second Coming of Christ would be preceded by an age of Mary. For example, Grignon de Montfort published in 1842 a manuscript entitled *Traité de la vraie dévotion à la sainte vièrge* which became extraordinarily popular. The manuscript made straightforward claims that the Second Coming of Christ and his reign on earth would be preceded by an age of Mary.[20] Accordingly the series of Marian apparitions and blossoming of fervent Marian piety in nineteenth-century France seemed to signal the dawning of this age of Mary with a corresponding rise in eschatological excitement.

Popular religious prophecy was active earlier in the century when in 1798 Napoleon banished Pope Pius VI from Rome to France. When the pope subsequently died a year later, religious prophets quickly connected these events with the Antichrist prophecy of Revelation 13:1-5: "And the beast . . . seemed to have a mortal wound . . ., and it was allowed to exercise authority for forty-two months. . . ." Prophets, counting from 538, calculated that the papacy had been permitted to reign for 1260 years and would then die of its "mortal wound." (The figure of 1260 was arrived at by multiplying 42 months by an average of 30 days for a month.)

In 1830 the prophetic tradition reappeared with prophecies about a "great king and angelic people."[21] The idea was common that France, piously considered the eldest daughter of the Church, was destined to play a decisive role in the providential events that would culminate in the Christian millennium. The various prophecies, however, never developed into a proper millenarian movement.

Four months after the revolution of 1830 and well before the anxieties about the future of France had receded, Sister Catherine Laboure, a novice of the Daughters of Charity in Paris, had a vision in which Mary reassured her that France had a special place in the Virgin's affections. In November 1830 a medal was revealed to Catherine, one side of which showed Mary standing on a globe extending her arms. Beams of light radiated from her open arms to the earth. During the 1830s millions of these Miraculous Medals were distributed, helping to keep alive the idea of France's special role in world history during the July Monarchy. The medals depicted Mary crushing the head of a serpent and wearing a crown of stars. This image could only evoke the woman of the Apocalypse: "And a great portent appeared in heaven, a woman clothed with the sun, with the moon under her feet, and on her head a crown of twelve stars. . . ." (Rev 12:1). The woman of the Apocalypse had at varying times been interpreted as representing God's people and then the Church in conflict with Satan; now

France

she was linked with Mary, and the Marian age was linked with the events of the End Time.

Catholic prelates had discussed the doctrine of Mary's Immaculate Conception, in part to counter the rationalism and irreligion that was felt to be a characteristic defect of modern times, especially in France where there was rising anticlericalism and a falling away of Catholics from the Church. The Church felt embattled against secular forces and disbelief. By the time the Church promulgated it as a dogma in 1854, the Immaculate Conception had become a popular doctrine whose cause was aided by prophecy, miraculous apparitions and cures, pious publications, and shrines that drew thousands of pilgrims. On the other hand the doctrine seems to have encouraged and fostered the insular, even bunker, mentality of nineteenth century Catholicism and encouraged a kind of triumphalism, that is, that the Church would surely triumph over its enemies.

In France, during the economic crises of the 1840s, there was a dramatic rise in Marian devotion. In the 1840s Alphonse Constant published apocalyptic visions in which the Virgin Mary seemed to connect Christianity and socialism in a way that would bring about the millennium. In 1846, there was a crop failure that caused much distress in the southeast region of the country. On September 19, 1846, the Virgin Mary appeared to two shepherd children on the mountain of La Salette. It became known that the Virgin criticized the irreligious behavior of the people and predicted further catastrophes if people did not change. Soon the shrine drew crowds of pilgrims. Pamphlets on the apparition soon circulated throughout France and created more excitement and religious devotion.

In 1858, in the small village of Lourdes in the southwest region of France, Mary announced to Bernadette: "I am the Immaculate Conception." The cult of the Virgin and the miraculous cures in the grotto made Lourdes an important center for pilgrims and confirmed for people that age of Mary had arrived.[22]

In spite, however, of the association between Mary and the End Times, the renewal of Marian piety with an emphasis on eschatology and the special destiny of religious France, no specifically millenarian cult or movement arose, most likely because no leader came forward with the vision and capacity to exploit the moment.

Conclusion

French millenarianism rests primarily on traditions of popular prophecy, traditions which flourished especially in the Protestant rebellion in the Cévennes mountains, among the Jansenistic sects of Paris, and more broadly around the popular Marian shrines and pilgrimages of the nineteenth century. Although the Jansenistic sects of Paris and the Marian apparitions did not result in a specifically millenarian group, their tone was apocalyptic and some of the religious excitement was present that might have moved believers to a more specific millenarian movement. But the French prophetic tradition with its millenarian concerns did get exported to England and revived English millenarianism.

NOTES

1. Hillel Schwartz, *The French Prophets: The History of a Millenarian Group in Eighteenth-Century England* (Berkeley, Los Angeles, London: University of California Press, 1980), pp 11-14. Hereafter, all references to *The French Prophets* will simply be Hillel Schwartz, unless otherwise indicated. See Philippe Joutard, *La Légende des Camisards* (Gallimard, 1977).

2. Emmanuel Le Roy Ladurie, *The Peasants of Languedoc* trans by John Day (University of Illinois Press: Urbana, Chicago and London, 1974), pp. 272-273; Hillel Schwartz, p. 16.

3. Hillel Schwartz, pp. 17-19.

4. Hillel Schwartz, pp. 20-21, and p. 23, footnote #29.

5. Hillel Schwartz, pp. 23, 29, 30, 34; Emmanuel Ladurie, p. 277.

6. Hillel Schwartz, pp. 27, 28, 31; Emmanuel Ladurie, p. 281; Ladurie, pp. 274-285, counts far fewer prophets, and also seems to emphasize the hysterical and pathological nature of their behavior.

7. Hillel Schwartz, pp. 32-34; Ladurie, p. 285, suggests sexual frustration as the explanation of prophetic behavior. He says that visions disappeared once young prophetesses lost their virginity. He links two great attacks of convulsionary fervor in seventeenth-century France (Camisards and Parisian Jansenism among the convulsionaries of Saint-Médard) to the areas of French culture where sexual morality was most demanding and vigorous.

8. Cf. Alexander Sedgwick, *Jansenism in Seventeenth-Century France* (Charlottesville: University Press of Virginia, 1977), pp. 193-203.

9. J.M. Neale, *A History of the So-Called Jansenist Church of Holland* (London, 1858; New York: AMS Press Reprint, 1970), p. 58; B. Robert Kreiser, *Miracles, Conversions and Ecclesiastical Politics in Early Eighteenth-Century Paris* (Princeton University Press, 1978), pp. xiii, 245; Clarke Garrett, p. 21. Hysteria in religion is an endlessly interesting topic; a recent addition to the field is Ian Wilson, *Stigmata: An Investigation into the Mysterious Appearance of Christ's Wounds in Hundreds of People from Medieval Italy to Modern America* (New York: Harper and Row, 1989).

10. Clarke Garrett, pp. 22, 25. I follow Garret closely in this discussion.

11. Clarke Garrett, pp. 26-27.

12. Clarke Garrett, pp. 27-29.

13. Clarke Garrett, pp. 11, 12, 31, 47, 49.

14. Clarke Garrett, pp. 33, 40, 45.

15. Clarke Garrett, pp. 32, 51, 72, 76.

16. Cited by Clarke Garrett, p. 85; cf. also pp. 77-81, 89-90.

17. Clarke Garrett, pp. 78, 83, 86, 89. Cf. Albert Mathiez, "New Evidence About Catherine Théot," in *The Fall of Robespierre and Other Essays* (New York: Alfred A. Knopf, 1927), 119-125; also, Albert Mathiez, "Robespierre et le proce's de Catherine Théot," *Annales Historiques de la Revolution Francaise* 6 (1929): 392-397.

18. Antoine Faivre, "Un familier des sociétés ésotériques au dix-huitième siècle: Bourrée de Corberon," *Revue des Sciences Humaines* 32 (1967): 282-3; Clarke Garrett, pp. 99, 111.

19. Clarke Garrett, pp. 107, 108; Antoine Faivre, pp. 274-7.

20. Thomas Kselman, *Miracles and Prophecies in Nineteenth-Century France* (New Jersey: Rutgers University Press, 1983), pp. 78, 90.

21. Thomas A. Kselman, p. 91.

22. Thomas Kselman, pp. 62-63, 80.

Chapter Nine
England from the Seventeenth to the Nineteenth Century

Once Charles II was restored to the English throne in 1660, millenarianism as a creed and program did not lose its vitality although it was not as intensely public or dramatic as the millenarian activity of the Civil War Period. Millenarian groups abandoned the center of the political stage, as it were, but individuals continued to speculate about the end times. Millenarian faith in one form or another continued to be respectable socially, theologically and intellectually as learned Englishmen continued the tradition of Foxe, Allstead, Mead, and Brightman—that is to say, the scholarly, respectable study of biblical prophecy for the sake of computing the signs and date of the world's end.

Indeed, Puritan traditions, including apocalypticism and millenarianism, persisted through the eighteenth century into the nineteenth.[1] The wide appeal of millenarian ideas and rhetoric and arguments perhaps was due to the disruption of social relationships of the Industrial Revolution and the Enlightenment and the rise of secularizing forces which made believers anxious.

But it was ultimately the other current of millenarianism, more common in France but not absent in England, a popular and prophetic, millenarianism that increasingly became dominant.

This chapter considers a few of the individuals and groups which illustrate the change in the English millenarian tradition from mainstream respectability to more ecstatic and prophetic and popular.

John Mason

Some of the most prominent men of seventeenth-century England such as Robert Boyle, Thomas Hobbes, Issac Newton, and some of the latitudinarian bishops speculated about the millennium. There was almost a consensus of opinion that the end was imminent. Some learned men favored a date in the 1690s. Around 1693 Sir Issac Newton began an intensive study of the Book of Daniel and the Book of Revelation to find out just when the end of the world was due. One Thomas Beverley, rector of Lilley in Hereford, predicted the end of the world for 1697. In 1698, he decided to write a book to prove that the world indeed had come to an end without anybody noticing it.[2]

John Mason, born in 1646, was the rector of the small village of Water Stratford, near Buckingham, whose normal population was about 100. Mason was well educated and pious, and he reflected on the writings of Bishop Ussher and the German theologian Alsted who had predicted from the safe distance of 1627 that Christ's reign of a thousand years on earth would begin in 1694.

In 1688 Mason's wife died. In the following year, Mason began to have intimations of the coming of the Kingdom. He began to hear voices and had visions of the New Jerusalem. (Modern psychologists would probably examine the role his grief played in shaping his perceptions of and beliefs about voices and visions.) In 1689 Mason believed a divine messenger declared to him that "the Lord would have a kingdom in this World, and the time draws near." He saw the signs of deliverance for the figurative church of Philadelphia, that faithful church which would be present at the Second Coming (cf.

Rev. 3:7-10). Believing himself inspired and the messenger of Christ's Second Coming he began to preach extemporaneously to a receptive audience of common people, the majority of whom were women.

Mason fixed on the year 1694 as the time of the millennium. He further believed that his own village, Water Stratford, was the "very Spot of Ground" where Christ's standard would be set up. On this Holy Ground, a plot south of the village, around the rectory, was the only place where safety and salvation were to be found. Mason held the rigid view that most people are so bad they could not be redeemed, as they could only corrupt God's chosen.

Early on Easter Monday morning, April 16, 1694, in the midst of the dancing and singing of his followers at Water Stratford, Mason had a vision. He predicted that Jesus's Second Advent would be on Pentecost Sunday, a few weeks away, when Jesus would gather together all His saints on the holy ground of the small village and inaugurate the millennium. Men and women flocked to the holy ground around Mason's rectory to await the Kingdom and "to live in imitation of the primitive saints," with all possessions in common and in continuous praise of the Lord. A clergyman named Henry Maurice came and observed believers running up and down excitedly, stretching their arms upwards to catch the Savior, others extending them forwards to meet Him, to grasp Him. They would leap and dance and clap their hands saying: "Appear, appear, appear."[3] By April 26 there were about 100 followers, mostly women and children who sang and danced around Mason's rectory, and hundreds of the curious came as spectators to watch the celebration and hear Mason prophesy.

Mason became increasingly odd and physically ill. He stayed in his room and only communicated with his followers through two lay disciples. In May he died, although he assured people that God said he would not die; his disciples expected him to rise on the third day. Some even believed they had seen him and spoken with him. Because some of Mason's followers waited for his return, the succeeding rector disinterred Mason to convince the faithful that their prophet had been an ordinary mortal. Those who believed in the second coming of John Mason were still dancing and singing at his house in Water Stratford in 1710, and the small sect survived until about 1740.[4]

The Philadelphians

Drawing their name from the model church at Philadelphia (cf. Rev. 3:7-13), English Philadelphians did not set themselves up as a church. Most of them were members of the Church of England but wished to establish a religious society for the "Reformation of Manners, for the Advancement of an Heroical Christian Piety, and Universal Love towards All."[5] They believed that the time allotted for the purification of Christianity would shortly expire, and they were perhaps the most important body of millenarians in England at the time to receive and to acclaim the French Prophets, Camisard refugees who added an ecstatic dimension to the English millenarian tradition.

Some of the ideas of the Philadelphians came from the German mystic Jacob Boehme (1575-1624). A few of his writings that had been translated during the 1640s had impressed English millenarians. Boehme, in a variation on Joachim of Fiore, contemplated a seventh period in human history when all would be happy and peaceful. This he called the Enochian time. His ideas were picked up by Dr. John Pordage (1607-81) at Bradfield, (Berkshire), a student of medicine and alchemy, and the founder of the Philadelphians. In 1654 he was ejected from his church for invoking spirits and claiming the power to bestow gifts of the Spirit upon whom he pleased. He first met Mrs. Jane Lead, a woman with mystic leanings and the central figure among the Philadelphians, in 1663. Over time, he transmitted to her his theosophical ideas, and when in 1681 he died, she, aged fifty-seven, assumed leadership of the small group of seekers, most of whom were well off.[6]

Her ideology was a complicated mix of mystical, prophetic and theosophical ideas, with a decided millenarian inclination. Essentially the Philadelphians conducted an inward search for revelation and the true peace of Philadelphia. Her writings included: *The Enochian Walks with God, found out by a Spiritual Traveller, whose Face towards Mount Sion above was set* (1694), *A Fountain of Gardens watered by the Rivers of Divine Pleasure, and springing up in all the variety of Spiritual Plants, blown up by the Pure Breath into a Paradise. . . .* (4 vols, 1696-1701), *The Signs of the Times: forerunning the Kingdom of Christ, and evidencing when it is to come,* (1699). Until 1697 the Philadelphians

England

convened privately at Jane Lead's house in Hoxton or at homes of Joanna Oxenbridge and Ann Bathurst in Baldwin Gardens, London. Their meetings were subdued, begun with prayer and scripture readings and followed by that silence familiar to Quakers in which the inspired might speak. By the 1690s Philadelphian circles existed in Holland, Germany, and Switzerland. A German branch in the summer of 1694 settled in Wissahickon, Pennsylvania.[7]

In 1697 Jane Lead prompted the English Philadelphians to give a more pubic testimony of their expectations, a message that God's love and mercy were breaking through. They moved some of their meetings to Hungerford Market and Westmoreland House which they duly licensed as places of religious worship under the Toleration Act. But ruffians who distrusted the group's millennial expectations disturbed the meetings and the Philadelphia Society had to abandon their Hungerford Market assemblies.

Philadelphians slowly retreat from public view, a retreat accelerated by the death of Jane Lead on August 8, 1704. Her death, like the death of other charismatic leaders, affected the group and no adequate replacement followed her. Philadelphians stopped holding public meetings, although they continued to gather in private. The Philadelphians pointed to the French Prophets (and their English associates) as a valid Christian movement that would lead to the millennial state. Some Philadelphians, along with some Anglicans and nonconformists and others who had continued the millenarian tradition, became followers of the French Prophets who had come to London spouting millenarian slogans and manifesting extravagant physical signs of inspiration.[8]

Attention can now be turned to the French Prophets and the reinvigorated group that grew up around them.

The French Prophets

The influence of the Camisards and of Pierre Jurieu spread far beyond France. Huguenot refugees and missionaries carried his ideas to Germany, Holland, and central Europe. Most important is the arrival in England of three French Huguenot Prophets or Camisards who were refugees from southeastern France where the Protestant Huguenots had been rebelling against Louis XIV's religious repression for more than twenty years. The three prophet-missionaries, Elie Marion, Jean Cavalier, and Durand Fage, arrived in London in 1706 predicting an imminent Second Coming.[9]

The three young prophets (the oldest was twenty-eight) came filled with the ideas of Jurieu who had recast King Louis XIV's repression in apocalyptic terms with the French king and his armies as the servants of the Beast of Revelation. The prophets' millenarianism, nurtured by years of bitterness and persecution, was turbulent and menacing. They predicted an imminent millennium to be preceded by the destruction of London and the wicked by famine, pestilence, and earthquake. Elie Marion warned prophetically that the Trumpet was ready to signal the end of the world, and that fire and terrible things were being prepared for the enemies of the Prophets and their followers. On November 4, Marion received a divine command to begin a fast and he immediately prophesied the London would soon be aflame, and that Christ's Kingdom was at hand.

The London that received the Prophets was a very different milieu from that of the Cévennes. London in the early 1700s was a diverse and sprawling city, growing in wealth, with a population of about half a million. New coffeehouses allowed businessmen and writers to gather, read the flood of pamphlets and publications and exchange ideas. A large portion of London's population was made up of religious dissenters and nonconformists who were receptive to new ideas. The new prophets could walk around the city safely, and they could make contact with Christians who were initially disposed to hear their message. And best of all was the presence of a large population of refugee Huguenots who were initially receptive of their co-religionists. The diversity and freedom of London contrasted with the mountains of the Cévennes whose embattled peasants had endured persecution while offering a sympathetic community and widespread support for their prophets.[10]

The cosmopolitan environment of London and the presence among the prophets of English converts eventually brought changes in the

Camisard message and style of assembly. It would also be necessary to reinterpret the function and style of prophecy as well as the meaning of millennium.

Initially Cavalier and Fage had established the procedure for meetings of the prophets during summer of 1706 before Marion arrived. A small group would gather in a drawing room of a private home, with two or three scribes ready to take notes. The focus of the group centered on divine inspiration. As one of the prophets became inspired he—and later, she—would succumb to shaking, jumping, gasping, convulsions, and eventually begin to speak. The scribes, jotting comments on the manner of agitation, would render in shorthand a faithful account of the inspired communication.

Later, meetings continued to be in small groups, often hosted by middle-aged women. Believers assembled to discuss and confirm what individual prophets had said. Regular meetings became somewhat formalized. After a reading of a prophetic warning, scripture, and letters from missionaries, the assembled faithful would sing a psalm, all the while expecting to be interrupted by someone among them seized by inspiration. If inspiration found no one, they would wait, sometimes for hours. Because of later distrust and some fears of false prophets, changes were made so that by 1712 only the inspired prophets and select scribes were to meet formally, and there were disputes over the criteria for true inspiration.[11]

As time went on the French Prophets continued to proclaim the coming of the Kingdom, but they also had to deal with unexpected opposition. The Huguenot refugee community of London turned against them for a variety of reasons. Some clergy were vexed that the unordained prophets had been conducting services that ordinarily required an ordained minister. Some Englishmen were upset by the presence in the movement of female prophets who made "indecent" agitations while inspired. Further, the situation of the Huguenots was precarious in the political environment of late Stuart England, and their leaders could not risk antagonizing English authorities. London weavers resented the Huguenot weavers, and Huguenot leaders could not risk seeming to support prophets whose millenarianism involved prophecies of violence.[12]

John Lacy and the English Prophets

The Prophets, however, did attract new followers, perhaps 20 by April of 1707, a hundred by autumn. Among the converts was John Lacy, a well-to-do Presbyterian, age forty-two, married and with a family. Lacy was to write a number of volumes of prophecies and testimonials of the "Miraculous Things lately come to pass in the Cevennes" and also would eventually become the foremost English prophet. Lacy's friend, Sir Richard Bulkeley, second baronet and holder of a large estate in Ireland and a country house in Surrey, also supported the prophets. Other literate and prominent men included Thomas Cotton, Richard Roach, Sir John Philipps, and Nicholas Fatio de Duillier, an internationally known mathematician and disciple of Sir Isaac Newton. The prominence of these men gave stature to the prophets. Other followers were from the ranks of artisans, shopkeepers, laborers, and refugees without work or money. Gradually this socially diverse group of English and French prophets and believers came to be known as the French Prophets regardless of nationality or actual gift of prophecy.[13]

London's scientific elite did not yet disdain millenarian ideas and sought to understand the universe through scripture as well as mathematics. But these educated men played a decreasing role in English millenarianism.

Difficulties and dissensions were present from the start within the small community of French Prophets. For example, in 1707-8 as the group became more diverse and differing prophecies emerged, the faithful did not have well-worked-out criteria to differentiate the genuineness of inspiration. Concerns about false prophets grew. In addition there was legal opposition and other hostility which they interpreted as a temporary trial in the process of universal renewal, that they were suffering from the plots of the ungodly. Further, tension between the English members and the French refugees developed because of the different orientations towards the millennium. Camisard millenarianism, in contrast to the English tradition, gave emphasis to violence and warfare. The French Prophets preached a punishing God who was the opposite of the loving God of the Philadelphians.[14]

England

Important support for the movement came when the Philadelphians reached out to them. Richard Roach, an Anglican clergymen and heir to Jane Lead's leadership of the Philadelphians, met with the Prophets in March 1707 along with several other Philadelphians. The Philadelphians brought their tradition of acceptance and the hope for universal spiritual change; they wanted to develop love and an apostolic faith that would hasten universal redemption and renewal. At least ten Philadelphians entered the ranks of the French Prophets while other English followers came to the fore.

The concern of the French Prophets and Camisards had been to broadcast news that these were the last days, that Judgment and the Kingdom were impending. If only people would harken to the warnings of the prophets, they would prepare themselves, they would lead pious lives and all could be saved, but those who hardened their hearts would be judged severely. The Prophets promised the faithful a heavenly Kingdom, but it was not entirely clear whether it would be on earth as presently known. Despite their confidence that the millennium was at hand, the doctrines of the Prophets were somewhat blurred. At best, the Prophets offered only a vague sequence of a Second Coming, followed by the millennium period, which, in turn, was followed by the final judgment. Few of the French Prophets bothered to struggle with Revelation's clues as to an exact schedule of how the world was to end. The distinguishing characteristic of the French Prophets (and the Camisards) was not their millenarianism but prophecy: the fact of inspiration in their midst. Their faith was a millenarian faith but above all a faith in the prophets who brought word of the millennium.[15]

Between June 1706 and June 1707 the Prophets created expectations of an imminent end, but refrained from predictions as to a specific time. Some predicted that the winter of 1706/7 would bring "pestilential Fogs or Mists, that should sweep away, like a Plague, a vast Number of the inhabitants" of London. But none of the prophecies demanded significant personal investment on the part of group members. Until late July 1707 few predictions held any real likelihood of being disconfirmed. Some thought Marion had in November 1706, predicted the burning of London, but the written version of his prophecy adds the bail-out words "in a few days."[16]

As legal and clerical opposition mounted, the leaders—especially Lacy—seemed pressed to find wonders that would be decisive proof to their persecutors of the divine call of the prophets as well as give encouragement to their followers. Lacy claimed to have cured the blindness and paralysis of Elizabeth Gray, a young woman alone in London and isolated from her family, but her illnesses seem to have been of a neurotic nature. Lacy's prophetic outpourings often were in bad French and worse Latin, but he nevertheless claimed they were directed by a foreign agent or the Spirit, which could even carry him across the room. Indeed, he did glide ten feet across the floor, claiming to levitate. Lacy spoke in tongues (possibly Latin and then later Greek) and supposedly performed automatic writing. Followers seized on any unusual happening as a sign. In the evening of July 19 a prophet recorded an extraordinary sign from heaven, that it had rained flies all over the city, leaving people's clothes covered with them.[17]

Some accounts also indicate that there was a great release of feelings during the meetings with much laughter. It was reported that Lacy laughted "when he saw *Elizabeth Gray* rolling her eyes about in a distorted manner in her *Agitations*. . . ."[18] Apparently the French but not the English Prophets "had Love Meetings . . . where they would meet, *Kiss* and *tickle* one another, *chucking* one another under the Chin, laughing and crying out, He, He, He, He . . . and using many lascivious Postures. . . ."[19]

When one of the English Prophets, Dr. Thomas Emes, died in December 1707, his death threatened the hope of believers that they would soon be participants in the coming Kingdom, just as deaths among the first Christians worried the small community at Thessalonia (cf 1 Thes. 4:13-18). Emes' death shook the faithful and made them insecure about how far off the End might be if an inspired man died before it come. Lacy made various predictions that he would raise Emes from the dead on the 25 of May, only forty-one days away.[20]

Believing they were living in the last days, the English Prophets expected the end to come on March 25 with the final resurrection to come on May 25. The English members left their jobs and spent money to gather food as they waited for the end. On March 24, surrounded by food, the English followers prayed and fasted. The world, however, continued to exist. Nevertheless, tension and expectation about May 25 continued high. Newspapers picked up the story and forecast that a throng of curious and excitable people would converge on Bunhill Fields and even suggested that this wonderful show would need grandstands and refreshments. Some were less amused, and Daniel Defoe, the author, feared mob violence. One contemporary witness estimated 20,000 milled about Dr. Emes' grave. To the disappointment of most, Dr. Emes neither rose nor appeared. What astonished people more was the lack of embarrassment on the part of the French Prophets who had nervously prepared for failure. Lacy blandly said the atmosphere of the day was inappropriate for a miracle.[21] The Prophets struggled with the incomprehensible ways of God and tried to live in a world whose ultimate renewal was constantly being deferred.

Later in that summer of 1708, the French Prophets received and obeyed a divine command to wear a yard-long green ribbon in public. The prophet Fatio de Duillier explained this as the livery of the Lord. Believers wore the ribbons "as a Mark for the destroying Angel to know us by, when he should come to execute the Judgments of the Lord."[22]

Although the Camisard Prophets and their English disciples travelled through England and Scotland proclaiming a message of imminent doom and destruction, these missions tended to be unsuccessful. Differences among members increased, and lack of success and unfulfilled prophecies drained their confidence. After all, the world had passed safely into 1710 even though the Camisard Elie Marion had vaguely predicted in 1706 that within three years the end would come. Disciples murmured and sought the reasons for unfulfilled prophecies. Internal disputes and external opposition seemed to exhaust the Prophets. They endured abuse, as they expected true prophets to receive such treatment. As the end of time seemed less imminent, believers fell back on the importance of seniority and experience in the movement.

Less and less did the group hold to the pentecostal idea, that all the faithful would be inspired. Even the first supporters of the Prophets, the Philadelphians, began to separate themselves from the French Prophets prior to 1710. In 1712 members of the Prophets learned that

John Lacy, by then the principal English Prophet, had received a divine command to leave his wife and sleep with Elizabeth Gray. To those who were disturbed by this news Lacy responded that he could no more refuse a divine command than deny the Lord's absolute sovereignty and that he would be threatened with everlasting destruction and hell if he disobeyed. Ever so slowly his followers were reconciled to the adultery.[23]

In comparison with other English religious groups the French Prophets stood out in granting considerable status and freedom to women. Only the Quakers and Philadelphians allowed women something approaching the same latitude and authority. Prophecy allowed women a way around the Pauline proscriptions against women in ministry (1 Cor 14:34-5), since another Pauline passage seems to allow for female prophets: "... Any woman who prays or prophesies with her head uncovered ...," (1 Cor 11:5). But the relatively enlightened attitude of the Prophets toward women also earned opposition for the movement. Women Prophets were more conspicuous than men since they in more obvious ways were deserting traditional roles in a patriarchal social and religious system. The women's youth and agitations during prophecy attracted suspicion and public opposition unknown in the original Camisard tradition as these women certainly abandoned English rules of deportment and constraints on physical movement and style of dress. The Prophets themselves expelled some women because of their extravagant agitations or failure to humble themselves to male prophets.[24]

In 1713 some of the original Camisard prophets returned to the Continent. For the six or seven years that they had been in England they re-energized English millenarianism. In the same year Marion died shortly after he left England; Pierre Jurieu died the year before, in 1712. In England the French Prophets gradually fell silent from 1715 to 1730, with less clamor and less cohesion, until a slight resurgence under the leadership of Hannah Wharton.[25]

Despite the fervor of those who belonged to the small group, the French Prophets failed to become a larger, more forceful movement in England for several reasons. They never developed criteria for admission, had no rigorous definition of membership, and made only simple theological demands of their adherents. The early English converts were Anglicans or moderate Presbyterians who tended to continue membership in their own church until that church excluded them. The influx of new converts into the Prophets affected its ideology, that is, the English converts brought traditions from English millenarianism which softened the urgent and violent expectations of the Camisard tradition. The agitations and prophetic warnings of the Camisards, developed in a milieu of persecution and war, were unsettling amidst the academic sermons and sedate ceremonies of London's churches in the early 1700s. With the gradual shift from Huguenot to English majority within the Prophets, the Camisard tradition of cataclysmic-type millenarianism gradually put more emphasis on a universalist church as espoused by the Philadelphians and by an English tradition more intent on personal faith.[26]

The Camisard tradition, in a convoluted way, touched and influenced other English groups of the period. French Prophets established ties with English, Scottish, and European pietists. They also encountered John Wesley and some of his early followers. Wesley met with members of the French Prophets and read Lacy's writings. The founder of Methodism, however, was ambivalent toward the French Prophets. He disapproved of their ways and he preached against religious enthusiasts who imagined they had divine gifts even as he accepted some of their tenets. Wesley and the French Prophets shared a common concern for spiritual revival and genuine religious experience. They also agreed that the Montanists, those early Christian millenarians with women prophets, had been genuine Christians. Wesley suggested that miraculous gifts were withdrawn from the Christian church for so long because the "dry, formal orthodoxy" of Catholicism had ridiculed them and decried them as madness.[27]

Wesley himself sometimes voiced premonitions about the imminence of Judgment Day. Some of his hymns reveal a proneness to millenarian ideas and imagery. Even if Wesley did not encourage literal belief in the millennium, the apocalyptic manner of Methodist revival meetings, as shall be seen below, inflamed the imagination of those attending and made the way easier for all those millenarian preachers of the late eighteenth century.

Perhaps more of interest is the claim by the Quakers of Manchester, England, that they received from the remnants of the French Prophets their illumination.[28] Indeed groups that had some contact and inspiration from the Camisard tradition resembled the Camisards and the French Prophets in a variety of ways: similarities in the style of worship, the status accorded to women, and confidence in the approach of the millennium. Perhaps most important was their emphasis on prophetic inspiration which was to become an important component of religious experience during this period and for the next century.

The Bolton Society

Scattered remnants of Prophets continued to hold semi-secret meetings in various parts of the British Isles. During their twilight years the French Prophets would gather silently around inspired women, waiting for agitations and some prophetic utterance. Some time in the 1740s Jane and James Wardley, Quaker tailors living in Bolton-on-the-Moors, a bleak town twelve miles northeast of Manchester in Lancashire, joined the French Prophets. They had visions of the Second Coming, of the downfall of the Antichrist, of the rise of the Church in transcendent glory. About 1747 the Wardleys received from the exiled Prophets that further "degree of light and power" which enabled them to separate from the Quakers (also known as the Society of Friends). Shortly afterwards the Wardleys gathered a small sect around them, never more than 50 people. The practices of both the Quakers and the worship assembly of the Prophets seems to have strongly affected the Bolton tailor and his wife. Their worship service had some of the frantic behavior of the Camisard tradition, agitations of head and limbs, and prophecies of the end of the world and the Second Coming of Christ.[29]

A Wardley meeting might begin in traditional Quaker fashion, with believers sitting in quiet meditation. They would be taken ". . . with a mighty trembling. . . . with a mighty shaking; and were occasionally exercised in singing, shouting, or walking the floor, under the influence of spiritual signs, shoving each other about,—or swiftlypassing and repassing each other, like clouds agitated by a mighty wind."[30]

Mother Jan Wardley eventually presided over the Bolton sect. She warned her followers of the approach of the Kingdom of God and exhorted them to:

> "... amend your lives. Repent. For the kingdom of God is at hand. The new heaven and new earth prophesied of old is about to come."[31]

These former Quakers (and pre-Shakers) had no clearly formulated doctrine. Their prophecies, which were often the passionate utterances of women members, shared the same millennial, apocalyptic, and anti-clerical character of the Camisards.

In 1758 a young, uneducated woman by the name of Ann Lee became a member of the Bolton sect. Lee, the daughter of a blacksmith, labored under a deep sense of sin, and her involvement with the Wardleys enabled her to have a conversion experience. She, too, gathered a small band about herself but, not finding much success in England, set off for America, where she called her followers the Millennial or Second Christian Church, more commonly known as the Shakers. Later, Shaker officials made the claim that there had been two witnesses chosen by God to prepare for the Second Coming: Quakers and French Prophets. Supposedly the Quakers lost their light as they compromised too much with secular society. It was the French Prophets, however, who awakened the Spirit in James and Jane Wardley who in turn prepared the way for Mother Ann Lee.[32]

Thus the Bolton sect, in its popular millenarianism, suggests the linkage between France with its Camisard tradition, England with its French Prophets and its Bolton Society, and finally America with Ann Lee's Shakers. The next chapter will treat further the Shakers in America.

Eve of the French Revolution

On the eve of the French Revolution the common populace experienced a rising expectation of the millennium. Popular periodicals like *Gentleman's Magazine* included essays on the signs of the times which indicated that God might be preparing to end history. In England, as in France, some viewed the early events of the French Revolution with great expectation and a sense that history was being either regenerated or expiring in a special way. Less and less were learned men seeking signs of the apocalyptic end, and more and more the common people sought out heavenly signs and warnings of the End Time. In 1793 and 1794 came a sudden flaming up again of millenarian expectations not unlike those of the seventeenth century, which had never been totally extinguished.[33]

The revolutionary excesses of 1790 caused a shift in French attitudes. By the end of the year, the confidence in the possibility of national regeneration which had helped to unite public opinion in support of the Revolution evaporated and would never reappear. A similar opinion shift also occurred in England where there had been initial enthusiasm for the Revolution. By the end of 1792 with France at war with half of Europe, the French king executed, and French orators proclaiming the liberation of oppressed peoples, England began to prepare for war. Part of this preparation involved the English tradition of interpreting biblical prophecies and applying them to current affairs for patriotic purposes. In a switch from the Protestant tradition, which cast the Church of Rome in the role of the Apocalyptic Beast, England's propagandists now saw the French Revolution in the role of the Beast of Revelation. (Later Napoleon was to inspire some to call him the Antichrist, but in general he did not inspire the same sorts of millenarian hopes and fears that the revolutionary Jacobins stirred up in 1794.) The international crisis of 1792 which brought England into a tacit alliance with the Catholic powers temporarily confused English millenarians who had long been accustomed to Rome and the pope as apocalyptic enemies.[34]

Richard Brothers

And again, just as French prophetic figures gained some following during the initial revolutionary excitement, so, too, in England several individuals were inspired to see themselves as prophets and to offer their followers a way of digesting and interpreting the great events on the Continent. Since the times were both exciting and confusing, it can cause no surprise that a disturbed prophet like Richard Brothers began to attract attention by 1794, especially among London's poor and credulous.

Brothers, although born in Placentia, Newfoundland, in 1757, grew up in England and seems to have seen action in the British navy during the American Revolution. About 1791 he had several visions. After one of these visions, in which he learned that London was to be destroyed, he lay in bed for three days and nights without eating. His landlady later testified to his strange behavior, but he claimed his actions were in response to divine warnings. One warning was a loud burst of thunder, the voice of a great angel (Rev. ch. 17). The angel informed Brothers that London was Babylon and God would destroy London by fire. Brothers saw "a large River run(ning) through London coloured with human blood," and he saw "Satan walking leisurely into London: his face had a smile. . . ."[35]

Brothers did attract one key disciple in 1795 whose prestige and lofty status as a member of Parliament gained Brothers a measure of respectability he probably would not have otherwise had. Nathaniel Brassey Halhed, former official of the East India Company and member of Parliament and the son of a director of the Bank of England, publicly declared his belief in the prophet's claims after reading Brothers' writings and speaking with him.[36]

Most of Richard Brothers's followers knew of his prophecies through his writings. He published *A Revealed Knowledge of the Prophecies and Times. Book the First. Wrote under the direction of the Lord God, and published by His sacred command. . . .* in 1794. The sixty-page pamphlet contained scriptural passages and his visions. He claimed to have predicted the death of Louis XVI and predicted that all monarchies would fall by 1798. In other writings Brothers also launched an attack upon the teachings of Copernicus and Newton. The notion that the earth revolved around the sun was the "most erroneous, wild and unnatural that ever entered the imagination."[37] His eight-page pamphlet appeared early in 1794, with a title almost as long as the text: *Brothers's Prophecy of all the Remarkable and Wonderful Events which will come to pass . . . foretelling the Downfall of the Pope; a Revolution in Spain, Portugal, and Germany; the Death* of Certain Great Persons in this and other Countries. Also a dreadful Famine, Pestilence, and Earthquake. . . . Brothers promised that at the end of great turmoil there would be an era of universal brotherhood.

Brothers's *Revealed Knowledge* reached many readers with its calculations of the millennium, its sense of identity between Englishmen and Jews, its translation of meteorology into prophecy, and the insistence that the Bible's prophecies be literally applied to current events. He gave fresh energy to that special English tradition, started by John Foxe's *Book of Martyrs*, that the English were God's chosen people, and England a New Israel. These kinds of speculations had always been intense in times of crisis, and England had seldom experienced a time as filled with distress and sense of disaster as 1795. Brothers' prophecies were vague enough to seem to be fulfilled, especially during the ominous times where French armies were victorious.[38]

Authorities found Brothers to have a "very methodical kind of madness." The Privy Council had him arrested in March 1795, and confined him in a lunatic asylum. Brothers spent the last thirty years of his life planning the New Jerusalem and designing its flags, uniforms, and palaces. He even made lists of the crops that should be grown in the Holy Land: parsnips, carrots, and cabbage. He called himself the Prince of the Hebrews and planned for the day God would enable him to rule the world from Jerusalem. For a while his followers agitated for his release, threatening violence if the prophet remained confined. His delusions eventually cost him his followers, however, and he was soon forgotten.[39]

Joanna Southcott

As Brothers's disciples fell away, many undoubtedly took up the cause of Joanna Southcott. Joanna Southcott came on the scene during a time of war-weariness and millenarian expectancy, which had in part been created by prophets like Brothers. In 1801 she published her first prophetic booklet, *The Strange Effects of Faith*. With great rapidity the fame of this Devon farmer's daughter and former domestic servant swept the country. As Brothers' communications deteriorated to mad proclamations about his kingly role, Southcott attracted followers by her assurances that the millennium was indeed at hand, and many expected that the Seven Seals were about to be opened.

Southcott gathered around her an entourage which included several educated men and women, but her appeal was felt strongest among working people of the west and north—Bristol, south Lancashire, West Riding, Stockton-on-Tees. Her appeal to the poor seems to have been based on a sense that divine revelation could fall upon a peasant's daughter as easily as a king.[40]

Southcott had been receiving and transcribing in a literal way divine messages or "voices" since 1792, when she was forty-two. Most of Joanna's prophecies convey little more than an apocalyptic mood, auguries of catastrophe so vague that they were easily applied to the crises and upheavals of Napoleonic Europe, with Napoleon as the Beast. Her style differed from the revolutionary specificity of Brothers' initial prophecies, as she raised anxieties about the final judgment of sinners. "O England!. . . The midnight-hour is coming for you all. . . . I warn you of dangers. . . ."[41]

Southcott was uneducated, simple, and credulous if not unbalanced. One day, while sweeping out a house, she was "permitted by the Lord" to find, "as if by accident," a commonplace seal. Thereafter her followers, the Southcottians, were able to obtain from her a special letter sealed with a wax imprint of this seal, a sort of promissory note which said that the bearer should "inherit the Tree of Life to be made Heirs of God and joint heirs with Jesus Christ."[42] The promise of the millennium was available only to "The Sealed People," while the scoffers received threats. Possibly as many as a hundred thousand were "sealed" this way. There was even a market in seals at one time not unlike the late medieval market in relics of the Cross. The emotional disequilibrium of the times is revealed, not only in the enthusiasm of her prophet disciples called "Joannas" but also in the corresponding violence of people who sometimes assaulted these Joannas.

Southcott spent much of 1803 traveling through western and northern England issuing her special sealed letters. She sought to give the faithful assurance that they would be preserved after the Second Coming. Her brand of millenarianism, which became the dominant current in millenarian popular religion in England, was not revolutionary. It did not inspire the lower classes to effective social action; indeed, it scarcely engaged the real world. Its apocalyptic spirit was closer to the Methodist revivalism of the time. It brought to a point of hysterical intensity people's concern for personal salvation.

After the intensity of 1801-1804, the Southcott movement achieved a second climax in 1814 when the ageing Joanna had an hysterical pregnancy and promised to give birth to "Shiloh," the Son of God. In West Riding the whole district "was infested with bearded prophets"—members of the movement were obliged to wear beards—while Ashton in Lancashire became a center for her prophet disciples in the north. Southcott died at the end of 1814, tragically disillusioned in her own "voice." But the cult proved to be extraordinarily deeply rooted, and successive claimants appeared to inherit her prophetic mantle, most notably a Bradford woolcomber, John Wroe. Many Methodists seem to have joined the movement, but as a whole Methodism had far greater organizational stability, money, the benign attitude of authorities, and a more reliable system for handing on its traditions.[43]

The Southcottian movement was a cult of the poor. Her God cursed the false "shepherds" of England, the landowners and governors who conspired to raise the price of bread. The Southcottian movement seems to have, in part, sprung from the terrible conditions of lower-class life during the early Industrial Revolution as well as from the failure of Jacobins, English radicals, and millenarians alike to achieve the earthly millennium envisaged in the 1790s. It was not the prophets, secular and religious, who failed but the Revolution.[44]

Other individuals, although also failing ultimately, more effectively helped people by means of radical experiments. In the early nineteenth century, as the effects of the Industrial Revolution began to be felt, several activists such as Robert Owen proposed a reordering of society along communitarian lines. The remarkable Owen gained a large fortune from cotton spinning but departed from the usual pattern of successful industrialists. Animated by millenialist fervor (but of a different kind than the usual religious millenarian), he planned for radical social reform and the reconstruction of society. Drawing on

England

the widespread ideas of the time, Owen developed a kind of social and secular millenarianism. He established socialistic communities on both sides of the Atlantic that would be models of ideal factory communities. Of the two dozen Owenite communities set up, however, all dissolved by 1830.[45]

Early Nineteenth Century

With prophetic and millenarian themes commonplace, it is not unexpected that many individuals claimed illumination and special knowledge of the end of the world. Such individuals usually did not attract a following. In 1800 a member of the Irish House of Commons named Francis Dobbs cited the Books of Revelation and Daniel against the proposed Act of Union between England and Ireland. He had temporarily left politics to study the fulfillment of millenarian prophecy in history. His religious convictions and Irish Patriotism combined to produce the belief that the Second Coming was imminent and would occur in Ireland. He predicted the Messiah would come in 1800 or 1801 in enough time to prevent the Act of Union. The Act of Union, however, did pass and Christ did not come to Ireland. Dobbs died mad and impoverished in 1811.[46]

In contrast to Mr. Dobbs was John Nelson Darby. Darby joined a sect called "The Brethren," being organized by A. N. Groves during the 1820s. Groves rejected all ecclesiastical forms and denominational distinctions. The Brethren became split because of the influence of Darby.

Darby devised a way of interpreting the Bible known as dispensationalism. For him the Bible was a history of God's dealings with humankind during seven periods or dispensations of history, from the first age of innocence before the flood, through the dispensation of the Gentiles down to the final age, the fullness of time. The first event of the final dispensation is the invisible coming of Christ to gather up his chosen, a lifting up known as the secret rapture. Once Jesus has taken up his saints, the Jews will convert to Christianity but there will be seven years of tribulation caused by Satan. At the end time, Christ and his army will do battle, and there will be a millennium of peace.

Darby's followers have been called Darbyites, and his network of local assemblies, tied to each other by consensus of doctrine and bonds of fellowship, are usually called by some variation on the name of Church of God or Plymouth Brethren. Darby visited the United States and Canada during the 1860s and 1870s. Many conservative Christians and clergymen of nineteenth-century America accepted Darby's dispensational thought, although they did not join his Brethren. Many Bible institutes and colleges were set up, perhaps most notably the Moody Bible Institute in Chicago.[47]

Edward Irving (1792-1834) was an effective if bizarre preacher and populariser in the 1820s. Prompted by a significant personal crisis, the death of his infant son, Irving underwent a religious conversion. He began to find millenarian ideas far more spiritually comforting than contemporary Christian orthodoxy. He saw death belonging to sin and Satan. On the other hand, the Second Coming of Christ would transfigure the earth. Christians, he argued, should hope for a union with Christ on a transfigured earth. Indeed, Christians should live as if that coming might occur at any moment.

In 1826 Irving gathered with others at Albury Park, at the home of Henry Drummond, for a conference on prophecy. In his church in London's Regent Square Irving's followers felt that their speaking in tongues and healings were clear signs of the Holy Spirit's presence and that the last days were near. Because of their excesses they were compelled to draw apart, gathering to await the end and believing they were the saving remnant. They called themselves the Catholic Apostolic Church (and sometimes were called Irvingites).

Conclusion

There were different kinds of millenarianism in England and on the Continent. England seems to have had a more continuous millenarian tradition, starting prior to the Civil War and extending well into the

England

nineteenth century by means of a steady stream of learned treatises, sermons, and popular tracts. The English tradition tended to be based more directly on Scripture, with specific attention to Daniel and the Book of Revelation. French millenarianism tended to derive from a wider variety of sources such as traditions of popular piety and from the eighteenth-century search for spiritual enlightenment in such areas as occultism and mesmerism. For a variety of reasons, England had a greater public circulation of printed material, even the most bizarre, so that millenarian ideas could be disseminated and thus survive to be examined by modern scholars with far greater ease than is true in France.[48]

England and America, and France to a lesser degree, witnessed during the middle years of the seventeenth century a "great awakening" of religion, even though different areas experienced this revival of religion in different ways and at varying times. From approximately 1760 to 1850, England and America possessed a popular millenarian culture which was quite extraordinary, with its various prophets and movements. Millenarian concerns and popular prophetism had become commonplace. But an extraordinary shift began to take place, from religious millenarianism to millenarianism based on a secular ideology. People continued to be religious, of course, but the revivalism of Methodism and the religion of Joanna Southcott tended to the desire of personal salvation. Other millenarians, like Robert Owen, sought to inspire people to effective social action using the words of millenariansim but without the religious faith. Around this time in London (1850), Friedrich Engels was establishing a link between religous millenarianism and the social millenarianism of the nineteenth century. In his book on the Peasant's Revolt he especially showed his admiration of the leader of the peasants, Thomas Müntzer.[49]

The next chapter turns to the American religious experience which, perhaps because of less repression and persecution, perhaps because of a more literalist and fundamentalist tradition, perhaps because of fewer established traditions, was more lush and diverse than that of England and the Continent, with a number of experiments in communial or communist living inspired by millenarian ideas.

NOTES

1. On this question of the persistence of millenarian concerns, indeed, their normalcy in English popular religion, see William M. Lamont, *Godly Rule: Politics and Religion, 1603-60* (New York: St. Martin's Press, 1969), p. 13, and John F.C. Harrison, *Quest for the New Moral World: Robert Owen and the Owenites in Britain and America* (New York: Charles Scribner's Sons, 1969), p. 138.

2. Christopher Hill, *Puritanism and Revolt* (London: Secker and Warburg, 1958), p. 329.

3. Christopher Hill, p. 328-332.

4. Christopher Hill, pp. 330-333; Hillel Schwartz, *The French Prophets: The History of a Millenarian Group in Eighteenth-Century England* (Berkeley, Los Angeles, London: University of California Press, 1980) pp. 43-45.

5. Hillel Schwartz, *The French Prophets*, p. 45.

6. D.P. Walker, "English Philadelphians," in *The Decline of Hell* (University of Chicago Press, 1964), pp. 245-257; Hillel Schwartz, *The French Prophets*, pp. 45-46, 49.

7. Cf. Don Yoder, "Sects and Religious Movements," *Encyclopedia of the American Religious Experience* ed. by Charles H. Lippy and Peter W. Williams (New York: Charles Scribner's Sons, 1988), Vol. 1, p. 620; Hillel Schwartz, *The French Prophets*, p. 47; cf. "Lead, or Leade, Mrs. Jane" in *Dictionary of National Biography* Vol. XI, pp. 753-754.

8. Hillel Schwartz, *The French Prophets*, pp. 21, 48-50. Hillel Schwartz, *Knaves, Fools, Madmen, and that Subtle Effluvium: A Study of the Opposition to the French Prophets in England, 1706-1710* (Gainesville, Florida: University of Florida Social Sciences Monograph Number 62, 1978), p. 5.

9. Hillel Schwartz, *The French Prophets*, p. 72; Clarke Garrett, *Spirit Possession and Popular Religion: From the Camisards to the Shakers* (Baltimore and London: Johns Hopkins Press, 1987), p. 41.

10. Hillel Schwartz, *Knaves and Fools*, p. 14; Hillel Schwartz, *The French Prophets*, pp. 70-72.

11. Hillel Schwartz, *The French Prophets*, pp. 73, 79, 147, 261.

England

12. Hillel Schwartz, *The French Prophets*, p. 91, 139; cf. also Hillel Schwartz *Knaves and Fools*, pp. 16-17.

13. Hillel Schwartz, *Knaves and Fools* pp. 16, 25-26; Hillel Schwartz, *The French Prophets*, pp. 105, 180; cf. also "Lacy, John" in *Dictionary of National Biography*, Vol. XI, pp. 382-383.

14. Hillel Schwartz, pp. 151, 241-242; E.P. Thompson, p. 257.

15. Hillel Schwartz, *The French Prophets*, pp. 85-6, 90; *Knaves and Fools*, pp. 25-6.

16. Hillel Schwartz, *The French Prophets*, p. 91.

17. Hillel Schwartz, *The French Prophets*, pp. 93-95; *Dictionary of National Biography*, p. 383.

18. Cited by E.P. Thompson, *The Making of the English Working Class* (New York: Pantheon Books, 1964), p. 256.

19. Cited by E.P. Thompson, p. 257.

20. Hillel Schwartz, *The French Prophets*, p. 113.

21. Hillel Schwartz, *The French Prophets*, pp. 119-123, 150.

22. Hillel Schwartz, *The French Prophets*, p. 128.

23. Hillel Schwartz, *The French Prophets*, pp. 142-145, 148-149.

24. Hillel Schwartz, *The French Prophets*, pp. 135, 139, 140, 143.

25. Clarke Garrett, p. 153; Hillel Schwartz, *The French Prophets*, pp. 180, 192, 196, 201.

26. Hillel Schwartz, *Knaves and Fools*, pp. 25-26; Hillel Schwartz, *The French Prophets*, pp. 87, 89.

27. Hillel Schwartz, *The French Prophets*, p. 207.

28. Cf. Hillel Schwartz, *The French Prophets*, p. 212, footnote #41, where Schwartz says he is unable to confirm any Wardley attachment to the Quakers or the French prophets; cf. also *Knaves and Fools*, p. 26.

29. Edward Deming Andrews, *The People Called Shakers: A Search for the Perfect Society* (New York: Dover Publications, 1953, 1963), p. 6.

30. Cited by Edward Deming Andrews, p. 6.

31. Edward Deming Andrews, p. 6.

32. Hillel Schwartz, *The French Prophets*, pp. 211-212; cf. "Lee, Ann" in *Dictionary of National Biography*, Vol. XI, p. 784.

33. E.P. Thompson, p. 117; Clarke Garrett, p. 163.

34. Clarke Garrett, pp. 167-8, 211.

35. Clarke Garrett, pp. 179-181; E.P. Thompson, p. 117.

36. Clarke Garrett, pp. 175, 191-192.

37. Clarke Garrett, pp. 189, 214; E.P. Thompson, p. 118; cf. "Brothers, Richard," in *Dictionary of National Biography*, Vol. II, pp. 1350-1353.

38. Clarke Garrett, pp. 184, 190; E.P. Thompson, p. 118. Garrett, p. 185, points out that Philosemitism had been an integral part of English millenarian thought since the 1600s. At the end of the eighteenth century there was widespread belief that the lost tribes of Israel would be found by European explorers, perhaps somewhere in the American wilderness. Some of these ideas showed up in the writings of the American prophet Joseph Smith.

39. Clarke Garrett, pp. 181-184, 209, 214; E.P. Thompson, p. 118.

40. James K. Hopkins, *A Woman to Deliver Her People: Joanna Southcott and English Millenarianism in an Era of Revolution* (Austin: University of Texas Press, 1982); E.P. Thompson, pp. 382-283; Clarke Garrett, pp. 216; cf. W.H. Oliver, *Prophets and Millennialists: The Uses of Biblical Prophecy in England from the 1790s to the 1840s* (Oxford University Press, 1978), p. 157.

41. Cited by E.P. Thompson, p. 384.

42. Cited by E.P. Thompson, p. 385; also Clarke Garrett, p. 221.

43. E.P. Thompson, pp. 386-387; Clarke Garrett, p. 321.

44. E.P. Thompson, p. 386; Clarke Garrett, p. 212.

45. Cf. J.F.C. Harrison, *Quest for the New Moral Order: Robert Owen and the Owenites in Britain and America* (New York: Charles Scribner's Sons, 1969), pp. 6-7, and especially pp. 92 ff. for Owen's millennialism; see also, W.H. Oliver, *Prophets and*

England

Millennialists: The Use of Biblical Prophecy in England from the 1790s to the 1840s (New Zealand: Auckland University Press, 1978), pp. 197-217.

46. Clarke Garrett, pp. 118-119.

47. Cf "Darby, John Nelson," in *Dictionary of National Biography*, Vol. V, pp. 493-494; J. Gordon Melton, *Biographical Dictionary of American Cult and Sect Leaders* (New York and London: Garland Publishing, Inc., 1986), p. 63-65.

48. Clarke Garrett, pp. 145-146.

49. Henri Desroche, *The American Shakers: From Neo-Christianity to Presocialism* translated by John K. Savacool (Amherst: University of Massachusetts Press, 1971), p. 59; also see E.P. Thompson, p. 386.

Chapter Ten
America, The Land of God's Chosen: The Early Period

The American landscape has been sprinkled with a bewildering diversity of religious movements, experimental communities, and curious sects. Not only did an abundance of homegrown movements sprout up, but it seemed as if every possible religious experiment in Europe had been put in a box, shaken, and strewn out lavishly over the American wilderness. The lushness and variety of all types of religious, utopian, and communitarian groups are a touching statement of the hope that the New World promised to immigrants and idealists and religious seekers of all kinds, even though that lush diversity sometimes makes a shambles of scholarly attempts at historical neatness and order.

This richness and diversity of American religious history necessitate a narrowing of focus on millenarian movements. The difficulty, however, is that millenarian ideas and groups so pervade the already lush religious history of eighteenth- and nineteenth-century America that we must recognize that millenarianism was an ongoing phenomenon in the American religious experience and, in comparison with Europe, closer to the center of religious experience than an aberration at the fringe.[1] But American millenarianism has many different threads, and in many ways differed from the European experience.

This chapter will look at first and briefly the Puritan heritage, then a few of the dozens of indigenous religious groups that sprouted in New England. Then attention will turn to the continuing waves of European immigrants who sought out American shores as a religious refuge.

Puritans in America

English religious Dissenters, that is, the Calvinists who followed the Puritan tradition of dissenting from the established Church of England populated New England, and their religion gave a tone and spirit to the region because they felt they had a mission to build a society in conformity with the demands of God. They were also unusually receptive to millenarianism. But perhaps the American Puritan millenarianism initially, like its English counterpart, was a bit too cerebral, concerned with an unravelling of scriptural puzzles. But that changed, and increasingly the millenarians in America adopted a more prophetic and enthusiastic style.

As the Puritan wave crested and waned in England it washed up on the shore of the New World, particularly in New England. English Puritan immigrants brought millenarianism with them as part of their baggage. After the King's dismissal of Parliament in 1629 it looked as though there was no longer any hope of revolution. The Puritan John Winthrop and his companions migrated to New England in 1630 with the apocalyptic vision of building a revolutionary city like the New Jerusalem, a "Citty vppon a Hill" (cf. Rev. 21:10).[2]

During England's Civil War, New England's Puritan divines were preoccupied with the same millenarian themes as their English counterparts. Indeed, some of the earliest works printed in the American Colonies expounded on the Book of Revelation. In Boston during the cold winter of 1639-1640 the Rev. Joseph Cotton gave weekly sermons on the Book of Revelation. He also published three treatises on the same subject. Cotton estimated that the millennium would begin after the destruction of Antichrist which he identified as the Papacy. About the same time, across the river from Boston in Cambridge, the Reverend Thomas Shepard wrote a work dealing with

America: The Early Period

the certainty of Christ's Second Coming and the duty of believers to be watchful for this event. Further up the coast of Massachusetts, the Reverend Thomas Parker of Newbury, in a book which he published in 1646, predicted the end of the world would come about 1859. Disagreeing with this date, William Aspinwall, a deacon in Boston as well as a member of the General Court of Massachusetts suggested it would not be later than 1673.[3]

That foremost American Puritan, Increase Mather, continued the tradition of learned speculation about the end of the world. In his *Mystery of Israel's Salvation, Explained and Applyed* (1669), Mather believed the millennium of chapter 20 of Revelation was still to come, that the conversion of the Jews, however, would precede the Second Advent of Christ and the glorious earthly kingdom. Increase Mather's son, Cotton, also had a lively sense of the approaching end and believed that the Great Day of the Lord was very close. English immigrants, like John Davenport, who founded New Haven in Connecticut, believed in the literal resurrection of the saints to reign with Christ on earth for a thousand years following His Second Advent. These New Haven Christians expected their city to be the seat of the millennial kingdom, that Christ would come in person and live with them for a thousand years.[4]

In addition to this current of learned men who continued to speculate and preach on the end time and the Second Coming of Christ, the other prophetic and enthusiastic current was beginning to rise. In fact, throughout Western Europe and the North American colonies, there was a spiritual ferment, as the upper classes and educated tired of the religious squabblings of the seventeenth century and turned to the abstractions of eighteenth-century rationalism. The spiritual hungers of the ordinary people were not being met, and consequently during the eighteenth century their aspirations found vent in a variety to popular religious movements and experiments of a highly emotional nature, not the least of which were the revivals. In New England it was as if many farmers and hardy backwoods folk were saying that the Harvard and Yale graduates were preaching a religion that was too academic.

Starting in the 1730s George Whitefield, an energetic itinerant evangelist, made a series of triumphant missionary tours across New

England that helped spark the so-called Great Awakening of the 1740s. Whitefield recast the Puritan religious experience. Hitherto Calvinist Puritans had identified salvation as depending upon the covenant between God and the human race, but they never had a secure sense of personal salvation. Whitefield now located the key transaction between God and man in the experience of conversion within one's soul, an experience he called the "New Birth." This emphasis on personal experience opened up New England Calvinism to a whole range of religious experiences that Puritans had hitherto dismissed as enthusiasm. Soon noisy, ecstatic, and zealous individuals enlivened—and disturbed—hitherto stern New England congregations, some of which split apart to form new churches.[5]

Perhaps the most dramatic and exciting eighteenth-century American theorist and preacher of the millennium was Jonathan Edwards. Edwards, a Calvinist and Puritan, put an American and postmillennial gloss on Puritan millenarianism by adding personal and emotional elements to the intellectual search for portents of the Second Coming. He intensified the subjective and personal aspects of spiritual renewal. He interpreted the widespread renewal of the Great Awakening as an eschatological sign of the Second Coming, especially as settlers populated North America and the idea of progress developed. Edwards was convinced that the prophecies of the last times were being fulfilled and considered the Great Awakening as prelude to the millennium.[6]

Although there were occasional scenes of emotional religion in Boston, it was the small country churches of the Connecticut Valley that experienced a frenzy of religious emotion. Jonathan Edwards delivered revival-type sermons with titles like "Sinners in the Hands of the Angry God." His small audiences yelled and shrieked, rolled in the aisles, crowded up to the pulpit, and begged him to stop. In the 1740s Edwards' influence dominated the region of Central New England. When Harvard faculty and graduates viewed or heard reports of people writhing in the churches, they could only consider the Great Awakening as an orgy of emotion, and they called it by a word that conveyed their contempt: enthusiasm. They believed it was a crisis and even feared that the excitement of overstimulated passions would slop over into activities other than ecclesiastical. Edwards thought it was an outpouring of the Spirit of God upon the land, a necessary prelude to the Second Coming. But by the 1750s Edwards was exiled, escaping to the frontier as did so many other misfits in American history. At Stockbridge, at the far western end of Massachusetts, he eked out his last years as a missionary among impoverished Indians. Then in 1758 as the still acknowledged leader of the nascent revival movement he was invited to become president of the newly founded Princeton College, but he died shortly after his inauguration.[7]

The period of 1730-1760 was swept, not just in America but in most of Western Europe, by some form of religious emotionalism. There were, however, still those who continued the tradition of learned men who speculated on the end time and its signs. Among them was Joseph Priestly. That distinguished scientist and theologian, before he migrated from England to Pennsylvania in 1794, delivered a sermon contending that the events of his time appeared to be foreshadowing the Second Advent. His book *The Present State of Europe Compared with the Ancient Prophecies* (1794) elaborated on his belief about the signs of the approach of the Second Coming. Especially significant, he felt, were the preaching of the Gospel to all nations, the seeming great prevalence of infidelity, and the undermining of antichristian Catholic power by the French Revolutionaries.

Other prominent, respectable, and learned men continued this current of speculation. Yale's president, Timothy Dwight, chose the Book of Revelation as the theme for his July 4th sermon in 1798 and related the prophecies of St. John to the suppression of the Catholic Church in France. The significant contemporary events in Revolutionary France persuaded him that "the advent of Christ was at least at our doors." He also speculated that the millennium would begin not far from the year 2000, that the millennium would be realized, not by miracles but gradually and through human efforts.

One New Haven divine had the confidence to fix an exact and imminent date for the Lord's return. The Reverend David Austin graduated from Yale in 1779, became a pastor at Elizabethtown, New Jersey, and in 1794 during the excitement of the early years of the American Republic, published *The Millennium; or, the Thousand Years of Prosperity, Promised to the Church of God, in the Old Testament and the New, Shortly to Commence*. He announced the date of the Second

Advent as May 15, 1796. His excited congregation joined him in church to await the event, but as the day wore on and nothing unusual happened he finally stood and preached from the text, "My Lord delayeth his coming." He admitted he made a mistake in calculations, but he did not lose faith. He returned to New Haven to build houses and wharfs for the Jews whom he expected to gather to meet the Messiah.[8]

Early "New Light" reformers followed Edwards against the "Old Lights" who resisted the revival excitement. "New Lights" welcomed individual inspiration and the enlightenment of the Holy Spirit, while Old Lights maintained traditional authority and resisted the need for an experience of conversion. During the years of the Great Awakening, traveling preachers gathered people in group revival meetings in which they aroused feelings of guilt and the hope of redemption through a transforming religious experience. Preachers demanded spiritual rebirth and an emotional engagement with religion. Religious excitement, the new religious style of revivalism, and a new realignment of churches in New England followed in the wake of the Great Awakening.

Jonathan Edwards looked for signs of that reign's beginning in history and saw the Great Awakening as one harbinger that the millennium was to begin in America by the year 2000. Attention on a "new birth" cloaked the American self in the garments of subjective individualism and gave revivalistic evangelism a lasting place in the American religious experience.[9]

Revolutionary Period Sects

The Revolutionary War years saw intense religious excitement and a flurry of millenarian expectations among the radical evangelicals of rural New England and southeastern Canada. In New England the excitement was called the New Light Stir and in maritime Canada the New Light Revival. The American Revolution brought unprecedented political and social changes, caused the movement of people to the frontier, and threw New England's cultural institutions into turmoil.

America: The Early Period

The Revolutionary War fired many American ministers' millenarian hopes. They interpreted the conflict as God's elect against the forces of Antichrist; America's victory would initiate Christ's millennial kingdom. New England sermons bristled with euphoric images of America's role in bringing the kingdom more quickly, that the American cause was God's cause, that British tyranny could only be the sign of the Antichrist.[10]

During the 1770s and immediately after the War, large numbers of people migrated into the hill country of the northern and western frontier, most for economic reasons and a few for political reasons. Hundreds of families from southeastern and coastal New England moved to newly opened lands in Maine, Vermont, and western Massachusetts. The resultant disruptions left no pattern of culture or tradition unchanged in northern and rural areas of New England. Change, the appearance of new settlers, and the inability of an overstretched Congregationalist establishment to pastor so many new communities created a vacuum that allowed for the rise of dozens of sects, mostly small and most with a very brief lifespan. These local sects transformed the Calvinist tradition, rejecting much of the Calvinist emphasis on innate human depravity by allowing for a religious experience that gave vent to feeling, sensation, and excitement. Now hysterical cries and emotional spasms, speaking in tongues, visionary trances, all were acceptable symptoms of spiritual transformation.[11]

The "New Lights" were primarily radical evangelicals among Puritan-tradition Congregational churches. The "New Lights" were reformers who believed in the imminent Second Coming and sought to bring new light and fervor into the established churches by sanctifying the "saved remnant" in the Last Days. This new movement began in Nova Scotia, ignited by the charismatic Henry Alline, an eccentric who typified the rural leaders of the New Light Stir. He had been born in Rhode Island in 1748, but when he was about twelve his family joined other southern New Englanders who emigrated to Nova Scotia because of social and economic limitations. When he was about twenty he had sexual fantasies about a young female friend which plunged him into an extended period of guilt and depression which his unsophisticated theology could not lighten. In 1775, when he was about twenty-seven, he underwent a religious conversion; inspired by the necessity for a "New Birth" and animated with a sense of the nearness of the Second Coming, he felt a special call to ministry.

Alline began his itinerant ministry in 1776, armed with little theological training but an effective preaching style. His own family rejected him, and other listeners were suspicious of any unlettered preacher. Despite opposition from "Old Light" Congregationalists, Alline's ministry spread in the vacuum caused by the inability of Congregationalists to staff rural parishes adequately. He visited eastern Canada and then northern New England in 1782. The meteoric success of his revival ministry came at the opportune time, a time of rural disruption and change; his gospel of pacifism spread through Nova Scotia, for instance, after the most serious threat of American invasion had passed. He gained many converts, although sometimes at the cost of schisms among local congregations.[12]

Significant differences separated Congregationalists and the radical evangelism of Alline and his "New Lights." The Congregational view, typified by Ezra Stiles's 1783 sermon *The United States Elevated to Glory and Honor* focused on America as the chosen nation of God, blessed by the Lord with millennial virtue and holiness. Congregationalists endorsed and supported the Revolution with a sanguine expectation of an earthly millennial kingdom in America. Alline's movement was eclectic, shaped by overwhelming personal experience rather than based on the Calvinist theology which dominated most Congregationalist ministers. Alline issued a charismatic gospel call that had millenarian expectations. Firm was his belief in the imminent Second Coming of Christ and in the necessity for the "saved remnant" to search for sanctification, especially in the last days when people were frightened of revolutionary wars and rumors of wars. Radical evangelicals held the premillennialist notions that humanity was sinful and depraved and that the religious revivals signaled the looming end of history and the imminent establishment of the Kingdom of the New Jerusalem.

Alline's confrontation of his mainstream opponents was a confrontation between his revivalist premillenarianism and their increasingly mainstream postmillenarianism. The rural saints of the New Light Stir were certain that the reign of glory would commence only after the imminent return of Christ. Unlike the Old Lights, they did not find

America: The Early Period

hope and solace in America's military triumph but rather gloomily sought "the signs of the times" in political events and natural omens in order to discern the moment of the millennial dawn. One such event, the Dark Day of 1780, occurred midway through the Stir and served to drive it to new heights of chiliastic fervor. May 19, 1780, from early morning to mid-afternoon, was an eerie day during which most of New England was plunged into darkness. To believers this was but one more dramatic sign that God had added to the other signs of war and renewal. Believers felt these omens were but the harbingers of the predicted Last Days. Millenarian expectation suffused the New Light Stir, and the larger and more intense the awakening became, the more self-validating evidence believers brought forth that God was preparing the end time.[13]

Alline died in New Hampshire in 1784, and the New Light Stir gradually weakened after 1782, never able to set itself up as a lasting establishment, even though significant local revivals continued sporadically throughout the 1780s and 1790s because rural isolation did not provide any institutional form or routinization for peoples' religious enthusiasm and desire for renewal. A number of these small, local sects merit some consideration.

Jemima Wilkinson's Universal Friends

An early indigenous American sect with some millenarian characteristics was the Universal Friends, which flourished in Rhode Island, New York, and Connecticut from 1776 to 1863. The charismatic prophetess Jemima Wilkinson founded and led the sect. She was the eighth child of prosperous Quaker parents and was born in 1752 at Cumberland, Rhode Island. As a teenager during the emotional revivals of radical evangelicals and New Lights in 1774, she experienced a series of visions that eventually led to her expulsion by the Quakers. She embraced the charismatic faith of a Separatist congregation. In 1776 Smithfield Lower Friends Meeting expelled Jemima's older sister Patience for bearing an illegitimate child. In July, the Continental Congress declared independence, and the British warship "Rose" plundered the islands and coastline of Narragansett Bay and upset Rhode Island's regular commerce. Thus, the outbreak of war, her sister's indiscretion and her own religious concerns caused the Quaker Wilkinson household to be in turmoil and stress. Not surprisingly, Jemima became ill in October of that year.[14]

Jemima's account of her "fatal fever" shows that she herself genuinely believed that she had died. In her delirium she had a vision of two Archangels who brought her the revelations of the will of God. Her account says that the angels announced the Last Days and that "the Spirit of Life from God, had descended to earth, to warn a lost and guilty, perishing and dying world, to flee from the wrath which is to come."[15] When she rose from her sick bed she told her family and acquaintances that they were not speaking to Jemima, that Jemima was dead and her soul was in heaven. The Spirit of God now inhabited her body and was to be called the Publick Universal Friend.[16] She spoke of herself in the third person and believed that "the tabernacle which Jemima had left behind was re-animated by the power and spirit of Jesus Christ, that this was the second coming of the Lord, who was to remain on earth and reign a thousand years, that it was the eleventh hour, and the last call of mercy that would ever be made to the human race."[17]

Immediately Wilkinson dressed herself in special robes and began her ministry of witnessing the Spirit messenger from Christ which inherited her body. She began to preach to any who would listen to her in the "eleventh hour." Her message at taverns and private homes was one of millenarianism and perfectionism, of holiness and preparation for the Last Judgment. Her prophecies, ecstatic prayer, spiritual discernment, costume, and genuine charm and dignity gave her a messianic impact on hearers. Distinguished by her rarity as a woman preacher, especially one who was notably attractive, and by her claim that she was restored from the dead, her preaching caused a sensation. To war-weary Narragansett society she offered a life of holiness and moral discipline in preparation for the Last Judgment. She didn't try to forgive sins but did, however, offer herself as an infallibly inspired guide in all sorts of affairs.[18]

When a wealthy and prominent Rhode Island judge, William Potter, became a convert, he provided a distinguished house for the Public Universal Friend and her other converts. Her first followers seem to have been, as one hostile source puts it, "dissenters from other denominations, those who had been suspended or excluded from church membership for their disorderly conduct—a few unprincipled adventurers, and a still greater number of weak men and women, and inexperienced girls and children."[19] But others followed her, and not just the kind of socially marginal people who gathered in a typical Radical Evangelical congregation, for all of her family joined her as well as several leading Narragansett families that were bound together by marriage. In 1783 the Universal Friends built a meeting house at East Greenwich and issued faith statements proclaiming that they were redeemed from the wrath to come.

Wilkinson fashioned her sect into an unusual group structure, a kinship network of nuclear families governed by a charismatic celibate matriarchy. The prophetess enjoined celibacy on her followers as the purest way of life, even though she did not outright forbid marriage and was rather lenient in enforcing celibacy, unlike her contemporary Mother Ann Lee of the Shakers who, like Jemima, also claimed to be an embodiment of Christ. Jemima may have chosen the path of celibacy because of her infatuation with a man who had been killed in the Revolution. After a period of depression Jemima began to be "disgusted with the idea of wedlock."[20] Because her followers lived in such close proximity, the Universal Public Friend regulated every aspect of behavior, issuing detailed, monastic-type rules for personal hygiene, dress, meals, work, and other matters.

Wilkinson traveled constantly and usually had from six to a dozen devoted female companions on a journey. She traveled on horseback through southern New England and Pennsylvania seeking new converts. Soon she obeyed a revelation to join together her followers, and she began to plan a communal settlement in the wilderness where the Universal Friend would initiate the millennial kingdom. In 1788 the sect purchased land in the Seneca Lake region of New York, and the following year, when George Washington was inaugurated as America's first president, she had gathered her followers into an enclave called the New Jerusalem. Although Wilkinson died in 1819, her prosperous utopian community on Lake Seneca and Keuka Lake (where her followers were the first white people to try to raise crops) managed to survive without her up to the Civil War. Lawsuits between her heirs and several opponents and apostates dragged in courts until

1828. Her appointed successor Rachel Malin apparently held a core of the society together until her death in 1843. The difficulty, as we shall see again, was the sect was too bound to the personal charisma of its founder to survive for very long as a cohesive community. She had never developed mechanisms to ensure continued commitment to and ongoing leadership for her evangelical, millennialist ideology.[21]

Other Minor Groups

Another radical sect appeared around 1775 at Harvard, Massachusetts, a small town about 30 miles northwest of Boston. This celibate perfectionistic sect rejected the biological family. The sect began with the eccentric teachings of a minister by the name of Shadrach Ireland. Around 1770 he abandoned his wife and family and professed the doctrine of spiritual wifery. He persuaded some followers to construct a large brick building which became known as the "Square House" and in which Ireland lived with his new spiritual wife and a retinue of other female disciples. About 1775 he felt moved to proclaim himself immortal and urged followers to obey his instructions so that they, too, would achieve spiritual and physical perfection. He banned marriage, and to those already married, he issued orders for the partners not to sleep with each other. The movement flourished for two more years, until Ireland's poor health made it impossible to sustain his claim to immortality. To prepare his followers for his death, Ireland took an increasingly apocalyptic focus: he predicted the imminent arrival of Christ. On his death bed Ireland gave instructions to his followers gathered about him: "I am going but don't bury me; for the time is short; God is coming to take the church."[22] He died in September 1778, and his followers left his corpse in a lime-filled box for more than six weeks before the indisputable evidence of decay finally compelled them to bury it. They regarded his passing as a prophetic sign of the Second Coming, and the sect continued on at Square House until 1781 when many joined the Shaker community.

Rural areas were especially rich in generating eccentric groups that readily made use of ecstatic practices and millenarian ideas. There was, for example, a brief flurry of Come-Outers and Merry Dancers who practiced ecstatic worship in 1779. In their religious rituals, the Come-Outers, mostly women, wrought themselves up to a frenzy, even to point of frothing at the mouth, dancing, leaping, stamping, and whirling around. This physical excitement brought about a trance state which they regarded as putting them in communion with God. At its peak the Come-Outer movement embraced strange notions of physical and spiritual perfection, and any millenarian ideas were not compelling or essential.[23]

About the same time in Maine, in the town of Sanford, ecstatic Radicals earned the name of Merry Dancers. A group comprised mainly of young veterans of the Revolution, the Merry Dancers disrupted the local Congregationalist parish in 1780 before gathering for their own meeting. The exuberance of the group got out of hand, and they began to drink to excess and engage in "indecent and immoral practices." The Dancers engaged in strange antics such as "hooting the Devil." Dressing in strange garb they would scream "Woe, woe, woe!" which could be heard in the night as far as a mile away. The Dancers explained, apparently without irony, that these were purification rites on the way to perfection, a sort of "carnal slough" through which they were doomed to pass on the way to spiritual regeneration.[24]

The "exercises" and loss of control of the Come-Outer movement and Merry Dancers differed from ecstatic Shaker dancing. The revival "dances" and exercises tended to be individualistic and a chaotic frenzy, even though the participants believed they were manifesting in a physical way the presence of the divine. Although the Shakers also engaged in dances which they believed to be a physical manifestation of the divine presence, they performed, however, structured dances with uniform and precise patterns of movement each week in preparation for the Sunday worship celebration. Involvement in such ritual activites, whatever their nature, tended to strengthen the participants' identification with the community since all were involved.

Other short-lived sects bloomed in western New England during the Stir. In the Berkshire Mountains of western Massachusetts and, in particular, New Lebanon, New York, six miles west of the Massachusetts border, a sect emerged of New Lebanon Lights. The focus was the imminent return of Christ and the search for millennial perfection. These New Light millenarians came together for long meetings in which glossolalia, visions, and prophecy were prominent gifts. Joseph Meacham was leader of this sect, son of a Baptist elder, from Enfield, Connecticut. Joseph left Enfield in 1776 and spent several years in pilgrimage. He arrived in New Lebanon just before the outbreak of the New Lift stir. Meacham's preaching brought millennial fervor to a feverish level with daily meetings in 1779 while the community awaited the Coming of Christ with ecstatic worship and charismatic gifts. Mary Andrus, a participant, recalled that Meacham and others gave assurances that the latter day of glory was near at hand, and that Christ would shortly set up his kingdom on earth and make an end of sin. But when Christ did not appear in 1779 the congregation and Meacham suffered a depression which left them troubled about their erroneous interpretation of signs but still clinging to the belief that God had indeed given warning of the end of the world. The excitement of the summer of 1779 passed into autumn disappointment, and extraordinary activities stopped, but Meacham's group held onto their firm conviction that Christ would appear shortly, even if they did not know in what manner.[25]

The disappointment and confusion of the new community at New Lebanon was not untypical. The influx of strangers and war-time conditions in rural areas fostered a fever-like intensity among new groups. New converts brought a concern for religion, and the institutional fluidity of rural areas allowed for heterodox ideas, heightened expectations, and orgiastic rites. The rural environment, isolated from tradition or established church structures, allowed deviant beliefs to go unchecked and various rites to get out of hand. These new groups typically ran the course rapidly from initial feverish intensity, and ecstatic excesses to bitter disappointment and a lapse into religious anxiety and doubt. In their doubt they urgently sought dramatic demonstrations of spiritual power, especially the millennial sign of experiencing freedom from sin. After the initial excesses and millenarian expectations had passed, the members of these groups typically felt at a loss, often either returning to a traditional congregation or perhaps remaining stranded in a spiritual limbo waiting for "further light."[26]

The New Light revival at New Lebanon finally proved so disturbing that it brought Meacham and several members of the congregation into the Shaker fold as the first significant American converts of Mother Lee. Henceforth New Lebanon was to be the Shaker headquarters. But even here the Shaker community continued to be in flux at this stage with regard to its perfectionism and millenarianism. It was not until 1787, three years after Mother Ann's death, that the informal Shaker community was constituted formally as the "United Society of Believers in Christ's Second Appearing." When Meacham took charge of the community, he imposed a strict regime and definitive shape on the Shakers.[27]

Other small, quirky sects continued to sprout in isolated areas. William Dorell, who had fought with Burgoyne at Saratoga, returned to his small hometown in Vermont. In visions he learned of his own immortality and physical invulnerability which he proclaimed to the world in 1794. His few followers seemed to believe that God would empower people to transcend the ordinary laws of nature, but when an angry hearer punched Dorell and bloodied his nose, the small sect was shaken. The Dorellites, however, continued to live together in belief of Dorell's revelations.[28]

Another Vermont sect was the New Israelites of Middletown. The sect originated when Nathan Wood led his three sons and their families from the local Congregationalist Church in 1780. Among his followers were Joseph Smith, Sr., father of the Mormon Prophet, and Oliver Crowdery, Sr., father of one of the three Mormon witnesses. Wood asserted his followers were modern Israelites or Jews who were under God's special protection, while the Gentiles, that is, all those opposed to them, would suffer. In addition to having his New Israelites follow the Mosaic law, Wood imposed other, increasingly bizarre demands on his followers. In 1799, for example, having became impressed with divining rods, he announced that these rods were instruments of God. The rods, for example, revealed to Wood that Satan was living in the clothes of two young female members of the sect, who were told to strip and walk naked over a nearby mountain to purify themselves. Under the guidance of the rods, Wood's New Israelites would dig for treasure during the summer. Woods finally predicted that on the night of January 14, 1801, the destroyer would appear and slay any unbelievers, a kind of second Passover, preparatory to the end of the world. The New Israelites abandoned their houses and gathered in a schoolhouse to pray and fast, but the night passed.

Wood accordingly declared that there had been a slight miscalculation, and two months later he instructed his followers to contribute to the paving of the streets of the New Jerusalem. Soon the Wood, Smith, and Crowdery families abandoned Vermont and went to upper New York State where the religious torch was picked up by the younger Joseph Smith.[29]

During the 1820s and '30s, years of great religious fertility in the American Republic, Joseph Smith, Jr., underwent a series of experiences and published a number of documents that resulted in the Church of the Latter Day Saints. Smith claimed to have deciphered from "reformed Egyptian" some gold plates that he found in the Hill Cumorah, in Manchester, New York. Early in 1830 he issued the Book of Mormon, the publishing of which was to be a sign that the Second Coming was here and that would inaugurate the final dispensation of the fullness of times. Other revelations in the 1830s called for a gathering of saints in one place to prepare for the Coming of Christ.

Initially the young prophet seemed to be attempting a restoration of the primitive Christian church. But the emerging Church of the Latter Day Saints had less and less of Christianity and Old Testament and more and more of its own quality and structures. Smith introduced such practices as plural marriages, and he sought to organize the political Kingdom of God. When he was murdered in 1844, one of his followers, Brigham Young, led the Saints to the Great Salt Lake to establish the Kingdom the prophet had envisioned. It was as if the Latter Day Saints had left nineteenth-century America for a promised land, where they organized a political religious kingdom superficially similar to that of King David and Solomon.[30]

Because Mormonism has such a tenuous relationship to the Judeo-Christian tradition of the millennium, it shall not be given consideration here, despite its millenarian elements. Increasingly in the American scene, as shown in the next chapter, groups emerged that had millenarian elements which were drawn less from the apocalyptic literature of the Scriptures and more from popular religion and non-Christian sources.

Before turning to immigrant groups arriving in America during this period, the paramount role played by women in these sects and local churches must be noted, however inadequately. Church activities allowed women their few emotional and spiritual outlets. In most local churches women constituted the majority of membership. In rural areas women had to make do with a nearly exclusive avocation of religion. If the only interesting and exciting alternative to mind-numbing drudgery was a camp meeting or a revival or a reforming crusade, a mother or wife or daughter could attain maximum concentration in this religious arena. Not enough scholarly work has been done on the religious experiences of women but in this period—and others as well—women played important roles in enthusiastic and millenarian movements. Their influence and service were paramount, even if they were not always the leaders.[31]

Communitarian Groups, Particularly German Groups

Attention can now be turned to the role played by immigrant groups, for American religious freedom offered European immigrants the chance to experiment with new practices and new institutions. What was theological speculation in the Old World became actual experiment in the New. Some immigrants brought a literal belief in the Second Coming of Christ, which reinforced the more common communitarian tendencies among expanding sects. In the wilderness of America, immigrant groups sought to develop the perfect social order as a refuge from a world of sin and darkness; if the world were about to pass away, they would be well prepared.

Many of the post-Reformation groups, with their alternative to traditional family structures, offered a Protestant substitute for monasticism. They voluntarily separated from the world, shared things in common, strove for perfection, and sought the religious regeneration of society. Distrusting secular authority, they often experienced persecution which in circular fashion reinforced their sense of the world as evil and sin-filled. Religious communitarian groups typically found their inspiration in the Christian tradition of Acts 2:44, a chosen people in Hebrew terms, a City of God in Augustinian terms, a

Benedictine-like community separated from a sinful world. Often a literal belief in the Second Coming of Christ reinforced their communitarian tendencies and millenarian beliefs. For example, the Shakers chose as their official name the "Millennial Church or United Society of Believers in Christ's Second Appearing." The Perfectionists who established the Oneida Community believed the Second Coming had occurred at the time of Fall of Jerusalem in 70 C.E.

It was not only immigrants from England, like the Puritans, who brought millenarian hopes. Later waves of German and Eastern European sectarians washed up on American shores, usually as transformed successors of sects described in earlier chapters.

In 1677 William Penn made a missionary tour up the Rhine and the Palatinate to invite persecuted groups to settle in his colony of Pennsylvania. His agent in Rotterdam, William Furly, working tirelessly at recruiting and publicizing Penn's new American colony, assisted a small German group. This group followed Johannes Kelpius who expected the millennium in 1694. Many of Kelpius's ideas were based on the Book of Revelation, and he gave special attention and his own eschatological interpretation to verses 12:1-6 which speak of the Woman in the wilderness. In his interpretation the American wilderness took on rich meaning, not unlike the remote and physical wilderness which the early Desert Fathers of Christianity extolled as so important for spiritual happenings.[32]

America's wilderness allowed the European imagination to soar, to develop, and implement alternate visions of what society should be. The vast forests and frontier conditions of parts of New England, upper New York State, Ohio, and Indiana allowed for ripe visions of perfect societies, utopian Edens, and millenarian kingdoms. Pennsylvania in particular seemed to offer to spiritual imaginations fertile ground and quickly bloomed with religious diversity.

William Penn and his agent Furly enabled a number of groups to seize the opportunity that emigration offered; thus a number of embattled sects took advantage of Penn's invitation, and steady streams of Germans left the Palatinate and other parts of Germany for Pennsylvania late in the seventeenth and early eighteenth centuries, carrying a heritage of religious radicalism and profound millenarian hope.

Sectarians arrived in waves to settle in different parts not only of Pennsylvania but also Delaware and Ohio. These sects, often based on Anabaptist theology or Pietist ideas, rejected the common culture of their age and quietly awaited the millennium.[33]

As with Puritanism, the Anabaptist movement had fractured into various traditions. Few if any remnants remained of the revolutionary millenarian wing of the Anabaptist movement such as the Münsterites, but the evangelical branch included such groups as the Mennonites with their conservative offspring the Amish and various other branches of the evangelical tradition such as the Swiss Brethren, Schwenkfelders, and the Hutterites.

The complicated processes of survival and transformation of some of these groups deserves a fuller treatment. The Unity of the Brethren (or the *Unitas Fratrum*), for example, was founded in Czechoslovakia in 1457 around the Archbishop-elect John Rokycana and was subjected to Taborite and Hussite influences. Religious persecution in Bohemia and Moravia drove the Brethren (variously called Bohemian Brethren and Moravian Brethren) to seek refuge in Bethelsdorf in Saxony. In 1741 communities of these Brethren set up settlements at Bethlehem and Nazareth in Northampton County, Pennsylvania, in the early 1740s.[34] The Moravians tended to be less radical than the German and Swiss Brethren; most of these groups were collectivist, pacifist, and opposed to any kind of revolution.

The Rappites

In 1805 Father George Rapp, a Würtemberger, led a small German sect, the Harmony Society (about 600 followers) from southern Germany across the Appalachian mountains to settle at Harmony in Beaver County, Pennsylvania.[35] The Book of Acts, especially 2:44: "And all who believed were together and had all things in common," described the kind of communitarian society which they believed was enjoined upon all believers. Rapp, a Lutheran dissident, drew his millenarian view of the future from the pietist teachings of Jacob Boehme and, of course, from the Book of Revelation. Under the near dictatorship of Rapp, the community saw itself as a righteous remnant that would be judged as pure and holy when the Lord returned to judge the human race. Father Rapp imposed a radical doctrine of purity similar to that of the Shakers such that after 1807 he opposed marriage and demanded strict celibacy. Thus the group had no internal means to increase its members, and curiously they seemed to show little inclination to proselytize to seek new converts to their way of life.

Rapp did not rely merely on his charisma to dominate his followers and promote cohesion but imposed regulations that would insure commitment to Harmony's vision of the pure life. Rapp wanted his community to increase daily in holiness, always progressing toward the first resurrection. Father Rapp insisted on rigid self-discipline with all property in common. Like other successful communitarian groups, the Rappites abandoned worldly fashions and had all their clothing made in a uniform style. Rapp kept his eye on his devotees, periodically appearing unannounced to make sure that all were adhering to the community's regime. A series of secret passages enabled him to move with ease from one part of the community to another without being observed and thus he would dramatically and unexpectedly appear from time to time. Rapp's dominance and personal charisma made him the first among equals in this community, and his was the largest residence. Nevertheless, the discipline of members and stern leadership of Rapp made Harmony widely known and economically successful.

In 1815 the Rappites joined the general westward migration and left Pennsylvania to establish a new Harmony colony on the Wabash River in Posey County, Indiana. Although this community was also successful, the Rappites or Harmonites felt they had ventured too far west. In a sermon on December 19, 1824, in justifying another move, Rapp said that the millennium had been in progress for thirty years: ten in Würtemberg, ten in Harmony and ten in Indiana; just as the Woman in Rev. 12:14 had fled twice, so, too, was the Harmony congregation a living realization of that Woman.

In 1824-5 the community sold their property to Robert Owen, thereby establishing direct contact with the secular branch of the communitarian movement in America. Robert Owen named the colony New Harmony and set up there his first American socialist Eden.

The Rappites migrated to Economy, Pennsylvania, on the Ohio River, about 18 miles south of Pittsburgh. Here they again built their community where they expected to remain until the millennium dawned. But by time they moved to Economy, signs of dissatisfaction were emerging in the Harmony community, most of which revolved around Rapp's authoritarian and sometimes bizarre leadership. Rappite discontent and expectations about the Second Coming and the millennium made members of Harmony ripe for the appearance of one Bernard Mueller. Mueller, who called himself Count Leon, proclaimed he was divinely sent to usher in the millennium. He had come directly from Germany, stayed at Economy in 1831-2, and, amidst increasing disharmony and internal dissension, won over many members of the community. In the spring of 1832, Leon led 176 of the total 800 members from Economy to found a community called the New Philadelphia Society at what is now Monaca, Pennsylvania, about 10 miles away from Economy. In 1833 Count Leon moved his followers to Louisiana to found a new settlement.

The original Rappite Community at Economy ultimately dissolved in 1905. The sacrificing of private property and a sex life, similar to the monastic demands of poverty and celibacy, were the powerful social mechanisms which the Rappites used to established a strong sense of commitment and community. But like other groups, the Rappites did not confront their overreliance on the guidance of a single individual, and they failed to provide structures to transmit authority to successors once the original charismatic leader died. Nevertheless, their survival for a century as a coherent group marks the Rappites as one of the more successful communitarian endeavors in American religious history.[36]

A communitarian group which succumbed to similar difficulties was the Zoarites. In 1817, a dozen years after the Rappites had arrived on American shores from Würtemberg, Joseph Michael Bimeler led another communitarian group from Würtemberg. This community, fleeing religious persecution, had trekked from Bavaria to Würtemberg and finally to Zoar, Ohio, where they purchased land with the aid of British and American Quakers. They organized themselves as the Society of Separatists of Zoar.

Numbering about 225, the Zoarites hoped to lead a simple life of religious perfection. They initially adopted celibacy, but the practice proved ultimately unworkable. Bimeler, like Father Rapp, enjoyed a position of authority and privilege. When he married in 1828 the practice of celibacy ended, and thus a powerful mechanism for community control was dismantled and not replaced. But other factors also caused a decline in the community which peaked at about 500 adherents. Not only did the community find that generational conflicts begun as the strict, narrow way of life of the elders did not appeal to the American-born youth, but they also failed to adopt to economic and manufacturing changes on the American scene. Perhaps easiest to see was the failure to provide for effective transmission of authority after Bimeler's death in 1853. Zoar counted 222 members when it disbanded in 1898.[37]

Other Utopian Experiments

The early years of the nineteenth century saw extraordinary social experimentation in America. As the effects of the industrial revolution rippled across Europe, utopian idealists sought to reorder society into more humane communities, because times of social upheaval and transition demonstrate how even established institutions no longer appear effective. During such turbulent times, radical reshapings of society seem to have greater appeal. Utopian ideas and communitarian dreams, many of which were conceived in the Old World, were brought to fulfillment as trial communities in the New World. In the United States, the period from the Revolution to at least the Civil War was an era of great social fluidity, of immigration, of national expansion, a time when distinctly American self-consciousness was replacing an outmoded colonial identity. In addition to the Rappites of Harmony and the Separatists of Zoar, other communitarian groups such as the Oneida Community and the Amana Community came to full bloom.[38]

Oneida

John Humphrey Noyes, the founder of the Oneida Community, was willing to recognize that other experiments might share his idealism. Noyes and a handful of followers arrived at Oneida, New York, in 1848, where in an isolated community they could live the perfect life now. Noyes became a religious convert at a revival in 1831, studied for the ministry at Yale and developed a perfectionistic theology. He believed that the Second Coming of Christ had transpired in 70 C.E. The millennium had begun then but was obscured by the errors of the second- and third-century Christians. Noyes became convinced that modern believers could achieve salvation from sin and could lead lives of perfection if they replicated the practices of the earliest Church.

To restore pure, primitive Christianity, Noyes promoted the communal possession of property and material things as well as a peculiar form of marriage. Like the Shakers' Ann Lee, Noyes' view of marriage was colored as much by his personal experience as by ideology. His ideas about sex were quite original, considering the Puritanism of the time, and he exercised the rights of "first husband" with a number of young women who reached puberty in the community and fathered at least fifteen children. However, he regarded marriage as an unholy institution. Within the ranks of the perfect in the Heavenly Kingdom, love must not be exclusive. Rather each man should regard each woman within the community as a wife, and each woman should regard each man as a husband. Noyes, perhaps more aptly than he realized, dubbed his alternative "complex marriage."[39]

Although outsiders condemned complex marriage as free love, within the community relations between the sexes were carefully regulated. Complex marriage was more a mechanism to maintain social control than it was an invitation to license. Men were expected to approach women through a third party, usually an older woman, and in theory any woman could decline to have sexual relations with any individual man. At the same time, older persons were expected to initiate younger persons into the procedures of complex marriage, the intricate procedures of which probably made as much demands on the Oneida members as celibacy did for the Shakers since individuals had to submit to a set of community regulations rather than yield to personal impulse. Only after a generation did the Oneida Community embark on a carefully structured program of internal propagation called stirpiculture, a form of eugenics in which a committee in consultation with Noyes authorized specific couples to have a child.

Under Noyes's enormous energy and inspired by his religious zeal, the Oneida Community developed a social framework that enhanced commitment to the Perfectionistic ideal. New members were required to sign over personal property to the community, a practice which required sacrificing individual control in exchange for a stake in the common success of the community. Clothing styles were also uniform within the community, with the practical pantaloons worn by women regarded as scandalous by outsiders in an age before bloomers became popular.

After a generation, problems emerged that ultimately brought an end to the Perfectionist experiment as a communitarian endeavor. Over the years the Perfectionist impulse became muted as Noyes became more concerned with the socialist economics that undergirded the community. The not-so-surprising ascendancy of secular communitarianism within Oneida eroded the religious dimension so important for community commitment and continuity. Thus once again, change, this time economic and social, contributed to a movement's decline. Further, exclusive attraction and parent-child bonding proved more powerful than Noyes' efforts to control. His authoritarian leadership began to provoke resentment among new and younger members. In 1877, Noyes resigned. He left the community secretly in the middle of the night on June 22, 1879. By 1881 the utopian experiment officially dissolved, although a publicly traded company with the Oneida name continues to exist and employs thousands of workers who produce copper wire and cooking utensils in addition to the sterling silverware that brought it initial success.[40]

Owenites

Robert Owen, neither a Christian nor a millennialist who accepted the apocalyptic literature of the Bible, announced the arrival of the millennium. He was a gifted, ambitious Welshman who owned textile mills in New Lanark, Scotland. By enhancing his workers' environment he increased his profits and productivity. Combining great energy with ideas about advancing humankind by improving peoples' personal circumstances, he began to preach as a secular evangelist a radical utopian idealism in the conviction that his new arrangements would usher in a future of unlimited abundance. In his *Address to the Inhabitants of New Lanark* in 1816, Owen began to use biblical expressions and said that even though he did not know what ideas individuals attached to the term "millennium," he was convinced that a society free from crime, poverty and misery was universally feasible. Eighteen months later he was declaring a "new religion" and the commencement of the millennium. He said these were the last days of misery on earth. In 1817 the first, short-lived Owenite journal, the *Mirror of Truth*, appeared, totally millennialist in tone and language and anticipating the imminent collapse of commercial civilization. From this point most of Owen's writings contained a millennial tone, and from time to time even he announced the commencement of the millennium. Curiously at the same time that he began to use millenarian language he denounced all other existing religions, and after 1835 Owenism acquired some of the characteristics of a religious cult.[41]

To advance his theories, in 1825 Owen bought 20,000 acres in Illinois and Indiana in order to establish a model community to be called New Harmony. Owen actually established some two dozen socialist experiments on both sides of Atlantic that would be models of ideal factory community. All of them came to an end by 1830.

What is worthy of note is the severing of the link between religiously inspired millenarianism and the social millenarianism or communism that began to be written about in the nineteenth century. Friedrich Engels, for example, in order to show that communism could be profitable and practical pointed to the American religious communities, in particular the Shakers. Marx essentially drew attention to the collapse of capitalism and the embryonic existence of a new order—a different kind of order, to be sure.[42]

The Shakers

Preceding the Millerites by about 50 years, the Shakers were probably the most important—and unique—communitarian and millenarian group of this period. The previous chapter recounted Ann Lee's roots in the dissident evangelical Quakerism of the Wardleys, who, in turn, had come under the influence of the Camisards or French Prophets. When Ann Lee led a small group to America in 1774 they established a curious blend of communitarianism and millennialism that doesn't fit into a neat scholarly category. Her millenarian movement, coming in the heart of the Industrial Revolution perhaps best is explained as a millenarianism of flight, a "chiliasm of despair."[43] That is, it turned inward from outward pain to become a mystical and realized eschatology that experienced Christ's Second Appearing in the present and not at the end of time.

Shaker tradition places Ann Lee's birth on the last day of February 1736. That tradition recalls her as a short, rather stout woman in later life with a fair complexion, blue eyes and light chestnut-brown hair. Her followers thought her to be beautiful, although others are less complimentary. She undoubtedly possessed great personal magnetism.[44]

A fervent religious awakening was washing over Lancashire, and Ann Lee joined the Wardley society of shaking Quakers. In 1762 Ann married a large Manchester blacksmith Abraham Stanley, a kindly man said to love his beef and beer and the village tavern. Ann soon gave birth to four children—all of whom died in infancy. This tragedy wrecked havoc on Ann's health, physical and mental, and irrevocably shaped her views on sex and marriage. She began to fear sex with her husband and avoided her bed "as if it had been made of embers." She was afraid to sleep lest she "awake in hell."[45] She tried to help herself by a regimen of mortification to purify her soul. She denied herself, ate poorly, and abstained from sleep. The result was a powerful sense of conversion, and she testified that her "soul broke forth to God," and she experienced a birth into a spiritual kingdom.

Ann Lee believed that the struggle she had undergone as an individual was the same for all people. She located sex as the central sin, the source of all evil. Needless to say, this provoked arguments between her husband and herself. Withdrawing from domestic life, she dedicated more energy to the Wardley community and gradually replaced Mother Jane as head of the sect. She increased discipline and sharpened the group's testimonies against the flesh. Membership increased and meetings grew more exuberant as their worship duplicated in its ecstasy of spirit and disorderly behavior the meetings of the French Prophets. They sang and danced, they shook and shouted, they prophesied and spoke with new tongues, they heard heavenly voices and believed in the Second Coming of Christ, and hoped for supernatural succor in their time of distress. From the beginning Ann Lee's followers believed that theirs was an extraordinary enterprise, an invitation to leave the life of this world and enter the millennial kingdom. As Lee denounced the Established Church's acquiescence to marriage, and as her worship meetings disturbed the neighborhood, people grew furious, tried to stone Ann, and charged the sect with fanaticism and heresy.[46]

Her imprisonment in the Manchester house of correction for blasphemy solidified her leadership, and her followers saw her as a martyr and saint. In her jail cell in 1770 Ann Lee underwent the mystical experience that guided her future leadership. She rapturously felt the spirit of Christ so suffused her being that henceforth she regarded herself as His special instrument, indeed that she herself *was* Christ come again as Holy Mother Wisdom destined to inaugurate the millennial kingdom on earth. She said "I converse with Christ! . . . I am married to the Lord Jesus Christ. He is my head and my husband, and I have no other! I have walked, hand in hand, with him in heaven. . . . I am Ann the Word."[47] She took the title Mother or Mother of the New Creation and formally assumed leadership of the sect. At this stage the movement revolved around her alone, and she had yet to formulate a theology or organize social structures.

Mother Ann developed a simple and straightforward doctrine. From her experience of Christ's presence, Ann concluded that he could be absent no longer. Her vision of Adam and Eve in Eden led her to conclude that lustful bonding was the cause of human sinfulness and women's burdens. Not unlike Joanna Southcott who came to a similar conclusion about human sexuality, Ann responded to the call to redeem the human race. The reader will recall how the Adamites had come to an opposite interpretation of human sexual impulse. Since "concupiscence" was the cause of evil in the world, of disease, war, slavery, Ann concluded that celibacy had to be the remedy. The mission of the true church was to expose the "glossy covering" which hid the "doleful works of the flesh."[48] Only by freeing oneself absolutely from the bondage of the flesh, could one achieve perfection.

Those who responded to her call were, with few exceptions, poor laborers, mill hands, mechanics, housewives and servants, people in debt and with little property, individuals who worked during the day and assembled in the evenings for worship. Because of the restrictions and opposition in England, Ann decided to leave for America and in August 1774, her small band arrived in New York. The little group of Believers in Christ's Second Coming had arrived in the New World.

Mother Lee, as she became known in America, remained in New York in poverty to earn her livlihood by washing and ironing, while a few followers bought a small tract of cheap land and started a small settlement at Niskeyuna (now Watervliet), about 8 miles from Albany. Ann the prophetess, on the eve of realizing her dream of a New Jerusalem, finally left New York and moved to the wilderness area where there were still Iroquois and only a few white families. Her small band, toiling as blacksmiths, weavers, and craftsmen, worked hard to survive.

It was the brink of the American Revolution, and Ann's timing was perfect. Religious excitement had peaked in the New York-New England area. One such revival had grown despondent. The New Light Baptists in New Lebanon, New York, and Hancock, Massachusetts, under the leadership of Joseph Meacham and Samuel Johnson had reached a frenzy in the summer of 1779. The excited preaching at summer meetings held in a barn led to prophetic shouting and the screaming of men and women "as if wounded in battle."[49] The devotees had hailed their revival as an event immediately preceding the millennium itself, when all religions would fall before the triumphant Second Coming of Christ. When nothing happened, in their disappointment and depression, they turned to Mother Ann's obscure community and were impressed by the testimony that the Christ for whom they waited in vain had already made his appearance in the person of Mother Lee. Mother Lee offered those who confessed their sin salvation and resurrection. The world was at an end for any who entered into the life of the spirit.

For the revivalists of New Lebanon, nurtured on the expectation of a universal judgment day, this was revolutionary doctrine. Indeed, Mother Ann proclaimed that "that we are the people who turn the world upside down." She also laid down the cost: Ann demanded that "You must forsake the marriage of the flesh, or you cannot be married to the Lamb, nor have any share in the resurrection of Christ."[50]

As excitement grew, so, too, did doctrinal inconsistency. Their early enthusiasm for what they believed to be divinely revealed truths led the early Shakers to quote the Book of Revelation more often than any other part of Bible—and often out of context. The Book of Revelation came to be the basis of Shaker theology, with the Wardleys as the "two witnesses;" the Catholic church was the "beast" of anti-Christ (13:1; 17:4), Babylon (14:8), and the Mother of harlots (17:1). Ann Lee was the "woman clothed with the sun" (12:1).

Shakers justified their withdrawal from the world into celibate enclaves by their conviction that the Second Coming of Christ had transpired in the person of Ann Lee. Mother Ann was revered as the one who revealed the reality of the returned Christ. The presence of Christ inaugurated a new age: the millennial kingdom had dawned. Shakers believed they were living in the heavenly sphere now, sharing in Mother Ann's mystical experience. To live in the millennial kingdom required firm boundaries to demarcate the millennial society from the outside world, which was polluted and distracting.

Shakers totally renounced sex and marriage. They proclaimed the "joys of celibacy" as part of their search for Edenic innocence. Segregation of the sexes, however, was not left to members' own discretion. Men and women used separate entrances and separate staircases, they ate silently at separate tables, and labored silently in separate areas. Even in their worship men and women formed separate ranks on opposite sides of the room and danced in separate lines. They dressed in plain clothing and followed a monastic-like daily order. It is noteworthy, however, that such practices of uniform clothing and celibacy underlined the then-radical belief that men and women were equal in the eyes of God and consequently the status of women was enhanced.[51]

As Ann Lee's fame as the female Messiah grew, increasing numbers of Americans were drawn to the Shaker way of life and practiced the strange mode of worship that had become even more extravagant than it had ever been in those early Manchester meetings under the aegis of the Wardleys. Early visitors described Shaker meetings, how they assembled and began their ritual dances. Valentine Rathbun, founder and minister of the Baptist church at Pittsfield, Mass., warned people of a "new and strange religion" and recounted what he experienced at a Shaker service on May 26, 1780:

> They begin by sitting down, and shaking their heads, in a violent manner, turning their heads half round, so that their face looks over each shoulder, their eyes being shut; while they are thus shaking, one will begin to sing some odd tune, without words or rule; after a while another will strike in; and then another; and after a while they all fall in, and make a strange charm .... Some singing without words, and some with an unknown tongue or mutter, and some with a mixture of English.... They fall a groaning and trembling, and everyone act alone for himself; one will fall prostrate on the floor, another on his knees and his head in his hands; another will be muttering ... sounds, which neither they nor any body else understand. Some will be singing, each one his own tune ... some will be dancing, and other stand laughing, heartily and loudly ... others will be shooing and hissing evil spirits out of the house, till the different tunes, groaning, jumping, dancing, drumming, laughing, talking and fluttering, shooing and hissing, makes a perfect bedlam; this they call the worship of God.[52]

When Mother Ann died at Niskeyuna on September 8, 1784, her passing rudely shocked her followers since they had believed that her ministry would be endless or at least a thousand years long. The Shaker leaders who immediately followed Mother Lee were quite capable, however. James Whittaker was dynamic, but obsessed with carnal pleasure as the cause of sin. He preached urgently against sin and thanked God that he himself never had "carnal knowledge of any woman." "Blessed are all those who are not defiled by women.... Blessed are all those young virgins that were never defiled by men."[53] So completely had he subdued the flesh, he claimed, that he had no more lust than an infant or unborn child. The competent Meachem and the beloved Lucy Wright followed in leadership, but when Mother Lucy died in 1821, no highly respected or charismatic individual was able to assume leadership and authority.

The subsequent leadership faced great difficulties. Not only did the community have to determine standards for admitting new members, but they had to establish structures for on-going leadership, for decision making and for dealing with the practical matters of organizational survival. The Shaker "Millennial Laws or Gospel Statutes and Ordinances" set down procedures, similar to those of monasteries and other idealistic communities, that were intended to bond the individual strongly to the community and facilitate the pursuit of the millennial life in general. Life in economically self-supporting communities allowed Shaker devotees to sever ties with the sinful world.[54]

After the first Shaker community at New Lebanon, New York, in 1785, communities were established at Harvard, Shirley, Hancock and Tyringham, all in Massachusetts, and Enfield, Conn., as well as other locales. At their peak in 1840s the number of Shakers living in 19 separate settlements reached 6000.[55] The Shaker lifestyle generated, however, not only great interest but also savage opposition and even beatings. It seems that eighteenth-century New Englanders could only view Shaker dissent from orthodox beliefs and their lively worship practices as extreme and heretical.

The Shaker survival for approximately two centuries marks their experiment as the longest communitarian venture in American religious history. Their decline, only in part, stems from the industrialization of American society and the change in values that sounded the death knell for the agrarian Shaker communities. As the new nation gained stability and the chaos of frontier life gave way to order, the need for the kind of security provided by the Shaker lifestyle diminished. As the Shaker vision failed to appeal to new potential converts, numbers dwindled as the way of life that depended on celibacy required the Shakers to depend exclusively on conversions rather than on internal propagation.

Conclusion

There occurred a flurry of rural religious excitement during he Revolutionary War period. The Second Great Awakening started about 1795, lasted for twenty, forty, or fifty years, depending on its locale, and culminated in the extraordinary Millerite movement that will be looked at in the next chapter. The years from the Revolutionary War up to the Civil War saw unprecedented religious, social, and political change and a blizzard of religious awakenings and revivals. As established political and social ways crumbled in the turmoil of the Revolution, sectarian movements came to the fore; some transplanted groups did thrive, such as Ann Lee's Shakers, and also indigenous sects like Joseph Smith's Church of Latter-Day Saints.

Religious communities like the Shakers, Oneida, Amana, Zoar, and the Rappites peaked prior to 1845. Millenarian and mystical ideas infused many of these groups, but their millenarianism was typically mystical rather than revolutionary. Communities based on a more secular ideology, such as those of Owen, came into being in the 1820s.

Other forms of American communitarianism would arise before and after World War II and would peak in the late 1960s. But the Marx-Engels communist movement in Europe, partly inspired by mystical and religious millenarianism, became the dominant form of social millenarianism of the nineteenth and twentieth centuries. Engels idealized the socio-economic success of the Rappites at Harmony-Economy, the Separatists of Zoar, and, especially, the Shakers. Writing in 1845 Engels shrugged off the religious premises of these communities as he celebrated the principle of common ownership of goods as practiced by these religious sects.[56] Increasingly communal and millenarian movements would be inspired by non-biblical and non-traditional ideologies.

The next chapter turns to the most extraordinary of American millenarian movement, a bible-based group that did not demand of its members to seek out a special community but appealed to thousands of average Americans.

NOTES

1. Ernest R. Sandeen, "Millennialism," in Edwin S. Gaustad, *The Rise of Adventism: Religion and Society in Mid-Nineteenth-Century America* (New York: Harper and Row, 1974), p. 104; cf. also, Ernest R. Sandeen, *The Roots of Fundamentalism: British and American Millenarianism 1800-1930* (Chicago and London: University of Chicago Press, 1970); Charles H. Lippy. "Millennialism and Adventism," in *Encyclopedia of the American Religious Experience: Studies of Traditions and Movements* ed. by Charles H. Lippy and Peter W. Williams (New York: Charles Scribner's Sons, 1988), Vol. 2, p. 842; Ronald L. Numbers and Jonathan M. Butler, editors, *The Disappointed: Millerism and Millenarianism in the Nineteenth Century* (Bloomington & Indianapolis: Indiana University Press, 1987), "Introduction," p. xvi.

2. Perry Miller, *Errand into the Wilderness* (Cambridge, Mass.: Harvard University Press, 1956), p. 158.

3. Ira V. Brown, "Watchers for the Second Coming: The Millenarian Tradition in America," *Mississippi Valley Historical Review* 39 (1952): 452.

4. Ira V. Brown, pp. 446-447.

5. Stephen A. Marini, *Radical Sects of Revolutionary New England* (Cambridge, Mass., and London: Harvard University Press, 1982), pp. 12-13; Marini is very helpful on the local sects of the Revolutionary period. Unless otherwise noted references to Marini are to *Radical Sects*. Cf. also, Michael Barkun, *Crucible of the Millennium: The Burned-Over District of New York in the 1840s* (Syracuse University Press, 1986), pp. 21-22.

6. Ira V. Brown, p. 447; Perry Miller, p. 154-157.

7. David S. Lovejoy, *Religious Enthusiasm in the New World: Heresy to Revolution* (Cambridge, Mass.: Harvard University Press: 1985), pp. 189-192; Perry Miller, p. 155.

8. Ira V. Brown, pp. 448-450.

9. Stephen A. Marini, "The Great Awakening," in *Encyclopedia of the American Religious Experience: Studies of Traditions and Movements* ed. by Charles H. Lippy and Peter W. Williams, (New York: Charles Scribner's Sons, 1988), Vol. 2, pp. 776-779.

10. Nathan O. Hatch, "The Origins of Civil Millennialism in America: New England Clergymen, War with France, and the Revolution," *William and Mary Quarterly* 31 (1974): 407-408.

11. Stephen A. Marini, *Radical Sects of Revolutionary New England* pp. 5-6, 56, and Whitney R. Cross, *The Burned-Over District: The Social and Intellectual History of Enthusiastic Religion in Western New York, 1800-1850* (Ithaca and London: Cornell University Press, 1950), p 39. I have relied on Marini heavily in this section.

12. Stephen Marini, *Radical Sects*, pp. 37-42, 46.

13. Stephen Marini, *Radical Sects*, pp. 46-47.

14. Herbert A. Wisbey, *Pioneer Prophetess: Jemima Wilkinson, the Publick Universal Friend* (Ithaca, N. Y.: Cornell University Press, 1964), p. 9.

15. Cited by Herbert A. Wisbey, pp. 12-13.

16. Stephen Marini, *Radical Sects*, p 48; also, Winthrop S. Hudson, "A Time of Religious Ferment," in Edwin S. Gaustad, *The Rise of Adventism: Religion and Society in Mid-Nineteenth-Century America* (New York: Harper and Row, 1974). p 9.

17. David Hudson, *Memoir of Jemima Wilkinson* (Bath, N.Y.: Richardson and Dow, 1844; New York: Ams Press Reprint Series, 1972), pp. 23-24. David Hudson's biography is hostile and not always very accurate.

18. Stephen Marini, *Radical Sects*, p 49; also Whitney R. Cross, p. 38.

19. David Hudson, p. 41; Stephen Marini, p. 49.

20. Herbert A. Wisbey, pp. 69, 209; Stephen Marini p. 50; David Hudson, p 41.

21. Stephen Marini, p. 50; Charles H. Lippy, "Millennialism and Adventism," p. 863; Herbert A. Wisbey, *passim*.

22. Cited by Stephen Marini, p. 51.

23. Stephen Marini, pp. 50-51; Charles H. Lippy, "Millennialism and Adventism," p. 865.

24. Stephen Marini, p. 53.

25. Stephen Marini, pp. 52-53.

26. Stephen Marini, p. 53.

27. Edwin S. Gaustad, *The Rise of Adventism: Religion and Society in Mid-Nineteenth-Century America*, p. 10.

28. Stephen Marini, p. 53.

29. Stephen Marini, pp. 54-55; Whitney R. Cross, p. 38.

30. Jan Shipps, "The Latter Day Saints" in *Encyclopedia of the American Religious Experience: Studies of Traditions and Movements*, ed. by Charles H. Lippy and Peter W. Williams (New York: Charles Scribner's Sons, 1988), Vol. 1, pp. 649-658.

31. Whitney R. Cross, pp. 38, 84, 87, 88, 93; cf. Louis J. Kern, *An Ordered Love: Sex Roles and Sexuality in Victorian Utopias—The Shakers, the Mormons, and the Oneida Community* (Chapel Hill: University of North Carolina Press, 1981).

32. Elizabeth W. Fisher, " 'Prophesies and Revelations:' German Cabbalists in Early Pennsylvania," *Pennsylvania Magazine of History and Biography* 109 (1985): 307; cf. Charles H. Lippy, "Millennialism and Adventism," pp. 859-860.

33. Arthur Eugene Bestor, *Backwoods Utopias: The Sectarian and Owenite Phases of Communitarian Socialism in America: 1663-1829* (Philadelphia: University of Pennsylvania Press, 1950), pp. 1, 3, 6, 22; also Don Yoder, "Sects and Religious Movements of German Origin," in *Encyclopedia of the American Religious Experience: Studies of Traditions and Movements*, ed. by Charles H. Lippy and Peter W. Williams (New York: Charles Scribner's Sons, 1988), Vol. 1, p. 615; also George H. Williams, *The Radical Reformation* (Philadelphia: The Westminster Press, 1962), pp. 853-860, 618. In 1986 the largest Mennonite Church in the United States numbered about 90,000, and the Amish about 34,000.

34. Arthur Eugene Bestor, pp. 22-23, and George H. Williams, pp. 212-218.

35. Karl J. R. Arndt, *George Rapp's Harmony Society 1785-1847* (Philadelphia: University of Pennsylvania Press, 1965); John S. Duss, *The Harmonists: A Personal History* (Ambridge, Pa.: The Harmonie Associates, Inc., Reprint, 1970); Charles H. Lippy "Communitarianism," in *Encyclopedia of the American Religious Experience: Studies of Traditions and Movements*, ed. Charles H. Lippy and Peter W. Williams, (New York: Charles Scribner's Sons, 1988), Vol. 2, p. 868; Arthur Eugene Bestor, p. 34.

36. Charles H. Lippy, "Communitarianism," p. 869-870; Karl J.R. Arndt, p. 353; Arthur Eugene Bestor, p. 35; John S. Duss, pp. xiii-xvi.

37. Charles H. Lippy, p. 871.

38. Charles H. Lippy, p. 861.

39. Arthur Eugene Bestor, pp. 50-51; Charles H. Lippy, "Communitarianism," pp. 865-7; Louis J. Kern, p. 249; William M. Kephart, "The Oneida Community," in *Extraordinary Groups: An Examination of Unconventional Life-Styles* (New York: St. Martin's Press, 1987), pp. 68, 89.

40. Charles H. Lippy, p. 867; William M. Kephart, pp. 84-89.

41. J.F.C. Harrison, *Quest for the New Moral World: Robert Owen and the Owenites in Britain and America* (New York: Charles Scribner's Sons, 1969), pp. 55, 81, 92-93. Owen was a prolific writer. Two of Robert Owen's books are: *Book of the New Moral World* (London, 1836) and *Lectures on the Rational System of Society* (London, 1841).

42. Cf. Henri Desroche, *The American Shakers: From Neo-Christianity to Presocialism*, trans. by John K. Savacool, (Amherst: University of Massachusetts Press, 1971), p. 293; W.H. Oliver, *Prophets and Millennialists: The Uses of Biblical Prophecy in England from the 1790s to the 1840s* (Oxford University Press, 1978), pp. 211-212.

43. Clarke Garrett, *Respectable Folly: Millenarians and the French Revolution in France and England* (Baltimore: The Johns Hopkins University press, 1975), p. 3; E.P. Thompson, *The Making of the English Working Class* (New York: Pantheon Books, 1964), p. 388.

44. Edward Deming Andrews, *The People Called Shakers* (New York: Dover Publications, 1963), pp. 4-5; Flo Morse, *The Shakers and the World's People* (Hanover, N.H.: University Press of New England, 1987), pp. 53-54.

45. Edward Deming Andrews, p. 8; Flo Morse, pp. 10-13.

46. Edward R. Horgan, *The Shaker Holy Land: A Community Portrait* (Harvard, Mass.: The Harvard Common Press, 1982), p. 12; Edward Deming Andrews, pp. 9-10, 12.

47. Cited by Edward Deming Andrews, p. 12.

48. *The Shakers: Two Centuries of Spiritual Reflection*, edited with an introduction by Robley Edward Whitson (New York: Paulist Press, Classics of Western Spirituality, 1983), "Introduction," pp. 5-12.

49. Edward Deming Andrews, p. 18.

50. Cited by Edward Deming Andrews, pp. 18, 20.

51. Louis J. Kern, pp. 91-94; William M. Kephart, pp. 203-204.

52. Valentine Rathbun, *Brief Hints of a Religious Scheme*, pp. 7-8, 12, cited by Edward Deming Andrews, pp. 27-28.

53. Cited by Edward Deming Andrews, p. 50.

54. Charles H. Lippy, "Communitarianism," pp. 860-865; William M. Kephart, pp. 201-208. As an appendix to his book Edward Deming Andrews, pp. 249-289, publishes the "Millennial Laws."

55. Edward R. Horgan, pp. 2, 197.

56. Friedrich Engels, *Beschreibung der in neurer Zeit enstandenen und noch bestehenden kommunistischen Anseidlungen*. See Henri Desroche, pp. 294-295, p. 351, footnote #12.

Chapter Eleven
America, Part Two:
From Millerism to Flying Saucers

Millerites

The largest nineteenth century American millenarian movement and perhaps the one most vilified by their opponents was the Millerites. The Millerites expanded rapidly in the late 1830s and early 1840s within the evangelism and reformism of antebellum Protestantism. No other group had specified such dramatic events as the Millerites: the breaking open of the heavens with the appearance of Christ, the ascent of the saints into heaven, and the descent of the wicked into hell. But many of their contemporaries ridiculed them and circulated delicious but untrue stories of Millerites wearing white ascension robes and climbing to the roofs of barns and into trees to be closer to the returning Jesus. The Millerites, numbering up to 50,000, actually were a varied group, with little consensus of belief or practice, and were probably fairly typical Americans of the time.[1]

The man whose private calculations resulted in this popular mass movement was William Miller, born in Pittsfield, Massachusetts, on February 15, 1782. When he was a small child his family moved to Hampton, New York, near the Vermont line. His resume, as it were, was solid. He married Lucy P. Smith on 29 June, 1803, and moved to nearby Poultney, Vt. He became a deputy sheriff in 1809, and in 1810 became a lieutenant in the militia of Vermont. After active service in the War of 1812, he left the army in 1815.[2]

In 1816, because of his conversion at a local revival, he joined the Hampton Baptist Church and soon became its leading member. Literate but scarcely learned, Miller remained within the narrow boundaries of the conservative Protestantism that prevailed at the time. He devoted himself to an exhaustive study of the Scriptures, assuming both their utter trustworthiness and the existence of the absolute reality of a supernatural order. He used just a Bible and *Cruden's Concordance*, and his biblical methodology, if he had one, emphasized the literal fulfillment of biblical prophecy. He began to center on millenarian prophecies and especially the biblical chronology of Archbishop James Ussher, the English authority on Biblical numbers. Ussher claimed that the world began in 4004 B.C. and would last 6000 years, and one of his conclusions placed the world's end in 1996.[3]

Using the same kind of biblical arithmetic that his contemporaries had long used, Miller corrected Ussher's calculations. He focused especially on such passages as Rev. 11:15 and Daniel 12:12. Daniel 8:14, for example, reads: "And he said to him, 'For two thousand and three hundred evenings and mornings; then the sanctuary shall be restored to its rightful state.' " Miller interpreted Daniel's 2300 days as the years that must pass before the final cleansing of the earth, that the sanctuary meant church, and cleansed referred to the complete redemption from sin. He calculated the original prophecy as dating from 457 B.C. Subtracting 457 from 2300 gave the figure of 1843. Miller rechecked his figures. Common orthodoxy allowed 6000 years from the time of creation to the end of the world. Miller argued that Ussher's figure of 4004 B.C. plus 1843 only gave a total of 5846. He argued that there had to be 4157 years between creation and the birth of Christ. This calculation provided the necessary 6000 years for the fullness of time from creation to the end.[4]

Miller arrived at the arresting conclusion that the end of the world was near. His discovery came in 1818 after two years of study. He solemnly concluded that "in about twenty-five years from that time all

From Millerism to Flying Saucers

the affairs of our present state would be wound up."[5] In spite of his discoveries, Miller continued his personal studies in private.

By 1831, however, he became convinced that he should go out and tell the world what he had learned. At the age of fifty, he began to preach or give "lectures," as he termed them. The Baptist Church in Low Hampton issued him as license to preach in 1833, and he began to travel in the New England area. He had both a sense of modest self-doubt as well as a sense of destiny. Andrew Jackson was president, and the country was optimistic about its future. Indeed, the years between the War of 1812 and the Civil War were years of expansiveness in the new nation. Boundaries of status eroded in the egalitarian celebration of common folk. Curiously in that time of buoyant optimism and progress and religious ferment, Miller seemed to have tapped into a darker side of the country with a contrary message, predicting with "proof" and "logic" that the world was not going to expand but rather going to end.[6]

When Miller had delivered one of his "lectures" in New York City in May 1840, a reporter from the *Herald Extra* was present and described Miller in this way: "In person he is about five feet seven inches in height, very thick set, broad shoulders; lightish brown hair, a little bald, a benevolent countenance, full of wrinkles, and his head shakes as though he was slightly afflicted with the palsy. His manners are very much in his favor; he is not a very well educated man; but he has read and studied history and prophecy very closely; has much strong common sense, and is evidently sincere in his belief."[7]

The great variety of people, doctrines and techniques under the umbrella of Millerism make it hard to define Millerism precisely, except in its central doctrine that the Second Coming of Christ was near.

Miller's Views

Miller's views did not deviate substantially from that of most conservative Protestants—except for his setting a specific time for the fulfillment of the Book of Revelation. Miller estimated that the Lord would come "about the year 1843." In 1832 Miller summarized his views about the date for the end of the world and how he arrived at them in a 64-page pamphlet *Evidence from Scripture and History of the Second Coming of Christ, About the Year 1843 and of His Personal Reign of 1000 Years* published by the Brandon Vermont Telegraph Office. His studies inescapably pointed to a pre- instead of a postmillennial Advent of Christ. His doctrines, however, in ever other way epitomized orthodoxy. His chronology merely elaborated and refined the kind of calculations of the end time his contemporaries had long been making. On only two points was he dogmatically insistent: that Christ would come ("He comes!—He comes!"),[8] and that He would come *about* 1843. On January 1, 1843, Miller had to try to be more precise as to the time, and he said again "sometime between March 21st, 1843, and March 21st, 1844, according to the Jewish mode of computation of time, Christ will come. . . ."[9] Miller steadfastly resisted the notion of people withdrawing from the churches that they were already members of, but he maintained a bias against the Catholic Church, seeing it as the "Mother of Harlots" and its progress as one of the prophetic signs of the approaching judgment of the world. He had other ideas that were liberal for his day, such as charitably sending "the Negro back to Africa." Miller was against the "fire-skulled, visionary, fanatical, abolitionists."[10]

Organization

By 1839 Miller had delivered about 800 "lectures" promoting his ideas on the advent year. His labors and energy were gradually turning Millerism from a single man's efforts to that of a growing national movement that involved increasing numbers of other people. One key recruit in 1839 was Joshua V. Himes, the pastor of Chardon Street Chapel in Boston. Once he was converted to Miller's chronology, Himes became the ideal number two man, a man of action with a gift for promotion. Every successful religious movement needs a person like Himes who proved to be a gifted publicist and organizer whose skills substantially helped make Miller a national figure and greatly expanded his movement. Himes started an eight-page newspaper early in 1840, the *Signs of the Times*, which continued uninterrupted throughout the history of movement. He changed the name to *The Advent Herald* in 1844. On November 17, 1842, Himes also started *The Midnight Cry* in New York City. In 1843 he started the *Philadelphia Alarm*.[11] Indeed, the extensive use of newspapers to spread Miller's ideas probably marks Millerism as the first religious movement to make extensive use of modern communications media, although the Puritan divines did publish their sermons and tracts in the seventeenth century. Not only did Himes start newspapers for the enterprise, but he arranged the various camp meetings and devised the extensive tours of a groups of evangelists, with the biggest tent the country had ever seen.

By the end of 1844 the Millerite movement had spread over the entire Northeast, with adventist journals thriving in New York, Philadelphia, Cincinnati, Cleveland, Rochester, and Montreal. Travelling preachers carried the message into Michigan, Illinois, and Wisconsin. Perhaps upstate New York and New England, having been washed over by previous adventist movements, gave the most intense support.[12]

In the Fall of 1840, as Millerism was slowly emerging as a well-defined movement and not just a local phenomenon, the presidential campaign between Van Buren and Harrison was being waged. The Harrison campaign made clever use of log cabins to dramatize Harrison's humble beginnings. Political supporters organized mass meetings to which from many miles around came farmers with families, singing songs at night. Some of these campaign techniques were borrowed from religious camp or revival meetings. Because revivalist groups, especially Methodists, had been conducting camp meetings for about forty years, the technique was not new and the public was accustomed to the emotional atmosphere, and for some it was stimulating entertainment as well as a religious release. Fires would blaze in the darkness, and the shouts and cries of the religious enthusiasts would cut through the night. Observers noted[13] "strange physical phenomenon" at many of these revival meetings, with the "falling exercise" being the most common. Indeed some felt that a preacher scarcely could consider his work that of God until "the slain" fell about him in a spiritual swoon.

The supporters of Miller also made use of such dramatic camp meetings to get their message out. The first Millerite Camp Meeting was held in the southern New Hampshire village of East Kingston from June 28 to July 5, 1842. The organizers wanted to "give the midnight cry," that is, to tell people of the immediate coming of Christ to judge the world, to say that He was near, "even at the door."[14] The Millerite organizers made arrangements to obtain a huge tent, one that could shelter between 3,000 and 4,000.

Other Ministers

In the late 1830s and early '40s other ministers began to accept Miller's views and make known the message of the coming of Christ. Prominent ministers like Henry Dana Ward, Henry Jones, Josiah Litch and Joseph Bates became active in the movement, even though not all agreed with Miller as to the exact time of Christ's advent. Charles Fitch, a Congregationalist minister had written to Miller in 1838 to clear up some of his uncertainties as to the time of the Second Coming. Some, like Himes, had been active in other causes of the times, such as the antislavery movement or the temperance movement. Josiah Litch, a prominent New England Methodist, joined the movement in 1838 and was one of the first New England ministers to preach on adventism from a Millerite perspective. He provided one of the most active pens of the movement. He edited the *Signs of the Times* in Boston, perhaps the most influential Adventist journal. Miller, Himes, Fitch and Litch were the big four, as it were. Dozens of other preachers, perhaps as many as a hundred, devoted full time to proclaiming the near Advent of Jesus and organizing camp meetings. Miller's supporters organized publications and second advent meetings and conferences in most of the major cities of the country.[15]

Size and Extent of the Movement

By the late 1830s, Miller with his tireless lectures and traveling had expanded his movement through northeastern New York, Vermont, and western Massachusetts. After he had been invited to Boston in 1839 and Himes had joined him the increased publicity allowed the movement to reach its peak in 1844. Across North America, at its broadest extent, the range of Millerite promotion stretched from the lower reaches of Canada, southward to Virginia and Kentucky, and westward as far as Ohio. During these years, other new ideas, fads, and movements competed for the attention of citizens. Appealing to idealists were the temperance and abolition movements, as well as such social experiments as Brook Farm, set up in 1841 a few miles from Boston. Men like Sylvester Graham, after whom the cracker was named, touted the health value of a vegetarian diet and the superiority of whole grains over refined flour products. In the fall of 1844 Polk and Clay were battling for the presidency while their followers organized torchlight processions and other novelties to attract the attention of voters.[16]

Who were the followers of William Miller? Millerism seems to have attracted a wide variety of Americans. Since there were no criteria for joining and no records were kept of who attended Miller's "lectures" or the various revivalist-style camp meetings, it is not possible to know if the majority of Millerites hailed from rural areas, as did some of their millenarian predecessors, although there is the impression of urban strength lent by the crowds who attended metropolitan meetings. Unlike earlier millenarian movements, there seems no evidence that Millerites were economically deprived. If anything, Millerites seem comfortably situated.[17]

Millerites seems to have come from all denominations, perhaps in their largest numbers from Baptist Churches. Indeed, Miller urged his followers to retain membership in their own churches, and Millerism, up to 1844, was antisectarian. The movement genuinely seems to have been a mass, interchurch movement with lay persons and ministers connecting themselves to the movement but still remaining as members in their own local church. It was only in 1844 with the Great Disappointment that the movement splintered.[18]

As many as 50,000 people in the United States became convinced of Miller's assertion that time would run out in 1844, while perhaps a million or more people were marginally curious or skeptically interested. In general, the followers of Miller seem to have been a sober group, unmarked by fanaticism, and in the initial stages at least clearly representative of nineteenth century American religion. The Millerites never manifested aggressiveness or violence. Possibly this was due to the fact that the level of opposition never evoked a violent response and perhaps because the poor and disadvantaged did not make up a large percentage of Millerites. Indeed, the followers of Miller seem to have been indistinguishable from their neighbors.[19]

It should be noted, however, that the movement did attract a number of enthusiasts and fanatics, so that some contemporaries claimed that Millerite doctrines caused insanity, partly because excessive religious enthusiasm had long been seen as a form of madness. Even Himes himself complained of being mired in "mesmerism seven feet deep." However, it seems more accurate to say that Millerism, rather than causing insanity, attracted some who may have already been mentally unstable.[20]

1843-1844 The Year of the End of the World

Miller had said that "sometime" between 1843 and 1844 the end of time would come. As his followers became more active in promoting his message, interest grew and crowds increased. Secular as well as adventist newspapers gave ample attention to the doctrines of Millerism. Newspapers in 1843 more frequently commented on such phenomena as comets, and Millerites believed that these sights were part of the heavenly signs foretold by biblical prophecies. In general, however, Miller and his spokesmen were restrained. They planned advent conferences, and during the summer of 1843 continued to actively give lectures and arrange camp meetings.

As crowds and attention increased, so did attacks from various clergy and the secular press. Miller's movement had in 1843 gained such proportions that mainstream clergy increased their criticism. Many clergy opposed the distinctive message of the nearness of the Advent. Stung by opposition from the unexpected direction of Protestant clergy, Millerites responded like earlier enthusiasts, that they had the light and any opposition to them could only be from deliberate sinfulness. Some Millerite preachers began to set forth the view that "Babylon" referred not only to the Catholic Church as Protestantism had long taught but also to the great body of "Protestant Christendom." Charles Fitch, one of the leading Millerite clergymen, said that both Catholic and Protestant branches of Christendom had fallen from the high spiritual state of pure Christianity and that he could only conclude that the symbolic "Babylon" now included Protestantism. Secular newspapers of the time often seemed bemused, printing cartoon-like gibes, referring to the end of the world in advertisements, and sometimes making ludicrous or ridiculing accusations that Millerite leaders were adventurers who had made money out of the whole scam. Despite opposition and ridicule Miller continued to be reluctant to start a new sectarian organization of those who would call themselves Adventists.[21]

The First Disappointment

As March of 1844 drew to an end, the world did not. But Miller, aged sixty-one and in poor health, showed no indication that he would stop his efforts to warn people that the next great event in the world's history was its ending. He was determined to continue to watch and pray. Perhaps, just perhaps, in the mysterious providence of God there might be a delay in the fulfillment of His plans in order to test the resolve and faith of believers. Miller was open to the fact that his calculations had an element of uncertainty, that errors in chronology may have crept into the reckoning of events over the centuries.

On May 2, six weeks after the fateful March 21, 1844, Miller confessed to his followers that somehow he had erred in his calculations. "I *confess my error*, and acknowledge *my disappointment*; yet I still believe that the day of the Lord is near, even at the door; and I exhort you, my brethren, to be watchful, and not let that day come upon you unawares."[22]

In the last week of May 1844, the leaders of the movement, including Himes and Miller, convened a large advent conference to try to puzzle out what had happened that the Lord had not come when expected.

In one of the meetings Miller arose and again frankly confessed his mistake at the defined time at which he supposed time would run out.

The year of the end of the world drew to a close, but Millerism continued. True, Millerites felt deep disappointment and concern that Miller's predictions failed, but also failing were the predictions of critics who said Millerites would burn their Bibles and give up their faith in disgust at their disappointment. Some who were lukewarm in the movement did leave. But many maintained their fervor and faith. They were ready to attribute the disappointing delay of the Lord's Coming as due to some minor human error in calculating chronology. The essential truth remained: Jesus was coming and coming soon; particulars were unimportant. Believers began to seek to be called Adventists, and the movement was larger than William Miller himself and any small details of time.

The summer of 1844 brought new hope and ardor, the movement continued to attract large crowds, 4000 at one meeting in Cincinnati alone. Miller and Himes and other leaders continued to add the proviso to their public statements: "providence permitting," or "if time lingers." In September, Miller and Himes reluctantly endorsed the revised calculations of one Brother Snow that pointed to October 22, 1844, as the fateful day of the Lord's Return. About thirty roving preachers continued their efforts into the fall, and Father Miller himself, despite his failing energies, conducted camp meetings in Cooperstown, Rochester, Buffalo and other upstate New York towns—over twenty-five meetings since May in preparation for the final climax of October 22, 1844.[23]

How did believers react to the apparent drawing near of the end of all things? Most who were pious seemed to be involved in prayer and spiritual activities with a lack of overt fanaticism. The faithful core were convinced that they were in the waning weeks of the world, and reports had it that in New Hampshire some farmers had not plowed their fields because the Lord would surely come "before another winter." This conviction grew among others in that areas so that even if they had planted their crops, they believed it would be inconsistent with their faith to take in their harvest. The majority of Millerites, however, seemed to continue in their various occupations.[24]

As they faced what they thought were their last few days on earth, true believers confronted the perplexing question of how completely they should withdraw from the world and its activites, and how they should make ready for the Advent of the Lord in the little time left. Their dilemma was whether they should go nonchalantly about their routine tasks until the last minute and thus be open to the charge of hypocrisy or whether they should cease all ordinary activites and rid themselves of worldly possessions, which would open them to a charge of fanaticism. Some Millerite merchants did indeed close their stores, to be free for spiritual activites and to provide a witness to the Lord's near coming. One sign read: "This shop is closed in honor of the King of kings, who will appear about the 20th of October. Get ready, friends, to crown Him Lord of all."[25]

Many believers had contributed money to support the four key journals that provided information on Millerism. Many Millerites wanted all their financial dealings concluded honorably and all debts paid before they would face their Lord when He came. A New York newspaper reported a dry goods store owner who offered his wares at bargain prices so that his conscience would be clear. Newspapers reported a few individuals resigning because the end was near. Stories spread of Millerites throwing their money out on the street and people confessing small crimes to cleanse their consciences.[26]

In the issue of the *Advent Herald* that came out 6 days before the expected end of the world, Himes wrote: "As the date of the present number of the *Herald* is our last day of publication before the tenth day of the seventh month, we shall make no provision for issuing a paper for the week following.... We feel called upon to suspend our labors and await the result."[27]

When at last the expected day came, most Millerites could be found gathered in their meeting places and churches to pray for themselves and for their unregenerate contemporaries. In New York the police had to close some of the Millerite meeting places because of the crowds. Some curious wanted to discuss the anticipated ascension expected on that day. Some believers met in small groups in private homes to comfort and accompany each other on their expected ascension. A reporter from the *Cincinnati Chronicle* attended a Millerite service on this day. "As the consummation of all terrestrial things was expected to have taken place last evening, and being desirous of seeing the effect of such belief upon its votaries at their last earthly meeting, I took the liberty . . . of being present. The assemblage, indoors and out, probably numbered 1,500 persons. . . . There was less excitement than I expected, and a great deal more cheerfulness manifested in the countenances of the believers than could have been supposed at the hour of so serious a crisis. . . . Considering the crowd, the meeting was very orderly. Two or three attempts were made by a set of rowdies outdoors to raise a breeze by noise and clamor, but the assertion of the preacher, that a strong police force was present, calmed the multitude, and he was enabled to proceed with what he at the close said was, in his opinion, his last warning to a sinful world. . . . By nine o'clock the benediction was pronounced, and the people advised to go quietly home and await the awful coming, which not unlikely might transpire at the hour of midnight. . . ."[28]

The Great Disappointment

Most Millerites had entered October 22 with fervor and the genuine expectation that they would soon see Him who had been the object of their prayers and adoration. When the Lord did not appear at midnight, and the next day dawned as usual, they could only feel great disappointment and confusion.

A Millerite named Hiram Edson said:

> Our fondest hopes and expectations were blasted, and such a spirit of weeping came over us as I never experienced before. It seemed that the loss of all earthly friends could have been no comparison. We wept, and wept, till the day dawn[ed]. I mused in my own heart, saying, My advent experience has been the richest and brightest of all my Christian experience. If this had proved a failure, what was the rest of my Christian experience worth? Has the Bible proved a failure? Is there no God, no heaven, no golden home city, no paradise? . . . And as I said, we wept till the day dawn[ed].[29]

Another Millerite, Washington Morse, reported:

> That day came and passed, and the darkness of another night closed in upon the world. . . . The passing of time was a bitter disappointment. True believers had given up all for Christ, and had shared His presence as never before. The love of Jesus filled every soul; and with inexpressible desire they prayed,'Come, Lord Jesus, and come quickly;' but He did not come. And now, to turn again to the cares, perplexities, and dangers of life, in full view of jeering and reviling unbelievers who scoffed as never before, was a terrible trial of faith and patience. . . . I left the place of meeting and wept like a child.[30]

After October 22 passed, shock, confusion and sorrow lay heavily on the Millerites, especially those who had given little thought to their future earthly needs. Had they not been most conscientious in their preparation for the Lord's Coming? What could have gone wrong? Their literal reading of the Bible had caused them to focus on the single doctrine of Jesus's Second Advent. Expressing faith in the imminent return of Christ was the same as expressing faith in God. When Jesus did not return as expected, it threw into question their entire faith as well as their assumptions about the reliability of the Bible.

The shaken Millerite movement fractured into several parts, with no clear breakdown possible of how many scattered into different branches. One group would have included those watchers of October 22 who were lukewarm or fearful of judgment day because of guilt rather than belief; many of these fell away from the Adventist ranks, either to return to their old churches or to abandon evangelical religion completely. Others joined the Shakers, often a final refuge for those who were disappointed by other religious experiments of the early years of the nineteenth century.[31]

But thousands of Millerites remained steadfast in their Adventist beliefs. For this core group, any doctrinal alternatives to Adventism were unacceptable and a return to orthodoxy unthinkable, so these believers could only hold on grittily to the essentials of their Adventist faith. Indeed, ridicule from scoffers and persecution from a hostile world only strengthened, by a process known as cognitive dissonance, their belief. Their issue, once they recovered from their initial dejection, was to discover an adequate explanation for the failure of October 22. Battered by opposition and the failure of their expectations, the faithful remnant, as it were, put forth many different ideas to explain what had happened. Some felt that an error had occurred in calculating the last day. Others concluded that no mistake in the date had been made, but that Christ had indeed come but in a spiritual way. Joseph Turner of Maine promoted the "Shut-Door" interpretation, namely that the Bridegroom had come, gone into the wedding, and shut the door with the result that no longer could there be probation for sinners.[32]

To attempt to unify the fragmented, confused and depleted movement, Miller himself, Himes, Litch, Fleming and other Millerites met on April 29, 1845, at Albany, New York. Controversy divided the conference. Those who advocated the "Shut-Door" theory—the idea that no one could be saved who had not entered the community of saints by 1844—refused to compromise with those who believed that salvation could still be attained. Miller reaffirmed his belief in the approaching personal return of Jesus, but after the Great Disappointment of October 22 he seems to have lost the position of eminence and authority he previously had held. Divisions among Adventists became more solidified, with the Millerite movement giving birth to several different sects.[33]

Remnants of Miller's movement formed a formal Adventist organization, the very thing that Miller had so long resisted. This General Conference of the Second Advent Believers held in loose affiliation for almost 20 years a scattering of groups. The bone of contention right from the beginning was the disagreement on chronology. Some abandoned the notion of a specific date for the return of the Lord and His millennium, preferring to be constantly ready for an event of unknown date. If individuals set dates for the Coming of Jesus, there was no unanimity and enthusiasm could not be sustained. When the Civil War broke out, Adventism was still in disarray, in spite of the wide interest and a flood of widely circulated journals and periodicals with millennial concerns such as the *Millennial Harbinger* and the Mormon *Millennial Star*. David Nevins Lord, president of Dartmouth College, established the *Theological and Literary Journal* in 1848 in an attempt to bring some order to the confusion among different millennial groups.[34]

There was indeed much confusion and fragmentation among groups and ideas. Alexander Campbell, the founder of the Disciples of Christ, in his *Millennial Harbinger*, broadcast his hope that Christians would come together in a unity that was indispensable to the dawning of the millennial age. In the early days of his movement there was the eager anticipation of a millennium of bliss on earth. As Campbell gradually lost faith in a radical restoration of the primitive church which would produce harmony and unity, he increasingly came to appreciate what later scholars have called the civil religion of the United States which allowed a plurality of religious opinions. Campbell anticipated in many ways themes which have been central to American civil religion and which in many ways have been expounded in presidential inaugural addresses.[35] John Thomas in 1844 led a few congregations out of Campbell's Disciples movement. Thomas elaborated a complex premillenarian theory and named his followers the Christadelphians. This group fell into an irresolvable schism over the issue of whether both the faithful and unfaithful would be raised to be judged by Christ.

Several of the offshoots of Millerism have survived to the present day; indeed, most modern American Adventist groups are the heirs of the Millerite tradition. One group became organized as the Advent Christian Association at Worcester, Massachusetts, on November 6, 1861. This church, known as the Advent Christian Church, constitutes today the principal segment of what might be described as First-day Adventists, in contrast to the other group, the Seventh-day Adventists, the largest and most widespread of Millerite offshoots.

There can be considerable diversity in the views of groups which share roots in the Millerite tradition, although most Adventists and apocalyptically oriented groups perceive natural disasters and political disorders as indicative of the time of trouble. For example, the First Day Adventists continued to hold a more traditional doctrine of the Second Coming of Christ. They believed that biblical prophecies indicate the approximate time of Christ's return, and the great duty of believers is to proclaim this soon-coming redemption. Central to their belief are chapters 2 and 7 of Daniel and the fulfillment of Matthew, chapter 24, and they consider that the seeming historic realization of many of the signs and symbols of Revelation indicates the near return of Christ.

Seventh-Day Adventists

While Miller focused on the imminence of Christ's return, Seventh-day Adventists originally had to face the disappointment of Christ's non-appearance and come to some understanding of the delay in Christ's return.

The Seventh-day Adventists developed out of discussions among small Adventist groups as to the correct interpretation of the key passage in Daniel 8:13 and 14: "Then I heard a holy one speaking; and another holy one said to the one that spoke, 'For how long is the vision concerning the continual burnt offering, the transgression that makes desolate, and the giving over of the sanctuary and host to be trampled under foot?' And he said to him, 'For two thousand and three hundred evenings and mornings; then the sanctuary shall be restored to its rightful state.' " These adventist believers concluded that there had been no mistake in regard to the prophecy of the 2300 days, just a mistake in interpretation.

The illumination as to the correct interpretation originally came to a disappointed Millerite by the name of Hiram Edson on the day after the Great Disappointment. His insight into the meaning of the prophet Daniel was that the cleaning of the sanctuary referred to the sanctuary in *heaven*. That is, on October 22, Jesus moved into the most holy place in heaven, an entry that marked the end of 2300 years to complete his mediatorial work before coming to earth for the second time.[36]

There were many strands in the tapestry of beliefs that Seventh-day Adventists were to hold. Another former Millerite, Ellen G. Harmon, gained a reputation as an adventist prophetess and gradually was accepted as an authoritative messenger from God in the emerging Seventh-day Adventist movement. Born in 1827, she began as a teenager to have visions. In one ecstatic experience she had a vision which connected the warning of the third angel of Revelations 14.9 to the observance of the true Sabbath. She believed that the failure to keep the Ten Commandments, especially the fourth, was the reason for the delay of Jesus' return. She accordingly insisted on the observance of the fourth commandment, that is, the observance of the

Sabbath on Saturday, the seventh day of the week, rather than on Sunday, the first day. Other visions followed which assured Adventist believers that despite their gloom, they would have eventual triumph. Indeed, through her visions of heaven, she informed her followers what was required on earth. Many disillusioned Millerites joined the growing movement.[37]

Ellen Harmon in 1846 married the Reverend James White, who was himself an Adventist and the owner of the company which published the *Adventist Review and Herald*. Her religious experiences became the raw material on which White's publishing company would flourish. Her support was also important for the growing organization of the movement. In general Adventists opposed organizing themselves into a denomination, fearing that moving in this direction might transform them into a "Babylon," a body that would conform to the world and be apostate. But the demands of ordaining clergy, supporting evangelization, legally holding meeting house properties, all the tasks necessary in institutionalized religion, increasingly led to a series of conferences that shaped the Seventh-day Adventist into a denominational organization. The group only adopted the name Seventh-day Adventists in September 1860, having previously called themselves Sabbatarian Adventists.[38]

After 1855, the headquarters of the movement guided by Mrs. White was centered in Battle Creek, Michigan. In a vision in June 1863, she received word that a change of diet would improve her poor health. She began to advocate vegetarianism, to warn against alcohol and tobacco, and to disparage contemporary medical practices. Her Adventist ideas soon became linked with the contemporary concern over diet, such as advocated by Sylvester Graham (known for his health crackers). Dr. John Harvey Kellogg, a follower of Mrs. White, became known for his cereal as well as transforming the Adventist water cure center in Battle Creek into a renowned sanitarium. As part of their slow but almost inexorable transition from sect to Church, the Seventh-day Adventists also made the leap from counter-establishment health reform to establishment medicine.[39]

By the middle 1860s Seventh-day Adventists, evolving from the discouragement and divisions of Millerism, had substantially consolidated themselves on doctrinal and organizational issues. Their main focus continued to be on biblical prophecies, especially those of Daniel and Revelation, but they worked out a careful theology of the end time. They expect the Lord will return for the second time only when the work of blotting out of human sin is completed. In the meantime, it is still possible to be saved, but as soon as the cleansing is complete, the door of salvation will close. Adventists feel they bear the credentials of the remnant, the "seal of God" by reason of their seventh-day observance, and will play a key role in the final struggle between good and evil. They regard the various Christian churches that force people to worship on Sunday bear the mark of the Beast. Indeed, the United States, the Catholic Church, and the mainline Protestant churches are all considered aspects of Babylon.

The Second Coming inaugurates the millennium, during which there will be three resurrections. In the first those who played the great roles in the battle between good and evil will be raised; the second resurrection is of the righteous only. At the third resurrection the damned of every generation are raised for the great battle of Gog and Magog, the equivalent of Armageddon. After the final defeat of Satan, Christ will reign for eternity with the righteous in a new heaven and new earth.[40]

The Sabbath is a key to gaining insight to the Seventh-day Adventist relationship with America. Puritan immigrants and evangelists during the Great Awakening had seen the proper observance of Sunday as part of perfecting the American people. Revivalists during the Second Great Awakening had called for the perfection of society and the reformation that would hasten the earthly millennium in which the American Republic would become the righteous empire. By contrast, the Seventh-day Adventists refuse to see American society as the means of universal redemption. Indeed, they identified America as one of Revelations's Beasts. They define themselves as a band of Sabbath keepers, in negation to the American nation which is in league with Satan. In opposition to this Beast there stands the remnant seeking perfection, a group whose defining characteristic was to observe the Sabbath on the seventh day. This group, not America, would share the key redemptive role, and the seventh-day Sabbath observance illustrates their difference from—even antagonism to—mainstream America, America the ultimate adversary. Indeed,

America would become, in Adventists' eyes, an instrument of the Antichrist before its destruction at the Second Coming.[41]

Because the Seventh-day Adventists hold that the exact time of Jesus' Second Coming cannot be discovered from the study of Biblical prophecy, the movement has not been subjected, as the Millerites were, to any climaxes of expectation on the part of the larger public. They still, however, are keen discerners of the "signs of the times" and give constant apocalyptic commentary on current events. They continue their mission work and have confidence that they are the inheritors of a sacred trust with the task of calling all people to make ready for the return of Christ and for a better world that God has prepared for those who love him. They believe that even though the Bridegroom is at the door, believers cannot know the day nor the hour of his coming.

The spiritual discipline of Seventh-day Adventists aims at self-improvement and perfection, to reassimilate a remnant of the human race into the divine realm, to be like the inhabitants of heaven, the angels. Angels are sexless, and so to be like the angels, to transform themselves, Adventists preach self-control. Virtue is to be practiced in readiness for heaven. Sexual activity, from the viewpoint of heaven, is "dysfunctional." To avoid activities that release sexual impulse, Seventh-day Adventists generally are instructed to avoid alcohol, tobacco, meat, and coffee. Activites such as dancing and popular entertainment can also stimulate passions which the angels shun. Seventh-day Adventists claim they do not eschew pleasure for its own sake but simply avoid those pleasures that might prevent them from being perfectly adapted to heavenly society.[42]

Seventh-day Adventism, although an offshoot of Millerism, has become very different from it. No millenarian movement can last long in a state of expectation. The diffusion and discouragement of the Millerite remnant of October 1844 have lead to the structured, stable, organized denomination with concerns very different from those of Miller, who would not recognize his spiritual grandchildren. The Seventh-day Adventists have more than five million members worldwide, an elaborate church administration, schools, and a medical establishment that has the hospitals and skills to perform the controversial transplant of a baboon's heart into the body of a baby girl, Baby Fae, in 1984.[43]

Other Millerite Offshoots

Most modern American Adventist bodies can trace their lineage back to the Millerite movement and William Miller's brand of popular Baptist theology. Some of the Adventist bodies, such as the Church of God (Holiness), espouse the Second Coming of Christ with a literal millennium but without the high intensity of the Millerite expectations. The Church of Universal Triumph/the Dominion of God was founded by Rev. James Francis Marion Jones, or the Prophet Jones, who was born in 1908. Jones claimed God instructed him in the form of a breeze. During the 1940s and '50s his church grew. He imposed very strict rules, of not smoking, of drinking neither coffee nor tea. The central belief is that in the year 2000 the millennium would begin and those who would be alive then will be immortal and live in an earthly paradise. Police, however, arrested Prophet Jones in his home in 1956 on indecency charges, and his church was shaken. Jones died in 1971.[44]

Various pentecostal assemblies which began in the 1930s have expectations of the millennium, but usually their emphasis is more on attention to the Holy Spirit and the experiencing of the signs of His presence, such as speaking in tongues. They do not set dates for nor stress the imminence of Christ's Second Coming.

Jehovah's Witnesses

Contrasting with the Seventh-day Adventists who do not calculate a precise date for the Second Coming are the Jehovah's Witnesses. It is very hard for millenarians to last as millenarians; they can endure only if they transform the millenarian outlook. Perhaps more than any other millenarian movement, the Witnesses have continued over considerable span of time to prophesy the end of the present world. Prophetic Witnesses have continually named specific dates as having definite eschatological significance, 1874, 1878, 1881, 1910, 1914, 1918 on up to the present. The Witnesses seem neither dissuaded from further date setting because of any past disappointments nor troubled that they must "adjust" prophetic chronology over and over. Indeed, their date-setting eschatology is probably the very basis of their existence as a separate religious community—although it has costs. Expectation and uncertainty had the effect early in the movement of sifting membership and producing various schisms, with some believers maintaining vigilance and others becoming disappointed and falling away.[45]

Charles Taze Russell was born in Pittsburgh, Pennsylvania, in 1852, eight years after the Great Disappointment of 1844. In his twenties he published a small pamphlet *The Object and Manner of Our Lord's Return* in which he outlined two stages of Christ's coming, namely his invisible presence prior to his Second Coming at end of the world. In part this doctrine developed out of a different way of translating the biblical word *parousia* as "presence" rather than as "coming" as had been traditional. Russell believed that the invisible presence of Christ began in 1874. Russell also taught the doctrine of the invisible rapture of the saints during Christ's invisible presence. Many of his ideas resembled those of Edmund Irving in England as promulgated by John Nelson Darby of the Plymouth Brethren.[46]

The work of Dr. Nelson H. Barbour, an Adventist preacher and former Millerite, very much influenced Russell. In a book called *Herald of the Morning*, published in Rochester, New York, Barbour made use of a chronology which concluded that 1873 was the 6000th year from Adam's creation. He accordingly had expected 1873 as the year of Christ's Second Coming and the end of the earth. When nothing happened, he began like Russell to translate *parousia* as "presence" and began to believe that the invisible presence of Christ began in 1874. Russell threw his support behind *Herald of the Morning* and helped Barbour write a book expressing his ideas on the end of the world. In a collaborative effort in 1877 Barbour and Russell published *Three Worlds and the Harvest of this World* that provided an elaborate chronology and prophetic speculation about the end of time. Barbour used the common idea that a biblical day equalled a year from Numbers 14:33-34 and Ezekiel 4.1-8 that prophet-like days really meant years. Barbour spent "one evening" with the Bible and corrected the chronology of Bishop James Ussher whose chronology was off by 124 years. Both Barbour and Russell sought to determine God's timetable for the second coming, the rapture (taking up) of the saints, and restoring of earth to a paradise-like Eden. They developed a system which they claim demonstrated amazing, mathematic "correspondences" between historic events and biblical prophecy. The three worlds in the title seem to refer to three periods, not unlike the ideas of Joachim of Fiore.[47]

Russell had no formal university or seminary training, and his "Bible students" have followed him in his intense scrutiny of the Bible while ignoring standard biblical and historical study. Even to this day Witnesses maintain a biblical chronology and history that essentially ignores the last 100 years of scholarship. Russell showed no interest in other theologians, even though his followers regard him with his enormous bulk of writings as one of those very theologians he despised. Indeed, Russell apparently abhorred the established Christian churches, and early in his career came to look on most clergy as false shepherds, who were not preaching Christ's kingdom and who were more and more influenced by the new biblical criticism which would undermine his literal reading of the Bible.

Russell seems unaware how much his doctrines resembled his Adventist and millenarian predecessors. He based his doctrines, a form of pre-millenarian eschatology, on his understanding of the teachings of Christ, the apostles and prophets as contained in the Bible, especially the Book of Revelation. He believed that Christ was choosing a church of 144,000 (Rev. 7:4, 14:1), spiritual Israelites who would rise to rule with Him as king-priests for a 1000 years. The rest of humanity would be raised during the millennium in order to learn God's will and to accept it or reject it. Those who put their faith in Christ and his kingdom were to pass through Armageddon into a new earth that is to become a new Eden. At the end of a 1000 years Satan will be loosed to deceive the nations, but finally God's wrath will destroy him, and those who are alive at that time will receive the reward of everlasting life.[48]

Russell began to differ from Barbour and added some new doctrines, for example, the idea that those dying from 1878 onward would have an immediate heavenly resurrection rather than have to sleep in their graves. He felt that the "higher calling" or harvest of the "elect 144,000" saints would be completed in 1881. Even though he changed his position, especially on the nature and timing of the rapture he felt the time for his ministry would be short, not more than a few years at most. In 1882 he rejected the traditional doctrine of the trinity and moved further away ideologically from his former Adventist associates. He concluded that 1914 was to be the year in which time would end, but before the end he expected much trouble in the world, such as never seen before.

Russell was a many-gifted man, with tireless zeal, great speaking ability, and a dynamic and warm personality. The fortune he earned in the clothing business allowed him to pursue his religious interests. He was not yet thirty when he took on a leadership role, motivated by a need to defend a doctrine that was not receiving attention as well as his sense of God guiding and directing him. He was not unlike William Miller in that he seemed to have had no interest in starting a movement, and initially his followers had few of the organizational marks of a sect. Soon they had to develop their own devotional practices and forms of governing themselves as a congregation just as Miller's followers eventually did in developing the Seventh-day Adventist denomination.

In 1881 he insisted that all who considered themselves members of Christ's Body and who regarded him as their pastor must preach to their neighbor, a practice which the Jehovah's Witnesses continue to this day. In spite of his insistence on his followers being a preaching brotherhood, Russell believed the vast majority of humans would be given an opportunity to attain salvation during the millennium, that there was no need to preach to everyone.

Russell was very active as a writer, evangelist, and organizer of the Zion's Watch Tower Tract Society. He published its official magazine, *Zion's Watch Tower and Herald of Christ's Presence*, starting in 1879. He sent missionaries to foreign countries and made numerous trips himself to Canada, Britain, Europe, and throughout the United States. Despite his great success and the adulation in which he was held by his "bible students," Russell's movement on least two occasions, in 1884 and 1908-1909, was split by schisms, in part because some of his followers thought Russell was too domineering.[49]

Russell seems not to have been very successful in his personal life. While he was genuinely an attractive and kind man who was sincerely devoted to his ministry, he also revealed qualities of arrogance as well as naivete. In his relationship with his wife he seems to have shown a lack of sensitivity and normal affection. He and she had entered an agreement not to consummate their marriage, ostensibly on the basis of Mt. 19:12. (". . . There are eunuchs who have made themselves eunuchs for the sake of the kingdom of heaven.") The reality seems to be that Russell, perhaps because of his consuming concern with religion, manifested little sexual interest. He said that he wished to live a celibate life but would have fulfilled his marital obligations if Maria had wished. He took pains not to be in a room alone with a woman, and he held very conservative views on the subordinate position of women in marriage. By 1879 he and Maria had separated. In 1903 she published an attack on him, depicting him as an arrogant tyrant, and she became his bitterest opponent.[50]

Russell had predicted that 1914 (or 1915) would see the destruction of the Gentile nations and the time of troubles that would lead to Armageddon. The saints were to be rapt up to heaven with Christ, and the millennial rule of Christ over the earth was to be inaugurated. As 1914 drew near Russell was nervous about the possible disconfirmation of his predictions. By 1913 the International Bible Students were experiencing great millenarian excitement. When World War I erupted, Russell and his Bible Students took it to be a confirmation of his prophecy and chronology. Russell and the Bible Students strongly opposed any involvement in the war because the war was the fulfillment of prophecy and warring nations were not in God's favor. Many Bible Students were harassed and attacked. Russell was not obviously discomforted by the delay of the rapture for himself and his followers. On Friday, October 2, 1914, he said, "Good morning" and clapping his hands happily announced that "The Gentile times have ended."[51] He expected the battle of Armageddon in 1918 with the rapture of the church but he died on October 31, 1916.

His followers did not expect to see their pastor die before the end of world and were not psychologically prepared to carry on his mission. Even more, they were disturbed that Christ did not take Russell up physically to heaven. In 1917 and 1918 his followers struggled over who was to succeed Russell.

Judge Joseph Rutherford, Russell's personal attorney, was chosen president of the Watch Tower Bible and Tract Society. With Rutherford a new era began for Russell's movement. Judge Rutherford promoted strong growth after the War, and in 1920s used a publicity campaign with the slogan: "Millions now living will never die," with the suggestion that the millennium would begin in 1925 and that there would be a full restoration of mankind. In July 1931 at a convention for members in Columbus, Ohio, Rutherford recommended a new name for the movement, "Jehovah's Witnesses."

Along with growth, Rutherford also brought more isolation and alienation from American society for the Witnesses. He fostered the view that the secular state was demonic and without redeeming features. The Judge bitterly attacked business, politics, and established churches. Different individuals and groups responded by attacking those Witnesses who more openly courted martyrdom—which recalls where this work began, that is, the efforts of some early Christians to court suffering for their beliefs. Some Witnesses manifested bizarre and extreme behavior, with attacks on religion and clergy, and savage attacks on the Roman Catholic Church as a harlot. Witnesses sometimes with militant fervor invaded towns carrying signs and fulfilling their preaching mission. Many were jailed. Judge Rutherford believed the apocalyptic end was near in the early 1940s. He died in 1942.[52]

Capable administrators succeeded the Judge, and they fostered the growth of the Jehovah's Witnesses worldwide so that they currently number about eight million. But the Witnesses continue to set prophetic dates, little troubled that they must time and again "adjust" their chronology. For example, they said that 1975 was the end of 6000 years of human existence. The group has lessened its tirades against vaccination but continues to emphasize the sacredness of life and to oppose blood transfusions (on the basis of Gen. 9:5-6, Lev. 17:10 and Acts 15:20, 28, 29). They refuse to serve in the military and are convinced that the secular state firmly opposes the Kingdom of Christ. It is as if the Witnesses do not have a good grasp on their own history with its contradictions and distortions. They are a world-denying group which tends to be psychologically isolated from the larger culture and promotes a seige mentality and a vigilance for any signs indicating the approach of the millennium. They believe God guides and directs all things to his divine purpose.[53]

Other North American Groups

The religious diversity in the United States during the second half of the twentieth century continues to be extraordinary. Amidst the hundreds of small cults in any large American city, a diversity and variety of religious experiences and groups can be found. New Age consciousness in various forms is yet another religious awakening on the American scene. Before closing this chapter on America and some of its millenarian groups, it is interesting to note a small 1950s flying saucer cult in which a curious secular kind of millennial ideas emerged.

Flying Saucer Cult

This small apocalyptic and millenarian group came to the attention of researchers in the 1950s when the Lake City *Herald* carried a story about a prophecy of the earth's end due to a great flood. The prophet was a fifty-year-old suburban housewife by the name of Marian Keech who claimed to have received messages by automatic writing from superior, nonterrestrial beings on planets called Clarion and Cerus.[54]

Mrs. Keech believed higher forces could communicate to her by using her hand: automatic writing for Mrs. Keech involved holding a pencil and seeing her hand write in a handwriting not her own. Initially the messages lacked clarity and coherence, but gradually she became aware that other beings or intelligences were trying "to get through" to her.

Initially, the messages from "Elder Brother" and "Sananda" were diverse, but some gave predictions of specific future events and others gave ideas about flying saucers and other intelligent beings in the universe. Gradually the messages began to predict cataclysmic disasters and worldwide upheaval and change. She and her two staunchest followers, Dr. Thomas Armstrong and his wife Daisy, received these momentous announcements with awe and reverence. They regarded this as perhaps the most important news in history, although they also they displayed a curious indifference about the terrible possibilities of world destruction. On August 30, Dr. Armstrong began to spread the word by means of a seven-page mimeographed statement that outlined the coming catastrophe which was "very, very near." His action was the first step in the formation of a movement.[55]

Dr. Armstrong began to be more active and somewhat more successful in proselytizing. If someone manifested interest, he would casually make it known that he had a friend who was in contact with people on another planet. If the potential recruit showed more interest, Dr. Armstrong would share his belief in the coming catastrophe, reincarnation, and flying saucers. New recruits would gradually learn about the communications brought to the group by Mrs. Keech's automatic writing. The messages, for example, brought by Mrs. Keech's automatic writing informed the group that she had been Mary, Jesus's mother. Messages further informed the group that smoking was bad, not only because it fouled the atmosphere but also because it was a yielding to the cravings of animal nature. Eating meat was also deleterious because it dampened spiritual development by incorporating the very elements people should be trying to rise above. The central issue, however, of Mrs. Keech's messages was that on December 21 a great flood would begin to cover the earth. Within a year the earth's surface would be under water, and the souls of the dead would be raised. The select who were ready and qualified would be taken to the planet Clarion and trained for the task of repopulating and ruling the cleansed earth.

A total of thirty-three people represented the largest number that ever attended meetings of Mrs. Keech's small band. Eight of these were heavily committed; seven were less committed and had some doubt about the predictions. Eighteen were curious or mere sightseers. Mrs. Keech's daughter Cleo wavered, while Bob Eastman, a student, believed and was ready to go anytime. He continued his classes only to preserve outward appearances and not to create panic. He sold some of his possessions and spent the Thanksgiving vacation winding up his affairs and bidding farewell to his parents and friends. Kitty O'Donnell had become convinced that the flood would come on the 21st, quit her job, and devoted all her time to the group. She honestly believed she might be picked up at any time by a flying saucer. Indeed, her motivation was high: "I have to believe the flood is coming . . . because I've spent nearly all my money. . . ."[56] Core member Mark Post soon gave up his job at a hardware store, and his mother Edna Post gave up her job as the director of a nursery school. Dr. Armstrong was asked to resign from his position at the local college health services because of complaints he was teaching strange religious beliefs. He interpreted this rebuff as a further loosening from the world and as confirmation of the validity of the messages.

Dr. Armstrong and Mrs. Keech announced at a meeting on November 23 that they believed they would soon receive their orders. It was possible, they said, that someone attending the meeting might be a possible messenger from the Guardians. Mrs. Keech said that if December 21 was the wrong date and the flood did not occur, it would be a test of their faith. Dr. Armstrong thought that some of their group would be picked up individually by flying saucers. Each member would probably receive instructions directly, that they would hear a voice telling him or her what to do. He added that members should be cautious in their efforts to proselytize; they should not force any one and they should avoid ridicule.

When the little band gathered to wait for the 21st, it was by now a relaxed and familiar group, even cheerful, as the end grew near. They had a sense that their future would be glorious and that as the chosen they would be engaged in happy, important work. The future would be a new age and the earth would be better. Dr. Armstrong, with a sense of the imminence of the disaster, was making detailed plans for their evacuation. Mrs. Keech gave instructions that all of them should remove any metal from their pockets and to cut out any metallic parts of their clothes such as the flies of pants or snaps of brassieres because riding in a flying saucer would cause metal to heat up so much so as possibly to cause burns.

Reporters began to telephone and appear at the door. Dr. Armstrong and Mrs. Keech tried to keep private their beliefs, and Dr. Armstrong actually denied the world would end on the 21st of December. He did allow that there would be a tidal wave and the earth's crust from Hudson Bay to the Gulf of Mexico would be displaced. The world, he said, was in a "mess," but the supreme Being would cleanse house by sinking all of the land masses. Some would be saved by being taken off the earth in a space craft.[57]

As the 21st drew near the group grew embattled and withdrew in the face of ridiculing publicity and pranksters and the curious. The group faced the difficulty of sorting out the chosen from the heathen. A practical joker who called himself Captain Video (the name of the main character of a popular TV science fiction program) telephoned and told them a saucer would pick up the group up at 4 P.M. After 5:30 the group gave up the wait and returned to Mrs. Keech's living room. They even watched the "Captain Video" TV program for any messages in code. The group expected to be rescued by flying saucers before the cataclysmic flood took place on the 21st.

In their efforts to explain the failure of the saucers to pick them up, they fell back on the explanation that it must have been a practice session and test of their faith. Soon Mrs. Keech received a midnight message of greatest importance—that a flying saucer was indeed on its way to her backyard to pick them up. The small group waited, free of any metal, in the cold. The were elated and excited and chilled. When they finally went back into the warm house, they could only conclude that it was another drill.

Mrs. Keech received another vital message. At midnight on December 20 the group was to be taken to a place where they were to board a flying saucer. That evening about 15 people gathered once again in Mrs. Keech's living room to prepare for their departure. Again they removed all metal from their clothes. At 11:15 PM Mrs. Keech received by automatic writing the order for them to get their overcoats on. They were tense with expectation. When midnight approached, they waited in silence. The cataclysmic flood was but seven hours away. Midnight passed. By 2:30 the little group was still reluctant to talk about the failure of another midnight prediction. They had in some way to come to terms with the failure of their expectations. The issue was to find an adequate way to reconcile the disconfirmation of belief.

Finally help came in the form of a message that announced that the world's destruction was called off. Because of the little group's faith, God had spared the world from destruction. The group was exhausted from fatigue and tension but also had a desire to spread the good word. They had to face the hard facts of life in the same old world that was not flooded or destroyed.[58]

Mrs. Keech and Dr. Armstrong were floundering. They still clung to their belief but searched desperately for guidance when succeeding predictions were not fulfilled. On December 23, Mrs. Keech received another message saying that momentous events would take place on Christmas Eve. The message commanded the little group to assemble on the sidewalk in front of Mrs. Keech's house at 6 PM on the 24th to sing Christmas carols. There the group would be visited by spacemen who would land in a flying saucer. The message told Mrs. Keech and Dr. Armstrong to invite the public. Accordingly the faithful band gathered on December 24, Mrs. Keech, the two Armstrongs and their children, Edna and Mark Post, and Bob Eastman. About 200 onlookers milled around the small band while they sang carols. After twenty minutes the small band re-entered the house, and Dr. Armstrong told reporters that he believed the spacemen had been in the crowd or perhaps they had refrained from landing for fear of creating panic among the onlookers.

Mrs. Keech's group began to disintegrate even as they continued to search for orders from the Guardians. Their attempts to explain what had gone wrong were less and less effective. Mrs. Keech and Dr. Armstrong continued to believe long after their followers departed, and Dr. Armstrong himself received a message that he would be picked up by a flying saucer at the garage ramp of the hotel in Collegeville. All one night he his wife, daughter Cleo, and one other woman waited. He had a boundless faith and a sublime resistance to disconfirmation. (Dr. Armstrong was later declared sane by two psychiatrists.)[59]

What is noticeable in this group is the absence of any biblical basis for their millenarian idea. It is debatable whether they are a millenarian cult in the usual sense of the word, as their ideas were rather muddled with only the vaguest religious sense. Their notion of the millennial period was even more underdeveloped.

Other groups, however, have developed or are developing with millenarian-like ideologies that are not scripturally based. For instance, at the end of the nineteenth century, Native Americans, responding to expansionist pressures of the white civilization, developed revitalization movements that had millenarian characteristics. The so-called Ghost Dance Movement offered Indians a myth of a great upheaval that would swallow up whites but permit indians to be saved to enjoy the earth and the fullness of the earth with all its good things.[60]

Members of an immigrant Canadian group, the Doukhobors, have been called "living examples of a type of messianic and millenarian Christianity that in western Europe was largely moribund by the end of the seventeenth century and that elsewhere has long lost its revolutionary character."[61]

This small Canadian group, numbering about 20,000, comes to attention because of their provocative and dramatic mass protests. For example, in 1932, roughly 600 were arrested for their nude parade before police, and in 1950, approximately 400 were arrested for a similar protest. They have also protested through the use of dynamite and arson as recently as 1979. It is likely that the extreme behavior—arson, nudism, dynamiting—never represented more than a small minority of an otherwise peaceful community, but some scholars have compared them to the Adamites.[62] Originating from various Russian sects dating back to the end of the fifteenth century or even earlier, this communitarian sect migrated to Canada in 1899 and settled in Saskatchewan. Because of their tradition of nonconformity and because they acknowledge only God's laws, they have on occasion strenuously opposed Canadian legislation of any kind and have struggled against assimilation.[63]

The forms and variations of millennial concerns increase and diversify. For example, members of Jim Jones's Peoples Temple believed the end was near and on November 18, 1978, committed mass suicide.[64] This group was an apocalyptic cult, whereas the Doukhobors comprise a communistic or communal sect. Mrs. Prophet's Church Universal and Triumphant appears to be primarily an apocalyptic group with scant millenarian ideology that can be traced to Scripture.

Conclusion

When Millerism swept various parts of the young American Republic, many Americans took its ideas seriously. With the Great Disappointment the Millerite movement fragmented but left an Adventist heritage that continues. It is hard for those who watch for the Bridegroom to wait very long; millenarian excitement tends to pass when the emergency passes. Adventist groups, however, by adjusting some of their millenarian concerns have become an important part of the American religious environment.

Merely believing that Jesus will eventually return or that the world is going to end does not make a person a millenarian, however. But it is hard not to notice the on-going phenomena of groups continuing to spread the word of the end times and of Jesus's Second Coming. For example, various conferences of prominent fundamentalist preachers have gathered in New York City to affirm that Americans are living in the end of times. Although there was little new about what they said or how they said it, there was a surprisingly warm response by New Yorkers in the worldly Wall Street area. In one small lower Manhattan Church, 150 people a day came to services sponsored by the Jack Wyrtzen Word of Life Bible Institute.[65]

The issue is not which Americans hold millennial ideas—and Adventist ideas—but rather the range and number of Americans who do espouse these ideas and how they gather together on that basis for the sake of action. A Gallup poll reported that a majority of Americans do not doubt that Jesus will return to earth; 62 percent of those responding to this nationwide poll said they had no doubts of Jesus' return.

Among those who say religion is very important in their lives, the percentage of those who are certain of Christ's return jumps to 79 percent.[66]

Perhaps American millenarianism or, perhaps more correctly, American premillennialism, reached its peak of success during the rise of the so-called New Christian Right, not unlike another Great Awakening. Evangelicals, more visible through an increased presence on radio and television, are more likely to have millenarian beliefs. Evangelicals are not a denomination but can be found in most Christian denominations. They usually define themselves by a "born again experience" in which they fervently commit themselves to Christ—reading the Bible literally, accepting the Bible as without error, and encouraging others to accept Christ as a savior. Evangelicals, representing perhaps between 25 percent to a third of the American population,[67] are receptive to apocalyptic and premillennial ideas. Hal Lindsey, a widely read premillennialist writer, fit nuclear war into his prophetic scenario of the end times. Jerry Falwell, an extraordinarily successful TV evangelist, connected nuclear war with the Second Coming of Christ. Another successful TV evangelist and staunch premillennialist, Pat Robertson, made a bid to be a candidate for the presidency of the United States. Perhaps most extraordinary in the link of politics and millenarian ideas was the expression by the President of the United States, Ronald Reagan, that he accepted a dispensational view on the imminence of the Battle of Armageddon that observers could only interpret in a premillennialist way.[68] Reagan believed Armageddon, as the forecast of the end of the world and the Second Coming of Christ, was inevitable and probably imminent. He seems to have understood Armageddon as a nuclear catastrophe, and during the 1984 presidential campaign he was challenged on the possible connections between his belief in Armageddon, his foreign policy, and U.S. planning for nuclear war. But the issue of a nuclear Armageddon did not catch on as a political or campaign issue.[69] Possibly Reagan's remarks about having discussions with theologians who were convinced that the prophetic end times were near was a mere political pitch to a sizable portion of the American electorate. Or perhaps it was a sign of the persistence and potency of millenarian ideas.

NOTES

1. Whitney R. Cross, *The Burned-over District: The Social and Intellectual History of Enthusiastic Religion in Western New York, 1800-1850* (Cornell University Press, 1950), p. 287; David L. Rowe, *Thunder and Trumpets: Millerites and Dissenting Religion in Upstate New York, 1800-1850* (Chico, Calif: Scholars Press, 1985), pp.ix & x); David L. Rowe, "Millerites: A Shadow Portrait," in *The Disappointed: Millerism and Millenarianism in the Nineteenth Century*, ed. by Ronald L. Numbers and Jonathan M. Butler (Bloomington & Indianapolis: Indiana University Press, 1987), pp. 7, 9.

2. Francis D. Nichol, *The Midnight Cry* (Washington, D.C.: Review and Herald Publishing Association, 1945), pp. 17-22. Although Nichol is a Seventh-day Adventist minister and not a professional historian, his book seems to make careful use of records, the correspondence of Miller and the newspapers of Miller's time. Until recently Nichol's book was the principal "modern" biography of Miller, based on Sylvester Bliss's biography of 1853, *Memoirs of William Miller*. The phrase the "Midnight Cry" was used by Millerites to describe their message to the world. The words come from Christ's parable of the wise and foolish virgins who were waiting for the bridegroom to come forth so that they might go with him to the marriage. At midnight the cry came to "Behold, the bridegroom cometh; go to meet him."

3. Whitney R. Cross, p. 60.

4. Ruth Alden Doan, *The Miller Heresy, Millennialism, and American Culture* (Philadelphia: Temple University Press, 1987). 41-42; cf. William Miller, *A Few Evidences of the Time of the Second Coming of Christ*, mss. dated Feb. 15, 1831. A further contemporary discussion of these prophetic numbers can be found in Alexander Campbell, "The Coming of the Lord," *The Millennial Harbinger: A Monthly Publication Devoted to Primitive Christianity*, Vol. 7, 1843, pp. 49-55 (reprinted by College Press Publishing Co., Joplin, Mo., 1987).

5. William Miller, *Apology and Defense*, pp. 11-12, quoted by Francis D. Nichol, p. 33.

6. Cf. Michael Barkun, *Crucible of the Millennium: The Burned-Over District of New York in the 1840s* (Syracuse University Press, 1986), pp. 31-311; Wayne R. Judd, "William Miller: Disappointed Prophet," in *The Disappointed: Millerism and Millenariainism in the Nineteenth Century*, ed. by Ronald L. Numbers and Jonathan M. Butler (Bloomington & Indianapolis: Indiana University Press, 1987), p. 20; Francis D. Nichol, pp. 41, 430.

7. Reporter in the New York *Herald Extra*, as quoted by Francis D. Nichol, p. 122.

8. Cf. William Miller, *Evidence from Scripture and History of the Second Coming of Christ, About the Year 1843* (Troy, 1838).

9. *Signs of the Times*, January 25, 1843, p. 147, as quoted by Francis D. Nichol, p. 126.

10. Francis D. Nichol, p. 54, and Whitney R. Cross, p. 291. Cf. William Miller, *Evidence from Scripture and History of the Second Coming of Christ, About the Year 1843* (Troy, 1838), as quoted by Whitney R. Cross, p. 233.

11. David T. Arthur, "Joshua V. Himes and the Cause of Adventism" in *The Disappointed: Millerism and Millenariainism in the Nineteenth Century*, ed. by Ronald L. Numbers and Jonathan M. Butler (Bloomington & Indianapolis, Indiana University Press, 1987), p. 38-39; Francis D. Nichol, pp. 46, 69, 70, 123.

12. Whitney R. Cross, p. 288; David L. Rowe, "Millerites: A Shadow Portrait," p. 2; Michael Barkun, pp. 37-38.

13. The Methodist Bishop Asbury in 1800, as quoted by Francis D. Nichol, p 294.

14. From *Signs of Times*, June 15, 1842, p. 88, as quoted by Francis D. Nichol, p. 104-105; cf. Michael Barkun, p. 38.

15. Francis D. Nichol, pp. 79-81, 154; on the complex relationship between abolitionists and Millerites, cf. Ronald D. Graybill, "The Abolitionist-Millerite Connection," in *The Disappointed: Millerism and Millenarianism in the Nineteenth Century*, ed. by Ronald L. Numbers and Jonathan M. Butler (Bloomington & Indianapolis, Indiana University Press, 1987), p. 139.

16. Whitney R. Cross, pp. 287-293.

17. David L. Rowe, *Thunder and Trumpets*, pp. 7, 106, 162; Whitney R. Cross, 263, Francis D. Nichol, p. 287.

18. Francis D. Nichol, p. 133, Whitney R. Cross, p. 263; David L. Rowe, "Millerites: A Shadow Portrait," p. 1-2; David L. Rowe, *Thunder and Trumpet*, p. 142.

19. David L. Rowe, "Millerites: A Shadow Portrait," p. 7; David L. Rowe, *Thunder and Trumpets*, pp. 47-48.

20. Ronald L. Numbers and Janet S. Numbers, "Millerism and Madness: A Study of 'Religious Insanity' in Nineteenth-Century America," *Bulletin of the Menninger Clinic* 49 (1985): 90-92; David L. Rowe, pp. 102-103.

21. David L. Rowe, *Thunder and Trumpets*, pp. 107-108; Francis D. Nichol, pp. 141, 148, 152, 167, 242; Whitney R. Cross, p. 302.

22. From Sylvester Bliss, *Memoirs of William Miller*, p. 256, as quoted by Francis D. Nichol, p. 171; cf. also Francis D. Nichol, pp. 158, 162-163.

23. Francis D. Nichol, pp. 206, 212-213; Whitney R. Cross, p. 304.

24. David L. Rowe, *Thunder and Trumpets*, pp. 138-139; Francis D. Nichol, pp. 217, 219, 221, 236-237.

25. From the *Philadelphia Public Ledger*, October 11, 1844, as quoted by Francis D. Nichol, p. 239.

26. Francis D. Nichol, pp. 238-240.

27. *The Advent Herald*, October 16, 1844, p. 81, as quoted by Francis D. Nichol, p. 243.

28. From the *Cincinnati Chronicle*, quoted in the *United States Saturday Post*, November 9, 1844; Francis D. Nichol, p. 245; Whitney R. Cross, p. 306.

29. As quoted by Francis D. Nichol, pp. 247-8.

30. As quoted by Francis D. Nichol, p. 248.

31. Ruth Alden Doan, *The Miller Heresy, Millennialism, and American Culture* (Philadelphia: Temple University Press, 1987), p. 202; Whitney R. Cross, p. 310; David L. Rowe, *Thunder and Trumpets*, pp. 142 ff.

32. Everett N. Dick, "The Millerite Movement, 1830-1845," in *Adventism in America: A History*, ed. by Gary Land (Grand Rapids, Michigan: William B. Eerdmans, 1986), pp. 31-33; Whitney R. Cross, pp. 308-9, and Ruth Alden Doan, p. 54.

33. Everett N. Dick, p. 33-5; Ruth Alden Doan, p. 203; Whitney R. Cross, p. 311.

34. Cf. Eric W. Gritsch, *Born-againism: Perspectives on a Movement* (Philadelphia: Fortress Press, 1982), p. 20.

35. Richard T. Hughes, "From Primitive Church to Civil Religion: The Millennial Odyssey of Alexander Campbell," *The Journal of the American Academy of Religion* 44 (1976): 87-103; cf. Robert N. Bellah, "Civil Religion in America," *Daedalus* 95 (1967): 1-8. David Edwin Harrell, Jr. "Dispensational Premillennialism and the Religious Right," in *Return of the Millennium*, ed. by Joseph Bettis and S.K. Johannesen (Barrytown, N.Y.: New Era Books, 1984), pp. 9-34.

36. See Malcolm Bull and Keith Lockhart, *Seeking a Sanctuary: Seventh-day Adventism and the American Dream* (New York: Harper and Row, 1989), pp. 45, 60.

37. Malcolm Bull and Keith Lockhart, pp. 20-21; Godfrey T. Anderson, "Sectarianism and Organization 1846-1864," in *Adventism in America*, ed. by Gary Land, p. 39.

38. Godfrey T. Anderson, pp. 46-52, 59-60.

39. Malcolm Bull and Keith Lockhart, pp. 9, 12, 21; Godfrey T. Anderson, p. 43; Jonathan M. Butler, "The Making of a New Order: Millerism and the Origins of Seventh-Day Adventism," in *The Disappointed: Millerism and Millenarianism in the Nineteenth Century*, p. 204.

40. Malcolm Bull and Keith Lockhart, pp. 44-45; see the especially helpful appendix in *Adventism in America: A History*, "Seventh-Day Adventist Statements of Belief," pp. 231-250.

41. Malcolm Bull and Keith Lockhart, pp. 166-167, 268.

42. Malcolm Bull and Keith Lockhart, pp. 168-169.

43. Jonathan M. Butler, pp. 190-192; Malcolm Bull and Keith Lockhart, p. 227.

44. J. Gordon Melton, *The Encyclopedia of American Religions* (Detroit, Michigan: Gale Research Company, 2nd Edition, 1986), pp. 287, 302.

45. M. J. Penton, "The Eschatology of Jehovah's Witnesses: A Short, Critical Analysis," in *The Coming Kingdom: Essays in American Millennialism & Eschatology*, ed. by M. Darrol Bryant and Donald W. Dayton, (New York: New Era Books, 1983), p. 169.

46. M. James Penton, *Apocalypse Delayed: The Story of Jehovah's Witnesses* (Toronto: University of Toronto Press, 1985), pp. 13-17.

47. M. James Penton, *Apocalypse Delayed*, pp. 18-19.

48. M. James Penton, *Apocalypse Delayed*, pp. 27, 33, 42, 180; M. James Penton, "The Eschatology of Jehovah's Witnesses," pp. 173-175.

49. M. James Penton, *Apocalypse Delayed*, pp. 24-35, 121.

50. M. James Penton, *Apocalypse Delayed*, pp. 35-44.

51. M. James Penton, *Apocalypse Delayed*, pp. 44-46; M. James Penton, "The Eschatology of Jehovah's Witnesses," p. 181.

52. M. James Penton, *Apocalypse Delayed*, pp. 47-46, 57, 62-65.

67. George Gallup, Jr. and Jim Castelli, pp. 92-93.

68. Timothy P. Weber, *Living in the Shadow of the Second Coming: American Premillennialism, 1875-1982* (Chicago and London: University of Chicago Press, 1987), pp. viii-x; cf. also *The Washington Post*, April 8, 1984, pp. C1, C4; *The New York Times*, October 24, 1984, pp. A1, A25, A28.

69. Lou Cannon, *President Reagan: The Role of a Lifetime* (New York: Simon & Schuster, 1991), pp. 288-290.

Conclusion

The Potency and Persistence of Millenarian Ideas

A review of millenarian movements reveals the tremendous potency and persistence of the idea of the millennium (and in varying degrees, related features of the millennium that are held in tension, such as Jesus's Second Coming, the end of the world, when judgment will be, who will be the elect).

Religious people have for two millennia sought signs of and precision about the end of the world and what follows. The idea of the millennium, rooted in ancient Hebrew and Christian apocalyptic literature, indicates that history is going somewhere, that there is purpose and meaning in the cosmos. The millennial myth has continually been revived as a statement about how, and sometimes when, the world ends. Coupled with the idea that the world will end is prophetic insight about the timing of the end and qualities necessary for preparing for the end.

Central to the millenarian idea is the transformation of the earth. During political and social changes, religious persecution or times of disaster, millenarian movements have made use of familiar biblical language to express their aspirations for imminent changes in society. Millenarianism is about the hope for a reorganized and regenerated society, for a new earth for the elect. When particular societies (for example, in the eighteenth century with the beginnings of the Industrial Revolution) faced unprecedented changes, when kings were giving way to parliaments, when agriculture was yielding to industry, millenarian imagery and language provided a way to articulate the new—or, at least, to allow familiar religious images to sustain people amidst profound change that seems of a cosmic proportion.[1]

Continuity

A review of millenarian movements in their historic context reveals the continuity of a complex millenarianism. Augustine set the tone for Western eschatological thinking when he identified the life of the Church with the thousand years in Revelation, chapter 20. The climax of history was Jesus's first coming, and the millennium was in the present. The influence of Augustine caused a pause in overt millenarianism for more than 700 years; although it is possible that careful research might find a few small cult-like groups during the Augustine lull.

Seven hundred years after Augustine, Joachim of Fiore challenged the Augustine view of time and history and established new images and categories. New ways of interpreting Scripture allowed a return of millenarian thinking and collective religious activism that became more frequent with the Protestant Reformation. Alternating with peaks of dynamic activity and with quiet periods, millenarian outbreaks became more frequent during the late medieval period, and millenarian ideas were a common concern. Groups such as the Fraticelli and, increasingly, groups within the Protestant tradition identified the papacy with the Antichrist.

The enthusiasm, excesses, and dramatic actions of some millenarians are more intelligible as scholars have come to recognize millenarianism as less a marginal impulse toward eccentricity and pathology than at times a sustained drive toward cultural revitalization and reform, such as the Taborite movement during the Hussite Revolution. In certain periods, such as during the Puritan Revolution from 1620 to

Conclusion

1660, millenarian concerns, as reflected in the sermons and writings of the time, were commonplace, normal, and not considered deviant.[2] During the American Revolution there were similar heightened millenarian images, tracts, and sermons.[3]

In America, especially, the millennial myth has proven so resilient and malleable that some observers seek to move it from the periphery to the center of the nation's self-understanding.[4]

The New World proved attractive for many of Europe's troubled and persecuted groups who sought a refuge, a utopia, the shining city upon a hill (Revelation, chapter 21). When the periods of Great Awakenings swept Europe and the New World, sects and millenarians and revivalists were not at the fringe of society, certainly not in nineteenth-century America, where immigrants and native groups made the American dream a millennial vision.[5]

During the past two centuries the millenarian tradition has continued to fractionalize, as it were, with some groups withdrawing from mainstream social and economic life while other groups remain acutely sensitive to social and economic upheavals.[6] But the major change is that, with the Bible no longer the common reference, many modern millenarian movements draw their ideology from sources other than the apocalyptic books of the Bible. To be sure, there are Christian sects that use undiluted the language and imagery of the Bible, but there has also been a rise in civil and secular millenarianism. The vision of a transformed society, the goal of political activity, has been held out with striking variations by communism, Hitler's National Socialism, and the secular millenarianism of American democracy. Within America, the contrasts between a religious fundamentalism and other secular streams of thought are striking. America with its "manifest destiny" from the colonial period onward, nurtured and fostered an optimistic belief in progress. But the optimism of America's civil millenialism contrasts with the essential pessimism of the premillennial groups of America, specifically Millerism.[7] By the end of the nineteenth century much Adventist theology tended to erode the scholarly millenarian tradition into a rather simple-minded adventist millenarianism, with predictions drawn almost exclusively from Daniel and Revelation. Since the 1960s America has witnessed an extraordinarily diverse new Great Awakening with the rise of various utopian communes and the apocalyptic visions of such public figures as televangelist Jerry Falwell and bestselling author Hal Lindsey, both of whom have a large following.[8]

Millenarian Diversity

Historical study reveals the extraordinary diversity of millenarian movements, movements that range from the fanatical Adamites to the relatively ordinary Millerites. The cause of that diversity, for the most part, is due to the context in which they arose and the particular social and religious functions which they served—and scholars disagree on these functions.

The European millenarian experience has differed from that of American groups. Early and medieval European millenarian movements tended to be more marginal in society, perhaps because of entrenched political and religious institutions like the Roman Catholic Church which did not tolerate alternative religious expressions and which often named new religious movements as heretical and deviant. When kings or emperors reigned there were few—if any—political means for change. When secular expressions and concrete steps cannot deal with changing political and social realities, vocabulary from a religious tradition seems to have been useful in a transitory way to express political revolution and activism. This would have been true of the Montanists, when a far-off Roman emperor was persecuting Christians and they had few ways of expressing their hopes and sense of being special.

In America, millenarian groups have tended to be less marginal, in part because there has been less violent repression and more religious toleration in contrast to Europe's more rigid class and social structures. Perhaps some American millenarian movements need to be understood as a different kind of reaction to change. Thus one might think of the Millerites as a kind of conservative reaction against social change and flux. As new immigrants and changes crossed the young American Republic, people tried to create a new sense of community in their own time, a community in which their status was absolutely clear. As individuals tried to adjust to a new and perhaps incomprehensible culture, the literal reading of scripture and sense of an approaching end gave them a sense of community and of their place in it.[9]

On the Origins of New Religions, Including Millenarian Groups

Why do people join a cult? How do new religions get born? What social or psychological factors give rise to religious creativity? Aside from theological considerations, the most common explanation is some form of deprivation. The broad generalization can be made that often social dissatisfaction and deprivation breed millenarian and messianic groups.

Scholars, especially those with a Marxist orientation, have pointed to the unique capacity of millenarian ideas to carry a message of political revolution; this orientation stressed qualities of being disinherited, disenfranchised, and deprived—in other words, something is wrong with society. Scholars with a Marxist orientation saw millenarian movements as a pre-political stage of political protests that developed toward the modern, secular, revolutionary consciousness. Indeed, some European millenarian movements, such as the Taborites and Camisards, occurred at times of political and social crisis. Such movements were able to use traditions of biblical prophecy and popular religion as a vocabulary to deal with a new socio-political consciousness that was emerging.[10] But the Marxist orientation often falls short in its explanatory efforts, especially in those movements, such as the Fifth Monarchy Men, with a membership that was not from the oppressed, politically disenfranchised class.

The deprivation theory suggests that millenarian groups have flared up when there is a cumulative deterioration in the quality of life with the likelihood of further declines. Sudden crises, be they disaster or plague, often supply the right fuel for flareups. Rapid social changes and attendant cultural disintegration produce the conditions for the emergence of messianic or millenarian groups.[11]

A millenarian movement can result as a complex psychic and religious response.[12] There must exist the possibility of some remedial change. When a society is made up of people who experience stress and emptiness, the promise of a total this-worldly salvation presents a powerful appeal. Millenarian movements, especially in Europe, often have attracted the oppressed, the peasants, the poor, the marginal people in society, those without hope, those with nothing but who have everything to gain,[13] although not infrequently the poor and marginal people in a society were the vast majority of that society and so were overly represented in such a movement. Nevertheless, millenarian movements tend to draw their membership from the deprived people in society if that deprivation is understood as people perceiving a discrepancy between what they might legitimately expect and what they might actually have.[14] The religious movement is a means to overcome the deprivation, the felt discrepancy between the way things are and the way they should be. Modern religious groups continue to attract the deprived, but that deprived group may increasingly draw from disenchanted members of the middle class who find reality dreary and flat and who seek some direct experience of wonder and mystery.[15] In other words, spiritual deprivation can also be an impetus for a person to join a new movement. No single cause or theory, however, can explain new movements.

The new and alien are threatening. However, what has at one time been considered deviant can become familiar and even normative. An exotic and once-marginal cult can sometimes evolve to become a successful mainstream church. Christianity was at one time a cult struggling for survival against the state religion and other exotic religions during an age of anxiety and the disintegration of the Roman Empire. Roman citizens and devout pagans regarded the new religion as deviant and threatening.[16]

It is likely that all religions originate as local cults, as small groups of individuals with common religious interests gather around a charismatic leader.[17] Almost invariably converts to new cults tend to be viewed as puzzling or even deviant by other members of society. Some scholars emphasize a cult's deviance or its fundamental break with the dominant religious culture of society. A cult initially focuses not on the problems of society but on individuals who have had or seek to have mystical, psychic, or ecstatic experiences. Cults tend to be short-lived groups, loosely structured movements with minimal organization. Those cults that are successful soon must turn their attention to maintaining the organization and the purity of teaching and so give less emphasis to the problems of individuals.[18] The movements investigated in these pages have an ideology drawn from the apocalyptic literature of the Bible and concerned with the millennium and the Second Coming of Jesus Christ.

Once a movement is born, various organizational changes can sweep the movement along. Leaders often transform the cult into an authoritarian group, with a centralization of authority and standardization of doctrine.[19] As the cult matures, it becomes more adapted to its society, more institutionalized and routinized, and may become a more communal and more cohesively organized group like a sect. As a group proceeds towards greater authority, organization, and social acceptability, it may attain the social status of an established church that accommodates to the prevailing culture. Seventh-day Adventists have resisted accommodating to society, but they no longer are the small sect that Mrs. White inspired. Because new movements change and are sometimes unstable, observers do not always use these descriptive categories precisely or consistently. The use of these categories in these pages has been intentionally open-ended rather than restrictive.

A group goes through a crisis when the expected appearance of the end time does not happen. Groups must establish institutions to preserve their vision and to survive. The Millerite movement after the Great Disappointment floundered until the different Adventist groups became organized. Charismatic cults dependent on their leader meet an early end when the leader loses his charisma or dies. Those local cults which survive do so as the result of a process of institutionalization. They must develop a formal organization which regulates procedures, ensures continuity of leadership, and establishes entrance requirements for new converts. When the founder of the Shakers died, Ann Lee's followers more successfully dealt with that transition than did the followers of Jemima Wilkinson.

Every movement, as it grows older, must either become more institutionalized and a part of the mainstream or somehow preserve its revolutionary, reformist fervor by splitting off new sectarian movements. The process is not conceptually neat, and overclassifying or overconceptualizing does not aid understanding religious enthusiasm and innovation.[20]

The Present Situation

Many mainline churches, such as liberal Protestant denominations and the Church of England, have declining memberships. Observers and church leaders wonder at the disaffection of many modern spiritual seekers who seem to find no outlet for their spiritual needs in these mainline churches. Even though conservative and fundamentalist churches have grown,[21] many people still seek new modes of spirituality to fill the voids in their lives in a culture that is secularized and disenchanted.

North America and Western Europe have experienced an explosion of new religious movements in the past 30 years in a new Great Awakening. Some of these new religious movements[22] include the Hare Krishna, the Unification Church of Rev. Moon; various Sikh, Yoga and Zen groups; neo-fundamentalist versions of Christianity and Judaism; and various human potential movements and quasi-religious movements like est, Scientology, and Arica. These various movements point to the possibility of achieving certain mental or spiritual states, and they promise the techniques to attain these goals.

Often new religious movements react to changes in society and, paradoxically, press for changes. Cults thrive where conventional faiths, once dominant, are weakened and less vital. When a theological consensus as well as a social consensus breaks down, people seek a new understanding of the cosmos, new ideas on how society should be maintained or transformed. Periods of history characterized by anxiety and disruption, when the world seems out of joint to many people, seem specially fertile in generating millennial enthusiasm.[23] The dominant faiths of today arose in turbulent times in obscurity as cults, well suited for the culture in which they arose. No sociologist was present when Jesus spoke or when Mohammed preached, but it is likely, even though no signs are apparent now, some major new world

Conclusion 353

faith or millenarian movement could be going through its infancy in obscurity.[24]

NOTES

1. Cf. Clarke Garrett, *Respectable Folly: Millenarians and the French Revolution in France and England* (Baltimore and London: Johns Hopkins University Press, 1975), pp. 225, 229.

2. Cf. Tai Liu, *Puritan London: A Study of Religion and Society in the City Parishes* (Newark: University of Delaware Press, 1986); William M. Lamont, *Godly Rule: Politics and Religion 1603-1660* (London, 1969).

3. Cf. Stephen A. Marini, *Radical Sects of Revolutionary New England* (Cambridge, Mass. and London: Harvard University Press, 1982); David S. Lovejoy, *Religious Enthusiasm in the New World: Heresy to Revolution* (Cambridge, Mass.: Harvard University Press, 1985).

4. Ronald L. Numbers and Jonathan M. Butler, eds., *The Disappointed: Millerism and Millenarianism in the Nineteenth Century* (Bloomington & Indianapolis: Indiana University Press, 1987), Introduction, p. xvi.

5. Jonathan M. Butler, "Adventism and the American Experience," in *The Rise of Adventism: Religion and Society in Mid-Nineteenth-Century America*, ed. by Edwin S. Gaustad (New York: Harper and Row, 1974), p. 173.

6. Michael Barkun, *Crucible of the Millennium: The Burned-Over District of New York in the 1840s* (Syracuse University Press, 1986), p. 139.

7. George Shepperson, "The Comparative Study of Millenarian Movements," in *Millennial Dreams in Action*, ed. by Sylvia L. Thrupp (New York: Schocken Books, 1970), pp. 50-51.

8. Cf. Michael Barkun, p. 156.

9. David L. Rowe, *Thunder and Trumpets: Millerites and Dissenting Religion in Upstate New York, 1800-1850* (Chico, California: Scholars Press, 1985), p. 163.

10. Clarke Garrett, p. 1. Cf. for example, Eric Hobsbawm, *Primitive Rebels: Studies in Archaic Forms of Social Movements* (New York: Norton, 1965), Peter Worsley, *The Trumpet Shall Sound: A Study of "Cargo" Cults in Melanesia* (New York: Schocken, 1968); Vittorio Lanternari, *The Religions of the Oppressed* (New York: Alfred A. Knopf, 1963).

11. Yonina Talmon, "Millenarism," *International Encyclopedia of Social Sciences*, p. 351.

12. Weston LaBarre, "Materials for a History of Studies of Crisis Cults: A Bibliographic Essay," *Current Anthropology* 12 (1971): 23; Joseph A. Dowling, "Millennialism and Psychology," *Journal of Psychohistory* 5 (1977): 126.

13. Yonina Talmon, "The Pursuit of the Millennium: The Relation between Religion and Social Change," in *Reader in Comparative Religion: Anthropological Approach*, ed. by W. Lessa and E. Vogt (New York, 2nd Edition, 1965), p. 530; also in *Archives Européennes de Sociologie* 3 (1962): 125-148.

14. David F. Aberle, "A Note on Relative Deprivation Theory as Applied to Millenarian and Other Cult Movements," in *Millennial Dreams in Action*, ed. by Sylvia Thrupp (The Hague: Monton, 1962), p. 209.

15. Daniel Bell, "The Return of the Sacred? The Argument on the Future of Religion," *British Journal of Sociology* 28 (1977): 422, 443, 445.

16. For a treatment of paganism's reaction to Christianity, cf. Robin Lane Fox, *Pagans and Christians* (New York: Alfred A. Knopf, 1986).

17. G.K. Nelson, "Cults and New Religions: Toward a Sociology of Religious Creativity," *Sociology and Social Research* 68 (1983/84): 305; cf. John A. Saliba, "The Christian Church and the New Religious Movements: Towards Theological Understanding," *Theological Studies* 43 (1982): 468-485.

18. Geoffrey K. Nelson, "The Spiritualist Movement and the Need for a Redefinition of Cult," *Journal for the Social Sciences of Religion* 8 (1969): 152-160. Cf. *Cults and New Religious Movements*, ed. by Marc Galanter (Washington, D. C.: American Psychiatric Association, 1989).

19. Thomas Robbins, Dick Anthony, and James Richardson, "Theory and Research on Today's 'New Religions,' " *Sociological Analysis* 39 (1978): 109.

20. Johannes Fabian, "Anthropological Approaches to Religious Movements," in David A. Halperin, ed., *Psychodynamic Perspectives on Religion, Sect and Cult* (Boston: John Wright-PSG Inc., 1983), p. 134.

21. Cf. Rodney Stark and William Sims Bainbridge, "Secularization, Revival and Cult Formation," *Annual Review of the Social Sciences of Religion* 4 (1980): 85-119; Dick Anthony, Thomas Robbins, and Paul Schwartz, "Contemporary Religious Movements and the Secularization Premise," in John Coleman and Gregory Baum, eds., *New Religious Movements* (New York: Seabury Press, 1983), pp. 1-8.

22. Cf. J. Gordon Melton, *Encyclopedic Handbook of Cults in America* (New York: Garland Publishing, Inc., 1986); Diane Choquette, *New Religious Movements in the United States and Canada: A Critical Assessment and Annotated Bibliography* (Westport, Conn.: Greenwood Press, 1985).

23. George Rosen, "Emotion and Sensibility in Ages of Anxiety: A Comparative Historical Review," *American Journal of Psychiatry* 124 (1967): 771-784.

24. Rodney Stark and William Sims Bainbridge, "Secularization, Revival, and Cult Formation," p. 93, 108, 116-117.

Selected Bibliography

Aberle, David. "A Note on Relative Deprivation Theory as Applied to Millenarian and Other Cult Movements." In Sylvia Thrupp, ed., *Millennial Dreams in Action*. The Hague: Mouton and Co., 1962, pp. 208-214.

Andrews, Edward Deming. *The People Called Shakers*. New York: Dover Publications, 1963.

Anthony, Dick, et al. "Contemporary Religious Movements and the Secularization Premise." In John Coleman and Gregory Baum, eds., *New Religious Movements*. New York: Seabury Press, 1983, pp. 1-8.

Barkun, Michael. *Crucible of the Millennium: The Burned-Over District of New York in the 1840s*. Syracuse University Press, 1986.

Barkun, Michael. *Disaster and the Millennium*. Yale University Press, 1974.

Bell, Daniel. "The Return of the Sacred? The Argument on the Future of Religion." *British Journal of Sociology*. 28 (1977): 419-448.

Bestor, Arthur Eugene. *Backwoods Utopias: The Sectarian and Owenite Phases of Communitarian Socialism in America: 1663-1829*. Philadelphia: University of Pennsylvania Press, 1950.

Bettis, Joseph and Johannesen, S.K., eds. *The Return of the Millennium*. Barrytown, New York: New Era Books, 1984.

Bietenhard, Hans. "The Millennial Hope in the Early Church." *Scottish Journal of Theology* 6 (1956): 12-30.

Bloomfield, Morton W. "Joachim of Flora: A Critical Survey of His Canon, Teachings, Sources, Biography and Influence." *Traditio* 8 (1957): 260-311.

Brandt, Otto. *Thomas Müntzer: Sein Leben und Seine Schriften*. Jena, 1933.

Brown, Ira V. "Watchers for the Second Coming: The Millenarian Tradition in America." *Mississippi Valley Historical Review* 39 (1952): 441-458.

Bryant, M. Darrol and Dayton, Donald W. *The Coming Kingdom: Essays in American Millennialism and Eschatology*. Barrytown, New York: New Era Books, 1983.

Burrage, Champlin. "The Fifth Monarchy Insurrections." *English Historical Review* 25 (1910): 722-747.

Burridge, Kenelm. *New Heaven, New Earth: A Study of Millenarian Activities*. Oxford: Basil Blackwell, 1980.

Capp, B.S. *The Fifth Monarchy Men: A Study in Seventeenth-Century English Millenarianism*. London: Faber and Faber, 1972.

Capp, B.S. "Extreme Millenarianism." In Peter Toon, ed. *Puritans, the Millennium and the Future of Israel: Puritan Eschatology 1600 to 1660*. Cambridge: James Clark & Co, 1970, pp. 66-90.

Choquette, Diane. *New Religious Movements in the United States and Canada: A Critical Assessment and Annotated Bibliography*. Westport, Conn.: Greenwood Press, 1985.

Christianson, Paul. *Reformers and Babylon: English Apocalyptic Visions from the Reformation to the Eve of the Civil War*. Toronto: University of Toronto Press, 1978.

Clouse, Robert G. "Johann Heinrich Alsted and English Millennialism." *Harvard Theological Review* 62 (1969): 189-207.

Cohen, Alfred. "Prophecy and Madness: Women Visionaries During the Puritan Revolution." *Journal of Psychohistory* 11 (1984): 411-430.

Cohn, Norman. *The Pursuit of the Millennium*. New York: Oxford University Press, 1957, 1970.

Collins, John J. *The Apocalyptic Imagination: An Introduction to the Jewish Matrix of Christianity*. New York: Crossroad, 1984.

Cross, Whitney R. *The Burned-Over District: The Social and Intellectual History of Enthusiastic Religion in Western New York, 1800-1850*. Ithaca and London: Cornell University Press, 1950.

de Labriolle, Pierre. *La Crise Montaniste*. Paris: Ernest Laroux, 1913.

de Labriolle, Pierre. *Les Sources de L'histoire du Montanisme*. Paris: Ernest Leroux, 1913.

Desroche, Henri. *The American Shakers: From Neo-Christianity to Presocialism*. Trans. by John K. Savacool. Amherst: University of Massachusetts Press, 1971.

Doan, Ruth Alden. *The Miller Heresy, Millennialism, and American Culture*. Philadelphia: Temple University Press, 1987.

Dodds, E. R. *Pagan and Christian in an Age of Anxiety*. Cambridge University Press, 1965.

Douie, Decima L. *The Nature and the Effect of the Heresy of the Fraticelli*. Manchester University Press, 1932; New York: AMS Press, 1978.

Dowling, Joseph A. "Millennialism and Psychology." *Journal of Psychohistory* 5 (1977): 121-130.

Fabian, Johannes. "Anthropological Approaches to Religious Movements." In David A. Halperin, ed. *Psychodynamic Perspectives on Religion, Sect and Cult*. Boston: John Wright-PSG Inc., 1983, pp. 132-145.

Faivre, Antoine. "Un familier des sociétés ésotériques au dix-huitième siècle: Bourrée de Corberon." *Revue des Sciences Humaines* 32 (1967): 259-287.

Festinger, Leon, et al. *When Prophecy Fails*. Minneapolis: University of Minnesota Press, 1956.

Firth, Katherine R. *The Apocalyptic Tradition in Reformation Britain 1530-1645*. Oxford: Oxford University Press, 1979.

Frend, W.H.C. "Heresy and Schism as Social and National Movements." *Studies in Church History* 9 (1972): 37-56.

Friedman, Jerome. *Blasphemy, Immorality, and Anarchy: The Ranters and the English Revolution*. Athens, Ohio: Ohio University Press, 1987.

Gager, John G. *Kingdom and Community: The Social World of Early Christianity*. Englewood Cliffs: Prentice Hall, 1975.

Galanter, Marc, ed. *Cults and New Religious Movements*. Washington, D. C.: American Psychiatric Association, 1989.

Garrett, Clarke. *Spirit Possession and Popular Religion: From the Camisards to the Shakers*. Baltimore and London: Johns Hopkins Press, 1987.

Garrett, Clarke. *Respectable Folly: Millenarians and the French Revolution in France and England*. Baltimore and London: Johns Hopkins University Press, 1975.

Gritsch, Eric W. *Reformer without a Church: The Life and Thought of Thomas Müntzer, 1488[?]-1525*. Philadelphia: Fortress Press, 1967.

Gritsch, Eric W. "Thomas Müntzer and the Origins of Protestant Spiritualism." *Mennonite Quarterly Review* 37 (1963): 172-194.

Harrison, J.F.C. *Quest for the New Moral World: Robert Owen and the Owenites in Britain and America*. New York: Charles Scribner's Sons, 1969.

Hatch, Nathan O. "The Origins of Civil Millennialism in America: New England Clergymen, War with France, and the Revolution." *William and Mary Quarterly* 31 (1974): 406-430.

Heymann, F. G. *John Zizka and the Hussite Revolution*. Princeton, New Jersey: Princeton University Press, 1955.

Hill, Christopher. *The World Turned Upside Down*. London: Maurice Temple Smith, 1972.

Hill, Christopher. *Antichrist in Seventeenth-Century England*. Oxford University Press, 1971.

Hill, Christopher. *Puritanism and Revolution*. London: Secker and Warburg, 1958.

Hine, Virginia H. "The Deprivation and Disorganization Theories of Social Movements." In Irving Zaretsky and Mark Leone, eds. *Religious Movements in Contemporary America*. Princeton University Press, 1974.
Hobsbawm, Eric. *Primitive Rebels: Studies in Archaic Forms of Social Movements*. New York: Norton, 1965.

Hopkins, James K. *A Woman to Deliver Her People: Joanna Southcott and English Millenarianism in an Era of Revolution*. Austin: University of Texas Press, 1982.

Horsch, John. "The Rise and Fall of the Anabaptists of Muenster." *Mennonite Quarterly Review* 9 (1935): 92-143.

Horsley, Richard A., and Hanson, John S. *Bandits, Prophets and Messiahs: Popular Movements in the Time of Jesus*. Minneapolis: Winston Press, 1985.

Isenberg, Sheldon R. "Millenarism in Greco-Roman Palestine." *Religion* 4 (1974): 26-46.

Jones, A.H.M. "Were Ancient Heresies National or Social Movements in Disguise?" *Journal of Theological Studies*, N.S. 10 (1959): 280-298.

Joutard, Philippe. *La Légende des Camisards*. Paris: Gallimard, 1977.

Kaminsky, Howard. *A History of the Hussite Revolution*. Berkley and Los Angeles: University of California Press, 1967.

Kaminsky, Howard. "The Religion of Hussite Tabor." In Miloslav Rechcigl, Jr., ed. *The Czechoslovak Contribution to World Culture*. The Hague: Mouton & Co., 1964, pp. 210-223.

Kaminsky, Howard. "Hussite Radicalism and the Origins of Tabor 1415-1418." *Medievalia et Humanistica* 10 (1956): 102-130.

Kieckhefer, Richard. *Repression of Heresy in Medieval Germany*. Liverpool University Press, 1979.

Kieckhefer, Richard. "Radical Tendencies in the Flagellant Movement of the Mid-Fourteenth Century." *Journal of Medieval and Renaissance Studies* 4 (1974): 157-176.

Kim, Chrysostom. "The Diggers, the Ranters and the Early Quakers." *The American Benedictine Review* 25 (1974): 461-465.

Knox, Ronald. *Enthusiasm*. Oxford University Press: Galaxy Books, 1961.

Kreiser, B. Robert. *Miracles, Conversions and Ecclesiastical Politics in Early Eighteenth-Century Paris*. Princeton University Press, 1978.

Kselman, Thomas. *Miracles and Prophecies in Nineteenth-Century France*. New Jersey: Rutgers University Press, 1983.

La Barre, Weston. "Materials for a History of Studies of Crisis Cults: A Bibliographic Essay." *Current Anthropology* 12 (1971): 3-44.

Ladurie, Emmanuel Le Roy. *The Peasants of Languedoc*. Trans. by John Day. University of Illinois Press: Urbana, Chicago and London, 1974.

Lambert, Malcolm. *Medieval Heresy: Popular Movements from the Bogomils to Hus*. New York: Holmes and Meier Publications, 1976.

Lamont, William M. *Godly Rule: Politics and Religion, 1603-60*. New York & London: Macmillan and St. Martin's Press, 1969.

Leff, Gordon. *Heresy in the Later Middle Ages*. Manchester University Press, 1967. 2 volumes.

Lerner, Robert E. "The Black Death and Western European Eschatological Mentalities." *American Historical Review* 86 (1981): 533-552.

Liu, Tai. *Puritan London: A Study of Religion and Society in the City Parishes*. Newark: University of Delaware Press, 1986.

Liu, Tai. *Discord in Zion: The Puritan Divines and the Puritan Revolution 1640-1660*. The Hague: Martinus Nijhoff, 1973.

Lovejoy, David S. *Religious Enthusiasm in the New World: Heresy to Revolution*. Cambridge, Mass.: Harvard University Press, 1985.

Marini, Stephen A. *Radical Sects of Revolutionary New England*. Cambridge, Mass., and London: Harvard University Press, 1982.

Mathiez, Albert. "Robespierre et le procès de Catherine Théot," *Annales Historiques de la Revolution Française* 6 (1929): 392-397.

McGuinn, Bernard. *Visions of the End: Apocalyptic Traditions in the Middle Ages*. New York: Columbia University Press, 1979.

McGuinn, Bernard. "Apocalypticism in the Middle Ages: An Historiographical Sketch." *Medieval Studies* 3 (1975): 252-286.

McGinn, Bernard. "The Abbot and the Doctors: Scholastic Reactions to the Radical Eschatology of Joachim of Fiore." *Church History* 4 (1971): 30-47.

Melton, J. Gordon. *Biographical Dictionary of American Cult and Sect Leaders*. New York and London: Garland Publishing, Inc., 1986.

Melton, J. Gordon. *Encyclopedic Handbook of Cults in America*. New York: Garland Publishing, Inc., 1986.

Nelson, G.K. "Cults and New Religions: Toward a Sociology of Religious Creativity." *Sociology and Social Research* 68 (1983/84): 301-325.

Niccoli, Ottavia. *Prophecy and People in Renaissance Italy*. Trans. by Lydia G. Cochrain. Princeton, N. J.: Princeton University Press, 1990.

Nichol, Francis D. *The Midnight Cry*. Washington, D.C.: Review and Herald Publishing Association, 1945.

Numbers, Ronald L. and Butler, Jonathan M., eds. *The Disappointed: Millerism and Millenarianism in the Nineteenth Century*. Bloomington & Indianapolis: Indiana University Press, 1987.

Penton, M. James. *Apocalypse Delayed: The Story of Jehovah's Witnesses*. Toronto: University of Toronto Press, 1985.

Reeves, Marjorie. *Joachim of Fiore and the Prophetic Future*. New York: Harper Torchbooks, 1977.

Reeves, Marjorie. *The Influence of Prophecy in the Later Middle Ages: A Study in Joachism*. Oxford: Clarendon Press, 1969.

Robbins, Thomas, et al. "Theory and Research on Today's 'New Religions.'" *Sociological Analysis* 39 (1978): 95-122.

Rogers, P. G. *The Fifth Monarchy Men*. London: Oxford University Press, 1966.

Rowe, David L. *Thunder and Trumpets: Millerites and Dissenting Religion in Upstate New York, 1800-1850*. Chico, California: Scholars Press, 1985.

Rupp, E. Gordon. "Thomas Müntzer: Prophet of Radical Christianity." *Bulletin of John Rylands Library* 48 (1966): 467-487.

Saliba, John A. "The Christian Church and the New Religious Movements: Towards Theological Understanding." *Theological Studies* 43 (1982): 468-485.

Sandeen, Ernest R. "Millennialism." In Edwin S. Gaustad, ed. *The Rise of Adventism: Religion and Society in Mid-Nineteenth-Century America*. New York: Harper and Row, 1974, pp. 104-118.

Sandeen, Ernest R. *The Roots of Fundamentalism: British and American Millenarianism 1800-1930*. Chicago and London: University of Chicago Press, 1970.

Schwartz, Hillel. *The French Prophets: The History of a Millenarian Group in Eighteenth-Century England*. Berkeley, Los Angeles, London: University of California Press, 1980.

Schwartz, Hillel. *Knaves, Fools, Madmen, and that Subtle Effluvium: A Study of the Opposition to the French Prophets in England, 1706-1710*. Gainesville, Florida: University of Florida Social Sciences Monograph, Number 62, 1978.

Scroggs, Robin. "The Earliest Christian Communities as Sectarian Movements." In Jacob Neusner, ed. *Christianity, Judaism and Other Greco-Roman Cults*. Leiden: E. J. Brill, 1975, pp. 1-23.

Shepperson, George. "The Comparative Study of Millenarian Movements." In Sylvia L. Thrupp, ed. *Millennial Dreams in Action*. New York: Schocken Books, 1970, pp. 44-54.

Stark, Rodney, and Bainbridge, William Sims. "Secularization, Revival and Cult Formation." *Annual Review of the Social Sciences of Religion* 4 (1980): 85-119.

Stayer, James M. "Thomas Müntzer's Theology and Revolution in Recent Non-Marxist Interpretation." *Mennonite Quarterly Review* 43 (1969): 142-152.

53. M. James Penton, *Apocalypse Delayed*, pp. 84, 199, 202, 153, 302-305; also Joseph F. Zygmunt, "Prophetic Failure and Chiliastic Identity: The Case of Jehovah's Witnesses," *American Journal of Sociology* 75 (1970): 926-948.

54. Leon Festinger, Henry W. Riecken and Stanley Schachter, *When Prophecy Fails* (Minneapolis: University of Minnesota Press, 1956 pp. 30-31.

55. Leon Festinger, et al., pp. 33-36, 43, 47, 55-59, 203.

56. Leon Festinger, et al., pp. 66-80, 86, 107.

57. Leon Festinger, et al, pp. 91-97, 100, 103, 108, 120, 122.

58. Leon Festinger, et al., pp. 132, 137-143, 158, 160-169, 176, 208. The authors stress that the group made efforts at proselytizing only after the disconfirmation of their expectations. Those who were lightly committed readily gave up their belief when it was disconfirmed. Those who were heavily committed (for example, they gave up their jobs) passed through a period of disconfirmation with faith intact.

59. Leon Festinger, et al., pp. 180, 186, 189-194, 232.

60. James Mooney, *The Ghost-Dance Religion and the Sioux Outbreak of 1890*, ed. with an introduction by F. C. Wallace (University of Chicago Press, 1965; original publication: Washington: Public Printing Office, 1896).

61. George Woodcock and Ivan Avakumovic, *The Doukhobors* (New York: Oxford University Press, 1968), p. 11.

62. George Woodcock and Ivan Avakumovic, pp. 10, 25.

63. Shirley Ardener, "Arson, Nudity and Bombs among the Canadian Doukhobors: A Question of Identity," *Threatened Identities*, ed. by Glennis M. Breakwell (New York: John Wiley and Sons, 1983), pp. 239-240.

64. On Jim Jones, see Judith Mary Weightman, *Making Sense of the Jonestown Suicides* (New York: Edwin Mellen Press, 1983); David Chidester, *Salvation and Suicide: An Interpretation of Jim Jones, the Peoples Temple, and Jonestown* (Bloomington: Indiana University Press, 1988).

65. *Christianity Today*, May 1982, p. 50.

66. *Christianity Today*, November 23, 1984, p. 46; George Gallup, Jr. and Jim Castelli, *The People's Religion: American Faith in the 90's* (New York: Macmillan Publishing Co., 1989), p. 66.

Stone, Michael Edward. *Scriptures, Sects and Visions: A Profile of Judaism from Ezra to the Jewish Revolts*. Philadelphia: Fortress Press, 1980.

Sweet, Leonard I. "Millennialism in America: Recent Studies." *Theological Studies* 40 (1979): 510-531.

Talmon, Yonina. "Millenarian Movements." *Archives Européennes de Sociologie* 7 (1966): 159-200.

Talmon, Yonina. "Pursuit of the Millennium: The Relation Between Religion and Social Change." *Archives Européennes de Sociologie* 3 (1962): 125-148.

Toon, Peter, ed. *Puritans, the Millennium and the Future of Israel: Puritan Eschatology 1600 to 1660*. Cambridge: James Clark and Co., 1970.

Troelsch, Ernest. *The Social Teaching of the Christian Churches*. New York: Macmillan, 1931.

Walker, D. P. "English Philadelphians." In *The Decline of Hell*. University of Chicago Press, 1964, pp. 245-257.

Wallace, Anthony F. C., "Revitalization Movements." *American Anthropologist* 58 (1954): 262-282;

Weber, Timothy P. *Living in the Shadow of the Second Coming: American Premillennialism, 1875-1982*. University of Chicago Press, 1987.

Weinstein, Donald. *Savonarola and Florence: Prophecy and Patriotism in the Renaissance*. Princeton, N. J.: Princeton University Press, 1970.

Weinstein, Donald. "Savonarola, Florence, and the Millenarian Tradition." *Church History* 27 (1958): 3-17.

Werner, Ernest. "Popular Ideologies in Late Medieval Europe: Taborite Chiliasm and Its Antecedents." *Comparative Studies in Society and History* 2 (1960): 344-363.

Williams, George Huntson. *The Radical Reformation*. Philadelphia: The Westminster Press, 1962.

Wilson, John F. *Pulpit in Parliament: Puritanism during the English Civil Wars, 1640-1648*. Princeton, N.J.: Princeton University Press, 1969.

Worsley, Peter. *The Trumpet Shall Sound: A Study of "Cargo" Cults in Melanesia*. New York: Schocken, 1968.

Zuck, Lowell H. *Christianity and Revolution: Radical Christian Testimonies 1520-1650*. Philadelphia: Temple University Press, 1975.

Zygmunt, Joseph F. "Prophetic Failure and Chiliastic Identity: The Case of Jehovah's Witnesses." *American Journal of Sociology* 75 (1970): 926-948.

Index

Adamites, 5, 14, 119-145, 293, 348, 349
adventist groups, *see* millenarian groups
Adventism, 317-324, 336, 351; *see* Seventh-day Adventist, First-day Adventist
Alline, Henry, 273-275
Amana, 288, 298
Amish, 6
Anabaptists, 153-156, 169-185, 191, 285
Antichrist:
    activity of, 131, 200, 201
    coming of, 106, 112, 113, 120
    papacy as, 97, 100, 107, 121, 162, 192, 194, 198, 234, 268, 346
    reign of, 78, 86, 101, 113, 120
    servants of, 97, 105, 135, 158
apocalypse:
    description of, 28
    hope, 84
    way of thinking and ideas, 31, 50, 168
apocalyptic groups, *see* millenarian groups
apocalyptic literature, 5, 19, 28-32, 54, 282, 290, 345, 351
    description of, 10
    see Book of Revelation, Book of Daniel
apocalypticism, 97, *see* millenarianism
Armageddon, 3, 63, 326, 328, 337
Armstrong, Thomas, 331-335
asceticism, 14, 36, 82, 89
Augustine (St.), 87, 88, 95, 98, 346

Barbour, Nelson, H., 325, 326, 327
Beast of the Apocalypse:
    eschatological figure, 134, 162, 212, 224, 226, 244, 322
    numbers and, 199, 234

Bolton Society, 252, 253
Book of Daniel, 8, 10, 11, 28-30, 155, 161, 192, 198, 199, 259
Book of Maccabees, 33, 34
Book of Revelation:
  as apocalyptic, 28, 81, 155, 158, 259, 284, 295
  use of, 76, 268, 271, 322, 326
Brothers, Richard, 254-256

Camisard, 224, 226-228, 243, 244, 247-252, 292, 349
Campbell, Alexander, 319
celibacy, 271, 277, 278, 286, 287, 289, 294, 295, 328
Charles I, King, 192-197, 202
chiliasm, 9, see millenarianism
Christians, early, 13, 49-67, 143
Church of Latter-Day Saints, 282
Church Universal and Triumphant, 3, 17
Circumcellions, 88
cognitive dissonance, 66, 317
Cohn, Norman, 18
Convulsionaries, 228, 229
Cromwell, Oliver, 192, 193, 195, 196, 201-213
cult, 9, 16, 349, 350, 351, 352

dancing, religious, 14, 111, 279, 296
Darby, John Nelson, 259, 260
Dead Sea Scrolls, 37
Didache, 77, 86
Diggers, 202-204, 216
Dionysus, 12, 80
dispensationalism, 259
Dorell, William, 281
Doukhobors, 335

Edwards, Jonathan, 7, 270-272
end of world, expectation of, 4, 91, 176, 281, 308, 312
English Prophets, 246, 248
Eusebius, 86, 159
End Time, 16, 31, 44, 54, 61, 68, 76, 84, 235, 254
Essenes, 19, 35-37

Falwell, Jerry, 348
fanaticism, 42, 86, 119, 133, 135, 137, 142, 146, 149, 153, 156, 172, 174, 177, 293, 312, 314
Fareinists, 229
Feake, Christopher, 203, 204, 206, 209, 210, 214, 217
Fifth Monarchy Men, 192-193, 200, 203-217, 227, 349
First-day Adventist, 319
Fitch, Charles, 310, 313
Flagellants, 108-112
flying saucer, cult, 330-335
Fourth Philosophy, 39, 40
Francis (St.), of Assisi, 98, 101-104
Franciscan Spirituals, 102-107
Fraticelli, 106-108, 346
French Prophets, 227, 242, 245-247, 249-253, 292, 293

Ghost Dance Movement, 335
Gray, Elizabeth, 246, 248, 249, 250

Harmon, Ellen G. (Mrs. White), 320-321
Harrison, Major-General, 206, 207, 208, 209, 210, 212
Himes, Joshua V., 308-310, 313, 314, 318

Index

Hoffman, Melchior, 170-172, 173
Hus, John, 121, 122, 148, 149, 159
Hussites, 119, 121-149
Hutterites, 6, 285

Italian prophets, 114

Jansenism, 228
Jehovah's Witnesses, 324-330
Jerome (St.), 87
Jerusalem, 25, 41, 43, 44, 64, 99, 110
   New, 36, 78, 82, 172, 176, 179, 180, 183, 185, 200, 240, 256, 294
Jesus:
   as King, 129, 204, 212, 315
   as Messiah, 52
   life and ministry of, 45, 49, 50, 58
   return of, 204, 336, 346, *see* Second Coming
Jewish:
   faith and fervor, 24, 41, 44
   groups, 9, 23, 31, 35, 66
   religious practices, 24-26, 32, 38, 214
Jews:
   ancient, 13, 24-33
   conversion of, 229, 269
Joachim of Fiore, 99-101, 103-105, 158, 231, 242, 346
Jones, Jim, 5, 178, 336
Josephus, 27, 33, 35, 40, 44
Jurieu, Pierre, 224, 225, 226, 243, 244, 250

Keech, Marian, 330-334

Kingdom, millennial, 54, 79, 98, 181-184, 195, 200, 204, 208, 213, 242, 245, 269, 277, 282, 284, 295
Koranda, Wenceslaus, 126, 130, 135, 137, 139

Lacy, John, 246, 248, 249, 250
Last Judgement, 11, 276
Lead, Jane, 242, 243, 247
Lee, Mother Ann, 228, 253, 281, 289, 292-296, 351
Levellers, 202, 203, 211, 215, 216
Leyden, John of, 8, 174, 177-184
Luther, Martin, 149, 153-154, 156, 160, 162, 163, 185-186

madness, prophetic and spiritual, 12, 82, 312
martyrs, 39, 78, 80, 87, 90, 147
Mason, John, 240-241
Matthys, Jan, 173-177
Maximilla, prophetess, 81-83
Messiah, 11, 40, 52, 105, 180, 272
millenarian:
   beliefs, 11, 51, 200, 203, 223
   concerns, 6, 192, 201, 204
   expectations, 60, 130, 169, 181, 192, 197, 204, 254, 272, 275, 280, 287
millenarian groups:
   American, 261, 267, 337, 348
   Anabaptists and, 155, 171
   characteristics of, 10, 12, 13, 15, 51, 61, 114
   definition of, 9
   diversity of, 9, 14, 232, 239, 347, 348
   English, 191-197, 240, 246, 250, 254, 260, 261

extremism, 5, 119, 183, 191, 193, 217
French, 223, 261
kinds of, 5, 6, 223, 232, 258, 260, 267, 336, 347
membership of, 17, 18, 63, 215, 250, 311
origins of, 16, 17, 62, 202, 349
radical, 130, 193
Taborites and other, 148
millenarian movements, *see* millenarian groups
millenarianism:
definition, 9
kinds of, 8, 258, 260, 261, 267, 270, 298
secular, 6, 261, 291, 298, 330, 347
social order and, 191, 203, 291
millenialism, *see* millenarianism
millennium:
description of, 5, 8, 10, 201
Doomsday and, 201
time of, 241, 247, 271, 272, 284, 324, 329
Miller, William, 6, 305-320, 323, 324, 327
Millerites, 5, 7, 305, 309-319, 321, 325, 336, 348, 351
monasticism, 90
Montanism, 76, 78-85, 251, 348
Montanus, 76, 78-85
Mormons, 282
Münster, 15, 155, 157, 172-184
Münsterites, 7, 172-184
Müntzer, Thomas, 7, 155, 156-168, 171, 226, 261

New Israelites, 281
New Lights, 272-274, 280
Newton, Isaac, 7, 255
Noyes, John Humphrey, 289-290

Olivi, Peter, 105-106
Oneida, 288-290, 298
Owen, Robert, 258-259, 261, 286, 287, 290-291

Parousia, 52, 54, 325, *see* Second Coming
Paul (St.), message and writings of, 52-64, 162, 250
Peasants' War, 163-167
Philadelphians, 242-243, 246, 247, 249, 250, 251
Pikarts, 145-146
Plymouth Brethren, 259, 260, 325
postmillenialist, 12, 270, 308
premillenialist, 12, 308, 326, 337, 347
Priestly, Joseph, 7, 271
Priscilla, prophetess, 81-83
prophecy, 12, 81, 82, 83, 177, 181, 199, 245, 247, 257, 276, 306, 328
lay, 225, 227, 230, 231, 260
Prophet, Elizabeth Claire, 3, 4, 336
Puritans, 192, 194-195, 197, 202-203, 267, 270, 284

Quakers, 202, 204, 214, 216, 243, 250, 251, 252, 288

Ranters, 202, 204
Rappites, 285-287, 298
rapture, 259, 325, 328
Reagan, Ronald, 337

Index

Rogers, John, 203, 206, 210, 212, 214, 217
Rothman, Bernard, 172, 181, 183, 185
Russell, Charles Taze, 325-329
Rutherford, Joseph, 329

Savonarola, of Florence, 112-115
Second Advent, *see* Second Coming
Second Coming:
  as imminent, 89, 137, 169, 155, 157, 199, 201, 271, 274, 278, 310
  belief in, 53, 171, 182, 197, 233, 253, 283, 293, 307, 314
  expectation of, 82, 83, 197, 198, 200, 214, 256, 269
  non-appearance of, 54, 169, 213, 226, 272, 313, 316, 320
  time of, 53, 114, 137, 169, 171, 200, 228, 233, 241, 244, 271, 284, 308, 318, 323, 324, 325
Seventh-day Adventist, 319, 320-323
Shakers, 5, 253, 279, 281, 286, 291-297, 317, 351
Sicarii, 37, 39
Sigismund, Emperor, 132, 121-122, 134, 137, 139, 141, 144
Southcott, Joanna, 228, 256-258, 261
speaking in tongues, 14, 57, 248, 273, 280
spirituals, *see* Franciscan spirituals
Storch, Nicholas, 159, 169

Tabor, 124, 125, 130, 132, 138, 140, 148
Taborites, 7, 15, 119, 124-148, 159, 346
  battle deployment of, 141
  beliefs of, 128-131, 142-144
Tertullian, 78-79
Théot, Catherine, 228, 230-232

Unity of the Brethren, 285
Ussher, Bishop James, 306, 326
Utraquists, 123-129, 159

Venner, Thomas, 211-214
violence, 5, 7, 14, 23, 40, 41, 45, 119, 125, 131, 133, 135, 136, 157, 160, 163, 165, 168, 192, 193, 204, 205, 212, 215, 312

Wardley, Jane, 252, 253, 292
Wesley, John, 251
White, Mrs., *see* Harmon, Ellen G.
Wilkinson, Jemima, 275-277, 351
women:
  as prophets, 82, 90, 227, 230, 245, 250, 252
  excesses of, 13, 90
  leadership of, 230, 227, 245
  prominence of, 80, 130, 141, 250, 279, 283, 296

Zealots, 9, 35, 40, 42-43, 103, 104
Želivský, John, 125, 132-136, 142
Zizka, John, 133-148
Zoarites, 287, 298